MW01006003

More Equal
Than Others

More Equal Than Others

America from Nixon to the New Century

Godfrey Hodgson

A Century Foundation Book

PRINCETON UNIVERSITY PRESS

PRINCETON AND OXFORD

Copyright © 2004 by The Century Foundation
Published by Princeton University Press,
41 William Street, Princeton, New Jersey 08540
In the United Kingdom: Princeton University Press,
3 Market Place, Woodstock, Oxfordshire OX20 1SY

Library of Congress Cataloging-in-Publication Data
Hodgson, Godfrey.
More equal than others : America from Nixon to the new century / Godfrey Hodgson.
p. cm. — (Politics and society in twentieth-century America)
Includes bibliographical references and index.
ISBN: 0-691-11788-8 (alk. paper)
1. United States—Politics and government—1945–1989.   2. United States—Politics and government—1989–   3. Political culture—United States—History—20th century.   4. United States—Social conditions—1980–   5. Equality—United States—History—20th century.   6. Social conflict—United States—History—20th century.   I. Title.   II. Series.
E839.5.H64 2004
305.8'00973'09045   2003055549
British Library Cataloging-in-Publication Data is available
This book has been composed in Electra
Printed on acid-free paper. ∞
pup.princeton.edu
Printed in the United States of America
1 3 5 7 9 10 8 6 4 2

For my family

Hilary, Pierre, Francis, Lindsay, Jessica, Laura, and Angus

Contents

FOREWORD ix

ACKNOWLEDGMENTS xiii

INTRODUCTION
Disappointment and Denial xvii

1 State of the Union 1

2 New Politics 29

3 New Technology 61

4 New Economics 87

5 New Immigrants 112

6 New Women 139

7 New South, Old Race 172

8 New Society 203

9 New World 249

10 New Century 288

NOTES 305

SELECT BIBLIOGRAPHY 349

INDEX 361

Foreword

By any measure the United States is a stupendously successful nation. Its citizens have been blessed with vast natural resources, renewed by waves of diverse and energetic immigration, guarded by two great oceans, and fortunate in the size and dynamism of their domestic marketplace. It is fair to say they have made the most of it. Today, the United States is recognized as uniquely powerful and influential.

Moreover, at least since John Winthrop's "City on the Hill" vision in 1630, a good deal of our national self-consciousness has involved the notion that we should be widely admired and even emulated. When we have found that others do not share our high opinion of ourselves, the explanation that comes readiest to hand is that the "erroneous" views are a consequence of ignorance, envy, or probably both. Serious hostility to America, in this view, often is understood to reflect the fact that America's enemies are, well, simply evil. This opinion has been reinforced by the fact that, for most of the past sixty years, virtually all of the major enemies that America actually confronted had in fact committed atrocities against their own people. They also were clearly foes of Western democracy and of liberty in general. In these circumstances, sustaining this rosy self-assessment has been relatively easy.

From time to time, however, the abiding self-confidence of the nation has been put to the test. The Great Depression was one such period. The tumult during the 1960s and early 1970s was another unsettling era of transition. During the past three decades, wage stagnation, the decline of the manufacturing sector, growing inequality, several painful recessions, and the sudden emergence of a terrorist threat have again raised questions about whether all is well with the Great Republic. There are scholars who have argued that, in the area of economic progress and equity, some aspects of American preeminence in recent years have been more theoretical than actual. And among foreign observers, there is an even more commonly held view that Americans are mistaken in the fervor with which they believe in the superiority of the structure, effectiveness, and leadership of their nation's government.

Some of those who raise these issues are among America's best friends in the scholarly and journalistic communities. Their work should be prized by Americans, for it often provides the missing perspective that is needed to understand our nation and its needs. Prominent in this group of "Americanists" is Godfrey Hodgson, a writer who has provided exactly this sort of friendly, thoughtful, and insightful writing.

Hodgson, a noted British journalist, has served as Washington correspondent of the *Observer*, the editor of *Insight* in the *Sunday Times*, the presenter of the London Programme and of Channel Four News, and foreign editor of the *Independent*. He also has taught in several universities in Britain and in the United States and explored the state of our nation in a number of important books, including *America in Our Time; The World Turned Right Side Up: A History of the Conservative Ascendancy in America;* and *All Things to All Men: The False Promise of the Modern American Presidency*.

One of Hodgson's most telling points in this book is the recognition of the reality that government and government regulation are the necessary foundation on which capitalism can flourish. As he puts it in his introduction: "Americans might dislike government, as many of them never ceased to repeat. But they experienced more government than anyone. This vast display of individual and institutional opportunities was organized and protected by the most elaborate and opulently funded pyramid of government in the world." One might add that American business has always looked to government for favorable treatment, from subsidized research to land grants to protection from competition—at home and abroad.

Hodgson stresses the dominance of the corporation both in economic and political fact and in the popular mythology about the way business functions. The most pervasive of these myths is that of the empowered stockholder as the functional equivalent of the citizen and the operations of the market as a surrogate for democracy. But as recurring corporate scandals remind us, the system is full of practical imperfections. More broadly, Hodgson's work emphasizes the costs and persistence of economic inequality as a central American problem. He asks: Is the United

States becoming, or has it become, a class-based society? If so, what does this mean for the future? The raising of this question (which American commentators typically skirt) is a major contribution of his book.

The Century Foundation has supported numerous studies of various aspects of these issues, including Robert Kuttner's *Everything for Sale;* Edward Wolff's *Top Heavy* and his forthcoming book on skill, work, and inequality; Jeff Madrick's *Why Economies Grow;* Jamie Galbraith's *Created Unequal;* and Paul Osterman's *Securing Prosperity.*

In addition to an insightful analysis of the American economy, Hodgson has a keen eye for political developments in the United States. His review of the rise and fall of southern power within the Democratic Party, followed by its rise to even greater heights among Republicans, is a central theme of the book. Thus one practical explanation for the growing strength of conservative politics in America during the past generation is the altered allegiance of the states of the old Confederacy. Indeed, the shattering of the liberal consensus, even as wages were stagnating and inequality was growing, can be understood only in these terms.

This is not a pessimistic book. Hodgson believes that the prospects for American progress remain bright, but he does raise a warning about the present course of the nation. At a time when patriotism is often equated with uncritical acceptance of the status quo, his arguments could not be more timely. On behalf of the Trustees of The Century Foundation, I thank him for this important contribution to our understanding of these critical issues.

Richard C. Leone, President
The Century Foundation
July 2003

Acknowledgments

The origin of this project was a phone call from The Century Foundation in New York, asking me whether I might be interested in writing a sequel to my 1976 book, *In Our Time*. My answer was to the effect of: "Can a duck swim"? This exchange led to a commission to write the book as a report for the foundation, with the idea that it would find a trade publisher for it. My gratitude therefore goes in the first place to Richard C. Leone, president of The Century Foundation, and to his colleagues, especially Leif Wellington Haase, Beverly Goldberg, and Greg Anrig; and then to my editor at Princeton University Press, Brigitta van Rheinberg, and to her colleagues.

I would like to thank all who agreed to be interviewed, too many to be mentioned individually; those cited in the book are identified in the notes. In a sense, of course, the book was made possible by all the friends in the United States who helped me with information, anecdotes, suggestions, and hospitality. In particular I would like to thank James V. Risser, James R. Bettinger, Henry S. Breitrose, and Henrietta Grant-Peterkin at the Department of Communications at Stanford University; Lee H. Hamilton and his colleagues at the Woodrow Wilson International Center for Scholars in Washington. The presence of the late senator Daniel Patrick Moynihan made the Wilson Center feel like home. As ever, I am more grateful than I can easily express for hospitality and advice to Harry and Tricia McPherson.

I am also indebted to Alan Ryan, the warden of New College, Oxford, and director of the Rothermere American Institute, for appointing me as a fellow and then as an associate fellow there, and to my colleagues there and among the Oxford Americanists generally. Thank you, too, to all the staff of the institute's Vere Harmsworth Library, an efficient and pleasant place to work.

Adam Fairclough, of the University of East Anglia, brought together a cast of friendly critics for a conference on my earlier book, *In Our Time*, which provided vital help with the revision process.

Brian Hickman, of Information Workshop, Oxford, has made it possible for me to keep in touch with the world's knowledge through the Internet.

My agent, Robert Ducas, has been a reassuring adviser as well as an old and valued friend.

I am grateful to those who have read parts of the book in manuscript, especially Professor Desmond King of St. College, Oxford, Professor Jay Kleinberg of Brunel University, and Professor Nelson Lichtenstein of the University of California at Santa Barbara. I don't know what confusion I might have fallen into but for the clear head of my friend Rosemary Allan.

My greatest thanks as ever go to my wife Hilary, a professional copy editor and proofreader as well as a beloved motivator, comforter, and counselor.

All animals are equal, but some animals are more equal than others.

—*George Orwell, Animal Farm*

Introduction: Disappointment and Denial

This book is an attempt to understand what has happened in the United States over the last quarter of the twentieth century. More specifically, it is an attempt to say some things that—I think—need to be said because they are not part of either of the two ruling narratives, the liberal recessional or conservative triumphalism. It is widely asserted that politics has become irrelevant to modern Americans and that government is not part of the solution but part of the problem. On the contrary, my central contention is that the power of democratic government, restrained by the American tradition of constitutional law and legitimized by fair and tolerant political conflict, to address troubles at home and internationally has never been more needed if we are to build a fairer and safer world.

I argue that the experience of the years from Richard Nixon's resignation of the presidency until the millennium, in contrast to the advertisement that was so often screened, of universal prosperity at home and cost-free triumph abroad, were in reality for many, probably for most Americans, years of disappointment and denial.

The most striking fact about the domestic economy was not that it grew, and for at least one brief period at the end of the 1990s quite rapidly, but that it grew far more slowly than had been the case in the previous quarter century, and far less equitably. The fruits of that growth were reaped by a small, and disproportionately by a relatively tiny, proportion of the population. Great and growing inequality has been the most salient social fact about the America of the conservative ascendancy. It is hard not to ask whether that was not one of the conservatives' strategic goals.

The existence of inequality, of a "winner-take-all" society, was widely acknowledged. But American media were generally in denial of its implications. Resentments were calmed by the idea that, if Americans were substantively more and more unequal, they had greater opportunities than ever to acquire status and possessions. The reality has been that gross and growing inequality, in a society where the rich were increasingly segregated—from the middling as well as from the poor—by geography, education, culture, and politics, amounted to nothing less than a reemergence of the class divisions that most Americans were proud to have put behind them decades before. Beyond a certain point, inequalities of money, especially in a society where so much was measured in terms of money, implied human inequality too. About this, however obvious it was, little or nothing was said in public discourse.

The high hopes held during the years of the liberal consensus for growing equality and broadening opportunities for excluded groups, above all for women and for ethnic minorities, were to a surprising extent resisted and substantially disappointed. And this, too, was denied. Progress for blacks, especially, simply slipped down the agenda. Labor unions, once cherished for the protection they afforded the citizen against business rapacity, lost much of their industrial power and with it their public credibility. Altruism, once again, as in the 1920s and 1950s, earlier decades of business hegemony, became suspect.

Domestic disappointment and denial were mirrored by a narrowing and hardening of American attitudes toward the outside world. This too, like the resurgence of class division, was a break with the best of American tradition. Where Woodrow Wilson called for a struggle against "militarism" (read "Germany") and "navalism" (read "Britain"), by the end of the twentieth century the United States was spending more on defense, or— to avoid euphemism—on military power, than the rest of the world put together. When the United States, better late than never, entered World War II, its armed forces were still smaller than those of minor European powers. America in 1940 was a profoundly civilian society. Well before the end of the twentieth century people spoke without discomfort of the "national security state," a euphemism, again, for a significantly militarized polity. But where in the late 1940s and the 1950s Americans shared their wealth and strength to build institutions to protect the common good, after the millennium allies were no longer wanted. The international institutions an earlier generation of Americans had built were derided. Unilateralism and power politics were in fashion.

If this account of what happened seems to stress disappointment and frustration, as opposed to the achievements of "the world's greatest economy" and the military triumphs of "the lone superpower," it is in part because it seems to me that there has been no shortage of writers keen to celebrate (transitory) rises in the stock market or (easy) military glory.

In part, too, this is no doubt due to the fact that, while I have been a student, an admirer, even a disciple of the United States for almost fifty years, I am not an American. Some Americans, it seems, have difficulty with the idea of a foreigner who is not either an immigrant or an enemy; I am neither. I have spent a total of some fifteen years in the United States over the past forty-eight years. In many ways, I have been proud to be treated as an insider. I have been privileged to have held a White House press card, teaching posts at Berkeley and Harvard, and contracts from the most respected publishers. I have been accorded an extraordinary measure of generosity from many American institutions, from the Woodrow Wilson Center in Washington to great American libraries to the *Washington Post*, from a desk in whose newsroom I was able to observe the world for years. I have been fortunate enough to know personally some of the most influential Americans of the later twentieth century, from Martin Luther King to Daniel Patrick Moynihan, and from Robert Kennedy to Irving Kristol. But I remain an outsider, not an American.

As a consequence, I am naturally skeptical of what is called "American exceptionalism," the essence of which I take to be the belief that the United States is not merely the richest, the most powerful, and the most successful of political societies, but at the same time the most virtuous and the most innocent, and one whose destiny it is to spread the enlightenment of its ways to a darkling world inhabited by the other 95 percent of the world's population.

Even I must admit, though, that there is indeed something exceptional about the American self-image. Americans do see themselves as pilgrims on a national spiritual journey. Nationality, nationhood, the idea of the American nation, are the altar of something akin to a political religion. It is a commonplace to observe that American patriotism shares many of the attributes of an organized cult: symbols like the flag, rituals, sacred texts (the Declaration of Independence, the Constitution, the Gettysburg Address), prophets, martyrs, apostles, and missionaries. Even a non-American must feel that there is something admirable and generous in the values and the aspirations of that tradition. (Senator Daniel Patrick Moynihan once wrote memorably about his hopes for an architecture to match the "dignity, enterprise, vigor, and stability of the American National Government."[1] Many of those who hold office in that government today might not understand that sentiment and, if they could, would recoil from it in horror.) Here, too, I sense a coarsening and a trivializing that has taken place in recent decades of the ideals of Woodrow Wilson and Franklin Delano Roosevelt, even of Lyndon Baines Johnson. Instead, a drum-banging triumphalism and commercialized populism seem to be what the men and women around George W. Bush most want to offer the world.

No doubt some of the fervor of American patriotism is due in part to the fact that Americans are a self-chosen people. To the general proposition that Americans are all immigrants or their descendants, there are, of course, two great exceptions, and there is also one less well known footnote. The twin exceptions are the one-eighth of the population descended, wholly or in part, from men and women brought to America as slaves against their will, and the smaller group of Native Americans, descended from those who were there all along. (It is a reflection of growing tolerance that the number of Americans who acknowledge native roots has more than doubled in a quite brief span of time.) The footnote is that, over almost a century and a half, roughly one-third of all immigrants to the United States went home again. Life for immigrants, as the black mother in Langston Hughes's poem put it, "ain't been no crystal stair." Whatever the multiple explanations of that fact, and the lesson it teaches about not sentimentalizing the struggle it took to build America, it remains essentially true that America is a nation of immigrants.

Immigration, as I have long thought, is only the first of the four great historical experiences that have shaped the American character and American society. None is exceptional. Each has been shared by many other countries. But together, in specific forms and ways, four strands have woven the distinctively American pattern.

The second formative experience, for better and for worse, was the epic of the frontier. The mobility of American society, and its persistent, imperfectly achieved aspiration toward equality, can be put down to the steady westward thrust of the frontier of settlement. So too can a certain hardness and a willingness to forget that the imperial resources on which American society has been built were taken from Native Americans and from Mexico at gunpoint. In the past few decades, the mighty course of empire westward has been tamed to the daily rhythm of the commuter suburbs. But the impulse to move on, to solve problems by leaving them behind, together with the daring and the aggression, has remained.

Third, just as Europe has been shaped and brutalized by five centuries of colonial expansion, so the United States has been indelibly marked by the historical fact of African slavery. That made inevitable the great conflict to preserve the Union. It shaped the political and economic geography of the continent. It also left a stubborn legacy of segregation and racism, and of subtle, deeply engrained devices for perpetuating them. One of the surprise developments of the past thirty years has been that, where it was once assumed that the South would become more like the rest of the country, in politics and in many aspects of culture, the rest of the country has come to resemble the South.

The fourth distinctive historical experience is that American political society and the American political religion have been guided by the values, one can even say by the ideology, of a noble eighteenth-century political experiment. The United States was born of a revolution against a distant and unreformed imperial power. But its founders brought with them from Britain and from Europe a rich heritage of law, political institutions, and ideas that were early codified into a new political system, founded on constitutional law and on the then novel idea of popular sovereignty. The world of the Founders has long crumbled away. But the ideas of Thomas Jefferson and James Madison are as lively as ever.

The ideas and ideals of the American Revolution have proved durable, because flexible. The paradoxical consequence of their success is that the titanic dynamism of a society, always driven by the push of immigration and the pull of the frontier, and haunted by the guilt and fear of racial conflict, has been contained and guided by political institutions that are relatively unchanging and in many ways remarkably conservative. One of the "conservative" ideas that has grown in influence over the past twenty-five years is the elevation, not of capitalism, which in its essentials, the coming together of buyer and seller in the market, and the concept of investing for the future in trust for a return, is arguably as old as human society, but of a particular, unregulated American version of capitalism as almost the consort of democracy on the throne of American belief.

This book attempts to chart, in what can only be the roughest of rough outlines, how these enduring experiences and forces operated upon American society in the last quarter of the twentieth century, that is, from the perceived crisis of the mid-1970s to the proclaimed coronation of the American Millennium.

The first four chapters seek to contrast the complacent political rhetoric of late-twentieth-century American politicians and media with the more checkered pattern of what was really happening: in politics, in the economy, in technology. Chapter 4 argues that, so far from being the child of the unregulated graduate-student capitalism of the myth, computers and the Internet were the long-gestated offspring of investments made by an alliance between the national security state and the institutions of social democracy. Chapter 5 examines the changes likely to be brought about by the new immigration. Chapters 6 and 7 show how the high hopes bred by the women's movement and the civil rights movement have been partially frustrated by division, resistance, and reaction. The reality for the majority, chapter 8 argues, may be full of pleasure, variety, and achievement. It is hardly the shining idyll portrayed by advertising or ideology, though, but rather an intricate pattern in which four ambiguous strands predominate: the emergence of the suburb, segregated by income, as the typical American habitat; the coronation of corporate power; the pervasive influence of both advertising and news media, themselves largely in the service of the corporate elite and its interests and beliefs; and the consequent slide toward a society horizontally divided by money and education into increasingly unequal social classes.

This, I believe, is nothing less than a betrayal of the society's long cherished and best instincts, those instincts that first drew me to it. All Americans may be equal, George Orwell might now say. But some Americans are so much more equal than others that the abyss between them can hardly be bridged, let alone stepped over as was once possible.

One large difficulty, suggested in chapter 9, is the growing slippage between how Americans see the rest of the world, and how the rest of the world sees them. The chapter makes the point that survey data show clearly that the harsh confrontational stance of modern Republican conservatives is not shared by the majority of Americans, even in the aftermath of September 11 and of war in Iraq. Nonetheless, the chapter suggests that, where once the United States was unquestioningly held up as a beacon by progressives everywhere, now it is the friend and guarantor of the relatively wealthy and conservative. The word "reform," once the banner of the champions of progress and equality, is now suspected as a "weasel word" for such changes as may profit American corporate business. Too often, a United States with conservative ideologists in the saddle is identified chiefly with the self-interest of the self-satisfied.

The major theme, left for the last chapter, is that growing inequality brings its own punishment. A small class of owners of wealth and their attendant corporate managers, professionals, publicists, and tame ideologues has steadily accumulated financial, industrial, media, and cultural power. These people are not well equipped to see clearly the reality of what is happening. "What do you mean, everyone is not rich and happy?" their spokesmen ask indignantly. "Why, everyone I know is doing just fine!" A society that does not see its own situation clearly, and is in denial about vital aspects of what is happening to it, must be storing up problems for its own future, and no doubt for others. Still less will it be able to command the respect, let alone the affection, in which it was held by the rest of the world in the days when it was a byword for equality and openness, generosity and candor. These virtues have not disappeared from the Republic. But they are not conspicuous among those into whose hands its power and its fortunes have fallen.

More Equal
Than Others

1

State of the Union

And so we have gone on, and so we will go on, puzzled and prospering beyond example in the history of man.
                    —*Thomas Jefferson to John Adams, January 21, 1812*

IN THE YEAR 1975, the mood of the United States was perplexed, morose,
and uncertain. For the first time in the modern era, the nation had lost a
war. For the first time, a president had been driven from office in disgrace. It was said that the American Dream would be denied to many, because for the first time a generation of Americans would be worse off than
their parents.[1] For the first time, Americans, "people of plenty,"[2] used to a
culture of abundance, confronted the prospect of not being self-sufficient
in energy and in some key raw materials.[3]

A quarter of a century later, the national mood was buoyant. The Soviet
Union had disintegrated, and its communist creed was utterly discredited.
Americans had not so much come to agree with one another about politics, as to lose interest in the political process. By the end of the twentieth
century there was an echo in the air of that epoch in nineteenth-century
French politics whose motto was "enrich yourselves."[4] Americans were
busy enriching themselves, and a significant minority did so to impressive
effect.

Most striking of all was the transformation of the nation's public philosophy from liberal to conservative. By the 1990s, few cared to identify

themselves as liberal. In 1992, for example, a poll showed that only 20 percent of the voters regarded themselves as liberals, compared with 31 percent who identified themselves as conservatives.[5] Whereas in 1973 only 32 percent agreed with the proposition that "the best government is the government that governs the least," by 1998 56 percent agreed.[6] In the middle 1970s Americans were just coming to the conclusion—painful for some, liberating for others—that the ideas of the New Deal had served their time.[7] People were turning from the warm inclusiveness of the liberal consensus to the energizing astringency of a new conservative philosophy. By the 1980s free-market capitalism was being enthroned, not just as a useful system for wealth creation that needed to be kept under watchful scrutiny, but also as one of the twin keys, with democracy, to the American belief system and the American future.[8]

In politics and journalism, and in a welter of what can only be called corporate propaganda, the idea was ceaselessly reiterated that giant corporations and the stock exchange were the true democracy, and that anyone who dared to challenge their hegemony was no friend to the working families of America, but an elitist and, as such, a traitor to the nation's best traditions. Thus a college professor or working journalist living on a few thousand dollars a month was condemned as an oppressor, whereas a CEO, who paid himself—with the connivance of an intimidated or collusive remuneration committee—several hundred times as much as his average employee, was held up to sycophantic praise as the working man's friend.[9]

By the late 1990s Americans had put the hesitations of the 1970s far behind them. They had made it, the majority felt. Whatever private fears or misgivings individuals might have, the public mood was robustly confident. It was never more trenchantly expressed than in the State of the Union Message with which President Bill Clinton celebrated the millennium on January 27, 2000, his last after eight helter-skelter years in the White House.[10]

His tone was triumphant, not to say triumphalist. It was as if the United States had finally attained a state of economic and social perfection, nirvana now.[11] We were, he said to an applauding audience of senators and members of Congress, "fortunate to be alive at this moment in history." Never before, Clinton went on, "has our nation enjoyed, at once, so much prosperity and social progress with so little internal crisis and so few external threats." Never before, he said, "have we had such a blessed opportunity to build the more perfect union of our founders' dreams."

This was, of course, political rhetoric. But it was not mere idle bragging. The United States really did enter the new millennium with impressive achievements to look back on, and exciting prospects for the future. The economy seemed to have overcome all hesitations. Clinton could claim, with some exaggeration, that under his administration the nation had achieved the "fastest economic growth in more than 30 years." In sober truth, the economy really had created some 20 million new jobs in a few years. As a consequence, the number of poor people had fallen to the lowest figure in twenty years and the unemployment rate to the lowest level in thirty years. What was more, unemployment for African Americans and for Hispanics was also lower than ever before. For the first time in forty-two years, there had been budget surpluses in two consecutive years, and—the president accurately predicted—in the very next month America would achieve the longest period of economic growth in its entire history.

That was not all. Economic revolution, Clinton claimed, had been matched by what he called "a revival of the American spirit." That might be hard to measure. But crime, for example, was said to be down by 20 percent, to its lowest level in twenty-five years. The number of children born to teenage mothers had fallen for seven years in a row, and the welfare rolls, those stubborn indicators of hidden misery, had been cut in half. Such statistical measures of societal, let alone spiritual, advancement are always suspect. But at home there certainly was a widespread sense of pride and optimism.

Abroad, the United States in 2000 was dominant in the world as never before. American military power was arguably greater, relative to all possible rivals, than ever. Even in 1945 the Soviet Union had formidable military forces under arms. At the beginning of the millennium the United States stood unchallenged. It had put down such truculent breakers of the peace as Iraq and Serbia with little help from allies and with few casualties. Less than two years later, American military supremacy was challenged once again, this time by terrorism. Once again, at least so far as war in Afghanistan and Iraq was concerned, it was confirmed.

The American economy, at least temporarily, had outdistanced former rivals in Europe and Asia.[12] Moreover, never before, unless perhaps in the first few years after World War II, had America been so much admired around the world. American fashions, American music, even American movies, were seen as the last thing in cool. America basked in the prestige earned, from Budapest to Bangalore, by American domination of the new frontiers of computing, information technology, and the Internet. The continued rise of the stock market seemed to confirm that the American economy defied the law of economic gravity.

President Clinton was quick to claim some of the credit for these achievements for his own administration. To renewed applause, he said, "We have built a new economy," and proceeded to set forth his vision of a social utopia as well: "We will make America the safest big country on earth, pay off the national debt, reverse the process of climatic change, and become at last what the Founding Fathers promised: 'one nation, under God, indivisible, with liberty and justice for all.'" With dollars cascading into the U.S. Treasury in a profusion that was unimaginable when his second term began, commented R. W. Apple Jr. in the *New York Times*, Clinton spoke "with all the expansiveness of a man who had hit the lottery."[13]

The president's euphoria was no doubt sharpened by relief, and his triumphant tone by an understandable desire to have his revenge on ruthlessly vindictive political opponents. Only weeks previously, after all, he had been acquitted in an impeachment trial before the United States Senate, the first chief executive to face that humiliating ordeal since Andrew Johnson more than 130 years earlier. He would not have been human if he had not taken advantage of the opportunity to confound his enemies and rub the doubters' noses in his success.

Yet Clinton's millennium speech by no means reflected a mere personal or partisan version of how things stood as the twentieth century ended. As early as 1997, *Fortune* magazine, for example, hardly a mouthpiece for the narrow political contentions of Democrats, claimed that the U.S. economy was "stronger than it's ever been,"[14] something it could in truth have said at most points in the past fifty years. *Business Week* consistently preached the gospel of the new economy. Gurus like Nicholas Negroponte of the Massachusetts Institute of Technology and innumerable brokers drummed away at the idea that, between them, the Internet and the stock market had changed the rules of the game of success.[15] From Wall Street the same message came drumming from the million hooves of Merrill Lynch, the thundering herd of people's capitalism. The broker proclaimed in a circular to its happy investors, that this was "Paradise Found: The Best of All Possible Economies"—except, presumably, for the next day's.[16] Later Merrill Lynch admitted to the government that its salesmen had been urging clients to "buy" or "accumulate" stocks its analysts privately regarded as "crap," "a dog," and even "a piece of shit."[17] Late in 2002 ten banks, including Credit Suisse First Boston, Merrill Lynch, and Salomon Smith Barney, agreed to pay $1.4 billion in a settlement that revealed that published research on stocks was "essentially bought and paid for by the issuer." One supposedly independent analyst at Goldman Sachs, the settlement found, was asked what his three most important goals for 2002 were. The response was "1. Get more investment banking revenue. 2. Get more investment banking revenue. 3. Get more investment banking revenue." Another analyst, at Lehmann Brothers, said that misleading "the little guy who isn't smart about the nuances" was "the nature of my business."[18]

Much media discourse in the 2000 election campaign took as real the idea that the country as a whole was enjoying unimaginable prosperity. This was an exaggeration. It might be more credible in Washington or Manhattan, Boston or Seattle, or the San Francisco Bay area, than in some less favored parts of the country. It might be truer of lawyers, doctors, and editorial writers than of Nebraska farmers, laid-off Indiana machinists, or Hispanic immigrants to southern California, let alone African American single mothers on the South Side of Chicago. But it was true enough for enough people that it became the key signal of the year, and even of the decade of the 1990s.

It was against this bass line of euphoria and optimism that Clinton moved to his peroration: "After 224 years," he declaimed to his applauding audience—made up in its majority of the Republicans who had opposed his policies every inch and actually prevented him from carrying out many of the policies he had advocated—"the American revolution continues. We remain a young nation. And as long as our dreams outweigh our memories, America will be forever young. That is our destiny. And this is our moment."

———•◆•———

LESS THAN TWO SHORT YEARS LATER, that shining moment was tarnished in many ways. Clinton's Democratic heir, Al Gore, had been defeated in the 2000 presidential campaign. The election itself was so close that its result was doubtful through weeks of litigation. On balance it is likely that the victor, George W. Bush, was not elected. One of the most careful and authoritative of the many analyses of the election result concluded that Gore was denied victory by a Supreme Court opinion "doomed to infamy" and that "the wrong man was inaugurated on January 20, 2001, and this is no small thing." No small thing, indeed, for a country that would be the teacher of democracy to the world.[19]

At the heart of the optimism so fervently expressed by Clinton in his State of the Union Address, but very widely shared in the nation, were two beliefs that had been sharply challenged, if not discredited, within months. One was the upward march of the stock market, rewarding the talent and enterprise of the few but also spreading its beneficence over the many. The Standard & Poor's composite stock price index, corrected for inflation, which trotted along modestly by comparison through the crash of 1929 and the boom of the 1960s and 1970s, soared dizzily from 1995 on to spike in the very month of Clinton's millennium speech.[20] The second idea behind the "irrational exuberance" of the market was the confidence that the new technology of the computer and the Internet promised a New Economy. By early 2001, the Dow Jones index of common stocks had fallen from its high by some 40 percent. The Nasdaq index, dedicated to charting the heroics of the new technology stocks, had fallen even more catastrophically. The Nasdaq composite index, to be specific, which passed 5000 in early 2000, had fallen below 2000 by late 2001, or by more than 60 percent in less than two years.[21] After the September 11 attacks, the markets rallied to the point where some investment analyses claimed to see the green shoots of a new bull market. Even if that were so, the idea that the new technology had simply abolished the laws of economic gravity had been exploded for good. And by the summer of 2002 the market had fallen to the point where it threatened the health of the economy as a whole.

The other heartening economic statistics Clinton cited had also been swept away. By March 2001 the economy was technically in recession.[22] Unemployment was rising, from 3.9 percent in October 2000 to 5.4 percent a year later. In October 2001 alone it rose half a percentage point, the biggest increase in a single month since February 1996.[23] And the economic climate was harshest for those very high technology sectors that had led the way in the boom of the later 1990s. "Dot.com" startups were worst hit. The major winners of the high-technology market—Yahoo!, AOL, Compaq, Sun, even Intel and Microsoft—all announced profit warnings, layoffs, even in some cases actual losses, and their stock fell heavily. Indeed, contradicting a central assumption of the boosters of the New Economy, the stock market would have done better without the new technology companies than with them.

By the summer of 2002 any talk of a New Economy would have appeared fatuous. The Dow Jones indeed had fallen below 8000. Disillusion had spread far beyond the overhyped dot.com stocks to most sectors of the market. Worse, the collapse of Enron and Worldcom, and serious problems in many other major corporations, had shaken public faith in Kenneth Lay of Enron, Bernie Ebbers of Worldcom, and Jack Welch of General Electric, all of whom, two short years earlier, had been credited with virtually magical powers. Those corporate meltdowns, in turn, exposed the collusive behavior of major accounting firms, especially Arthur Andersen.

In the summer of 2002, the economist-turned-columnist Paul Krugman, writing in the *New York Times*, drew a political moral from the economic events: "The current crisis in American capitalism isn't just about the specific details—about tricky accounting, stock options, loans to executives, and so on. It is about the way the game has been rigged on behalf of insiders."[24]

As Krugman and many others pointed out, the Bush administration was full of insiders. George W. Bush's secretary of the army, Thomas White, came from Enron, where he headed a division whose profits were manipulated to the tune of $500 million, and who sold $12 million of stock before the company collapsed. His vice president, Richard Cheney, was chairman and chief executive of Halliburton, whose stock was one of the hottest counters in the boom, and where dubious accounting turned a loss into a profit. The president himself was not above suspicion. He had been a typical player in the same corporate world. He profited from insider knowledge to unload stock in his own company, Harken Energy. He made $15 million personally out of the sale of the Texas Rangers baseball club, which benefited from favors squeezed out of a suburban community

government. And as governor of Texas, he allowed a friend and major political contributor, Tom Hicks, to benefit financially from the privatization
of a large portion of the University of Texas's substantial endowment.[25]

So far from demonstrating the brilliance of the New Economy, the
Bush administration seemed to be drawing on Republican traditions as
old as Teapot Dome[26] and Credit Mobilier.[27] And, to judge by the polls,
the public seemed to draw its own conclusions.

As for Clinton's rhetoric about the United States remaining "forever
young," it is tempting to quote Oscar Wilde's cynical witticism: "[T]he
youth of America," he said more than a hundred years ago, "is its oldest
tradition."[28] Certainly the graying of America was attested by the new political clout of the American Association of Retired Persons. Without the
new immigrants who continued to pour in, especially from Mexico, Central America, and the Caribbean, for the first time the birthrate in the
United States would have fallen, as it had done in some countries in
Western Europe, below the point where it guaranteed a natural increase
in population. As for Clinton's confidence that the country faced no external threat, that too was to be disproved in a bizarre and terrifying way
less than two years later, on September 11, 2001.

———◆———

AT THE BEGINNING of the twenty-first century, the United States was a mature civilization marked by striking, well-rooted contradictions. It is (and
the list of pairs by no means exhausts the difficulties facing anyone who
attempts a simplistic analysis) generally pacific but occasionally bellicose;
religious yet secular; innovative but conservative; tough but tender; aggressive yet reluctant to incur casualties; egalitarian by instinct but stratified in tiers of wide and growing inequality; puritan yet self-indulgent;
conformist but full of independent-minded people; devoted to justice, yet
in many ways remarkably unfair; idealistic yet given to cynicism. ("Nice
guys finish last" is almost a national motto.) At some times it can be self-
confident to the verge of complacency, at others self-doubting to the point
of neurosis.

A quarter of a century ago, while Richard Nixon was falling from grace,
I was at work on a book published just as Jimmy Carter was on course for
the White House and the intractable problems he found waiting for him

there.[29] Its main argument was that, by the early 1950s, the Depression, the New Deal, World War II, and the Cold War had forged what, for want of a more precise term, I called a "liberal consensus" and that this was a victim of the tumultuous events of the 1960s. The consensus I had in mind was in effect a gigantic deal, by which conservatives accepted the main principles of a welfare state, made necessary by the Depression, and in return liberals accepted the need for the national security state, demanded by the Cold War. The book described how that consensus was shattered by three converging crises. There was the upheaval against racial oppression, first in the rural South, then in the great cities of the north and West. There was the long agony of the Vietnam War and the growing opposition to it, culminating in the humiliation of defeat. And there was a pervasive crisis of authority. That had its roots, no doubt, in gradual, subtle changes inside the nation's families and schoolrooms. But it was brought home by a series of political shocks, among them the assassinations of John F. Kennedy, Robert Kennedy, and Martin Luther King, and the rise of a new, defiantly intransigent conservatism that directly challenged both liberalism and consensus. There was a fourth crisis gathering like a storm over the horizon: the 1960s saw the first widespread expressions of concern at the impact American industry and the American consumption of water, forests, fossil fuels, and other natural resources were having on the environment.

In the last words of that book, I summed up the prospect from the middle 1970s in a phrase from a letter that Thomas Jefferson wrote to his former antagonist and later friend, John Adams. "So we shall go on," Jefferson predicted, "puzzled and prospering beyond example in the history of man." Puzzled and prospering? Prospering, certainly, in the aggregate, but still puzzled. That is another pair of contrasts that describes the true state of the Union over the last quarter of the twentieth century.

One obvious clue to resolving this endless string of apparent contradictions, of course, lies in the sheer size and diversity of America. "Do I contradict myself?" asked the preeminent national poet, Walt Whitman. "Very well, I contradict myself. I am large, I contain multitudes."[30] By the end of the twentieth century the United States contained some twenty times more people than when Whitman wrote those lines, and those people lived in an infinitely richer variety of ways.

This is a nation on a continental scale, a country uniquely devoted to change, extraordinarily quick to adopt new fashions—including new fashions in thinking about itself. Yet the United States at the close of the twentieth century had assumed the patterns of belief and practice of a mature society, patterns that were strongly established, even when they were contradictory. In certain respects, it was even an imperial society, led by a self-confident elite, sure that its destiny was to lead and, if necessary, to dominate the world. In economic, intellectual, and cultural life its achievements were extraordinary. Not the least of them was the freedom that not just allowed but actually encouraged people to explore many different ways of living their lives.

Perhaps it was this freedom, rather than a fluctuating and ill-distributed prosperity, that accounted for the buoyancy and cheerfulness of many individual lives and for the resilience and adventurousness of America as a whole. It was on the whole an unprecedentedly tolerant society. It was one in which social arrangements made it possible for trout fishermen, dancers, scholars, architects, oceanographers, gamblers, golfers, grandmothers, writers, musicians, rock climbers, theologians, stockbrokers and many others—even, within limits, radicals—to pursue their diverse personal grails.

This was a rich vein of individualism. What was less often celebrated was the remarkable array of institutions through which individuals could achieve their diverse goals. Universities, graduate schools, night schools, foundations, charities, websites, and chatrooms were all dedicated to supporting individual obsessions and making individual dreams come true. So was an extraordinary range of commercial institutions. Pension plans, savings companies, trust companies, brokerages, real estate agencies, insurance policies, mutual funds, hedge funds, and every other instrument imaginable for saving and investing money were all in the dream business, while malls, markets, stores tiny and titanic, travel agents, and fashion emporia offered every kind of temptation to spend. This proliferation of commercial energy, dramatized by downtown towers with marble atriums as well as by suburban temples to consumption, was supported by an immense, only half-visible infrastructure of financial institutions. Collisions were avoided or mitigated by those pillars of American rectitude (also exemplars of American competitiveness), law firms of all shapes and sizes.

Science was passing through a golden age in the late twentieth century. Foundations and universities vied with one another to encourage original work and to recruit donors to finance it. Secondary and undergraduate education were less impressive. Research depended heavily on immigrant scientists, but as long as they continued to be attracted to work in America, there seemed no cause for concern.

This was a civilization on the move. An immense web of communications was already in place by the beginning of the period we are examining. Indeed, by the 1970s infrastructure was beginning to show signs of wear and tear. The interstate highway system, like the Internet a spin-off of Cold War expenditure, was approaching completion.[31] But the ingenuity of the franchising system was creating a national network of predictable caravanserais: the traveling businessman could eat, drink, sleep, use his laptop, and watch movies on TV in an environment as far as possible identical from Key West to the Puget Sound.

This rich abundance of provision and the unprecedented personal freedom of American life in the late twentieth century had not come about by accident. They were the willed consequences of tens of millions of lives devoted to foresight, hard work, planning, and, above all, investment. This was a society that had focused on its future even more than on its past. But here, too, there were contradictions. One was that it chose not to have any detailed blueprint for planning that future. Another was that Americans saved less than citizens of other developed countries, relying instead on the willingness of foreigners, especially the Japanese, to invest in America.

Americans might dislike government, as many of them never ceased to repeat. But they experienced more government than anyone. This vast display of individual and institutional opportunities was organized and protected by the most elaborate and opulently funded pyramid of government in the world. It rose from the minimalist administrations of poor counties and dying towns to state governments like those in Albany or Sacramento that challenged comparison with all but a handful of foreign capitals. At the apex stood the grand vistas and marble palaces of the federal government in imperial Washington.

By the end of the century, government, while widely derided, had become one of the nation's most prosperous businesses, as witness the great arc of office buildings that stretches for twenty miles from Dulles to Reagan airports on the west side of Washington. They accommodate enterprises that live by selling goods and services to the federal government, even as their occupants grumble about it. Four of the twenty richest counties in America are contiguous to the federal capital.[32]

Yet here too contrast and contradiction are everywhere. Washington is resented by the voters who in theory control it and is accused of every corruption by the citizens it serves. For years the preferred strategy for politicians hoping to be elected to national office in Washington has been to campaign against the Beltway Babylon and all its works. Yet on any summer weekend, the well-educated government interns playing their rowdy softball on the Mall can see, decanted from tour buses, the plain folks who have brought their well-scrubbed children to stare at the White House and tour the Capitol, like pilgrims to the shrines of the national political religion.

———◆◆———

AMID THIS WELTER of diversity and contradiction, two massive changes stand out between the middle 1970s and the end of the century. The first is the revival of national confidence, so shaken by the events of the 1960s and the 1970s. The second was the replacement of the liberal consensus by the conservative ascendancy.

The coming of the millennium, said Bill Clinton, was America's moment. His older listeners would have been struck by the contrast with the state of the Union little more than twenty years earlier. Throughout the 1970s, Americans' self-esteem was punctured with a frequency that damaged the national psyche and indeed the national credibility in the outside world.

The blows were internal and external, economic and political, public and psychic, and they fell relentlessly. With the fall of Saigon in the summer of 1975, the United States had lost a war, for the first time. The might of an American expeditionary force with carriers, fighter aircraft, helicopters, and more than half a million men had been defeated by small, lightly armed men in black pajamas.[33] Among other things, Vietnam seemed to mean "the end of exceptionalism."[34]

Everywhere in the world the Soviet Union seemed to be on the attack—in Afghanistan and at half a dozen points in Africa, in Chile, and in the Middle East.[35] The Democratic Party, in the ascendancy since 1933, was discredited in the eyes of many of its core supporters because of its ambitious dreams of building a Great Society. In 1968, partly because of its own internal divisions, it lost the presidency to its archenemy, Richard Nixon. Then the integrity of the U.S. government at its highest level was soiled by the Watergate scandal. Nixon himself escaped impeachment only by a humiliating resignation. But it is probable that, if Nixon's personal insecurity had not led him to misuse his power, a conservative turnover would have come seven years earlier than it did.[36]

As it was, the Watergate debacle both enabled the Democrats to win the presidency against Nixon's successor, Gerald Ford, and created the circumstances in which they chose as their candidate Jimmy Carter. Pious and self-denying, he was well cast as the symbolic leader of that element in the nation that had lost all confidence in itself.

The background to this nadir of frustration and failure was the oil crisis that resulted from the boycott by the Organization of Petroleum Exporting Countries in 1973–74. Americans were used to an unthinking abundance in energy and other natural resources. Few noticed that, even before the oil price rise, their country had ceased to be self-sufficient. Now they were suddenly obliged to import more than half of their oil. They could scarcely comprehend what was happening when gas lines appeared even in the most affluent suburbs. A handful of oil-producing countries, many of them desert kingdoms, which as enemies of Israel rated low on any measure of American sympathy, had shown that they were far from powerless. They succeeded in forcing up the price of oil by a factor of four in 1973. After the fall of the shah of Iran in 1979 the price doubled again. No economy could have survived an eightfold increase in its basic fuel in less than seven lean years without being severely shaken. "I could feel it everywhere," said a Gulf Oil executive, "it was the ebbing of American power—the Romans retreating from Hadrian's Wall."[37]

Oil was only part of the shock. American industry faced the unfamiliar problem of a lack of competitiveness in the face of exports from Europe and Japan. Helped by American aid and American investments, not to mention by the lessons they had learned from American business economy, first the Europeans and then the Japanese and Koreans began to pour their exports into the American market. It was the first time since the nineteenth century that any foreign industries had shown an ability to compete successfully with Americans. Military expenditure, tourism, increased imports, and the loss of competitiveness all weakened the dollar. In 1971 Nixon devalued it for the first time since World War I. By the middle 1970s the American economy faced a new danger, the combination of low growth and high inflation known as "stagflation."

That was not all. Many Americans were shocked and alarmed by changes in society. They were disproportionately to be found among traditional Democratic voters both in the South and among the unionized working class in the north and Middle West, the very people whose loyalty had sustained Democratic presidents from Franklin Roosevelt to Lyndon Johnson. Many combined liberal ideas about economics with deeply conservative social values. They venerated American patriotism. They cherished marriage and the family. Many of them, even those who could not by any stretch of language be called racist, nevertheless felt uncomfortable about the accelerated social change brought about by the civil rights movement and the physical movement of black people into their neighborhoods.

The radical ideas, the demeanor and the language of the "counterculture" appalled them. In this, there was often an element of class resentment. Men and women who had worked hard and never expected to study at Berkeley or Columbia resented it when students at such institutions flouted deeply held values, seeming ungrateful to the system that had afforded them privileged opportunity.

To crown everything, it began to be said that, for the first time in American history, a new generation might not be as well off as its predecessor. Substantial groups of voters, in short, were jolted by events at home and abroad into reconsidering their basic political allegiance. They included unionized workers; white inner city dwellers; white southerners alienated by black enfranchisement; southern Baptists and other evangelicals angry at the decline in public morals and especially at the Carter administration's withdrawal of tax immunity from church schools; Jews angered by black hostility at home and alarmed by developments in the Middle East. Such voters, many of them for the first time in their lives, were available to listen to the arguments of the missionary new conservatism. For many, the evidence of America's apparent impotence when faced with Islamic militancy and communist aggression was the last straw.

Energy was the issue that brought home to many Americans both the threat to America's position in the world and a perceived threat to the comfortable American way of life at home.

In 1979 President Jimmy Carter returned from an ill-tempered summit with the world's leading industrial nations in Tokyo to scare headlines about the energy crisis. Canceling yet another announced energy speech to the nation, he retreated to the presidential hideaway at Camp David. There, sitting on the floor in his trademark cardigan, he conferred with a shifting cast of pundits and wise men.[38] After ten days of something approaching a national panic, he emerged on July 15, 1979, and summed up the nature of the problem as he saw it. There was, he said, a growing disrespect for churches, schools, news media, and other institutions, and not without cause.

> We were sure that ours was a nation of the ballot, not the bullet, until the murders of John Kennedy, Robert Kennedy and Martin Luther King, Jr. We were taught that our armies were always invincible and our causes always just, only to suffer the agony of Vietnam. We respected the Presidency as a place of honor until the shock of Watergate. We remember when the phrase "sound as a dollar" was an expression of absolute dependability, until the years of inflation begin to shrink our dollar and our savings. We believed that our nation's resources were limitless until 1973, when we had to face a growing dependence on foreign oil. The wounds are still very deep. They have never been healed.[39]

Carter's analysis of the situation was true enough at the time, so far as it went, but he was never forgiven for it. His trouble was that no one really believed he knew what to do about what came to be called "the national malaise."[40] With puritanical rigor, he insisted that salvation would have to come not just from the White House but from every house in America. It was not what the American majority wanted to hear. With relief, many voters turned from this painfully honest man and his awkward truths to the genial simplicities of Ronald Reagan and his assurance that it was, after all, "morning in America."

There were many causes of the conservative ascendancy. The widespread popular reaction against the social upheavals of the 1960s and also against the liberal agenda of the Johnson administration would probably have led to a Republican victory in the 1976 presidential elections and also to mass defections from the Democratic Party in Congress, perhaps even earlier.[41] Anger at the national humiliation in Vietnam and at other perceived defeats abroad, including the Carter administration's renegotiation of the Panama Canal treaties, stirred in a fiery condiment of outraged patriotism. But it was economic discontent and a revolution in economic thinking that did most to prepare the ground for the sweeping ideological change of the 1970s.

In the course of that decade, the faith in a mixed economy that had sustained a broadly liberal consensus since the New Deal was replaced by a new belief in the superior ability of "the market" to allocate resources and make social as well as economic decisions. The causes of this ideological revolution were exceptionally complex. Some lay in the disappointing performance of the American economy. Some could be traced to populist politics, like the tax revolt that spread like wildfire after the success of Proposition 13 in California. The rebellion of businessmen against what they saw as the constricting regime of high taxation, greedy unions, and heavy-handed regulation played its part.[42]

Most important of all, perhaps, was the reaction to "stagflation" among academic economists, politicians, and the more thoughtful businessmen. For a generation, we had all been Keynesians, as even Richard Nixon put it. The real John Maynard Keynes was a subtle, sometimes apparently self-contradictory thinker, far more conservative than—in the United States, at least—he was popularly supposed to be. But the heart of American neo-Keynesian doctrine was the idea that there was a trade-off between unemployment and inflation. The implication, and this was central to the economic orthodoxy of the liberal consensus, was that government could reduce unemployment and stimulate economic activity by administering careful doses of inflationary stimulation. "Stagflation," that is, the plain fact, evident to all in the 1970s, that one could have rising inflation *and* a sluggish economy at the same time, seemed utterly to disprove the central plank of the prevailing Keynesian doctrine. This intellectual shock made economists and others who thought about economic policy open to conversion to conservative doctrines they previously rejected.

Now the hour had struck for conservative theorists, like Milton Friedman and his followers in the Chicago school, like monetarists and all others who rejected the ideal of a mixed economy, in which the free market was directed and restrained by public action. According to Robert Kuttner:

> When economic growth faltered after 1973, a new radically classical economics gradually gained influence in the academy and in politics. Resurgent business groups, once cowed by the New Deal–Great Society era, became unabashed crusaders for laissez-faire. The increasing marketization of global commerce undermined the institutional capacity of nation-states to manage a mixed economy, and discredited center-left parties.[43]

The ascendancy of free-market economics in academic and business circles was firmly established even before Ronald Reagan became president in 1981. Enthusiastically, if not always consistently, the Reagan administration did all it could to demean and diminish government itself. It cut back on both the regulatory and the redistributive functions of the welfare state. The famous decision in August 1981 to dismiss more than 11,000 air traffic controllers, which led to the bankruptcy and collapse of their union, and subsequent tough action in response to other transportation strikes, sent a powerful message. The airline and banking industries were radically deregulated in response to free-market theory. Long before Bill Clinton defeated George Bush senior in 1992, two Republican administrations had fully adopted conservative social theory and an uncompromising version of free-market economics as taught by the University of Chicago, whose leaders succeeded one another on the podium in Stockholm as Nobel laureates.[44]

By the end of the 1980s, the economy and society had been dramatically changed by the ascendancy not only of free-market theory but also of markets, and in particular financial markets. When money is short, as it was in the 1980s, the power of those who have it increases. The people with the money were in the first place the banks and the other financial institutions, and—more broadly—the well-to-do. The thirty years after World War II had been a golden age for big industrial corporations and their largely unionized workers. It was a time of regulation and imperfect competition but also of low unemployment and high growth in output and productivity. The last quarter of the twentieth century, in contrast, was a flush time for the financial sector.

Virtually every important change in the structure and performance of the economy was better for Wall Street than for anyone else.[45] Lower taxes disproportionately favored the wealthy and those with high incomes, leaving them with more funds to invest. With the exception of a few years after the sharp market break in October 1987, the stock market rose precipitously. The gains went to all shareholders, including the growing number of Americans who owned stock indirectly through mutual funds, but they went disproportionately to a small number of big shareholders. If by the end of the century almost half of all Americans had some stake, direct or indirect, in the stock market, for most the stake was small: for half of the stock-owning half, it was worth less than $5,000, or less than the value of a second-hand automobile.[46] No doubt it was to be expected that new investors would have a small stake. But this was hardly what was suggested by the promoters of a stock-owning democracy.

The big prizes went disproportionately to the insiders: to the bankers, the brokers, the arbitrageurs, the speculators, and those directors who were lucky enough to hold stock when it was run up by one financial operation or another.[47] Luckiest of all were those—bankers, lawyers, accountants, and other professionals—who commanded large fees for their role in facilitating the endless series of mergers, acquisitions, hostile takeovers, leveraged buyouts, and other even more recondite exploits of financial engineering. Inequality was further increased by the regressive character of the tax code, especially after the George W. Bush administration's selective tax cut of 2001, which raised the after-tax income of households in the top 1 percent by 6.3 per cent, compared with 2.8 percent for other groups. This was a $45,000 a year bonus for the wealthiest 1 percent of American families.

In free-market theory, what was happening was that the pitiless but ultimately benevolent "creative destruction"[48] of capitalism was allocating investment funds to the best-managed companies where they could earn the highest returns. All too often the process benefited not the shareholders, still less the corporation's employees or the economy as a whole, but the corporate raiders. The latter could borrow the money to take a company over and then leave it, panting for life like a beached whale, with a mountain of debt. Often, too, they could take advantage of some tax break, making the money cheap to them.

Deregulation and globalization together meant that virtually all the money in the world was available for speculation on the New York Stock

Exchange. The orgy of financial imprudence has been well charted in a number of accounts, some disapproving, others unable to conceal their admiration.[49] That was part of the cultural shift to the free market. Americans had first admired, then pilloried the Robber Barons of the Gilded Age and first followed, then blamed the unscrupulous businessmen responsible for the Great Crash. Now the heroes of Wall Street were cultural icons, and to disapprove of them smacked of either envy or leftism. Tom Frank summed up the doctrine of what he called "market populism":

> From Deadheads to Nobel laureate economists, from paleoconservatives to New Democrats, American leaders in the nineties came to believe that markets were a popular system, a far more democratic form of organization than (democratically elected) governments. . . . That in addition to being mediums of exchange, markets were mediums of consent. . . . markets were a friend of the little guy; markets brought down the pompous and the snooty; markets gave us what we wanted; markets looked out for our interests.[50]

The financial insanity culminated in the collapse of Long Term Capital Management in 1998.[51] This was a so-called hedge fund, constructed according to the precepts of two academic economists, Robert Merton and Myron Scholes. (They were awarded the Nobel Prize for the ingenuity of their theories about the new derivative instruments that were all the rage.) Months later, the fund was obliged to reveal that by pyramiding and kiting investments in time-honored fashion, albeit under cover of a barrage of newly coined pseudoscientific jargon, it was in danger of collapse. Its portfolio was valued at $200 billion. The derivatives hanging from it like baubles from a Christmas tree were put at $1.2 trillion. Putting ideological commitments to free-market theory aside, the great and the good of Wall Street loyally got together to bail out their overeager competitors. Broke or not, LTCM was too big to be allowed to fail.

Such casino capitalism in the financial markets earned great fortunes for those whom the novelist Tom Wolfe called the new Masters of the Universe. These ruthless raiders sacked venerable companies like financial Mongols. Greed is good, was their motto. They produced rich profits for shareholders, though in the nature of things only those who could afford to invest large sums made enough money to make much difference to their life-style.

The effect on the employees of once solid corporations in the real economy was not happy. One easy way for management, under pressure from such raiders, to cut costs was to reduce the work force. Unions in many industries were no longer in a position to protect their members. "For much of the union movement," wrote labor historian Nelson Lichtenstein, "the 1970s and 1980s were a disaster."[52] Union membership as a proportion of the entire work force fell from 29 percent in 1973 to just above 16 percent in 1991. In traditionally unionized industries (the needle trades, meat-packing, engineering, and the trucking and warehousing organized by the Teamsters, as well as automobiles) the losses were proportionately more severe. Membership in the International Ladies' Garment Workers Union fell by no less than two-thirds.[53] In the construction industry, too, traditionally dominated by the conservative craft unions, as early as the late 1960s employers consciously set out to break the unions. "It's time for a showdown," said Winton Blount, the Alabama contractor who became Nixon's secretary of labor.[54]

The unions' political clout fell commensurately. New jobs were being created and at an impressive clip. But many of the new jobs were at or even (in the underground economy) below the minimum wage, while many of the jobs that were disappearing were well-paid jobs with fringe benefits covered by union contracts.

Manufacturing jobs were being "exported" to developing countries, in two ways. Sometimes the U.S. corporation physically moved plants abroad to take advantage of far lower wages. Many manufacturers, for example, moved production to *maquiladora* plants in Mexico where workers, using the same equipment as in the United States, were paid one-seventh as much. Sometimes it was easier to buy semifinished or finished products from countries with even lower wages and with minimal or nonexistent costs for health and safety regulation, taxes, or environmental protection. Scanning the labels of garments in mass market stores like Gap or Banana Republic became a geography lesson, as U.S. retailers brought in goods from Surinam or the Andaman Islands.

This "outsourcing" to lower-cost foreign producers was a major reason why domestic employment in manufacturing fell from 27 percent in 1970 to 19 percent in 1986.[55] Moreover a Brookings Institution study showed that the trend toward assembly in low-wage foreign countries was encouraged by a favorable tax and tariff regime. Under tariff regulations, U.S. companies are permitted to reimport, without duty, goods that originate in the United States if they are fabricated or assembled overseas. While half of these duty-free goods were assembled in Japan, Germany, or Canada, half came from developing countries, notably Mexico, Malaysia, Singapore, the Philippines, Korea, Taiwan, and Hong Kong.[56]

Back home, corporate management systematically replaced unionized workers with unprotected "consultants" or contracted workers, often with no pension or health plan rights. Sometimes employers in effect asked existing workers to bid for their own jobs at lower wages. Sometimes even unionized plants installed two-tier wage patterns whereby older workers retained higher rates but newcomers entered at a lower wage that would never catch up.[57]

In obedience to the ancient philosophical fallacy that to name something is to explain it, some analysts attributed the decline in union membership to something called "post-industrial society."[58] Others saw it as the result of conscious strategies on the part of management to weaken labor.[59]

According to Barry Bluestone and Bennett Harrison,

[M]ost mainstream economists have rather cavalierly concluded that globalization (in both trade and investment) has not brought much downward pressure on the wages of lower-skilled American workers. One noteworthy exception is Harvard's Dani Rodrik, otherwise very much the orthodox economist, who surprised his colleagues with the publication in 1997 of an argument that more open trade . . . reduces the domestic bargaining power of labor, possibly leading to lower wages or lower growth in wages.[60]

Enthusiasts for the free market praised the new labor market for its realism or flexibility, and no doubt there had been plants and whole industries where wage costs were unrealistically high in a globalized world. That, after all, was what had made management go global: to drive down U.S. wages with competition from developing or scarcely developing countries.

Undeniably, however, what this added up to was a massive shift of economic and ultimately political power from labor to management, from the industrial sector to the financial, from the unionized North and Midwest to the largely nonunion South and the less unionized West, from workers and middle managers to top managers, major shareholders, and bankers—in short, from poor to rich. Overall, the effect of the free-market ideology in a deregulated economy was absolutely predictable, because intended. It was sharply to increase inequality.

———◆———

THIS RIGHTWARD SHIFT was not just a matter of conservatives winning more elections. It was also a matter of those who had called themselves liberals being converted to conservative ideas. There was no more interesting example than President Clinton himself. By stages, although originally an economic populist of a kind, he espoused the free-market creed. He belonged to that faction in the Democratic Party that had responded to the decline in the Democratic vote, and especially among white males, by moving to centrist positions. Clinton won in 1992 by repeating the mantra that it was "the economy, stupid." He accepted the strategy of the Democratic Leadership Council and was much influenced by its leader, Al From. Even so, the decisive stage in the framing of his economic policy came not from within the Democratic Party but from Wall Street.[61]

In his 1992 election campaign and in his manifesto, *Putting People First*, Clinton promised a middle-class tax cut and, at the same time, elimination of three-quarters of the deficit. Even before he was inaugurated, the Congressional Budget Office warned that the deficit would be much higher than expected. Next, the Office of Management and Budget predicted that the federal deficit would rise sharply, to more than $300 billion. Clinton's own budget chief, Leon E. Panetta, a former chairman of the House budget committee, and the holdover Republican chairman of the Federal Reserve, Alan Greenspan, agreed that long-term interest rates would rise. The danger was that stock and bond markets would lose confidence and might fall catastrophically.

Greenspan was a lifelong Wall Street conservative and disciple of the ultraconservative novelist and guru Ayn Rand. He was first appointed as chairman of the Fed by Ronald Reagan and then reappointed by George Bush senior and by Clinton. Clinton's first treasury secretary was the conservative Texas Democrat, Senator Lloyd Bentsen; and Robert Rubin, a Wall Street Democrat who had been chairman of Goldman Sachs, was brought in as chairman of a new body, the National Economic Council, before succeeding Bentsen two years later. These advisers persuaded Clinton that his first priority must be to reduce the federal deficit.

Suddenly Clinton's problem was how to persuade Congress not to cut taxes, as he had promised, but to increase them. In a startling turnaround, Clinton in effect abandoned Democratic economic and budget policy and adopted Wall Street orthodoxy. In the near term, it was a brilliantly successful move. Clinton's policies can be credited with having played a large part in making possible the stock market spike of the late 1990s. They reduced the burden of servicing the government's debt and so made more money available to lower taxes. They increased savings and damped down inflation and so contributed to creating a favorable impression on Wall Street.

After the Republican successes in the 1994 mid-term elections, widely attributed to Newt Gingrich and his Contract with America, Clinton again moved to the right.[62]

It was a good time for corporate profits, and good, exceptionally good, for the stock market. The most spectacular rises were in high-technology stocks, and especially in initial public offerings like those of Yahoo! (1996) and America Online (1995). The rise in equity values made people feel rich. Consumer spending roared ahead, much of it financed by credit card debt. But the newly tough management ethos, coupled with global competition and such technical innovations as sophisticated inventory management, not to mention the constant raider warfare on Wall Street, made people's jobs less secure. They might continue to spend. But they saved far less than their parents, and they went far deeper into debt.

So the economic policies of the 1990s caused, or at least allowed, a spectacular boom, especially on Wall Street. But they also did nothing to reverse the steady rise in inequality. Income inequality has increased since the 1970s. By 1997, the first year of Clinton's second term, a careful study showed that this had already extended to inequality of wealth. "The gap between haves and have-nots," it concluded, "is greater than at any time since 1929. The sharp increase in inequality since the late 1970s has made wealth distribution in the United States more unequal than in what used to be perceived as the class-ridden societies of northwestern Europe."[63]

Under Reagan and George Bush senior and their allies in Congress and in the conservative think tanks, the Republicans had set out to reverse what seemed to them an unhealthy trend toward equality. And in that they had succeeded.

Now the boom is over, but the inequality remains. It is clear that the increase in inequality is squarely the consequence of free-market policies promoted by conservatives in politics and by their allies in the economics profession. It is also plain that mainstream Democrats, including President Clinton, have to some extent adopted this ideology. In a number of major speeches, Clinton buckled together, as essentials of the American belief system, political democracy and free-market capitalism.

"We have a free market now," says Gordon Gekko, the antihero of Oliver Stone's movie, *Wall Street*. "We don't have a democracy."[64] America has always been a capitalist country. But it has not always been usual to couple free-market economics with democracy as the two coequal and essential foundations of the American public philosophy. Once, wrote one of the few who dared to challenge the omnipotence of the market at the very height of the great 1990s bull market, "Americans imagined that economic democracy meant a reasonable standard of living for all. . . . Today, however, American opinion leaders seem generally convinced that democracy and the free market are simply identical."[65]

Between 1975 and the end of the century, many Americans, including many who previously thought of themselves in some way as liberals, espoused the quintessentially conservative belief that business knows best and that the imperfect competition between giant corporations, guided by a few thousand stock market professionals trying to make their own fortunes, could do more to promote the prosperity of the many than a democratically elected government.

———•◆•———

THE THEME of this book, then, is the way the American polity has changed over the past twenty-five years. It argues that those changes have been misunderstood, largely because of a sometimes naive, often self-interested, adoption of conservative free-market ideology.[66] Between Richard Nixon's departure from the White House in 1974 and the return of the Republican George W. Bush in 2001, a new conservative consensus was forged. Some Democrats felt they had no alternative but to join it. In place of the New Deal philosophy, in which the workings of the free market were to be restrained and controlled by government intervention, the new public philosophy sought to set the market free. Whereas in the middle third of the century the political consensus encouraged modest redistribution of wealth, in its last quarter the free market was set free. If the result was a winner-take-all society, in which the devil took the hindmost, that was acceptable. The new assumption was that, left to itself, the mighty engine of free-market capitalism would generate wealth on a scale that would make redistribution unnecessary, even unpopular.

This book argues that this new worship of the market was doubly mistaken. While unrestrained markets and a deregulated economy could indeed create wealth on a dazzling scale, they could not abolish the laws of economic gravity. Bust would still follow boom, and perhaps in a cycle that was even more destructive than in the past. At the same time, the working of the free market, and of the conservative political philosophy that imposed it and made propaganda for it, would cause—had indeed already caused—social consequences that would be undesirable and in the end dangerous.

——◆——

PART OF THE OVERCOOKED triumphalism of the late 1990s was based on a misunderstanding of the genuinely thrilling opportunities afforded by new technology in general and especially the Internet. Chapter 3 traces the history of the new technology, and argues that this history has been misunderstood. Credit for its dramatic achievements has been wrongly awarded. It shows that, so far from being mainly the product of youthful entrepreneurs taking advantage of a deregulated free-market economy, both the basic science and the technology of the Internet were largely the products of research and development done under the impetus of the Cold War. Furthermore they can hardly be claimed as evidence of the creative élan of deregulated free-market capitalism, because the essential work was done either in government institutions or in universities or industrial laboratories shielded from the operations of the free market by government contracts. It was not the market but the government that built the Internet.

Chapter 4 shows that, in spite of the dizzy stock market boom and the really favorable economic conditions in the middle and late 1990s—low unemployment, relatively high productivity, low inflation—it is an illusion to see the economic record of the past twenty-five years as a brilliant one. To the contrary, until the mid-1990s the economy performed in only a mediocre way. Substantial gains for the wealthiest few in society concealed the fact that the situation for the majority of Americans actually got worse over most of the period. The spectacular gains of the last half-dozen years of the twentieth century compare very unfavorably with the record of the years after World War II, when—under a mixed economy philosophy— productivity and economic growth achieved a far superior record to those boasted of by conservatives in more recent years. In short, the New Economy is largely an illusion, and talk of new parameters is intellectually disreputable.

Contrary to President Clinton's predictions of lasting prosperity, and in spite of widespread self-congratulation in conservative and business circles, a sudden, short-lived spike in financial markets benefited the few rather than the many. And this is against the American grain. For the life-giving strength of the American economy has always been, until the past few decades, the breadth of its benevolence. The genius of the American economy has not lain in the ruthlessness with which the few were allowed to trample on their defeated competitors but in the generosity in which the many were allowed to share in the common prosperity.

Three chapters look at how the promise of real progress for significant groups in society, together making up a large majority of the population, has been disappointed by the reactionary character of the political revolution since the 1970s. Chapter 5 looks at the consequences of the new immigration, which has added more than 30 million people to the population since the late 1960s. It will transform the American gene pool, turning what was statistically a population of transplanted Europeans into one in which people of European descent will probably be a minority within half a century. It will also change American politics by concentrating immigrants and their descendants in a few metropolitan areas, rather as the last mass immigration of the early twentieth century did, but in the future migrants will be drawn in the majority from the developing world. And, of course, immigration will introduce new issues and new stresses into American politics.

Chapter 6 shows how the high hopes of the women's movement in the 1960s have given way to division and frustration. It argues that there have been in effect two women's movements. The first, largely confined to a small group of highly educated women in metropolitan areas, evoked a backlash by its unwisely enthusiastic adoption of radical rhetoric and tactics. The far larger movement of women into the work force has done more to change the status and expectations of all women. Yet it, too, has encountered frustration.

The argument of chapter 7 is that something similar has happened to the hopes of African Americans. Here the contrast, and the inequality, is even greater than for women. There are now almost no heights a black man or even a black woman cannot aspire to in America—Colin Powell, after all, is secretary of state and was a credible candidate for president. Black actors, entertainers, musicians, sportsmen and sportswomen have achieved astonishing feats. Yet equality of condition and equality of esteem remain elusive for all minorities. And a proportion of all African Americans that is depressingly high in the light of the ambitions of the civil rights movement has drifted down into the condition of an underclass, without jobs, without opportunities, too often without hope.

Chapter 8 returns to the mainstream. It looks at changes in the way all Americans live at the beginning of a new century. It examines the decline of civic engagement. It inquires into the responsibility of media, especially news media, for some disquieting trends. It confronts the implications of the fact that a growing majority of Americans live neither in cities nor in the countryside, but in suburbs. It suggests that one reason why such social issues as poverty have disappeared from the agenda is because the poor, and other unfortunate groups, are geographically remote and largely invisible. It asks, too, whether the economic inequality of the past few decades may not be reintroducing those hierarchies of social class Americans were so proud of abolishing.

The paradox of American power is that, at the very moment when American influence in the world is greater than ever, Americans seem less and less interested in the rest of the world: more self-sufficient, but also more self-satisfied. Chapter 9 points out some implications of this paradox for the United States and for the rest of the world and inquires into the revival of American exceptionalism. Finally, chapter 10 seeks to tie these themes together in the context of Jefferson's vision of a nation still sorely puzzled in many ways, even though prospering "beyond example in the history of man." But first we must analyze some of the changes in the political system over the past quarter of a century, and how they have converted the American majority to a new public philosophy that is willing to trade inequality for prosperity.

2

New Politics

Those of the top economic groups—particularly the new indus-
trialists—are to be found in communion with the advocates of
white supremacy. In the chaos and demoralization that ensue alert
men with a sharp eye for immediate advantage take and count their
gains.

—*V. O. Key Jr., Southern Politics in State and Nation*

THE "NEOCONSERVATIVES" OF THE 1970S liked to speak of the law of
unintended consequences. There is no such law, of course. They meant
simply that you could argue against any proposal for government action,
and they disapproved of most on principle, by suggesting that no one
could be sure what its consequences would be.

The logic is fallacious. But it is certainly true that many acts of public
policy do have consequences that are unintended, and few major pieces
of legislation have had as many of those as the Voting Rights Act of 1965.
Its consequences for American politics have been vast. (If they were not
intended, at least they were by no means wholly unanticipated.)

In the last third of the twentieth century, American politics changed in
many ways. Three of them can be pulled out as the most salient. The first
was the new national alignment symbolized and in part created by the
Voting Rights Act. That ended the solid Democratic South, and also
turned the Republican Party into a national conservative party. The old
party loyalties, ultimately traceable to memories of the Civil War, were
replaced by a modern alignment, based on an ideological rivalry between conservatives and liberals. That in turn fundamentally reflected,

for the first time for a century or so, a class division between haves and have-nots.

The second, in part a consequence of the first, was the triumph of conservative ideology. Conservatism conquered the Republican Party. After an interval, the Democratic Party moved in response to the right. The whole center of gravity of American politics moved with it. In response to national revulsion—it is not too strong a word—against the perceived errors and dangers of the Kennedy-Johnson Great Society programs and of the political turmoil of the 1960s, the American majority accepted a political culture dominated by corporate business and dedicated to proclaiming the supremacy of free-market capitalism as a value equal to democracy itself.

An account of the middle-class and working-class voters who broke ranks with their Democratic allegiance in 1965 to vote for William F. Buckley as mayor of New York sums up their feelings succinctly:

> Having prospered since the war, these second- and third-generation Americans no longer felt the pull of New Deal democracy. They were worried about higher taxes rather than unemployment. They wanted a fiscally responsible rather than socially committed administration. Many of them had started to move into the Republican column during the 1950s. They were also vexed by what they saw as the decline of the city manifested in both the growing crime rate and the deterioration of the schools.[1]

To be sure, those voters who rejected the New Deal ideals did not see themselves as voting for corporate power. But that was the inevitable, if unintended, consequence of their rejection of thirty years of Democratic policies—ironically the very policies that had put them in a position where they could afford to turn their back on a "socially committed administration."

The third great change was the growing dependence of the political process, as a practical matter, on paid political television advertising, and the consequent obsession with raising the money needed to pay for it. Although unions, too, were major contributors, on balance this greatly increased the influence of corporate business, through various spokesmen and surrogates, and of wealthy individuals on the fortunes of politicians, and therefore on the political process.

These three tectonic shifts were interconnected. The shift to the right was a consequence of widespread rejection of the Great Society's reforms. The monetization of politics was partly due to changes in media but more to the ascendancy of the view that there was nothing wrong with a democracy dominated by the people with money. It was a view symbolized by the victory, in *Buckley v. Valeo,* in 1976—the very year that opened the period under review in this book—of an ultraconservative who successfully argued, before a new Supreme Court with a Republican-appointed majority, that spending money on elections was a form of political expression, and so protected by the First Amendment guarantee of free speech.[2]

———•◦•———

PRESIDENT LYNDON JOHNSON chose to sign the Voting Rights Act on August 6, 1965 in the very room off the rotunda of the Capitol where Abraham Lincoln signed the first bill freeing southern slaves.[3] Whether or not as he signed it he muttered under his breath, "There goes the South,"[4] he certainly understood all too well that, by enfranchising African American voters in the South, he might well be destroying the traditional Democratic Party that had brought him to power.

What few, if any, predicted was that the Voting Rights Act (or rather the end of the one-party South, a process that had begun well before 1965, but that was decisively achieved by that legislation) would not only change the Democratic Party. It would transform the Republican Party as well. As a consequence it would play a crucial part in shifting American politics in a conservative direction.

The Deep South had fought in the last ditch to keep black citizens from voting. As late as that spring of 1965 Martin Luther King Jr. led a march in Selma, in the middle of the Alabama Black Belt, to demand the vote for black men and women. They were set upon by the local sheriff and his men with clubs and bullwhips. Fifty of them were injured. In the ensuing outrage, two northern demonstrators were murdered.[5] In a passionate speech to a joint session of Congress,[6] President Johnson called for bipartisan support, and in under five months he had signed the bill into law.[7]

The Voting Rights Act of 1965 did not, alone and of itself, transform the alignment of parties in America. Social, demographic, and legal factors had been preparing the way for decades. As long ago as the 1920s the formula was, in the casually racist language of the day, "the Yankees came South, the boll weevil came East, the cotton went West and the niggers went North." U.S. cotton production has largely shifted to irrigated lands in Arizona and California. African Americans have been migrating to the great northern cities since World War I. In recent decades there has also been heavy white migration into the South, and considerable reverse migration of African Americans moving back into a South they feel to be more congenial than North or West.

Analysts distinguish between different subregions of the South. The political culture of the Deep South, meaning those parts of South Carolina, Georgia, Alabama, Mississippi, and Louisiana, and smaller parts of other states such as Tennessee, Arkansas, and Texas, where the plantation system left very high proportions of black population,[8] was by no means the same as that of the upper South,[9] where the process of enfranchising black citizens advanced much faster. Even within the Deep South, the Black Belt counties, home until well into the twentieth century of a plantation system, were very different from the "piney woods" or "up country" districts, where there were fewer black people, and where the political creed of the whites at the forks of the creeks was a sockless populism, very different from the patrician paternalism of the Black Belt bourbons.[10] Both cultures were utterly different from that of the Appalachian and Ozark Mountains, where slavery hardly penetrated. Many in some mountain counties fought for the Union in the Civil War. In such places, a Republican tradition survived. Again, town was very different politically from country. Each region, and each state, had its distinctive political style. Finally, party loyalties in state and local elections were far more rigid than in presidential elections.

While the Democratic Party was losing control of the South in presidential elections, it continued to fare better in both houses of Congress and in many state houses. In 1972, when the Nixon national victory confirmed the emerging Republican hegemony, Democrats still won 68 percent of House and Senate seats in the South and virtually all state legislatures.[11] Long service and personal popularity presumably contributed to this result. So did atavistic Southern memories of Reconstruction. In 1980, when Reagan led a veritable Republican landslide, the Republicans won control of the Senate and if they failed to do so in the House it was in part because seventy of the seventy-eight southern Democrats were conservatives who duly supported Reagan's conservative agenda of cuts in taxes and spending.[12]

By the 1950s, demographic and cultural change had already begun to increase the number of black voters in the upper South, and in the cities. Only in the rural Black Belt were virtually all blacks prevented from voting. In presidential campaigns, well before 1965, Eisenhower in 1952 and Nixon in 1960 had made inroads into the Democratic allegiance of the South, and so did Barry Goldwater in 1964. Slowly, under the pressure of the civil rights movement and its Voter Education Project, the number of blacks registered to vote did grow, from 30 percent in 1962 to 43 percent in 1964. Even so, as late as 1964 there was no city in the Deep South where the percentage of blacks who were registered to vote reached 40 percent.[13]

After the Voting Rights Act, things changed quickly and decisively. Within weeks, President Johnson was able to boast that one-third of potential black voters in the first target districts had been registered.[14] It was plain that the white South was no longer in open revolt. Federal registrars needed to go into only 60 of more than 500 counties affected by the law. By 1968 there were only 14 counties (out of more than 1,000) in which massive black exclusion from electoral registers persisted.[15] By 1974 67 percent of blacks in the entire South were registered voters—only 1 percent less than the figure for white voters.[16] By 1968 blacks were voting in significant numbers in every southern state.

The effect on the composition and ideological tone of the Democratic Party in the South was predictable. Until 1965 it had been an all-white party, and the South had been a one-party region. The Republican Party, as the "party of Lincoln," was still largely beyond the pale for southern white voters. Before 1965 the eleven states of the former Confederacy sent seventeen or eighteen staunch conservative Democrats to the Senate, and close to a hundred staunch, mainly conservative Democrats to the House. (Southern Democrats were conservative on racial and constitutional questions but, as was natural in a poor, largely agricultural region, were often quite liberal on economic ones.) Governors and members of state legislatures were equally all white. Now, with surprising speed, that changed. But it changed in two ways.

By the 1972 elections, a handful of black men and women were elected to Congress, to state legislatures, and to other important offices. In Houston, Barbara Jordan was elected to a new congressional district, and in Georgia Andrew Young was elected to an Atlanta district.[17] Both were the first African Americans to represent their state since Reconstruction. But in that same year seven Republicans took congressional seats that had been safe for the Democrats since the end of Reconstruction, among them Trent Lott and Thad Cochran in Mississippi (both later senators). (In 2003 Senator Lott was unwise enough to say, in the unguarded moment of a tribute to Senator Strom Thurmond, that it would have been better for the region if Thurmond's "Dixiecrat" segregationist party had won the 1948 election.)

The ballast shifted. Before, a region with one-third of the nation's population was in the grip of a network of interlocking Democratic state leaderships,[18] each—at least in the Deep South—more conservative than the next. Afterward, the Democratic Party was a more or less uneasy coalition between "core" Democrats, a sprinkling of white liberals, and an African American vote that varied from 10 percent to more than a quarter of the vote from state to state. As a result of the same process, the Republicans captured the South, especially in presidential elections. Until Clinton's victories of 1992 and 1996, indeed, many commentators believed that the Republican breakthrough in the South gave the party a "lock" on presidential elections. The same process brought to Congress the new generation of intransigent Republican conservatives, culminating in the "freshman" generation of 1994, who stoked up the sulphurously ideological politics of the late 1990s.

Until the 1980s there were plenty of moderate and even liberal Republicans in Congress. Few survived after the 1980s.[19] So the new southern conservatives, allied to the metropolitan neoconservatives, were able to make the party over in their own image. The unintended consequence of the enfranchisement of southern blacks, in a word, was the "conservatization" of American politics as a whole. Before the Republican breakthrough in the South, both parties were defined by history. In the South, Democrats kept alive for a hundred years bad dreams of carpetbaggers, Radical Republicans, and their black protégés. In the North, even after Republicans had ceased to "wave the bloody shirt," their pride in the memory of Abraham Lincoln and abolition meant that they continued to think of themselves as a radical party long after they had become conservatives in all but name.

Party allegiance in some parts of the country, even as late as President Kennedy's term, still had almost as much to do with the alignment of parties during the Civil War as with contemporary economic or social issues. To many southerners, the Republicans, as the "party of Lincoln," were pariahs. In the North, party allegiances went back to some history that was almost as ancient, the suspicion and fear aroused in the Old American, Protestant middle class by the arrival of waves of immigrants, first Irish and German, then Scandinavian, later Italians, Slavs, Greeks, and Jews from southern and eastern Europe. The newcomers might be Catholic or Orthodox or Jewish. They might even be socialists. The great majority were not Protestants. Republicans looked askance at the foreign values of these newcomers. Democrats, the party, it was said, of "Rum, Romanism and Rebellion,"[20] represented their interests, and reflected the resentment felt by the newcomers at the resistance they had encountered in their search for prosperity and acceptance.

So until the 1980s there were both liberals and conservatives in each of the two main parties. Only after the end of the solid Democratic South were American politics divided, like the politics of most other democratic countries, on broadly ideological lines. Behind ideology, for the first time since the nineteenth century, party politics reflected a broad class division, between the haves and the have-nots, the inevitable political consequence of growing economic inequality.[21]

It is true that many Republican conservatives indignantly rejected the imputation that they were patricians. Especially in the South, a populist tradition lingered on. Many conservative Republicans clung to the "market populism" that associated liberalism with social privilege.[22] Equally, northern Democrats were by no means exclusively recruited from the ranks of labor. The paramount importance of fund-raising would have guaranteed that, if nothing else.

Some commentators have been misled by the relative lack of interest in pocketbook issues into supposing that the country is "fat and happy" and that economic issues are now less important than cultural ones, such as attitudes to religion, abortion, or the family.[23] To some extent, of course, cultural

factors have always played an important part in American politics. Massachusetts is not Louisiana, and New York is not Minnesota. History, economics, ethnicity, and climate guarantee that. But the supposed disappearance of
economic issues is also in part an illusion created by widespread political
indifference and low voting turnouts. It is not so much that the voters are
contented as that the discontented do not vote. In recent years voting has
been so strongly correlated with economic and social status that one can be
elected to many offices without needing to win more than a comparatively
small number of votes from the lower half of the income distribution curve.
This has reinforced the conservatization of American politics.

———•—

UNTIL THE 1960S, American politics were powerfully shaped by the
memories, and myths, of the Depression and the New Deal. The Democrats were numerically dominant but ideologically divided. The Republicans still presented the appearance of a party in decline. They had still not
quite thrown off the imputation of responsibility for the Depression. For
the most part they represented big corporate business, uneasily allied with
small-town business oligarchies, Old American gentility, and the more
conservative of the patricians who identified with the mainstream northern
Protestant churches and old money.[24]

There were ideological differences within the Republican Party. Both
in Congress and in state and local governments, there were in 1961 many
liberal or moderate Republicans who harked back to the Progressive and
"good government" traditions, themselves not wholly free from hostility to
the new immigrants or at least to the slums and the urban machine politics they were blamed for bringing with them. This group included many
politicians of vision and ideals, such as Senator Charles "Mac" Mathias of
Maryland and Mayor John Lindsay of New York, and governors like Earl
Warren of California and Nelson Rockefeller of New York.

Pockets of unreconstructed Republicanism survived, especially in the
Middle West, in the 1950s. But, especially after the rejection of Robert Taft
and the election of General Eisenhower in 1952, national politics were ruled
by a consensus that, at least domestically, was essentially liberal. The political landscape had been transformed by the great events of the 1930s and
1940s: severe economic depression, World War II, and the Cold War. In

effect, the Democrats—shaken by Republican accusations of disloyalty—adopted a conservative anticommunist foreign policy. The majority of Republicans, with many mental reservations and occasional rebellions, went along with the liberal Democratic policies that had created a welfare state in America. Decades later Ronald Reagan's conservative budget director, David Stockman, put it like this: "Why did the conservative, anti-spending [Republican] party . . . end up ratifying a half-trillion-dollar per year welfare state? In the answer lies the modern dirty little secret of the Republican Party: the conservative opposition helped to build the American welfare state brick by brick during the three decades prior to 1980."[25]

That Republican acceptance of the New Deal was, however, grudging and contingent. In the 1950s Republicans sought to limit labor unions through the Taft-Hartley bill (1947).[26] It was only a matter of time before the party's conservative wing gathered itself to throw off the liberal yoke.

In 1964 the Republicans nominated their first unequivocally conservative presidential candidate since Alf Landon, and Barry Goldwater was almost as badly beaten as Landon. Lyndon Johnson's landslide victory in that year made possible his ambitious liberal program before the Vietnam War limited his domestic ambitions. It also concealed the conservative insurrection that was brewing within the Republican Party. Starting on a small scale in the tiny, enclosed world of the conservative intellectuals, this movement would before long transform both the party's ideology and its electoral prospects.

In New York, the group of anticommunist intellectuals around William Buckley's *National Review* brokered differences between traditional and religious conservatives on the one hand, and libertarians and business conservatives on the other, skillfully exploiting the shared anticommunism of the two traditions.[27] Thus armed with confidence and a clear, if somewhat self-contradictory, political philosophy, the conservative movement set out to reverse the achievements of the New Deal. It inspired the Goldwater campaign, powered Ronald Reagan's victory in the California gubernatorial election of 1966, and helped to carry Richard Nixon into the White House in 1968. Had it not been for the follies encouraged by the darker side of Nixon's nature, it is likely that a conservative revolution in the tone and agenda of American politics would have followed Nixon's devastating victory in 1972.

As it was, the conservative movement came of age. In the 1970s it captured the Republican Party. Its ideas fell on fertile ground among all those who were shocked by what they saw as the excesses of Democrats and liberals. In three areas especially it responded to angry concerns: about the economy; about what was seen as moral and social decay; and about the perceived decline of American power and prestige in the outside world.

The U.S. economy was already experiencing competition from Western Europe and Japan when the two oil price rises, in 1973 and 1979, hit home to ordinary people. The unprecedented combination of inflation and stagnation triggered a tax revolt that spread swiftly from California, where it had passed Proposition 13, to other states. Corporate management and its political representatives, fearing that it was no longer master in its own house, launched a determined counterattack against unions, government regulation, and the environmental movement.[28]

Abroad, the Soviet Union under Leonid Brezhnev was challenging aggressively from Africa to Afghanistan. A series of painful humiliations began with the final collapse of the U.S.-backed regime in South Vietnam and the fall of Saigon in 1975 and culminated in the capture of fifty-three U.S. embassy staff in Iran in 1979. This, and the renegotiation of the Panama Canal treaties, made many Americans hungry for strong, patriotic leadership. Republicans and especially conservatives were able to capitalize on a widespread sense that something had gone badly wrong in society. They were able to take advantage of a public mood that shared their angry focus on what were labeled moral issues, such as divorce, single-parent families, the abuse of welfare, homosexuality, drugs, and above all abortion. Feminism, radical politics, opposition to the war and the draft, the counterculture, and new assaults on sexual mores and religious values were all seen as threatening chaos and social breakdown, not least by those very working-class ethnic families that had been the backbone of the support for the Democratic Party since the New Deal.

There has been a disillusion with the public sector, says David Smith, research director of the AFL-CIO: "You can trace its roots to the Vietnam war and to the civil rights issues. People have a 'money's worth' criterion for judging government. It is the middle class saying, 'You all are spending too much time worrying about poor people, and not enough worrying about us.'"[29]

This disillusion with government, says Smith, was born of the growing economic insecurity of the 1970s and 1980s. In the 1980s there was a fall in real wages. And there was insecurity caused by massive reorganization. Reaganism, especially the "Reagan Democrat" phenomenon, fed on economic insecurity. According to Smith,

> That was the domestic mood. But you mustn't confuse the very real underlying anxieties with the way they were exploited by the politicians. People told whoppers, about government being the only kind of bureaucracy, about the growth of the federal government. They said "if the government didn't spend so much money on lazy so-and-sos and welfare queens, there would be more for you, or taxes would not be so high. And so these whoppers resonated with people who were hurting. Management was trying to keep costs under control by downsizing, outsourcing. Then you should not underestimate the bitterness of the McGovern campaign. There was hostility to the intelligentsia. "They paid no price." People said the folks who were "talking down America," were not at risk.[30]

The extent to which the turn away from New Deal politics, and specifically the phenomenon of the Reagan Democrats, was racial in origin is angrily disputed. It seems to me indisputable that racial fears and antipathies played a part, sometimes crudely, more often subtly and in half-conscious ways. For one thing, white working-class people felt they bore the brunt of the social tensions created by black residential in-migration and by black mobility in the workplace. The white working class also felt disproportionately victimized by crime, which was—fairly or unfairly—blamed on black people. And both black politics, and the political stance of white liberals engaged in defending black people, often offended deeply held working-class beliefs about patriotism, the family, and self-help. The career of George Wallace offers evidence of how crude southern populist racism resonated with the northern white working class. As Dan T. Carter has written, Wallace was "the alchemist of the new social conservatism as he compounded racial fear, anti-communism, cultural nostalgia, and traditional right-wing economics into a movement that laid the foundation for the conservative counter-revolution that reshaped American politics in the 1970s and 1980s."[31]

At the same time, as the AFL-CIO's David Smith insisted, just because politicians were exploiting racial fears, that did not mean those fears were not real and to some extent justified. A *Time* magazine report from Macomb County, Michigan, just before the 1988 presidential campaign illustrates this. Asked why she was not, after all, voting for the Democratic candidate, Michael Dukakis, a young mother in Warren, Michigan, answered firmly: "Dukakis's views on crime."[32]

In the late 1960s and 1970s the "politics of rage" occasionally spilled over into violence and truculent, threatening populism. This mood was somewhat calmed by Ronald Reagan's election as president in 1980. Many, especially working-class "Reagan Democrats," welcomed his claim, in his successful 1984 reelection campaign, that it was "Morning in America." And many were persuaded by Reagan's clever formulation of a core conservative value, that "government is not the solution to our problem, government is the problem."[33]

With Reagan in the White House many conservatives believed that the longed-for counterrevolution had happened.[34] Many who were not committed conservatives agreed. On Inauguration Day in 1981, Hedrick Smith, the *New York Times*'s bureau chief in Washington, divined that Reagan was "a crusader" and called him "the first missionary conservative to be elected with the aim of reversing the liberal New Deal revolution of government activism and Democratic party dominance established by Franklin D. Roosevelt." Reagan's popularity was enormously enhanced by the unsuccessful attempt on his life by a deranged Yale student called John W. Hinckley in March 1981. He was able to use it to dominate the Congress as no president had done since Lyndon Johnson in 1964 and 1965.

Reagan's administration had its failures as well as its successes. It would be a mistake to credit it with the collapse of the Soviet Union, which began to happen as a result of the collapse of the Soviet economy and Mikhail Gorbachev's commitment to *perestroika* in the mid-1980s.[35] But most historians agree that Reagan's combination of firmness and openness toward the Soviet Union worked. With the Middle East and Latin America he dealt much less effectively. Indeed Reagan was lucky not to face impeachment as a result of the undisciplined and illegal antics of his staff in the Iran-Contra affair.[36]

The Reagan administration's economic policy was less successful. Reagan had set out to be fiscally prudent. Indeed, he favored a constitutional amendment to mandate a balanced budget. Unfortunately, he combined a tax cut with accelerated spending on defense and a failure to fulfill his promises of deep cuts in domestic spending. The result was exactly the opposite of what he said he wanted: a high and continuing budget deficit.[37] There is, to be sure, a school of thought that holds that the Reagan administration knew exactly what it was doing: that it meant to create a deficit so as to coerce the Democrats in Congress into abjuring high spending on social policies.[38]

Certainly Reagan's victory in 1980 had been accompanied by much conservative economic theorizing. There were enthusiasts for monetarism, for "supply-side" economic policy and, in academia, for "rational choice theory." The orthodoxy of "Keynesianism," which had reigned since the New Deal, was dethroned in favor of the economics of the free market, as advocated notably by the economics department of the University of Chicago.[39]

Reagan was replaced by his vice president, George H. W. Bush, in 1989. Bush was a classic Republican, as opposed to a conservative. He had no time for what he called "voodoo economics." A large share of his energies was devoted to foreign affairs. The collapse of the communist empire in Eastern Europe, the dissolution of the Soviet Union, and the Gulf War all happened on his watch. Bush's handling of these world events was not above criticism. He was slow, first to recognize the importance of what Gorbachev had done, and then to realize that, however impressive his achievement, Gorbachev was yesterday's man. Nevertheless, in the international arena Bush was courageous and honorable.[40] Politically, however, this inevitable absorption in the affairs of the world was a disaster. In the 1992 presidential election he was swept away by young Bill Clinton, who took advantage of the relatively mild recession of 1990–91 with the slogan, "It's the economy, stupid!"

———•◆•———

WAS THERE a Reagan revolution? Certainly Reagan was never either as popular or as effective as his formidable conservative claque in the media liked to suggest.[41] Some of the conservative theories he adopted proved overstated or even absurd. His "supply-side" belief that lower taxes would bring in more revenue was plain wrong. Clinton's victories in 1992 and 1996 would seem to give the lie to conservative hopes of an irreversible conservative tide. Yet Ronald Reagan's two terms, and even more the events that led up to them, do constitute a major turning point in American politics.

After Reagan, liberal ideas were on the defensive for more than twenty years. (As we shall see, that tide may be turning at last.)[42] The proportion of Americans who called themselves liberal had been declining even before 1980. By 1990 it was 16 percent.[43] Since the 1970s, substantial majorities disapproved of affirmative actions for minorities. There was a broad and growing assumption that government was often not the right agent to provide solutions for social problems. Instead, there was a new consensus that the "free market"—a term loosely used to describe extremely complex phenomena, and even more loosely invoked to propose solutions that were often unproved—was the place to find answers.

At the same time American society seemed to be becoming more conservative in certain other ways. Widespread support for the death penalty after 1979 was one example.[44] In the sixteen years from 1966 to 1982 just nine prisoners were executed in the United States. In 1984 the annual total was twenty-one; in 1993, thirty-eight; in 1997, seventy-four; in 1998, sixty-eight; in 1999, ninety-eight; and in 2000, eighty-five. Calls for tough policing and sentencing policy were other indications of the same socially conservative mood. The background was widespread concern about drug use and the connection between drugs and violent crime, although many of the murderers executed had killed in the course of petty robberies or domestic disputes. A high proportion—42 percent by 2000—were African Americans. At the same time it became fashionable to deride attempts to make discourse more sensitive to minorities as "political correctness."

From the 1970s on there was a huge shift in voters' attitudes to government, on the one hand, and to corporate business, on the other. Since 1932 the great majority of Americans had accepted the idea of a welfare state.[45] That implied, at least in principle, willingness to pay the taxes that would enable government to provide the services people could not provide for themselves. By the middle 1970s, that fundamental assumption was already under attack.

The great tax rebellion started in California, with the overwhelming approval by California's voters of Proposition 13 in June 1978.[46] The most obvious consequence was to release substantial sums into the pockets of a large number of middle class, mostly elderly, Californians. They had been the ones worst hit by the "bracket creep" in tax assessments due to the inflation of real estate prices. (Between 1974 and 1978 the average price of a home in California more than doubled.)[47] Now they had their reward. Estimates vary, but ten years later the California Taxpayers Association calculated that taxpayers had saved more than $200 billion.[48] Only a quarter of that went to individuals. The biggest winners were the state's biggest corporations. Pacific Telephone saved $130 million, Pacific Gas & Electric $90 million, and the state's other big interests profited in proportion.[49]

This was not just a tax rebellion. It was a political earthquake. It may have started as a reaction to the impact of the inflation of property taxes in California, heated up by some scandals in tax assessment. It turned into a rebellion against government itself. "It set the stage," wrote Peter Shrag, "for the Reagan era, and became both fact and symbol of a radical shift in government priorities, public attitudes and social relationships that is as nearly fundamental in American politics as the changes brought by the New Deal."[50]

Its implications for public services in California, and especially for the state's once superb public education system, were nothing less than catastrophic. In the early 1990s, the University of California at Berkeley lost 40 percent of its physics department, 30 percent of its historians; many of its faculty stars, including Nobel Prize winners, were persuaded to take early retirement.[51]

Even before Proposition 13, California's property-based education system was discriminatory in crude class terms. The better-off paid less and got more. In 1972 and again in 1976 lawyers for working-class parents persuaded California's supreme court that it was in violation of the constitutional requirement of equal protection and ordered the legislature to reform it. They developed evidence that an affluent suburb like Beverly Hills, where property values were sky-high, could generate more than $1,300 per pupil in revenue, whereas a working-class district (Baldwin Park, east of Los Angeles city center) would generate only $170 per child. "Affluent districts," the court found, "can have their cake and eat it too. They can provide a high quality education for their children while paying lower taxes. . . . Poor districts, by contrast, have no cake at all."[52]

Since 1960, Californians enjoyed free education from kindergarten through college. Not after Proposition 13. "Over the past three decades," one journalist reported, "California's commitment to its future has steadily eroded as 'student fees' first crept, then shot upward."[53]

Between 1970 and 1998, thanks to complex social changes but also to conservative social policies, while spending on higher education fell, spending on prisons shot up. In 1970 California spent 4 percent of its general fund on "corrections" and 14 percent on higher education. By 1998 expenditure on higher education had fallen as a proportion, to 12.9 percent, while expenditure on prisons had more than tripled to 14.5 percent. In 1988 the number of prisoners in the state was estimated to have exceeded the number of students at the University of California. In 1994, in response to public anger at the drug-induced crime rate,[54] the state legislature passed the toughest "three-strikes" sentencing law, subsequently confirmed by an initiative.

The tax rebellion may have started in California. It owed some of its vehemence to local causes. What it amounted to, said one sociologist, was "the California dreamers waking up."[55] But it soon spread to many parts of the country. Howard Jarvis, who had led the campaign for Proposition 13, became overnight a celebrity and a political power nationally. Within months his new American Tax Reduction Movement had cabled every member of Congress demanding support for a $100 billion cut in federal spending. Within a year there were tax limitation measures on the ballot in seventeen states. By 1980 that had spread to forty-three states. By 1994 "virtually all states had imposed some new constitutional restrictions on local or state taxes and/or imposed spending restrictions."[56]

Many, in the depressed climate that followed the oil price rises of the 1970s, held corporate business responsible for the fact that they had lost their jobs. Yet Ronald Reagan tapped into a rich vein of popular feeling when he pronounced that government was not the solution but the problem.

Union membership, one of the essential supports for New Deal–Fair Deal "welfare state" policies, collapsed. In the 1950s some 35 percent of American wage earners, more than one in three, were enrolled in unions. By the end of the century the proportion was 14 percent, or about one in seven.[57] Among industrial workers, union membership fell from just under half in 1955 to 16 percent in 1998. "Leaving out government employment," a Century Foundation report found in 1999, "union membership dropped below 10 percent of the private sector work force for the first time since before World War II."[58] In the late 1990s the AFL-CIO made increasing membership its top priority. But new recruits, many of them women, have not yet outnumbered the members lost because of shutdowns, downsizing, or the export of jobs abroad.[59] Unions were widely discredited, even among their own members, because of the concessionary agreements they felt obliged to negotiate. From 1964 to 1980, wage cuts were virtually unknown for unionized American workers. During the 1981–82 recession, virtually all sectors of industry saw unions grant concessions to employers. In 1982 44 percent of all unions negotiating new contracts either accepted wage cuts or agreed to do without a wage increase for the first year of the contract.[60]

From the late 1970s on, management became more aggressive. Once chief executives vied with one another to be "enlightened" in their relations with labor unions. As the competitive situation got tougher and the corporate raiders circled, life in the boardroom and on the factory floor approached the "war of every man against every man," described by the seventeenth-century English philosopher Thomas Hobbes. Persons of sovereign authority, wrote Hobbes, "are in continual jealousies, and in the state and posture of gladiators, having their weapons pointed, and their eyes fixed on one another."[61] The admired corporate leader was not, as in the 1950s, the industrial statesman, in the manner of Robert B. Anderson of Atlantic Richfield or J. Irwin Miller of Cummins Diesel, but more the ruthless captains of industry like Lee Iacocca, who said "Hey, boys, I've got a shotgun at your head. I've got thousands of jobs available at seventeen bucks an hour. I've got none at twenty. So you better come to your senses."[62]

A hatred of taxes. A suspicion, amounting sometimes to hatred, of government. A resentment of government intervention to help the underprivileged, seen as discrimination against the working poor, and especially of affirmative action. A climate of fear: fear of crime, of drugs, of a loosening of the bonds of society. But also economic fear: of competition, of losing one's job, of poverty, of the boss. Fear of communism, and of the frustrating complexities of the outside world, from Beirut to Panama. Strangest of all, perhaps, a disposition to blame government for one's troubles, and to give to corporate management the rather wary trust that Americans traditionally gave to their elected politicians. This was all part of the new political mood as the country entered the last quarter of the twentieth century. It was influenced by the new conservatism. And it was the soil in which the new conservative politics could flourish.

The new mood was specifically hostile to the politics of presidents Kennedy and Johnson and their interventionist, liberal policies. There was, too, vague, evanescent but unmistakable, a racial dimension to the new mood. It was not often openly, still less viciously racist. It was rather a reaction against some of the rhetoric of the civil rights movement—black power—and some of the social pathology of the ghetto: crime, drugs, welfare, single mothers. Of course, many who shared the new mood had little or no personal knowledge of these frightening phenomena. They reacted not to experience but to the representations of it by politicians and by the media. And the tone of the media changed. While conservative columnists and radio hosts continued to denounce the "liberal media," the media were in reality less sympathetic to the underprivileged and conspicuously more uncritical of corporate management. Large sections of the media were uncritically admiring of "the rich and famous."

All of this presented the Democratic Party with what looked to some of its thinkers a potentially mortal threat. The two main wings of the party in its happy days had been the South and the northern labor unions. Now the white South was apparently going over to the Republicans. And the labor unions were melting away. As union membership declined, so did white, male support for the Democrats. By the early 1980s, many moderate Democrats were afraid that their party might never again be able to elect a president.

Their gloom was deepened by Kevin Phillips's prophecy, in his influential 1969 book, *The Emerging Republican Majority*, that the future of American politics lay with what he called the Sunbelt.[63] That was his name for the old South, plus the rapidly expanding Southwest. In 1932, the year Democratic hegemony began with the election of Franklin Roosevelt, the Northeast and the Midwest, which Phillips unkindly dubbed the Rust Belt or the Snow Belt, accounted for a clear majority, 54 percent, of the nation's electoral votes. By 1960 the South and West had pulled up equal in population. By 1988 the proportion would be exactly reversed: 54 percent of the population was in the Sunbelt. In the 1950s more than twice as many votes in presidential elections were cast in the north and the Midwest as in the South and West. By the 1980s roughly as many people voted in the South and West. And the Sunbelt, as we have seen, was not only getting more populous. It was also getting more Republican, especially but not only in presidential elections, as conservative southerners abandoned their Democratic heritage.

As early as one month before the 1980 election, one of the shrewdest Democratic consultants in Washington, Lyndon Johnson's former speech-writer, Horace Busby, prophesied that "The hard-to-accept truth is that Democratic candidacies for the White House may no longer be viable. The Republican lock is about to close; it will be hard for anyone to open over the four elections between now and the year 2000."[64] In a number of speeches to increasingly worried Democratic politicians Busby continued to point out that their party was attracting the votes of fewer than 40 percent of the white males who voted. In the three presidential elections of the 1980s, only a rough half of all those entitled to vote did so. In 1988 Busby told the political reporter William Greider that, in spite of wide-spread disillusion with Ronald Reagan as a result of his economic man-agement and of the Iran-Contra affair, the Democratic Party was in such a parlous long-term condition that it would not be able to take advantage of Republican embarrassment. A growing number of moderate to conserva-tive Democrats were listening. Many had been seriously put off by the so-called reforms in the party in the 1970s, and especially by the fact that these mandated a certain level of representation for women, for minorities, and for the young.

In December 1976, no sooner had Jimmy Carter reached the White House than he received a fifty-six-page memorandum from his top strate-gist, Patrick H. Caddell, that was widely circulated to big Democratic fi-nancial contributors. "The unpleasant truth is this," Caddell wrote, "The party has never been weaker in our lifetime and the array of obstacles and trends never more alarming." Curiously, in view of events in 2000, both Caddell and Busby focused on the electoral college. They saw it as the "lock" that would prevent Democratic victories in presidential races. Caddell called the college an "electoral Matterhorn" for Democrats to climb. Twenty-three states with a total of 202 electoral college votes, including the most populous state, California, had voted Republican every time for the past twenty years. If you added in the states that had voted Republican four times out of five in that period, then the Republicans had a majority of safe electoral votes, comfortably over the 270 votes needed for victory. In Busby's calculation, the Republican advantage was even greater.

By the 1980s influential leaders in the Democratic Party, both in Washington and in state capitals, especially in the South, were coming to accept that there were strategic reasons, in terms of demography and also of policy, why the Democrats could never hope to recapture power nationally unless they changed their spots.

The key group in selling this idea was the Democratic Leadership Council (DLC). This was a body that began by attracting Democratic senators, congressmen, and especially governors who were worried about the danger of total eclipse for the party. Both as organizer and strategist, the key figure was Al From, a midwesterner who went to work on the staff of the House Democratic caucus in 1980. From 1981 he also worked for a group called the Committee on Party Effectiveness. This was composed of able congressmen from the center and center-right of the Democratic Party: among them Gillis Long of Louisiana, Dick Gephardt of Missouri, Tim Wirth of Colorado, Geraldine Ferraro of New York, and Bill Gray of Pennsylvania. They met once a week in the Longworth House office building. Later, From worked for Senator Gary Hart and for Chuck Robb and Lawton Chiles, governors of Virginia and Florida respectively.

In 1984 the Democrats faced annihilation, at least in national politics. They lost forty-nine out of the fifty states, and came within 2,500 votes of losing all fifty. Immediately after the election, the DLC was formed. Its membership was recruited from those Democrats who were afraid that the long-predicted party realignment, the "Reagan revolution" promised, or threatened, by conservative champions, might really be on its way. Among them were another southern governor, Bill Clinton of Arkansas, who became the DLC's chair in 1990, and a freshman senator from Tennessee, Al Gore. The DLC had a distinctly southern flavor, as was natural. (Jesse Jackson referred to it, only half in jest, as the "Southern White Boys.") After all nowhere were Democrats more in danger of losing their natural constituency to Republicans than in the South. Among its brightest lights were Robb, Chiles, Senator John Breaux from Louisiana, Sam Nunn of Georgia, and Clinton. Strategically, it aimed to recapture the suburbs, where at least half of all Americans now lived. Ideologically, it wanted to shift the party not to the right but to the center. It sought to float away from those planks of the Great Society program that had lost it southern whites, Reagan Democrats, and all those who were attracted by the tough, traditionalist, patriotic reaction against the liberal tradition.

The DLC had one other valuable asset: the ebullient charm and substantial fortune of Pamela Harriman, daughter of the eleventh Lord Digby, daughter-in-law of Winston Churchill, and wife of Averell Harriman. Altogether Mrs. Harriman raised a reported $12 million for the Democrats in the 1980s, and in 1986 Harriman left her $75 million.[65] The considerable influence that brought her, in a party strapped for cash, was thrown toward the DLC. She liked Bill Clinton and helped him to emerge as the leading candidate for 1992.

The Mondale debacle in 1984 was not the nadir. The Dukakis campaign was in some respects even worse. At that point the Democrats had lost five out of the last six presidential elections. In each of the last three, they had lost more than forty states. "We hit bedrock," said Al From simply.[66]

In 1989 the DLC set about rebuilding the party "by redefining and reclaiming the political center." A key part of that effort (made possible in large measure by Pamela Harriman's fund-raising) was the foundation of the Progressive Policy Institute (PPI). In September 1989 the PPI published a strategy paper by William Galston and Elaine Ciulla Kamarck that laid out several key points both of the DLC's analysis of the Democratic crisis and of its strategic plan for overcoming it. Liberalism had played an honorable role in the past, Galston and Kamarck conceded. But contemporary liberals had lost touch with the American people. The public had come "to associate liberalism with tax and spending policies that contradict the interests of average families." What the authors called "liberal fundamentalism" had meant a coalition composed not of "the working class and minorities with a smattering of professionals and reformers" but a new coalition "increasingly dominated by minority groups and white elites." The paper demolished various analyses it called "the politics of evasion," such as the idea that the Democrats could win back the White House if only they got out their vote. Instead it called for the party to "convey a clear understanding of, and identification with, the social values and moral sentiments of average Americans."[67] In 1990 the DLC gave expression to this new strategy in a statement of Democratic principles endorsed at a conference (chaired by Bill Clinton) in New Orleans.

It was the first statement of a new, middle-of-the-road Democratic party: "We believe the promise of America is equal opportunity, not equal outcomes. We believe the Democratic Party's fundamental mission is to expand opportunity, not government." And the declaration concluded that "the free market, regulated in the public interest, is the best engine of general prosperity."

Less than ten years after Ronald Reagan's first inauguration as president, the rising conservative tide had forced the Democrats to borrow two key conservative ideas: hostility to government and faith in the free market. Now, with Bill Clinton as their standard-bearer, the Democrats were indeed back in a position to recapture the White House. The new Democrats' "third way" centrism had made shrewd adjustments to the mood of the electorate. That, however, implied adopting a large part of their opponents' political baggage and jettisoning much of their own. It also meant accepting that the center of gravity of American politics had shifted to the right.

—•—

THE THIRD MAJOR CHANGE in politics was the growing influence of money. By the late 1990s an impressive chorus of voices, from right to left and far beyond the politics of party, agreed that American politics and especially Washington politics, were seriously corrupted by the ubiquitous influence of money on politicians and the politicians' obsession with raising it.[68]

In an interview I suggested to David Smith of the AFL-CIO that one of the key changes over the past quarter of a century was the growing influence of the corporate sector in politics. He demurred. "I'm not sure the phenomenon is corporate dominance so much as the enormous transformation of American politics by money. It is not just the electoral arena. It is also the enormous amounts of money spent by business in Washington. And it is not just direct lobbying. It is also agenda setting."[69]

The respected columnist and television commentator, Elizabeth Drew, who has been watching Washington politics closely since the 1960s, put it strongly in a book she called *The Corruption of American Politics:*

The most important change is that the quality of politicians in Washington has declined during the past twenty-five years, and that the rate of decline has accelerated. The country has paid a big price for that—in ways that are largely invisible to the citizens. In general, the newer politicians are less grounded on issues, and many have scant interest in governing. A growing number have had no experience in government, which in this anti-government era is supposed to be an advantage, but it leads many of them to be at sea—or simply destructive—when they reach Washington.[70]

Drew went further.

Indisputably, the greatest change in Washington over the past twenty-five years—in its culture, in the way it does business, and the ever-burgeoning amount of business transactions that go on here—has been in the preoccupation with money. Striving for and obtaining money has become the predominant activity—and not just in electoral politics—and its effects are pernicious. The culture of money now dominates Washington as never before; money now rivals or even exceeds power as the pre-eminent goal. It affects the issues raised and their outcome; it has changed employment patterns in Washington; it has transformed politics; and it has subverted values."[71]

Elizabeth Drew is generally regarded as a liberal commentator. But her harsh and worrying judgment is not one confined to liberals. Many conservatives agree. Jeffrey H. Birnbaum, for example, who has covered Washington for nearly twenty years for the *Wall Street Journal*, has expressed his concern in even stronger terms than Drew:

Washington is awash in campaign cash. It has flooded over the gunwales of the ship of state and threatens to sink the entire vessel. Political donations determine the course and speed of many government actions that—though we often forget—will deeply affect our daily lives. The deluge of dollars pouring into lobbying and elections is one of the main reasons Americans are turned off by Washington and its arcane ways.[72]

The fundamental problem is the politicians' dependence on paid television advertising to be elected and reelected. Starting in California in the late

1950s, politicians found they could no longer rely on reaching the voters through direct personal contact. Nor could they depend on contacting and persuading voters through organizations, whether they were old-fashioned party machines, unions, or ethnic or fraternal groups of one kind or another. Now that a growing proportion of the voters lived in the suburbs, the best way of getting a message to them was through advertising. At first this was done with billboards, then with newspaper ads, then on radio. But television was the ideal medium for sending strong, simple, often simplified, messages across.

The cost of space grew. So did the number of cities ("markets") where you had to advertise. The whole business became professionalized. Space buyers had to be found to negotiate the best price. Advertising agencies had to be hired to design and produce the ads. Sometimes politicians used simple ads they designed themselves. More often they found that didn't work. Politicians came to rely on consultants, including pollsters and experts in focus group analysis, to decide how to tailor their ads and their campaign generally. For all of these reasons, a raging inflation in campaign costs began to be felt from the 1970s on.

As early as 1971 Congress tried to get a grip on the issue. It passed the Federal Election Campaign Act. It introduced more stringent disclosure requirements for candidates for federal office, political parties and political action committees (PACs). In 1974, as a result of the serious financial abuses in the 1972 presidential campaign (Watergate), Congress tightened the limits on contributions and set up the Federal Election Commission to administer public funding and enforce the law. A quarter of a century later the system is seen as in dire need of further reform. Many people in Congress believe new legislation is needed that will respond to contemporary realities. Charles Lewis, of Washington's Center for Public Integrity, holds that the regulatory system has completely broken down.

> The post-Watergate reforms have been eroded and trivialized, with debilitating repercussions. Today's unvarnished political realities are: 1. Politicians and their parties can collect and spend as much money as they want. . . . 2. Candidates and their campaigns are raising and spending secret money. . . . 3. The enforcement of election laws is almost always too little, too late. . . . 4. Political accountability itself is in danger of becoming a lost virtue.[73]

The first attempts to reform campaign finance in the Watergate era were hamstrung by the Supreme Court's decision in *Buckley v. Valeo* (1976). It established advertising as tantamount to the "speech" whose freedom is guaranteed by the First Amendment. The politicians, desperate for money with which to pay for television advertising, mostly opposed reform.[74] The growing part played by money, and by fund-raising, in politics militated in favor of special interests in general, and of corporate and union interests in particular.

In the 2000 election cycle, six of the top ten donors were unions. They gave all or most of their money to the Democrats. AFSCME gave 99 percent of its $8.5 million (the biggest contribution) to Democrats, and the Service Employees, the Carpenters, the International Brotherhood of Electrical Workers, the Communications Workers, and the United Food and Commercial Workers gave between 94 and 100 percent of contributions ranging from just under $4 million to over $6 million to the Democrats. Nine of the ten top individual donors (including six of the seven who contributed $1 million or more) also gave almost all of it to the Democrats. Several of the biggest individual Democratic donors were movie producers from Hollywood.

It would be a mistake, however, to conclude simply that the Democrats, backed by Big Labor and Hollywood, competed on equal terms with Republicans, backed by Big Business. The lion's share of all contributions went to the Republicans. AT&T and Microsoft, both with vital issues before the government, split their donations, as did the two biggest bank donors. Philip Morris gave 81 per cent of its $3.8 million to the Republicans, and the National Rifle Association gave 92 per cent of its $3 million to the Republicans too. The Republican Party is heavily dependent on tobacco money. Between 1991 and 1999 Philip Morris was the biggest soft money donor with $6.2 million. Nabisco/R. J. Reynolds came fourth with $3.2 million, the United States Tobacco Corporation eighth with $1.9 million, and the Brown & Williamson Tobacco Corporation twelfth with $1.5 million.[75]

The pattern of political giving reinforces a vicious circle. The more politics seemed to become a sham battle between spokesmen for more or less shadowy corporate interests (such as the health insurance industry, tobacco, the oil and gas industry, Hollywood, defense contractors, trial lawyers, telecommunications companies, and many, many others) and for organized lobbies (the National Rifle Association, the Christian Coalition, the AFL-CIO, the teachers' unions, and many more of all persuasions), the more voters were turned off. The more money politicians would then need to woo them back to the voting booth. By 2000 it was knowledgeably estimated that there were 14,000 lobbyists at work in Washington.[76]

The financial numbers are certainly striking. In 1952 the presidential primary contest between General Eisenhower and Senator Robert A. Taft cost about $5 million.[77] In 1960 John Kennedy spent a whisker under $10 million and Richard Nixon a whisker over. In 1964 the Republican, Barry Goldwater, outspent Lyndon Johnson by almost two to one ($16 million to $8.8 million), and lost catastrophically. But in 1972 Richard Nixon, helped by the financial shenanigans that formed part of the gravamen of Watergate, outspent George McGovern by two to one ($61.4 million to $30 million) and drowned him. By 1996 all the Democratic, Republican, and Reform party candidates for president spent a total of $453 million, $234 million of it on seeking their parties' nomination, and $163 million in the general election.

Altogether, spending over the 1995–96 election cycle, both on behalf of candidates for the presidency, the Senate, and the House of Representatives, and by political parties, came to $2.2 billion.

Full details of expenditure for the 1999–2000 cycle are not available. But enough is known to make it plain that expenditure was substantially higher than in 1996 — perhaps as much as one-third higher. Spending on congressional campaigns was up from $765.3 million in 1995–96 to just over $1 billion in 1999–2000. (Hillary Rodham Clinton spent $41.5 million to be elected to Daniel Patrick Moynihan's New York Senate seat.)

One of the most striking features of the 2000 elections was the astronomical sums spent by wealthy individuals on their own campaigns. Banker Jon Corzine spent $60 million of his own money to be elected to the Senate from New Jersey. Malcolm "Steve" Forbes paid $38 million of his own on his futile race for president. And in 2001 Michael Bloomberg is said to have spent more than $70 million to be elected mayor of New York.

By the end of the 2000 primary campaign, a total of $337.6 million had been spent by all presidential candidates. By the end of the year, George W. Bush's campaign had spent $186.7 million, against $120.3

million disbursed by the Gore campaign. Steve Forbes spent $86 million altogether on his campaign for president, and both John McCain and Bill Bradley spent over $50 million each on their challenges to Bush and Gore respectively.

It is true that it has been calculated that this amounts to no more than the cost of a pizza, without topping, for every man, woman, and child in the United States.[78] The United States is a rich country and can afford to spend such a sum on elections. The point of interest in the sheer amount of money spent on elections, however, is not that they cost citizens more than they can afford. It is that money, the search for money, and its differential effects in terms of influence on policy and appointments, distort and corrupt the political process. Defenders of the Supreme Court's decision in *Buckley v. Valeo*, such as Senator Mitchell McConnell of Kentucky, insist that "money equals speech,"[79] or in other words that the right to spend money on a party or a candidate's campaign is tantamount to the freedom of speech proclaimed by the First Amendment.

It is a false analogy. Each citizen has exactly one vote. But Steve Forbes or Michael Bloomberg, or for that matter Mr. and Mrs. S. Daniel Abraham of West Palm Beach, Florida, who gave $1.6 million to the Democrats in 2000,[80] acquire substantially more political influence than their fellow citizens. Heavy political giving, by individuals, corporations, political action committees, or any other entity, is a direct contradiction of the principle of one man, one vote. Fund-raisers and lobbyists insist that "money doesn't buy votes." They are quite right. They buy influence. And they buy access. Wealthy individuals love to be able to say that they know leading politicians in their state personally. How much more do they like to drop the fact that they stayed a night in the Lincoln bedroom, a favor that the Clinton administration offered to more well-wishers than ever before? And a lobbyist or trade association executive knows that if he can raise $100,000 for a politician's reelection campaign, his calls are not likely to be put on hold. Money bought Denise Rich access to President Clinton as he left office, access she used to plead pardon for her ex-husband, one of the biggest tax-dodgers in history. And money bought Kenneth Lay, the CEO of the foundering energy trading company, Enron, access to President George W. Bush's vice president, Richard Cheney, in six secret meetings after the company's peculiar accounting practices had begun to be known.

There are many undesirable consequences of the politicians' need for money. One glaring loophole in the campaign spending legislation was "soft money." Under a 1978 law, donors are allowed to give money above the individual limit for party building, but not for individual candidates. The concession was used as an excuse for raising tens of millions of dollars for presidential candidates in the fall, when donations to individual candidates are forbidden, and for congressional candidates in key races.

In 1995–96 the Clinton administration, badly behind the Republicans in fund-raising, was tempted to accept large sums from Chinese and other foreign contributors from Asia. The area is murky and highly controversial, and the reporting of it not always clear. Soft money is not covered by the ban on foreign contributors. But it appears that both the Beijing and Taiwan governments, as well as a number of overseas Chinese groups and individuals, made determined efforts to influence the Clinton administration's policy of most-favored-nation treatment for Chinese and other strategic issues. This was only the most egregious example of the scandalous degree to which the political agenda was dictated by the willingness of wealthy corporate or individual donors to pay politicians to follow *their* agenda. Between them, the Republican champions of the free market and the Democrats who had been forced to imitate them had succeeded in setting up a free market in political decision making.

On March 27, 2002, President George W. Bush signed what became known as the McCain-Feingold bill.[81] This was hailed as a major reform of campaign finance, and in particular as closing the "soft money" loophole. The president made it plain he was less than enthusiastic: he called the bill "far from perfect." It soon became clear that his own appointees to the Federal Election Commission would do all they could to hamper enforcement of the law.[82] A few weeks later the Republican National Committee, in an unusually aggressive breach of Washington conventions, sent subpoenas to a number of liberal organizations, including the pro-choice National Abortion and Reproductive Rights Action League, the National Education Association, the public service union AFSCME, and the lobby for women's representation, Emily's List, demanding detailed financial records and internal strategic documents and asking whether the groups believed their activities "corrupt . . . any federal candidate or federal office holder."[83] As of the time of writing, two things are plain: that while Democrats receive substantial funding, Republicans oppose campaign finance reform; and that the battle over political funding is by no means over.

———•◆•———

THE WORD "POLITICS" in the United States has come to have two distinguishable meanings. One is the democratic system, which includes the electoral process by which public officials are chosen, but also the whole course of their policies and actions in office. That is politics as it should be: the adjustment of interests and the choice of policies for the good of the society as a whole.

In another sense, "politics" is the name of a species of industry, in which men and women compete for office. They do this with the help of large teams of professional advisers, consultants, and experts in such skills as writing copy for ads; shooting and editing TV spots; and sampling and manipulating public opinion through sophisticated management and interpretation of polls, focus groups, and other evidence about public preferences. Lawyers play a large part in these processes. They advise on what you may and may not do under electoral law. They act as brokers, advising interest groups and wealthy individual donors where their contributions can be most advantageously bestowed. Fund-raising, too, has been professionalized. Fund-raisers make an excellent living by connecting politicians in need of money with monied persons and groups in need of politicians. Then there are lobbyists and the organizers and spokesmen for an infinity of pressure groups, interest groups, and advocates for and against everything from abortion and guns to tort law reform and environmental pollution controls. To an increasing extent, it is politics in this sense that is the subject of study by academic political scientists. The new political science appears increasingly uninterested in policies, even value-free.

There is a widespread suspicion that there ought to be more democracy, and less business, about the political process. Many citizens feel that it ought not to be, to the extent it now seems to be, a market in which the wealthy and powerful purchase policies, tax rates, regulations, and the government subsidies and contracts they desire. No doubt it can be argued, is indeed vociferously argued, that in a democracy every man and every interest has a right to be represented, just as every man and woman has a right to legal representation. Yet the suspicion remains that politics in this sense has only the most tenuous connection with democracy as it has traditionally been interpreted in the United States. Between the individual citizen with his or her constitutional rights and duties and the legitimate working of democracy there has grown up an industry, the politics business.

Certainly over the course of the last three or four decades the public perception that this is so, manifesting itself as suspicion amounting in some cases almost to paranoia in relation to what goes on, or is suspected of going on, inside the Washington Beltway, has itself become a major factor in the reality of politics. Politicians themselves are painfully aware of this. After all, most presidential candidates of recent decades, even those whose careers owed everything to achievements inside the Beltway and to their influence in the capital, have campaigned against Washington. The spectacle of Al Gore Jr., brought up in a senatorial family in the Fairfax Hotel on Pennsylvania Avenue in northwest Washington, retreating to campaign from Carthage, Tennessee, in the hope of returning to the capital, may seem absurd to the remote observer. But Gore knew very well what he was doing. He is only the most recent of a long series of politicians who get to Washington by denouncing it as Sodom on the Potomac, and, having reached it, stay there and enjoy its Babylonian delights.

The consequence is that politics in the United States has been moving in two opposite directions. On the one hand, the two major parties have never been more sharply divided in terms of their ideology and, as a consequence, in terms of the social and economic groupings they represent. In the past quarter of a century, for the first time since the Civil War, American politics has been, broadly speaking, a contest for power between the representatives of the haves, called Republicans, and the representatives of the have-nots, known as Democrats. This contest has been, again speaking generally, a conflict of ideology: between those who sought to diminish the role and power of government, so as to leave as many decisions as possible to the power of "the market," which is to say, to the power of money, and those who sought to interpose protection for those who stood to be hurt by the untrammeled action of markets, and especially of the market for labor in the United States and abroad: in two words, between conservatives and liberals.

Yet the politicians of all parties, all now by definition haves, have never been more alike in their complicity in the business of politics. The paradox of modern American politics is that while the gap between the policies advocated by the politicians has rarely been smaller, the ideological divide is greater and more bitter than ever.

The two parties are evenly poised, and the political conflict has never been more angry or more vicious. Congressmen, once courteous to a fault, now bellow insults across the chamber, and wrangle over who should apologize. The impeachment of Bill Clinton backfired against the Republicans because the great majority of Americans thought it was a partisan maneuver.

How, again, to explain why in a society that is said to be so contented and prosperous, political fortunes change so abruptly? In 1980 conservatives proclaimed the victory of what they called the Reagan revolution. By the end of the 1980s, Democratic strategists supposed that they could survive only by abandoning large tracts of their political credo. Yet in 1992 Bill Clinton was elected as only the second Democratic president in twenty-four years. Two years later, the Republicans recaptured both houses of Congress for the first time since the early 1950s. It was the first time for more than sixty years that they had really controlled the Congress. It was as if an ideological metronome had been set to mark a two-year beat. Within two years Newt Gingrich, the architect of that stunning Republican triumph, was utterly discredited. Within four years, he was history. In 1998 the Republicans succeeded in impeaching a Democratic president and failed to remove him from office, mainly because the crude partisanship of their tactics revolted the voters.

In 2000 two lackluster presidential candidates fought each other to a standstill in a campaign notable for an extreme absence of intelligent discourse. In what would be called in athletics a dead heat, the new president was chosen after journalistic incompetence, legal chicanery, and judicial bias that would have been thought embarrassing in the municipal politics of the days when Lincoln Steffens was writing *The Shame of Our Cities*. Why, if society is so prosperous and contented, have politics become so uncivil and so volatile? And why are the citizens so indifferent? George W. Bush was elected by a mere 24 percent of the electorate.

Of course, dramatic events, not least those of September 11, 2001, had their effect. But one explanation, no doubt, lies in the very monetization of politics that has just been described. Without necessarily following all the inward deals and machinations of the politics business in Washington and, for that matter, in their state capital, the citizens understand very well that the public interest is low on many politicians' scale of priorities much of the time. There is tension between an increasingly sharp ideological argument about equality and fairness in an increasingly unequal and unfair society, and a political class that has become members, as never since the Gilded Age, in the world of the well-tailored and the well-shod. No doubt that, too, helps to explain both the volatility and the bitterness of the political game in the last quarter of the twentieth century—unprecedented since the end of Reconstruction.

Something, again, must be put down to the style in which the political process is now covered by the news media and especially by television. There is little explanation, little context. Politics is presented as drama, even as melodrama. Ideological opponents are portrayed as implacably dedicated to each other's destruction. Personality is everything. The steady working of the political process is ruthlessly dismissed as boring, the most deadly epithet in the television producer's vocabulary. More of the media later.

There is a further cause, however, to which we must now turn. The political and business elites were largely converted, in the last years of the twentieth century, to the comforting theory that the United States now lived in what magazine writers (though not many economists) called a New Economy. That happy state was seen as guaranteed by the convergence of free-market economic theory and practice with the bounty of new technology. Unfortunately, this confident political philosophy was based on naive triumphalism about what free markets can and cannot do, and on a complete misunderstanding of the sources of the new technology. Successful high-tech investors, conservative ideologues, and the publicists of the bull market deluded themselves that the laptop and the Internet sprang fully formed into existence, like the Greek goddess of wisdom from the head of Zeus. It is to the reality behind the myth of the virgin birth of technology that we must now turn.

3

New Technology

America's leadership in information technology is the result of an extraordinarily complex and fruitful long-term partnership among government, industry and academia.
— *Edward D. Lazowska, Computing Research Association*

A NEW TECHNOLOGY promised a new economy, and the new economy in turn would make possible a new politics and a new society. That was the dream that inspired President Clinton and many others as the old century ended and a new millennium began.

To be sure, such idealistic visions of a new society were mixed up in many minds with more material dreams. The illusion that new technology could indefinitely improve productivity translated into the hope of a bull run on the stock market that would be projected to infinity, or at least to "the Dow at 36,000."[1] But that illusion, in turn, was fed by a misunderstanding of the history of the new technology.[2]

The technological revolution impacted public consciousness in general only in the late 1990s. It tended to be narrowly identified, with two dramatic phenomena. One was the Internet, with all of its easily observed consequences for people's lives in the office and at home. The other was the extraordinary boom in the stock price of companies seen as likely to benefit from the Internet. That boom started in the middle 1990s, but only thoroughly caught the public imagination nationwide between 1998 and early 2000.

The Internet's real impact does not need to be labored. After all, I am writing this looking out at the stone houses and a flock of sheep in a Cotswold village. Thanks to the Internet I can call up U.S. government statistics, the websites of organizations, companies, and associations of every kind, and the catalog of libraries from Oxford to Stanford, and I can have books sent to me from all over the world within days. All of that would have been inconceivable thirty years ago and difficult even five years ago. Now it is banal.

The Internet's impact through e-mail and e-commerce, in consumer marketing and in business-to-business trading, for education and research, and for the exchange of every conceivable kind of data at virtually instantaneous speeds, is revolutionary and irreversible. It can be usefully compared, perhaps, with only a handful of innovations in the whole history of technology: to the inventions of printing, the steam engine, railroads, the electric motor, the internal combustion engine, and aviation. In certain respects, indeed, because of its almost universal applicability, it may be the most important single innovation there has ever been. In at least two respects, however, the nature of the Internet revolution, or rather of the revolution in information technology of which the Internet is only the most exciting and visible part at present, has been seriously misunderstood.

For one thing it has been largely seen as the cause and the central feature of an admittedly dramatic stock market boom. It is much more than that. It has also been widely identified with the activities of a few entrepreneurs, mostly very young, in the United States in the late 1990s. So it has even been seen as validating the elevation of the free market to a status equal to that of democratic life itself. Only a society whose eyes were so resolutely kept on the future, and where the past was so readily dismissed as in the United States, could have made these mistakes. (The key motto of Microsoft, the most successful of all the new technology companies, is "Attack the future!")[3] Their eyes fixed on future horizons, prophets and public alike showed little interest in the history of the technological revolution. Indeed, to many of them, an interest in the past raised a suspicion of not "getting it." Surely the glory of American civilization was that its eyes were firmly on the future?

Few, in that heady atmosphere, were interested in what had actually happened. Fewer still wanted to hear about the downsides and difficulties.

Almost none reflected that a few people making paper fortunes in Initial Public Offerings (IPOs) hardly validated everything that went with a particular model of free-market capitalism. The demand was for prediction, and the more bullish, the better.

Brokers extolled the potential of Microsoft and Sun Microsystems, of Cisco and Oracle, America Online and Yahoo! All were abruptly promoted to the ranks of the very wealthiest of American corporations, some before they had so much as earned significant profits. Customers profited mightily, and brokers even more so. Each new trend was projected to infinity. Futurologists and academics, who ought to have been asking the tough questions, vied with one another to produce ever more enticing visions. Often they sounded less like scholars than like customers' men or brokers' shills.

Their come-on to the investors was a science fiction fantasy. Comfortably ensconced in a computer-controlled, largely work-free environment—this was the picture painted by the cheerleaders of the digital industry, often disguised as academics—the citizens of the day after tomorrow, nay of tomorrow, would be able to use computers to smooth the smallest frictions in their life, to switch on the microwave and calculate the income tax, and, at minimal cost, to browse through the wisdom of the ages in an infinite virtual library of film, audio and videotape, and even, if it suited their whimsy, text, and to summon up whatever might be their pleasure. Business, meanwhile, to listen to these gurus and promoters, would levitate to a weightless world of low friction, low costs, high turnover, and ever expanding profit.

These myths translated into wholly unrealistic valuations of businesses, some of which amounted to not much more than a single more or less plausible idea. Some entrepreneurs, to be sure, were able to use wildly inflated paper assets to buy solid businesses. An example was the successful takeover, by America Online, of one of the world's half-dozen most powerful media companies, Time-Warner. Take the massive circulation, the national reach, the advertising revenue, the editorial mystique, and the talented journalists of *Time, Fortune, Sports Illustrated,* and the other Time Inc. publications. Stir in the technical wizardry and global reach of CNN. Add the legendary glamor and market presence of Warner Brothers, the classic and classy Hollywood studio, not to mention its portfolio of actors' and directors' contracts. In the judgment of the market, all this was worth less than the inflated paper of an enterprise that had not even existed a few short years before. In the fourth quarter of 1998, just over a year before taking over Time-Warner, AOL earned profits of $68 million. Yet it was valued by the New York Stock Exchange at $66 *billion*, twice the worth of General Motors. Later, with the sad inevitability such business fantasies always leave behind, it turned out that the profits, exiguous as they were by comparison with older and less glamorous businesses, were inflated by the usual accounting dodges.

——•◆•——

TWO MYTHS, especially, were allowed to obsess the country's imagination. It was not, of course, that the myths were wholly without foundation. Myths rarely are. It was simply that they accentuated the positive to the point of distracting attention from the realities and the limitations of the revolution they were preaching. This chapter is written in the faith that by trying to understand what has really happened, one has a slightly better chance of understanding what is likely to happen in the future, and indeed what is happening as we watch. It is also written in the sure belief that the wildly gyrating valuations of the stock market are not necessarily the soundest guide to what will work in the long run, and what will not. If, as enthusiasts for the free market like to claim, there is such a thing as a "perfect" market, with perfect knowledge of all relevant factors affecting the values of investment products, the Nasdaq exchange in the last years of the 1990s was assuredly not such a market.

The first myth was that the Net and the Web were invented by graduate students: by youthful, informal, and irreverent hackers in chinos, in epic "night marches" sustained by Diet Coke and pizza, and that these innocents effortlessly changed the world as a by-product, an unintended consequence, of carving out prodigious fortunes for themselves.

The second, following logically from this first misapprehension, was that the Internet and its promise were quintessentially the creation of, and therefore the ultimate justification of, entrepreneurial capitalism, operating in the free market, unaided and unaffected by government.

The first proposition is not wholly untrue, but it is wildly exaggerated. The activities of Bill Gates and Steve Wozniak, Marc Andreessen, Jerry Yang, and their like did help to spread the popularity of the Internet in the process of making mighty fortunes for themselves. By turning it into a series of successful businesses, they found out how to make the technology work commercially.

The second myth is almost wholly false. The emergence of the Internet has been pictured as a sudden starburst, like a Chinese firework. In reality, the technologies necessary to make the Internet possible took decades to evolve. Entrepreneurs certainly played their part in developing the new technologies. But many of the crucial innovations were inspired by intellectual curiosity, by ingenuity for the sake of it, by the need to solve professional problems, even sometimes by boredom, rather than by an entrepreneurial desire for financial gain. Nor was the work mainly done by irreverent young entrepreneurs. The bulk of it was done either by the government, by large, well-established corporations, or by universities, on contract from the government. The impulse, and most of the funding, came initially, not from the securities markets, but from the flood of federal spending motivated by the fear, after the explosion of the Soviet atomic bomb in 1949 and the launch of the Sputnik satellite in 1957, of the (again largely mythical) missile gap. In retrospect, it is hard to believe how many people who should have known better, from President Eisenhower on down, persuaded themselves that the United States was being left behind by Soviet science.

Nor were the science and engineering programs necessary to make the Internet possible mainly financed by venture capitalists. They came into their own, and made their fortunes, only after decades of investment, much of it with public funds. While equity markets have certainly demonstrated their ability to reward technological advance (IBM, Xerox, and Polaroid were all favorites of the trust funds of the 1950s), no one has yet figured out any sure-fire way of making money out of the Internet—except, of course, by persuading someone else that you are about to make money, and so selling him your stock.[4]

The point, very simply, is that the myth says that the Internet was made possible by free-market capitalism. On the contrary, it is a classic product of the age of social democracy and of the mixed economy. Brought about by the government's military needs in the Cold War, the research was largely funded with the government's tax revenues. Quite a lot of it, incidentally, was funded by foreign governments. It was carried out by giant corporations that existed in a state of cozy symbiosis with government and by universities that grew rich on research contracts. The point has been well summarized by one of the leading experts in the history of computing, Edward D. Lazowska, of the University of Washington:

> America's leadership in information technology is the result of an extraordinarily complex and fruitful long-term partnership among government, industry and academia. . . . Because the financial rewards in the information technology industry are so great, it is tempting to believe that industry must have been responsible for most of the fundamental innovations, and can be relied on exclusively in the future. In fact, the contributions of federally-sponsored university research are pivotal.[5]

———·◆·———

THE HISTORY of computing is full of brilliant individual insights. But it is emphatically not the story of individual geniuses, jumping to brilliant conclusions in total isolation from the work of others. It has been the collective achievement of many thousands of clever and dedicated people, most of whom never earned or even dreamed of earning more than a decent salary. To the extent that individuals have made crucial contributions, they are by no means identical with those who have made great fortunes out of their achievements. To be sure, the investments of venture capitalists, attracted by the prospect of eventual stock market capitalization, helped to disseminate ideas. But venture capital is not available until the ideas have been born and nourished to adolescence.

And it has taken a long time. There have been dynasties, successions, inheritances, some of them going back fifty years and even longer. Vannevar Bush, for example, later president of MIT and a key figure in the Manhattan Project to build an atomic bomb, built what was in effect an electromechanical computer as early as 1935. His 1939 paper, published in 1945, "As We May Think," imagined something like an Internet but one in electromechanical terms. Bush inspired the Harvard and MIT polymath, J.C.R. Licklider, who played a crucial role in developing the Internet.

On the island of Leyte in the Philippines, as World War II was ending, Vannevar Bush's article was read by a twenty-year-old navy electronic technician called Doug Englebart. He in turn influenced Alan Kay at the University of Utah, who played a crucial part in conceptualizing the personal computer. The same connections, going back many years, can be traced in the prehistory of the computer, of the "mouse," the "graphic user interface" (GUI), and the Internet itself. The history of computing is part of the history of science, which has always been a collective story. It is not the history of geniuses or individual entrepreneurs, although there have been plenty of both. Still less is it the history of capitalist entrepreneurs, although there have been many of them, too. It is above all the history of *teams*.

Second, software develops sequentially. Computer languages, for example, evolve. James Gosling developed Java for Sun Microsystems from Oak. Oak derives from C++, which is part of the C language of families, which descends from Basic CPL, developed at MIT by the British scientist Martin Richards, which in turn has an ancestry dating back to CPL, developed at Cambridge and University College, London, under Christopher Strachey in the 1950s. Crucial ideas have a long and complex ancestry, reaching back decades and involving numerous individuals and institutions. But this plain and utterly unsurprising fact is obscured by the requirements of protecting corporate intellectual property and of marketing. These commercial imperatives, not to mention the vanity of very wealthy individuals, have concealed the fact that computer history is not sui generis. Like other branches of science, it is an incredibly demanding area of human activity where the latest geniuses are—as a twelfth-century saint said about his theological contemporaries—"dwarves sitting on the shoulders of giants."[6] Sometimes the dwarves became billionaires, and the giants had to content themselves with modest prosperity and with the comforting thought that talent, like virtue, is its own reward. A clear understanding of what happened is not helped by the fact that journalists have more patience with tales of sudden wealth on an Arabian Nights scale than with the complexities of mathematical techniques, the frontiers of metallurgy, or abstruse engineering concepts, all of which have helped to make the magic of e-mail or the Internet possible.

It follows that, third, every major step has been the result of multiple inputs. For decades, to take one crucial development, researchers and their corporate and government employers could see how desirable it was that there should be small, individual, *personal* computers. The dream was there, even before it had been established that computers would be either digital or electronic. That was the idea that possessed Vannevar

Bush as early as the 1930s. To create a viable personal computer, though, demanded the convergence of many concepts and many technologies.

At least eight stages on this journey can be distinguished: (1) all modern computing follows from the creation of the electronic data processing computer, based on digital technology and ultimately on binary arithmetic; (2) computers had to be programmed with "languages"; (3) the vacuum tube had to be replaced with the silicon chip; (4) in 1960 it became possible to put a miniature computer onto a single chip, thus creating a "microcomputer"; (5) a whole gamut of techniques (miniaturization, screen, mouse, pull-down menus) made possible a true personal computer, to replace time-sharing on mainframes; (6) packet switching made possible the Internet; (7) a World Wide Web posited the four basic ideas represented by the codes www., http., html, and URL; and (8) search engines made it easier to use the Web. At least two other applications have proved crucial in spreading the popularity of the personal computer and the Internet: spreadsheets and databases.

In every case, the lion's share of the vital work was done not by entrepreneurs but by professors and researchers, corporate executives and research employees, and, yes, government bureaucrats, working for the most part on salary. (One of the reasons for the irritating opacity of much computerspeak is that it was developed by engineers and mathematicians for other engineers and mathematicians who did not care whether laymen could understand.) Only at quite a late stage were any of the significant breakthroughs achieved by classic entrepreneurs on the pattern touted by what might be called the *Wall Street Journal* school of history: Bill Gates, for example, Larry Ellison, Marc Andreessen. Even in those cases, the achievements and the subsequent prodigious wealth of the celebrity entrepreneurs often owed as much to their ability to figure out how to market a technique, an invention, or an idea, as to any originality or ingenuity in thinking it up in the first place. Conversely, many of the best-known names in this history are famous for the amount of money they have made, while equal or even greater contributions have been made by people who made little or no money out of them. The classic example is Tim Berners-Lee, the inventor of the World Wide Web. It has been said of him that "as technologists and entrepreneurs were launching or merging companies to exploit the web, they seemed fixated on one question: 'How can I make the Web mine?' Meanwhile, Tim was asking, 'How can I make the Web yours?'"[7]

To be sure, the legendary entrepreneurs deserve every bit of their fame and fortune. Often they saw and exploited an opportunity that a big corporation (IBM or Xerox) had failed to see or been slow to seize. But Bill Gates's original achievement—to take the most obvious example—was not to write BASIC but to rewrite a commercial version of BASIC for the Altair personal computer.[8] His great breakthrough came not as a result of originating the operating system that became the industry standard for personal computers, but because he had the foresight to sign a contract to supply an operating system to IBM and then the nimbleness to buy one from Seattle Computer and to develop it.[9] Ellison was not a database pioneer but an entrepreneur who saw the potential of database research done at IBM and in the Berkeley Ingres project.[10] Andreessen did not invent the World Wide Web; he (and the more experienced businessmen who became his partners)[11] saw how to market it.[12] Yang's Yahoo! started life as "Jerry's Fast Track to Mosaic,"[13] and Mosaic in turn owed a great deal to Tim Berners-Lee's creation of the World Wide Web. The great fortunes have tended to go not to the true innovators but to the business strategists and to a few imaginative suppliers of bells and whistles. Long before the end of the century, the carefree spirit of the graduate student and the entrepreneur had been replaced by the culture of the corporation and the business school, not to mention the law firm.

———•◆•———

WE MUST LOOK at this historical progression in a little more detail. The United States has not had a monopoly of invention over the past century. Electricity, the automobile, film, the radio, television, jet aircraft, nuclear energy, computers, and even the World Wide Web were all invented in Europe. What has been truly unique about the United States has not been invention (it turns out it may not even be true that Eli Whitney invented interchangeable engineering parts).[14] It has been the speed and enthusiasm with which inventions, innovations, even fashions of every kind, from hemlines to catchphrases to hardware and software, are disseminated, marketed, and adopted in every corner of a country of continental size.

Even if one skips the ancient history of the computer itself, the story begins more than sixty years ago, with academic research into a number of areas, including the physical properties of materials, stimulated by the

U.S. government's voracious need for new products and processes as it faced breakneck expansion on the eve of American involvement in World War II. In historical fact, as opposed to the self-interested mythology of the stock market, the new technology developed in three fairly distinct phases. In only one of the three did the lone entrepreneur play a decisive part.

In the first phase, government and big university and corporate labs, often founded in whole or in part by government contracts, made the running. The many different new technologies that made the Internet possible were developed by the Pentagon's Advanced Research Projects Agency (ARPA), as is well known, but also out of work done at Bell Labs and Xerox PARC, as well as at MIT, Stanford, Harvard, Berkeley, Carnegie-Mellon (previously the Carnegie Institute of Technology), and at many other universities in the United States and abroad.[15]

Indeed, it is hardly possible to overstate the contribution of two universities in particular, MIT and Stanford. The Massachusetts Institute of Technology, on a big city campus on the banks of the Charles River in Cambridge, a mile or so closer to Boston than Harvard, was founded in 1861 by a scientist called William Barton Rogers. It was already recognized by the 1920s as one of the world's great engineering schools, but it really came into its own during World War II and the Cold War, in part because of the work of Vannevar Bush, to whom President Franklin D. Roosevelt delegated the responsibility for building the atomic bomb.[16]

Bush was originally an electrical engineer, and in the 1920s he was interested in the problems presented by long-distance power lines and how they were affected by power surges and other events. The mathematics involved was exceptionally complex, and in the hope of solving this Bush came up with what he called a differential analyzer. In effect it was an analog computer, attempting to achieve with wheels, pulleys, and other mechanical devices what would be much more efficiently and very much more rapidly done with digital technology.[17] In the 1930s Bush was also thinking about information retrieval. In a 1933 published article he dreamed with amazing prescience of "a thousand volumes located in a couple of cubic feet in a desk, so that by depressing a few keys one could have a given page instantly projected before him." After World War II, in a popular article written for *Fortune* magazine, later published in an even more popular form in *Life*, Bush addressed the inadequacy of paper records for the information explosion he could already see happening around him. Although he had still not cottoned that digital technology would make his dreams come true, Bush did envision—in the form of what he called "trails"—something uncannily similar to the hyperlinks that would ultimately make the World Wide Web a reality.[18] From 1950 on, after the creation of the Lincoln Laboratory, MIT became heavily involved in Cold War research. It was there, and at Boston research consultancies like Bolt, Beranek & Newman (BBN), largely staffed by MIT people and paid for by government contracts, that many of the key concepts that would ultimately lead to the creation of the Internet were developed. Incidentally, e-mail was first developed at BBN.

Although MIT's Media Lab, the trampoline of that most gifted publicist of the digital revolution, Nicholas Negroponte, remained in the forefront of thinking about the new technologies, MIT was gradually surpassed as the most important single test bed of information technology by Stanford University, on the peninsula, thirty-five miles south of San Francisco. In the popular mind, the home of information technology in general, and of the Internet in particular, is thought of as "Silicon Valley," and in recent years the industry has spread south to San Jose and far beyond. But when people use the journalistic label, they are describing not really a valley but the immediate environment of the 6,500 acre ranch with which Leland Stanford's family endowed its foundation, on the western side of El Camino Real, the old Spanish road up the peninsula. An enormous proportion, sometimes estimated at as much as three-quarters, of all the major innovations in information technology since World War II has come from Stanford labs, Stanford patents, or Stanford alumni. Stanford has witnessed every stage of the revolution. It was in a nearby Palo Alto garage in 1939 that David Packard and Bill Hewlett first started manufacturing radio oscillators. (They sold eight of them to Walt Disney for use in the movie *Fantasia*.)[19] Today the Hewlett Packard Company dominates the Stanford industrial park, a model for academic imitators all over the world. Across Page Mill Road are the offices of Wilson, Sonsini, Goodrich & Rosati, the law firm that has almost a corner in Silicon Valley's legal work. Hewlett Packard and Apple Computer are among its clients, and the firm has been called "the leading global law firm advising information technology companies at all stages of their growth."[20] (It was Wilson, Sonsini who filed the historic antitrust suit against Microsoft on behalf of Netscape and other clients.) Up Sand Hill Road toward U.S. 101, on the north side of the campus, is Kleiner, Perkins, Caulfield & Byers (KPCB), the venture capital firm that has been the leading supplier of funds to information technology startups, including Yahoo! and America Online.

Stanford University not only educated many Silicon Valley entrepreneurs. It is also a major investor in new technology through KPCB funds, as are other major universities (Harvard, Yale, Emory, Duke), pension funds (AT&T, General Motors), foundations (Ford, Mellon), and major individual information technology entrepreneurs (Marc Andreessen and Jim Barksdale of Netscape, Michael Dell of Dell Computers, Jerry Yang of Yahoo! among many others). Yahoo! incidentally is one of many high-tech firms that actually started on the Stanford campus.

This roll of honor suggests just how deeply the Stanford campus has penetrated the American business establishment. Xerox PARC, the Palo Alto Research Center, is a few hundred yards off campus at 3180 Porter Drive. Gordon Moore Jr., of Moore's Law, the founder of Intel and reputedly the richest man in California, lives across Route 101 in Woodside, one of the horse-riding capitals of the United States. Steve Wozniak lives in nearby Los Gatos and teaches computing to fifth-graders. His partner in the founding of Apple, Steve Jobs, lives in Palo Alto, the Stanford college town. He has reminisced in a nostalgic vein about the Stanford ambience of his youth. "There used to be something magical here—scientific and cultural. You could smell it, feel it. When I was in high school, I would ride my bicycle to the Stanford artificial intelligence lab on weekends and hang out. You could feel the magic in the air."[21] It was to a computer at the Stanford Research Institute, in October 1969, that Charles Kiley of UCLA typed the very first message sent over ARPANET, the military ancestor of the Internet and the World Wide Web. After accepting just the first three letters of the instruction l-o-g-in, the Stanford machine crashed. Even Homer nods.

———•—•———

IN THE SECOND PHASE, for a decade and half or so, roughly from the middle 1970s to the early 1990s, the computing initiative did lie with the classic entrepreneurs of the familiar legend. It was in 1975 that Bill Gates and Paul Allen formed Microsoft. They had just written a version of the BASIC computer language for the new Intel 8080 chip. The entrepreneurial heroic age can be said to have ended with the launch of Microsoft's Windows 3.0, a program that sold 2 million copies in six months, in 1990. In the same year Microsoft rolled out Word for Windows, its word-processing software. In 1975 Microsoft had three employees and revenues of $16,000. By 1990 there were 5,635 employees and revenues had passed $1 billion.[22]

Admiration for Gates's business genius should not be allowed to conceal the fact that his career depended heavily on IBM. Xerox PARC's contribution to the evolution of a usable personal computer was ultimately frustrated by Xerox's failure to appreciate its importance. IBM, so dilatory and mistaken in many of its business decisions, did beat Xerox to the production of a workable personal computer. But it was in 1972 that Charles Thacker at PARC started designing the Alto, an effective and elegant personal computer. Seven years later as Xerox was already losing interest, or losing confidence in its brilliant research team, Steven Jobs paid a visit to PARC. The visit has passed into legend. But it is clear that it was a passing of the keys to the personal computer. Jobs and his engineers were deeply impressed by PARC's Alto personal computer and by its Smalltalk language. It is also clear that the two demos Jobs was shown at PARC critically influenced the Lisa and its successor, the Apple. But in 1981 IBM came out with its personal computer. The dream of so many individual engineers, programmers, and visionary entrepreneurs was over. The personal computer battle would go to the big battalions. Big Blue had won after all.

LATE IN 1993 Tim Berners-Lee, the English physicist working at CERN just outside Geneva, had finished writing a point-and-click browser-editor he called the World Wide Web. He had also written the hypertext transfer protocol (http), the hypertext mark-up language (html), the first URLs (universal resource identifiers), and the first Web server. A new heroic age was about to begin: the age of the Internet.[23]

For a brief interval, the Internet, in its turn, was a field for individual enterprise. Ideas and skill, not capital and massive business organization, were what counted at first. Within a few short years, access to the Web had been largely cornered by gigantic corporate bureaucracies. Some graduate students may have become CEOs in double-quick time. But it was unlikely that their successors would be chiefly recruited from the ranks of Ph.D. students.

The individual inventor and the isolated entrepreneur of the myth did play an important part in the history of the new technology. But it was briefer than the myth would have it. And it was made possible only by decades of earlier work, much of it in the public sector or in the research labs of giant corporations like Bell Labs or Xerox PARC. For the Internet, and the digital revolution more broadly, depended on scientific and technological advances in three closely linked fields: microelectronics, computers, and telecommunications.[24]

The first key invention built on the progress that had been made even before World War II in solid-state physics. In 1947 three researchers at Bell Labs in New Jersey, the research arm of AT&T (which then owned a monopoly on telephone service in the United States), John Bardeen, Walter Brattan, and William Shockley, developed the transistor. This is a device that enables electrical impulses to be processed very rapidly in the binary mode of interruption and amplification. The telephone company had an obvious interest in any technology that might reduce electronic "noise" in copper telephone wires. Transistors could not be manufactured in quantity until it had been discovered how to use silicon, which was accomplished in 1954 at Texas Instruments by Gordon Teal, a scientist recruited from Bell Labs.

For a time, manufacturing transistors, or semiconductors, remained a labor-intensive business. It was largely done by women using tweezers and peering through microscopes to fasten wire to silicon chips. The decisive step that made bulk manufacture possible was the invention by Jack Kilby of Texas Instruments in September 1964 of the integrated circuit, in which gold wire was soldered to connect components on the same chip. From the beginning, however, semiconductors were more efficiently manufactured by Bob Noyce of Fairchild, a company started by renegades from Bill Shockley's firm. It was Noyce who learned how to lay different materials on top of the silicon, engrave circuits on them with photolithography, and connect the layers with microscopic aluminum wires. This made mass production possible. So the price of ever more powerful chips fell, in accordance with the law formulated by Gordon Moore of Intel, that the speed of semiconductors would double, and their price halve, every year for a generation.

Already between 1959 and 1962 the price of semiconductors fell by 85 percent.

The next dramatic step forward came with the invention of the microprocessor, a tiny computer on a single chip, by Marcian E. "Ted" Hoff, a Stanford Ph.D., at Intel.[25] Hoff's breakthrough came as a result of the demands of a Japanese desk calculator manufacturer. In effect, by early 1971 Hoff had succeeded in miniaturizing the central processing unity of a computer. By 1974 the Intel 8080 chip, incorporating this computing function, was selling in the thousands. Even the earliest of Hoff's microprocessors had capabilities comparable with those of an IBM mainframe of a decade earlier but cost less to buy than the mainframe cost to rent for a single day. The implication was clear. The reign of the massive mainframe computer was over.

Computers had been built, mainly for code breaking, in both Britain and Germany during World War II. Konrad Zuse built a computer in Germany in the late 1930s.[26] But these had to be specially programmed for each task. The first stored program computer was built by Maurice Wilkes's team at Cambridge University in 1949, beating by weeks another at Manchester University. The first computer in the United States was the ENIAC, at the University of Pennsylvania, which was used to calculate the trajectories of ballistic missiles and firing tables for artillery. (No graduate students having fun there.) It weighed thirty tons.[27] For the next quarter of a century computers were massive machines, the size of a three-story house—not tools, someone said, but demigods. Prodigious efforts went into developing "timesharing," that is, ways of enabling several programmers to work on the same machine simultaneously, and this was a considerable part of the motivation for developing the personal computer.

The first computers had to be programmed in esoteric languages, comprehensible only to highly trained mathematicians. Two scholars at Dartmouth, a predominantly liberal arts university, Thomas Kurtz and John Kemeny, were influenced by C. P. Snow's 1959 lecture, "The Two Cultures," which lamented the widening gap between science and liberal arts graduates. They decided to write a computer language that would be accessible to all, or nearly all. The language was BASIC.[28] Other early languages were FORTRAN, designed for research scientists, and COBOL, aimed at business users.

In the early 1970s, thanks to the research that had drastically reduced the price and increased the power of semiconductors, the big companies that were making commercial calculators, in the United States and Japan, got into a price war. One of those who was hurt by this cutthroat competition was a certain Ed Roberts of Albuquerque, New Mexico, an electronic hobby manufacturer whose company was called MITS. In 1974 Roberts decided to build a computer kit for hobbyists using the new and powerful Intel 8080 chip. He shipped the only working model of his product, which he called the Altair, to New York to be displayed in *Popular Electronics* magazine, where it was advertised as retailing for $397. Altair was made possible by the compressed version of BASIC written by one Bill Gates and his friend Paul Allen. In 1975 they formed Microsoft, Inc., and signed an agreement with Roberts's company covering their rights to the software. The agreement led both to a dispute with Roberts and to widespread pirating of the new version of BASIC. In 1977 the retailer Radio Shack brought out a plug-in personal computer (not a kit like Altair). It sold 10,000 copies in the first month. Gates and Allen got the contract to supply the BASIC software, and shortly afterward moved to Bellevue, Washington, near Seattle, their hometown. That was when they got the contract to provide the software for an IBM personal computer. Gates was so keen to close the deal that he bought his first tie to impress the suits from IBM.

Meanwhile Apple Computer had been founded by two young men, Steve Jobs and Steve Wozniak. As we have seen, they came from the Stanford hotbed. Wozniak was an inspired tinkerer and idealist, Jobs a retired hippy who had returned to California from India and Oregon, whither he had journeyed in the classic search for meditation and enlightenment. Jobs went to work for a slightly older entrepreneur, Nolan Bushnell, the inventor of Pong and other Atari games. "Atari!" is what you shout in the Japanese game of *go* when you are about to take the opponent's stones, so it is roughly the equivalent of "Check!" in chess. It was not long before the Japanese games manufacturers had their revenge, calling *atari* for Atari, and cornering the market with Nintendo and Sega.

So Jobs and Wozniak moved on. They founded their Apple company and (helped by their visit to Xerox PARC) rolled out the stylish Apple II in 1977. Next they started work on the Macintosh. Microsoft, in the meantime, was not idle. In 1983 Gates introduced the word-processing program,

Word, with a mouse. He spent $450,000 at the COMDEX computer exhibition in Las Vegas, promoting the first version of Windows, a revolutionary concept based on work done at Xerox PARC on the Alto. But Windows 1.0 was not shipped until 1985. By then Apple had rolled out the Mac, which the *New York Times* called "a revolution in computing."

In the meantime, Apple's success with its earlier models had roused the sleeping giant, IBM. It drove IBM into competing, and competing directly, with its personal computer. But then IBM made what has been called "the single worst mistake in the history of enterprise on Earth."[29] Because it did not demand exclusivity for either the chip or the software used, it allowed Intel and Microsoft to have machines made by a number of hardware manufacturers such as Compaq and Dell. The intellectual property situation was such that there was nothing to stop these companies jumping into the market with "clones" that were in general as good as, and much cheaper than, IBM's original. The decision cost IBM its long-held primary position in the American computer industry. It also allowed for the phenomenal growth that made Microsoft its most obvious successor.

There was an important cultural aspect to these business contests. Apple's Mac was in many respects a superior and certainly a more elegant product than the IBM personal computer. The former seemed designed for the pleasurable explorations of individualists, the latter for the ordered labors of robots. Apple cleverly marketed the Mac as something more than a superior product: as David taking on Goliath, as Robin Hood against the sheriff of Nottingham, as the eternal Chaplinesque little man pitted against power and privilege. Slick ads openly portrayed IBM as the Establishment, and Apple as a crusader against pomposity. Never mind that its key technology, the "graphical user interface" (GUI) that used icons, pull-down menus, and a mouse, was not invented by a genius in a garret or even a Stanford graduate student, but by Xerox Corporation's Palo Alto Research Center.[30]

If Apple cast IBM as the heavy, Bill Gates and his skilled publicists also presented themselves as New Men, outsiders riding roughshod over the traditional structures of industrial hierarchy. Thus corporate strategy, too, has contributed to the myth of the graduate student culture. It takes its place neatly in the "market populism" thesis that presents the new Masters of the Universe as underprivileged strivers against privilege and pomposity.

Much stress, for example, has been laid on the fact that Gates was a "dropout" from Harvard. In fact, of course, he was a dropout only in the sense that he had discovered lucrative alternative possibilities outside the university and, coming from a wealthy family that had endowed him with a trust fund, he could afford to pursue them. A surprisingly high proportion of the pioneers of the new industries came from established and financially comfortable backgrounds. Many of them were graduates of Harvard, Princeton, or Stanford, among the most expensive colleges in the land.[31] It was, after all, on the whole the elite universities that had captured the lion's share of Cold War defense appropriations. That was where you could best study the new, defense-related technologies.

More to the point, in terms of putting into context romantic "market populist" claims about the "outsider" character of the Internet pioneers, is the part played—inadvertently—by the most "insiderish" of all corporations, IBM, in the rise of Microsoft.

Microsoft actually owed its success to a partnership with IBM. The story involves operating systems, the software that controls a microprocessor's basic functions.[32] Once again, the technology came out of the public sector. In 1975 Gary Kildall was teaching computer sciences at the U.S. Navy's Postgraduate School in Monterey, California. There he invented an operating system he called CP/M. It soon became the industry standard. In 1980, as we have seen, IBM was secretly working on its own personal computer. It wanted CP/M as its operating system but wrongly imagined that the rights belonged to Microsoft. Gates told them, correctly, that the rights belonged to Kildall's company, DRI. But when IBM approached Kildall, he at first was away flying and later refused to give IBM a license for a flat fee. IBM went back to Microsoft. That was how Gates and Allen were able to make what may have been their most decisive move. They knew of a version of CP/M, Seattle Computer's 86-DOS. Without mentioning IBM, they bought 86-DOS for $75,000 and eventually renamed it MS/DOS.

In 1981 IBM duly released its PC, using Microsoft's MS/DOS 1.0. IBM had hoped to acquire CP/M for a flat fee in the thousands of dollars. Instead Microsoft was able to negotiate a license that would attract payments of $10 every time the operating system was copied. As a result, Microsoft was able to keep ownership of the operating system (which it had not written) and charge IBM huge royalty payments. Gary Kildall was not happy. It was, he wrote angrily in an unpublished memoir, "a blatant misappropriation of proprietary materials—and of my personal pride and achievements."[33]

It was, of course, a legitimate as well as an astute business maneuver. But it had little to do with invention, and nothing whatever to do with outsiders challenging an *ancien régime*. Microsoft was not so much a young stag challenging the leadership of the oldest male in the herd as a hungry parasite, growing inside the hypertrophied body of IBM until it had reached giant size itself and could challenge for the succession to IBM's near monopoly.

The possibility of something like an Internet, however, would depend on new technologies that could link computers together. In the meantime, the world's telecommunications companies and their researchers, led as so often by AT&T's Bell Labs, had made advances in both switching and transmission technology comparable with those made in the design and manufacture of the chips themselves. The pace of progress was accelerated by the interaction between the two technologies. But the indispensable boost that made the Internet happen came, directly and unambiguously, from the government in the shape of the Department of Defense—with assistance at critical moments from abroad.

In 1960 Bell Labs produced the first electronic switch, and by the middle 1970s digital switches were available. However, Bell Labs's parent, AT&T, was at first reluctant to introduce digital switches because of its vast investment in analog switches. It was only when, in 1977, the Canadian telephone company, Nortel, captured a large share of the U.S. market with its digital switches that AT&T joined in and digital switches became the standard. AT&T's attitude to the matter was summed up, with devastating honesty, by one of the company's top executives, Jack Osterman. "First, it can't possibly work, and if it did, damned if we're going to allow the creation of a competitor to ourselves."[34]

The linking of computers into a national, then international, network was the work of the Pentagon's Defense Advanced Research Projects Agency (DARPA), the agency created by President Eisenhower as a response to the Russian Sputnik. By the 1960s it was estimated that 70 percent of all research into computers and related science in the United States was being funded by

DARPA.[35] One of the key technologies it was investigating was time-sharing. In 1962 Jack Ruina, the third director of DARPA, persuaded MIT's already legendary J.C.R. Licklider, an expert on time-sharing among many other fields, to come down to Washington to run the agency's command-and-control division.

Licklider, universally known as "Lick," changed the name of the division to the Information Processing Technology Office (IPTO) and took the vital step toward creating a linked computer network. In 1964 (two years after Licklider had returned to MIT) IPTO started a project for linking the big mainframes, funded by the Pentagon on some university campuses, into a network. The first problem was that the giant mainframes were all different and mostly incompatible. A solution was soon found. Each of these monster "nodes" would be linked to an "interface message processor" or IMP, in effect a small standard computer that would pass messages on to the local mainframe. The IMPs would all be compatible. All that remained to be done was to find a way of sending messages out to this network of IMPs.

As early as 1960–64 Paul Baran at the RAND Corporation in Santa Monica, California, was working on a problem confronting DARPA called "nuclear resilience." The Pentagon wanted to find ways in which military command-and-control networks could survive nuclear attack. Baran came up with a solution that depended on a technology Bell Labs had been slow to accept, packet switching. The concept relied on network architecture radically different from the obvious model, the Bell system's phone lines. Instead of centralized networks linking hubs by radial lines, Baran and his colleagues came up with the idea of cutting information up into tiny modules called "packets" that would bounce from computer to computer through what was called a "distributed network," until they landed on their destination computer, where they could be reassembled into the original message.

Unfortunately, Baran's pioneering work was forgotten or lost somewhere in the Pentagon's files. At a conference in Gatlinburg, Tennessee, the answer came instead from a British scientist, Roger Scantlebury. He explained that his colleagues, led by Donald Davis, at the National Physical Laboratory (NPL) at Teddington, in the London suburbs, had successfully developed the technique that came to be called "packet switching." Data were divided into sets of a standard length and transmitted over a distributed network. Each packet would be identified so that the receiving computer could put the full message together correctly. Scantlebury was able to reveal that the NPL already had a system up and running between ten of its own computers.

In August 1968 DARPA sent out formal requests for proposals to build a packet-switched network. The contract went to the MIT-linked consultancy, Bolt, Beranek & Newman (BBN), who hastily recruited a network of graduate students across the country to work out the "protocols," as they were called: codes to enable computers to link up and transfer files. The work went at high speed. By October 1969 the historic first message, mentioned earlier, had been exchanged between computers at UCLA and Stanford.

The technology of transmission was also leaping ahead. Optical fiber made possible dramatic improvements in the number of circuits that could be carried by a given cable. Where the first transatlantic cable carried 50 compressed voice circuits, by the mid-1990s fiber-optic cables could carry 85,000 circuits. The integrated broadband networks (IBNs) envisioned in the 1990s offered the prospect of quadrillions of circuits. Packet-switching technology kept pace with the transmission capacity of the fiber-optic cable itself. At first these new technologies offered new possibilities for military communications and to such comparatively humdrum operations as the transmission of bank data or news. It was not to be long before they made possible the spectacular promise of the Internet.

Before long many universities joined ARPANET. They soon constituted a new network, funded by the National Science Foundation (NSF), called Usenet. Before long both universities and research institutions abroad (for example, in Norway and the United Kingdom)[36] and many corporations were on the net. As graduate students took their e-mail addresses with them to more and more companies and other employers, questions were raised about security. But in 1993 the NSF cleared the Internet for nonacademic use. In the middle 1980s computer bulletin boards had ramified into an informal connection among computers known as Fidonet.

Increasingly, after the splitting up of AT&T, the new commercial telecommunications companies like MCI began to install high-speed trunk lines that linked hubs in centers like Washington, New York, Houston, the Bay Area, and Seattle. But no commercial use was made of the net until after 1991, when Berners-Lee invented the World Wide Web.

At the time the Internet could be run only on big computers, using Unix computers and software originally developed at Woolongong University in Australia.[37] This was the kind of hardware and software found in university physics departments and research labs, and you needed engineers to run them. Late in 1993, however, a University of Illinois undergraduate called Marc Andreessen took a hand. He had been working, for $6.85 an hour, on a government-funded project called the National Center for Supercomputing Applications. But now, with the end of the Cold War, no one except the government and a few big corporations was interested in supercomputing any more. Andreessen was technically knowledgeable and was familiar with the Internet. He thought it would be fun if, instead of the forbidding scientists' flavor it had to start with, he could give the Web the graphics-rich software it lacked. Working with Eric Bina and four other friends, Andreessen posted a Unix version of this software, called Mosaic,[38] and by late spring 1993 PC and Macintosh versions were also available. Tim Berners-Lee had written software that anyone could use. Mosaic, with its graphics, made people want to use it, and on their personal computers at that.

It is revealing that Berners-Lee, the trained research physicist, was mildly shocked by the graphics. "This was supposed to be a serious medium," he protested. "This is serious information."[39] He saw the Web as a way of communicating knowledge, in the sense of scientific or cultural information, not where you could find the coolest pizzas or the cheapest CDs. People ask him whether he is upset that he has not made a lot of money from the Web. What distresses him, he said in his autobiography, is how important the question seems, and it happens mostly in America, not in Europe, he says. "What is maddening is the terrible notion that a person's value depends on how important and financially successful they are, and that that is measured in terms of money. That suggests disrespect for the researchers across the globe developing ideas for the next leaps in science and technology."[40]

Andreessen saw the Web differently: as a business opportunity. After graduating, he went out to California.[41] There he met Jim Clark, who was running a firm called Silicon Graphics in Mountain View, just south of the Stanford campus. Clark had been in the U.S. Navy, then taught at both Berkeley and Stanford.[42] He was intrigued by President Clinton's talk of an information superhighway, and he was interested in doing something simple with mass-market appeal.[43] Clark saw the potential of Mosaic. He quickly recruited a public relations woman, Roseanne Simo, and with her and John Doerr of the venture capitalists KPCB he flew to Seattle to recruit Jim Barksdale as a high profile CEO.[44] In October 1994 Mosaic's software was launched as Netscape. After a dispute with the University of Illinois, which claimed rights to Mosaic, had been settled for $2 million, Netscape was soon outselling its competitors by ten to one.[45]

At this point, the Web's infrastructure was mostly in place. Commercial servers like CompuServe and AOL already had some 3.5 million subscribers. But commercial rivalry got in their way. The commercial services were not mutually interactive; and they could not claim the infinite diversity of the Web. So far from free-market capitalism making the Internet possible, in this instance it was holding things up.

Netscape's success was to trigger off the Last Battle with Microsoft, the pitiless struggle for domination that led in May 1998 to civil action 98-1232, *United States v. Microsoft Corporation*. This was the federal government's most ambitious antitrust action since its Pyrrhic thirteen-year suit against IBM, launched in the late 1960s, and a successor of the earlier efforts to break up AT&T and, decades earlier, to break up Standard Oil. For a long time, Gates and Microsoft had seemed strangely indifferent to the way the Internet was changing the world. Then, without warning, on May 26, 1995, Gates announced his full conversion in a memo, "The Internet Tidal Wave," that sounded like the Tablets of the Law, brought down from Sinai. Whereas over the past twenty years, the voice from out of the thundercloud proclaimed, it had been increases in computer power that had driven forward the revolution, in the future "it would be outpaced by the exponential improvements in communications networks." Now, Gates said, "I assign the internet the highest level of importance. I want to make it clear that our focus on the internet is critical to every part of our business. The internet is the most important single development since the IBM PC was introduced in 1981."[46]

That historical judgment is hard to fault in its own terms. But it was clear from the context that Gates's conversion to the importance of the Internet was also bound up in his own mind with what he saw as a dangerous commercial threat from Netscape. He acknowledged that philosophically the Internet, like a tidal wave, "changed everything." But he also identified the Internet with the competitive challenge from Netscape and moved to destroy that rival.

Implacably, Gates tied Internet browsers, first MSN, then Internet Explorer, to his own products. Relations between Microsoft and Netscape became more than usually bitter. The directors of Netscape felt as if they were trapped on a fishing smack that could not get out of the course of a supertanker bearing relentlessly down on them. Eventually the company merged with another adolescent mastodon, America Online. The quarrel between Netscape and Microsoft became merged in the greater antitrust suit between Microsoft and the federal government.

Several more historic fortunes were made before the shadows of recession began to cloud the sunlit uplands of the Valley. Jerry Yang and David Filo started a combination directory and search engine for the Internet they called, first, "Jerry's Fast Track to Mosaic," and later, Yahoo! Appropriately they started out in a trailer behind the Bill Gates building on the Stanford campus. A venture capitalist saw that they possessed that most precious of commercial assets, access to eyeballs. The venture capitalist invested $1 million. Within four years the business was worth $8 billion. Others were as successful, some even more so.

At first it looked as though the majesty of government, acting through the agency of the very tough Judge Thomas Penfold Jackson, might achieve what the government had done with earlier "overmighty subjects," Standard Oil, American Telephone & Telegraph, and International Business Machines. At the time of writing, the final solution of the lawsuit is uncertain. But the probable resolution is clear. Microsoft will not be split up yet.[47]

In the end, no doubt, technological change will afford some as yet unknown opportunity to some younger Bill Gates. Microsoft will continue to give comfort to its shareholders as a very big, very well managed, and profitable company, or perhaps eventually as two or more such companies. In the long run, no doubt, it/they will encounter competition that it/they cannot defeat. In the meantime, Bill Gates has not only created this spectacularly successful company, he has also decided a question of some importance. He and his fellow entrepreneurs, turned corporate strategists, have won. They have resolved a conflict that long divided the creators of computer networks.

On the one side stood those like Tim Berners-Lee, and the creators of open-access networks, countless bulletin boards and chatrooms, and Fidonet before them, who dreamed of the Internet as a liberating force, a revolution that would empower the citizen, free from the grip of corporate business. They insisted that software ought to be free. Some spoke of "copyleft" instead of "copyright" and dreamed of an egalitarian world in which every man would be his own publisher.

At the other end of the field, armed with the big stick of intellectual property law and waving the golden carrot of stock options, initial public offerings, and an instant share in what has been called the largest legal creation of wealth in the history of the planet, there rode those who wanted to turn the Internet into the greatest business America had ever seen.

The "free market," in this instance not so clearly identified with what people understand instinctively by personal freedom, has triumphed. The inside-out language of market populism, with its contention that it is the big corporations who are on the side of the "little man," and the improving tales of graduate students and their "death marches," sustained by Diet Coke and pizza, may have veiled from the public for a time what has actually happened. But it is plain enough to anyone who looks at the history. The researchers and engineers of the Cold War period, sustained by a patient partnership between government and business, endowed us with the most potentially liberating technology history has seen. That precious public asset has now been largely captured and appropriated by a handful of corporate masters. Will they show as enlightened an attitude toward science, research, and development as the generation that made it possible for them to cash in so spectacularly? Will they allow opinions that do not suit their corporate interests to be spread?[48]

———•◆•———

IN THE BEGINNING, the Internet was indeed seen as a force for personal liberation. The word that recurs again and again in the accounts of its enthusiasts is "empowerment." They saw, rightly, that the personal computer, as opposed to the massive mainframe, would tend to destroy the power monopoly both of the modern state and the modern corporation. The same claim was made on behalf of the Internet. It is true that the Internet does give anyone—anyone, that is, who can afford a computer and has access to the Internet, which means many people in developed countries but few in the developing world—the freedom of an unimaginably vast store of information, serious and frivolous, idealistic and self-interested, true and false. But by the end of the century that optimistic perception of the Internet was beginning to be seriously questioned, and from many different ideological and cultural perspectives.

For one thing, it turns out that states are not quite so impotent to control the Internet as libertarians at first assumed. Even democratic governments responded to whatever they saw as particularly sensitive material on the Internet by intervening. The French government succeeded in forcing Yahoo! to remove sales of Nazi impedimenta. The German government was less effective in its attempt to prosecute a student whose Web page contained a link to a radical magazine that had published hints on how to make bombs and derail trains. The British government tried in vain to keep secret intelligence information off the Web. Authoritarian governments in Asia have taken harsh and rather effective steps to control use of the Internet in their countries. Even in the United States, with its exceptional tradition of protecting freedom of speech, has passed legislation to ban indecency on the Internet. The campaign against terrorism will certainly end by making it plain that the federal government, with the full approval of the American majority, gives national security priority over the freedom and empowerment once promised by the Internet.

Governments, however, are not likely to be the main threat to the freedom of cyberspace. Corporations, in their endless struggle to control as much of the Internet as possible and to protect their business against all competition, foreign and domestic, are likely, unless restrained, to threaten individual freedom to use current and future technologies far more frequently and directly than government. In practice the courts are likely to give less practical redress to the citizen as customer against corporations than the political process does against the oppression of government. There will always be local and marginal efforts to reclaim the Internet for communities and civil society. But we can now see that they will not be allowed to be more than marginal, like public television and public radio. The prime purpose of those who have real power over the Internet will be quite simple: to make money, for themselves and for their shareholders. That is the inevitable consequence of the politics of free-market capitalism as it is now understood.

4

New Economics

I can see computers everywhere—except in the productivity statistics!
—Robert Solow, the "Solow Paradox,"
speech on receiving the Nobel Prize, 1987

BY THE BEGINNING of the new century it was all but official. The United States had developed a New Economy. The stock market seemed to confirm it. Business was sure of it, and business's favorite publications—the *Wall Street Journal, Fortune,* and *Business Week* foremost among them— enthusiastically embroidered the theme. The president and his men endorsed the New Economy,[1] and so did the chairman of the Federal Reserve.

For some years it had been apparent that the economy was going well. Unemployment was low, and falling. Inflation was low. Economic activity was high, and so, higher and higher, were the securities markets.

As early as the summer of 1997 journalists began to write of a "new era economy." *Business Week,* the home of some of the strongest optimists about the economy, picked up the phrase from two articles in the *Boston Globe* in July, and in the following month the highly respected economic commentator Paul Krugman, then at the Massachusetts Institute of Technology, gave the term wide currency by attacking the concept.[2]

In his acceptance speech to the Republican nominating convention in Philadelphia on August 3, 2000, for example, presidential candidate

George W. Bush did not attempt to deny that the country had prospered under the Democrats.[3] Instead he accused his opponents of failing to use what he attributed to their good fortune, and of "coasting" their way through prosperity. "This is a remarkable moment in the life of our nation," Bush said. "Never has the promise of prosperity been so vivid. . . . Our opportunities are too great, our lives too short, to waste this moment."

His opponent, Vice President Al Gore, similarly took prosperity for granted. The Clinton administration, he boasted, had "moved us out of the valley of recession and into the longest period of prosperity in American history."[4] Only, of course, instead of treating prosperity as an accidental blessing, he vigorously claimed credit for it as a Democratic achievement.

The man who may have had as much to do with bringing the good times about, the Republican-appointed chairman of the Federal Reserve, Alan Greenspan, took no position on where the credit belonged. By mid-2000, however, he too was claiming that the United States had entered a "new economy." He added that it was characterized not only by an unprecedentedly favorable combination of economic factors but also by the impact of a technological revolution. "The new current economic expansion," he told the national Governors' Association annual meeting, "has not simply set a new record for longevity. More important, the recent period has been marked by a transition to an economy that is more productive as competitive forces become increasingly intense and new technologies raise the efficiency of our businesses."[5] Although these tendencies had no doubt been at work for many years, the Fed's chairman argued, now they had reached what the nuclear physicists call "critical mass" and were changing the way the economy creates value in ways that were not foreseeable even a decade ago.

Bill Clinton had become president, in 1992, by repeating like a mantra "it's the economy, stupid." It's worth recalling that what he meant by that was "it's the economy that needs fixing." In 1993, prompted by the Federal Reserve chairman, Alan Greenspan, and by his Wall Street–bred treasury secretary, Robert Rubin, President Clinton had taken the fated decision to reduce the deficit, as a higher priority than reducing taxes. To the surprise of many of his own keenest supporters, it worked.[6]

By the time he came to make the first State of the Union Address of the new millennium, which was also his own last opportunity to present his record to the country for its posthumous approval, as we have seen, Clinton was able to claim that the country had never been better off. It became one of the premises of the 2000 presidential campaign that the country was rolling in prosperity, and that the major issue for its leaders to decide was merely how to spend it.

—•◆•—

THE REALITY was subtly different from this widespread assumption that all was for the best in the best of all possible economic worlds. In the second half of the 1990s there was certainly some very good news. Unemployment remained low, dropping to 4.2 percent in 1999. More important, it stayed low for several years in a row, the first time since 1970. As a result, it produced beneficial effects on both wages and productivity.

Wages rose, as you would expect them to do under the pressure of continuing low unemployment. They rose for everyone. But the best news was that they rose most for those who needed it most. In a sharp break from what had been happening over the past three decades, the wages of low-wage men, which actually fell by 0.9 percent between 1989 and 1995, grew by 1.7 percent between 1995 and 1999. The wages of low-paid women similarly grew faster (2.0 percent) than those of middle-wage women (1.4 percent) and slightly faster even than those of the highest-paid women (1.9 percent).[7]

Low unemployment helped single mothers affected by the Clinton administration's welfare "reform" to find work. Their employment rate rose from 40 percent in 1995 to 56 percent in 1998. Tight labor markets also helped African Americans. Median family income for that group grew more than twice as fast in those same four years as for white families. As a result poverty fell faster for minorities than for whites. (It fell by 4.7 percentage points among Hispanics and 3.2 percent among African Americans but only by 0.7 percent among whites.)

Productivity grew too. That was not nothing. Productivity—the measure of the goods and services produced by the average worker in a given time—is a key indicator, arguably *the* key indicator, of economic health. Since 1995 it grew at about 2.5 percent, well above the 1.4 percent rate maintained from the mid-1970s to the mid-1990s. (Since then, some research has suggested that the increase in the productivity rate has been exaggerated.[8] A report by the McKinsey Global Institute found that virtually all—99 percent—of the increase in productivity growth had come in only six sectors: retail, wholesale, telecoms, financial securities, semiconductors, and computers. In many businesses, such as banking and hotels, heavy investment in information technology produced no increase in productivity.)[9] Even so, had productivity risen by no more than 2.25 percent or even 2.0 percent that, if sustained, would have a huge and beneficial effect on national income and on America's competitiveness.

That was the good news. But not all the news was good.

For one thing, though the economy had returned to growth for five years, after twenty years in which there was almost no growth in real incomes, the growth was not unusually rapid by earlier standards.

The most significant characteristic of the American economy in the 1990s was its persistent and growing inequality. Wages, income, and wealth were all very unequal indeed, both by the standards of anything seen in America since the 1920s and by the standards of other developed countries. And the gap between a small group of big winners and the population as a whole was widening faster than ever.

In fact, the most salient fact about the economy of the boom years in the late 1990s was not broad advance, although low unemployment did bring relief to some of the poorest. In spite of the intentions, the hopes, and the rhetoric of the Clinton administration, the most striking development was the continuation of what had been achieved by a dozen years of conservative Republican management of the national economy: the consolidation of the domination of society by a new class of plutocrats, masters of American society as well as of the universe. The election of George W. Bush promised to accentuate this trend.

True, the shape of inequality had shifted in the second half of the 1990s. Whereas in the 1980s wages spread, with the highest earners pulling away from the middle-ranking Americans, as the middle-earners pulled away from the lowest-paid, now the poor were closing the gap with the middle class, but the rich were pulling away from everyone else.

This was true of *wages*. The smallest gains went to workers in the middle of the wage distribution. Above that level, the higher you look, the wider the gap. At the very top, corporate chief executives (CEOs) increased their pay over the ten years from 1989 to 1999 by a remarkable 62.7 percent, against 12.9 percent for the mere "upper middles" who earned more than 90 percent of their fellow citizens, and 2.6 percent for the population as a whole. By 1999 the average CEO earned a remarkable 107 times more than the average worker, double the ratio in 1989 and five times that in 1962.

The same pattern of rapidly growing inequality—strongly against the earlier American tradition—was even more marked if one looks at *income*, which includes earnings from dividends, interest, and capital gains, all of which accrue overwhelmingly to the top few percentiles of the population. There are several different ways of measuring income. By any of them, income inequality grew. By the most comprehensive measure, the incomes of the top 5 percent rose steadily over the 1990s, from under seven times that of the middle 20 percent of all Americans in 1989 to almost eight times in 1999. During the decade from 1989 to 1998, the average family's income grew by 3.9 percent. The income of a family at the ninety-fifth percentile (that is, a family whose income was greater than that of 95 percent of families) grew by 11.6 percent, or almost three times as fast.

Above all it was true of *wealth*.

The inequality of wealth in America is even greater than the inequality of income. In 1998, for example, the top 1 percent of Americans by income received 14 percent of all income, but enjoyed 38.5 percent of all net worth and 47.2 percent of all net financial assets. The top 10 percent received roughly 40 percent of all income, but owned 83 percent of all financial assets.

Wealth, like income, is getting more unequal, not less, as the champions of the free market like to suggest. Between 1989 and 1997, the share of wealth owned by the top 1 percent of American households grew from 37.4 percent of the total national wealth to 39.1 percent. Over the same period, the total share in the national wealth of the middle fifth of American families (twenty times as many families) fell from 4.8 percent to 4.4 percent, or little more than one-tenth as much wealth in total. Indeed, the wealth of these "middle Americans" actually fell, chiefly because these middle Americans were getting deeper and deeper into debt. Overall, the total sum of all debt (mostly mortgage and credit card debt) was greater than the total disposable income of all households. The comparable figure for the period after World War II was 20 percent.[10] The proportion of all

Americans with zero wealth or negative wealth (that is, where the family's debt exceeded its worth) had grown in a few short years from 15.5 to 18.5 percent, not far short of one in five, by 1995.[11] Middle-class households received 2.8 percent of the growth in stock market holdings in the decade to 1998, and took on 38.8 percent of the increase in debt.[12]

The biggest winners of all were the top 1 percent. One of the most popular media myths of the late 1990s, that most Americans were getting rich on the stock market, is demolished by the statistics. It was often said that half of all American families had portfolios of stocks. Almost true: while 51.8 percent owned no stocks at all (not even in 401(k)s or pension plans or IRAs) only 36.3 percent owned stocks thus generously defined worth $5,000. Contrary to happy myths about a stock-owning democracy, the concentration of ownership of stocks is even greater than the concentration of ownership of wealth generally. The wealthiest 1 percent of all American households control about 38 percent of national wealth, but almost half of all stocks.[13] The bottom 80 percent own just 4 percent of all stocks. The vast majority of the dizzy gains in the market over the second half of the 1990s went not to a sturdy stock-owning people but to a tiny proportion of the population, most of whom were wealthy already.

One key indication that the boom of the late 1990s left profound inequalities not just in paper wealth but also in well-being was the number of families who did not have health insurance. In 1998 fewer than two-third of all workers in the private sector (62.9 percent) had employer-provided health insurance. The proportion was slightly *lower* than in 1989. The likelihood of having health insurance went down from over 80 percent in the top fifth of the wage distribution to less than 30 percent in the lowest fifth. Similarly, in 1999 fewer than half of all workers in the private sector had an employer-provided pension plan, varying from three-quarters of the best-paid to less than one-fifth of the worst-paid.

Change was certainly overdue. Even a few years earlier, such bold optimism would have been unusual.[14] Amid the din of upbeat and self-congratulatory assessments it is hard to recall it now. But from the first oil crisis in 1973 until well after President Clinton's inauguration twenty years later, the performance of the U.S. economy was dismal. For under-average and average earners the experience had been little short of catastrophic. By the end of that period, it was becoming commonplace to say that those who came to adulthood during it would be the first generation in American history to be worse off than their parents.

The boom of the late 1990s was strong enough to end such gloomy prognostications. Yet, until that rather brief leap forward in the last few years of the twentieth century, the American economy had indeed come very close to stagnation in the single respect that matters most to ordinary people. The most shocking single statistic is that in 1999 average wages, discounted for inflation, had still not caught up with the level they had reached in 1973.[15] Indeed, as late as the spring of 1999, average wages were actually 10 percent *lower* than in 1973. In 1997, median family income was only $285 a year higher than it had been in 1989, at the peak of the previous business cycle, and that was only because on the average, more family members were working. All workers, too, on the average, were working longer hours.

Few Americans, and almost no foreigners, would believe that statistic, and yet it is true. Even less would most Americans, or foreigners for that matter, believe how mediocre the performance of the American economy was by international comparative standards. By two leading measures of economic success, the United States had fallen back at the very time when the conventional wisdom was that it was teaching the world economic lessons. By one measure—the measure of the free market—average income in the United States had actually fallen behind average income in half a dozen European countries. In terms of market exchange rates, Norway, Switzerland, Denmark, Finland, Sweden, and Luxemburg had higher annual per capita income than the United States.[16] That was something that had not been true since the nineteenth, indeed perhaps not since the eighteenth century.

If that comparison seems dubious, another is even more striking. Ever since the introduction of the assembly line and modern management in the United States in the 1920s, it was popularly assumed that American productivity was the key to American economic success. Indeed, in 1960 the productivity of American workers was five times higher than that of the Japanese, and more than twice as high as that of Europeans.[17] According to numbers from the Organization for Economic Cooperation and Development, however, over the whole period from 1960 to 1996, productivity in the United States grew slower than in Canada, the United

Kingdom, Germany, France, Italy, and Japan.[18] Even at the higher rate of 2.5 percent claimed for the last five years of the twentieth century, productivity grew slower in the United States than the rate of growth in the United Kingdom since 1960 (2.6 percent), and far slower than in France (3.4 percent) or Italy (3.8 percent).

A final international comparison demolishes another cherished belief. The myth is that the United States is a land of opportunity where people do not stay poor for long, in comparison with more rigid European economies. The numbers say otherwise. The United States had in 1994 the highest poverty rate of sixteen developed countries. It had the second lowest (after Canada) rate of escape from poverty. And American tax and financial transfer systems reduced poverty by less than half as much as provisions in Western Europe, Australia, and Japan.[19]

To summarize these surprising figures, the following statements would appear to be established. The United States remains the country with the highest per capita income in the world by a measure that favors the price of consumer goods, but not by the measure of the market, a measure that takes account of public service provision. The inequality of wages, income, and wealth in the United States is in each case the greatest in the world, and inequality is in general getting greater. Real wages did grow in the second half of the 1990s, and at a faster rate than in 1989–95, or over the two business cycles of 1973 to 1979 or 1979 to 1989. Over a longer period, though, the growth in U.S. incomes was feeble, and, specifically, worse than in other developed countries. The one area where U.S. performance was truly spectacular, the spiking of stock market indexes, benefited only the minority who owned stocks, and made a significant difference only to those in the highest income and wealth brackets.

———————— ◆ ————————

ALAN GREENSPAN'S acceptance that the digital revolution in information technology really had changed things decisively was spelled out in greater detail by his vice-chairman, Roger W. Ferguson Jr., in May 2000.[20] Since 1995, he pointed out, real gross domestic product had grown by more than 4.25 percent a year, while unemployment had fallen to 4 percent, and the underlying rate of price inflation still managed to slow. "You have to go back to the decade of the 1960s," he said, "to find even closely comparable periods of consistently robust economic expansion." Why? Because new technology was increasing the pace of growth in productivity, he suggested. Output per hour in the nonfarm sector, Ferguson reported, which had been running at the rate of 1.6 percent in the first half of the 1990s, had gone up by some 60 percent in the second half of the decade, to 2.6 percent. And Ferguson thought that this sharp upshift could be traced to structural changes and in particular the revolution in information technology. In support of this claim he revealed that two Federal Reserve economists, Steve Oliner and Dan Sichel,[21] had calculated that between 1995 and 1999 half of the 1 percent increase in the rate of productivity growth could be traced to what is known as "capital deepening," that is, to the capital invested in equipment per worker, while the other half-percentage point reflected technological innovations in the "actual production of computer hardware and semiconductors as well as better management," itself perhaps affected by these improved information systems. Altogether, Oliner and Sichel estimated, two-thirds of the acceleration in productivity growth since 1995 could be put down to high-tech investments. This research, Ferguson said, "supports the view that fundamental changes are under way in our economy."

Perhaps. There is no question that computers, the Internet, and many less visible new technologies, including improved control of tools, flow processes, and many other industrial activities, are changing the way Americans (and foreigners) work. But how "fundamental" are these changes? How much of a step change do they amount to? What, in short, are we to make of the talk of a "new economy" that was so fashionable among financial service workers, politicians, journalists, and others (most of them in high-income brackets) in the last years of the twentieth century?

A central assumption of New Economy talk was that it was computers and the Internet that made the difference. Not only were technology stocks responsible for the bull run in the markets. The theory also was that information technology employers competed fiercely for workers with special skills, bidding up their compensation to levels the rest of the economy had to match. No doubt that happened. But the evidence is that it did not happen enough to create anything that could be called a new economy, even for a few short years. It is likely—even if it is hard to demonstrate—that investments in new technology were a major factor in the increase in productivity growth. A reasonable estimate is that the increase in the use of new technology accounted for between one-third and one-half of the over-all growth in productivity. But the high-technology sector was simply not large enough to explain the increase in wages. Information technology jobs amounted to only 2 percent of all employment in 1999, and that was almost 50 percent up from 1990. But altogether information technology created only 7.5 percent of the new jobs between 1992 and 1999. Other factors must have been more important. Surprisingly, perhaps, the most important, and probably by far the most important, was an old friend: low unemployment. A tight labor market makes management think harder about how to get the most out of its workers. It provides an incentive for management to invest more in machinery (of all sorts, not just computers) to help boost those workers' productivity. So in a limited sense it is true, and of course it is not in the least surprising, that the technological revolu-tion of the 1990s did help to cause the increase in productivity. But it was not a simple story of cause and effect. Part of the welcome improvement in productivity was cyclical. Some was structural. Some good new things were happening in the economy. But talk of a New Economy was essen-tially political.

———◆———

IN A 1995 BOOK two academics argued that patterns of competition caused the concept of exceptional rewards for the few to spread from a number of sectors, such as professional sports and entertainment, where they had long been prevalent, to other fields, making the United States "the winner-take-all society."[22] Others would argue that there is nothing in-evitable about this development. They would see it as the consequence of those with power in the marketplace, such as executives and chief execu-tives, exacting higher compensation for themselves while holding down wage and salary increases for others. There is one telling statistic here. "For the first time in the postwar period the division of total corporate in-come between income paid to workers and income paid to owners of cap-ital shifted strongly in favor of owners of capital during the 1990s. In 1999, owners of capital received 20.5 percent of the income paid out by the cor-porate sector, up from 18.2 percent in 1989."[23] This increase was four times greater—2.3 percent as against 0.5 percent from 1979 to 1989—than in the

1980s, a decade that was itself regarded as marking a shift of power from labor to capital.

One of the main achievements of social policy in the middle third of the century was precisely to limit the ability of those with market power to help themselves to an excessive share of the pie. So others again would attribute this power shift to the decline of labor unions.

This gap, moreover, was twice as high in the United States, a country with a historically egalitarian tradition, than in any other country.[24] No wonder another observer could conclude that "we have entered a winner-take-all market in which the very highest incomes grow enormously while all other incomes stagnate."[25] Such statistics suggest just how far traditional assumptions about the relatively greater fairness and opportunities in American society have been challenged by social progress elsewhere and by the operation of the free market in the United States.[26]

Historically, inequality of incomes in America fell steadily from the 1920s, when the wealthiest 5 percent of American families enjoyed 30 percent of all family income, until 1969, when, symbolically, the inauguration of Richard Nixon ended the New Deal era. By that year, the share of the richest 5 percent had almost halved, to 15.6 percent. Since then, however, it has grown again, and is now once again over 20 percent. It may be morning again in America, as Ronald Reagan proclaimed. But unlike its natural model, the political sun does not shine with equal warmth on rich and poor alike.

So widespread was the belief in progress that it would have come as a total surprise to most American newspaper readers in 2000 to learn that in many respects the economy had been in better shape in the 1950s and 1960s. The statement that in real terms American workers were worse off than in the half-forgotten year of Watergate would have been simply incredible. As for the idea that in several crucial respects the U.S. economy had done less well for its workers than the economies of other industrial nations, that would have been greeted with derision. For years, mainstream American journalism had constantly repeated that the economies of Western Europe needed "reform," meaning adoption of something closer to the American model. Yet in the 1990s, while almost every voice in the United States was trumpeting about the superiority of the new American economy, national income per person actually grew at about the same rate as in France, Italy, and the United Kingdom and more slowly than in Germany, Japan, and the average rate for all advanced economies.[27]

While American economists were exaggerating the U.S. rate of productivity and arguing how much of it should be attributed to the miracles of technology, productivity growth rates in the United States averaged only half the rate of the other advanced countries. At least four European countries (Belgium, France, the Netherlands, and western Germany, all habitually dismissed in the United States as in dire need of instruction) had apparently caught up with U.S. productivity. The United States, in terms of productivity, was in the position of a track competitor who, at the very moment when the other runners are catching up, stops and offers to explain to the crowd the causes of his exceptional performance.

How could such a skewed version of reality become so unchallenged? One explanation lies in the changing shape of American society itself. (We return to this in chapter 8.) Once upon a time, if men and women were being laid off, you saw them. There were plenty of manufacturing plants no farther from the haunts of the media than lower Manhattan or inner Chicago. Now manufacturing has moved away from the metropolitan cities. Much of it, indeed, has moved across the Rio Grande or even across the Pacific. Opinion formers live in affluent suburbs and work in air-conditioned office towers. The poor and the unemployed are invisible and often geographically distant. Culturally, too, they are inaccessible. People who lived and worked in Washington, New York, the Bay Area, or southern California found it easier to assume that American society was so fair a society, and the free market, including the market for labor, worked so well, that if anyone was not doing well it was their own fault.

Then again, in spite of the "market populist" theory that the media were disproportionately controlled by liberals, trends in the ownership and consolidation of media meant that news media were increasingly in the hands of those who uncritically bought the free-market ideology and the market populist screen that protected it from criticism.

The collapse of communism at the end of the 1980s and the subsequent discrediting of socialism made any criticism of the free market and of the inevitable triumph of globalized American capitalism seem outdated, in a society where media people dreaded that above all else.

The illusion that all was for the best in the best of American worlds was also sustained by the change (noted earlier) in the coinage in which comparative economic performance was measured. In the past, the gross products of different countries were compared in terms of market exchange rates. Increasingly, such comparisons are made in terms of purchasing power parity (PPP). This seems fair. It takes account of lower prices in the United States. It does, however, conceal the fact that in what used to be the generally used criterion, namely exchange rate comparison, workers in several countries, including Norway, Switzerland, Sweden, Denmark, and Japan, earned more than Americans, while the average per capita income of employees in all eighteen developed countries, excluding the United States, at $25,969, was in 1996 breathing hard down the neck of the American income level at $28,553. It is true that PPP (originally adopted by international organizations for comparisons between developing countries) more accurately represents lower prices for food and many manufactured goods in the United States. It also tends to conceal the monetary value of services, such as health care, more generally provided free or cheaply by public bodies in other countries. So when Seymour Martin Lipset, for example, in his 2000 book *Why It Didn't Happen Here*, suggests that Americans have higher incomes than those of all other countries except Luxemburg, he does not seem to be aware that this is not true by other, once generally used, measures. Again, the low price of many goods in the United States, such as imported textiles and electronic equipment, reflects not so much greater American efficiency as the greater ability of American multinationals to drive down prices of their suppliers abroad by use of market power. It is true that the economies of Japan and much of Western Europe did not share the boom the United States experienced in the late 1990s. Unemployment, in particular, stayed stubbornly high in many parts of Western Europe, and Japan languished in recession. There may be some truth (especially in the case of Japan) in the idea that relatively uncompetitive practices have held back job creation in some foreign countries. This hardly justifies the widespread American assumption that the whole of Europe is still under the heel of socialism. But at the very least, it would appear that the economic success of the U.S. economy, both absolute and relative, was exaggerated in the public mind by the way economic issues were reported and discussed in the late 1990s.

In 1998 the economist Paul Krugman, then at MIT, wrote a thoughtful column that he called "America the Boastful":

> After a mere two years of good news America's mood has become startlingly triumphalist. In the view of many business and political leaders (though few academic economists) we have entered the era of the New Economy, an era in which traditional limits to economic expansion are no longer relevant. And because we have a New Economy and the rest of the world does not, we have also entered an era in which America is once more indisputably Number One—and the rest of the world must adopt our values, emulate our institutions, if it wants to compete.[28]

Krugman urged his readers to ask soberly what has gone right and what has gone wrong.

ONE THING that has clearly gone wrong, for all but the most tough-minded conservative thinkers, is that inequality has increased to a startling extent in the United States over the past quarter of a century. There are several reasons for this. The most obvious is that those with power in the society have taken care that it should do so.

They have consistently paid themselves historically large salaries, at an ever increasing multiple of the compensation of their employees. They had worked hard to make their employees' status more vulnerable, although in the late 1990s (perhaps temporarily) the trend toward "nonstandard work," including self-employment, contract work, temping, and "on call" work (a particularly unfair practice), declined slightly. They have succeeded in reducing the proportion of workers protected by unions. Not all of the news is bad. On balance, the lowest-paid workers recovered some ground in the low-employment conditions of the late 1990s. But the decline of union membership must be one of the major causes of the relative decline of wages over the quarter of a century before the short-lived boom of the late 1990s. Union wages, after all, are almost 30 percent higher than those of nonunion workers.

Another way in which those who hold power in American society have helped themselves at the expense of the majority is by making the tax burden conspicuously unfair. Average tax rates have changed little for the average American. But change in tax law (tax "reform"!) has sharply reduced the tax burden for the better off. To be specific, between 1977 and 1985, the tax payment of the bottom 80 percent of families actually *increased* by an average of $221. Over that same period, the tax bill for the richest 1 percent fell by an average of almost $100,000 per family.[29]

What is more, income inequality has risen sharply at a time when powerful structural and demographic forces were at work that ought to have made it fall. For one thing, incomes in the South were once far lower than in the North, Midwest, and West: on the average, little more than half the national average in the 1940s, and even further below the wages in states like California and Michigan. That sectional difference has disappeared. While great rural poverty is still present in parts of the Appalachians and the Mississippi Delta, metropolitan areas like those surrounding Houston and Atlanta have now achieved or even outstripped northern and western economic standards. Then, too, traditionally low-income farm families are a far smaller proportion of the population than they used to be. Older Americans, thanks to Social Security and private pensions, are no longer relatively as poor as they used to be.[30]

For decades, Republican politicians subscribed to the comforting theory of "trickle-down." That was another way of putting the hope comfortably expressed by Democratic President John F. Kennedy (given a $10 million trust fund by his father) that "a rising tide lifts all the boats": that is, that rising prosperity would help the poor as well as (though not as much as) the wealthy. At least until the very end of the twentieth century, there was little evidence that this happened. While the rich (including, in that emotive term, highly paid professionals, managers, and corporate executives) got richer, the poor not only stayed poor, but also got relatively and even in some cases absolutely poorer.

Changes in the tax code in 1993 reversed some of the inequities built into the federal tax structure in the 1980s. Also, after a decade of neglect, four increases in the minimum wage have boosted the incomes of millions of low-wage workers. The similar expansion of the earned-income tax credit has further improved the earnings of low-wage workers in the poorest families.

So the last few years of the twentieth century did see significant growth in real wages at all levels, especially at the bottom. A slight reduction in inequality of *pay*, however, has not reduced inequalities of *income*, which continue to grow wider. So the heavy concentration of such income in the hands of a very few at the very top of the income structure increases inequality even if salaries and wages are becoming more equal.[31] But these increases have not yet been sufficient to counteract the effects of two decades of stagnant and declining real wages.

Moreover, there is an important question whether the most recent (quite small) improvement in the income of the poorest is structural or cyclical in nature. The authoritative Economic Policy Institute assessment points out that "low and falling unemployment coupled with a higher minimum wage and an unexpected slowdown in inflation have combined to generate real wage gains since 1996." But it also warns that "these increases may prove short-lived and evaporate as unemployment rises in the next recession."[32]

There is, to complicate understanding further, a statistical sleeper. The consumer price index (CPI) is not only the most popular index of inflation in the public mind; it is also the one on which a number of very important government interventions, such as increases in Social Security pensions, are calculated. In the 1990s economists (led by the commission chaired by economist Michael Boskin of Stanford University) came to a consensus, or as close as the economics profession ever comes to a consensus, that the CPI had for many years systematically overestimated the inflation of prices. There are several technical reasons for this, the most important of which is the fact that the index, conscientiously calculated on thousands of prices, nevertheless underestimates the effects of innovation. If more Americans abandon restaurants and go to fast food outlets for their lunch, for example, or if they abandon higher-priced in-town stores in favor of suburban malls, or even if they take to communicating by e-mail rather than by telephone, these changes, which may lower the cost of living, are not fully reflected in the index. The degree of this overestimate was variously estimated at between 0.5 and 1 percent of price inflation. That is not a marginal distortion. It represents something between one-sixth and one-third of the inflation rate. The government has now accepted the (lower) figure of 0.4 percent. Even that represents an exaggeration of something like 12.5 percent of true recent inflation rates. This has wide-ranging implications. An awkward one from the politicians' point of view is that it suggests that recent increases in Social Security pensions may have been excessive; small chance, however, of persuading the many congressmen who are sensitive to the pressure of the active and feisty American Association of Retired Persons to go along with a compensating reduction in pensions.

The revision of the CPI has already had a positive effect on growth statistics. We have been doing—this revision suggests—better than we thought. But the catch is that the government, sensibly enough given the massive task involved in adjusting all economic statistics to take account of the revision, started with the most recent years. This first stage of the revision makes recent growth look better than we thought it was. But as revisions are made to earlier statistics, recent improvement will once again be diminished.[33] This recalculation is not likely to eliminate the recent positive economic statistics altogether. But its effect is bound to be negative. To that extent, for purely technical reasons, recent upbeat estimations of the economy's performance will have to be modified.

On May 8, 2001, the government announced that productivity actually declined in the first quarter of 2001. So much for the idea that the sustainable rate of productivity growth would settle at 3 percent per annum. So much for the idea that information technology had abolished recessions and that the information technology industry was recession-proof. In this instance, it would be closer to the truth to say that the information technology industry, or at least the absurd hyping of it by stockbrokers, journalists, and other interested parties, had caused the downturn, or at least determined its timing. What has really produced an improvement in wages, and one that has specially helped the poorest, is low unemployment.

———⬥———

IF PRODUCTIVITY has indeed been growing at a more rapid rate in the 1990s than in the 1980s, it is not growing as fast as at several previous periods of American economic history. The statistical record is not easy to read. Outcomes depend on which periods precisely are chosen for comparison, because they are so affected by where precisely in the business cycle the periods compared are located. Even so, if we take the business cycle as a whole, recent productivity growth has been unspectacular compared with that in the immediate post–World War II period and in the 1960s. Between the middle of 1960 and the end of 1969, for example, U.S. productivity grew by 2.7 percent per annum. In the next period, from the last quarter of 1969 to the last quarter of 1973 (before the oil price rise had had time to bite deep), productivity growth was again 2.7 percent. Earlier still, between the last quarter of 1948 and the third quarter of 1953 it was even higher at 3.3 percent.

Exaggerated conclusions should not be drawn from such comparisons. No doubt the U.S. economy then continued to enjoy the yield of the massive investments made in productive machinery to win World War II. No doubt, too, in the immediate aftermath of the war, it was possible to improve production methods by incorporating techniques into production practice that could not be adopted under wartime conditions. But such comparisons do serve, at the very least, as a warning against accepting too readily simplistic or triumphalist claims that we are now in a New Economy with wholly different rules from those of the past, or that the economy is doing significantly better than in the past.

It is fashionable to compare the digital revolution, for example, with the invention of printing. Certainly digital calculations and communications have already transformed the way most people work, just as printing eventually did. No doubt, too, the digital revolution will eventually transform teaching and research, social science and medicine, communications and entertainment. It has already had large effects. The question is whether this transformation is unique or to be compared only with a discovery made more than half a millennium ago. Steam power in the eighteenth century, the agricultural revolution in the nineteenth century, the electric motor, the automobile, and electronics all changed economies, not only by creating new products but also by transforming processes. The computer has certainly done both of those things, and the Internet is in the process of doing so even more. But it would be a bold economic or social historian who would assert that the process is incomparably more revolutionary than, its consequences too great even to be compared with, those earlier industrial and economic transformations. The first duty of those who would understand what has happened in the age of hype is to beware of hype.

Intuitively, we may sense that the New Economy is utterly different from the old. But so far the evidence is both scanty and drawn from a very brief period. At most, there is evidence only of an increase in productivity for fewer than ten years and that at a rate lower than in many previous periods. The evidence for technology-induced productivity growth is to be found only in a restricted number of industries and sectors.

Productivity has indeed been growing in manufacturing industries, especially (and that is no surprise) in computer manufacturing. There is little sign so far of rapidly increasing productivity in service industries. Roger Ferguson, the Federal Reserve vice-chairman quoted earlier, argues that the New Economy is a reality because of a revolution in information technology that has brought it along.

That is very plausible. Anyone who surveys a large office with dozens of workers bowed over computer screens, or watches robot machine tools responding swiftly and silently to CAD/CAM instructions, is ready to be persuaded of that. Yet the impact of the Internet in other areas has been disappointing. E-commerce, for example, touted as a tidal wave that would sweep away all previous forms of retailing, has been a conspicuous disappointment so far except in a narrow range of sectors.

Even the Fed's Roger Ferguson, however, confesses to being unsure just what is so special about the technological innovations and why they should have produced a spurt in productivity growth in the past few years. He expressed his uncertainty in a series of very good questions. How much can the economy continue to benefit in the future from the diffusion of current technologies? Specifically, does the Internet have the potential to improve business processes continuously? Can new innovations emerging from the research and development process deliver more productivity gains in the future? And, given the volatility of equity markets where new technology is at issue—a volatility dramatically demonstrated since Ferguson spoke—will capital continue to be invested in technological innovation at the same rate in the future?

These are all good questions, and so are two simpler ones. Exactly where has the new technology produced measurable net growth in productivity? And exactly where will it do so in the near future?

It is widely assumed that the recent acceleration in economic growth, combined with low inflation and low unemployment, is the consequence of productivity growth, itself the result of the computer revolution in general and of the Internet in particular. Some go further and argue that because of faster productivity growth, the United States could afford a higher growth rate without risking higher inflation, and that therefore the Federal Reserve should allow a looser monetary policy than it would be able to do if productivity growth were slower. In analyzing these arguments, Princeton's Alan Blinder, formerly a member of the Clinton administration's Council of Economic Advisers, has come up with a cautious statement that probably states a minimum consensus among experts.

> We have a tantalizing fact that productivity accelerated at about the time the Internet burst on the scene. Whether or not the Internet was the cause of the speedup will be a matter for economic historians to sort out some years from now; there are competing explanations. For now, however, it appears that the economy can sustain a higher growth rate than most people thought plausible just a year or two ago. In that limited respect, at least, we appear to be in a "New Economy."[34]

Such skeptical approaches may seem perverse, even eccentric. For many people, in the late 1990s, the economy was quite simply in the greatest boom in history. The great bonanza, they assumed, has been directly created by the digital revolution in general, and the Internet in particular. Why fuss and quibble? This was a time to rejoice and enjoy.

Over the past decade, securities markets, especially in the United States but also elsewhere, have been in a historic boom. The Dow-Jones index of equities rose from around 3,600 in early 1994 to 11,000 in 1999, and in 2000 it passed 11,700. The Standard & Poor's composite stock price index rose in an equally spectacular manner from under 500 in 1995 to over 1400 in 2000. And the Nasdaq index, disproportionately reflecting high-technology stocks, has risen even faster.

The direct beneficiaries of these stock price rises have included leading businessmen, journalists, publicists, even academics and politicians. To the extent that those rises have reflected the dramatic upward movement of mutual funds and other financial institutions, the paper wealth created by the stock market has also indirectly enriched a wider swathe than ever before of the American public. It is proudly claimed that half the American population has benefited from the rise in equity values. If so, half of the population has not, at least not directly; as we have seen, fewer than a third of Americans had as much as $5,000 invested in the market. Even if that had doubled and stayed doubled, it would not have made every man and woman a Rockefeller or a Gates. But the massive coverage of markets (in newspapers and other media that benefit from the need of brokerages, mutual funds, and other financial institutions to advertise heavily in those media), while understandable from a journalistic point of view, has undoubtedly had the inadvertent effect of persuading the American public that the economy as a whole has been advancing as rapidly as the equity markets, and that is not so.

This can be easily shown.[35] Stock prices have risen many times faster than earnings. And the prices of stock in the leading corporations of the New Economy, stocks like Microsoft, Cisco, Sun Microsystems, Yahoo!, and America Online, rose most precipitously of all. Overall, the price-earnings ratio, as measured by the relationship between the stock price of all companies in the S&P composite index and their earnings, rose from around 10 in the early 1980s to 44 times earnings in 2000. (Indeed, the ratios of many New Economy stocks rose for a time to infinity, since they had not yet made any profits at all!) The only remotely comparable spike in the price-earnings ratio was in September 1929, on the eve of the Great Crash. It took almost thirty years for the market to reach that level again.

It is, of course, possible that the market's exuberance is not, as Alan Greenspan called it, irrational, and that technological innovation will lead to a torrent of solid profit that will fully justify the recent levels of stock prices and price-earnings ratios. It is possible. No one knows. On balance it seems unlikely. And the fact that the Nasdaq index and other indexes around the world that disproportionately represent speculative high-technology stocks fell by 30 percent and even more from their 2000 peaks before rising, though not to their earlier peaks, after September 11 would tend to confirm a pessimistic or at least a skeptical view of future market levels.

This is not, however, an exercise in market forecasting. The relevant point here is that the market's exuberant performance has served to distort understanding of the history of the technological revolution, and so of its real future significance. Stock market prices reflect guesses, whether by ignorant citizens using methods of divination that have not improved since the days of the Chaldeans, or by consummate Wall Street professionals using giant computers and even (in the case of the most dramatic splash-down of recent years) relying on the supposedly scientific calculations of Nobel laureates in economics.[36] Productivity gains, in contrast, reflect actual corporate investments, in plant, software, or training. There is room for argument at the margin about methodology, but no guesswork whatever is involved.

A second factor has reinforced bullish sentiment. Over the dozen years since the fall of communism the United States has become the "last superpower" (a concept we examine in more detail in a later chapter). The most dangerous enemy, the Soviet Union, has imploded. Saddam Hussein's Iraq, Slobodan Milosevic's Serbia, the Taliban in Afghanistan have been easily defeated. Economic rivals, such as Japan and Western Europe, have been less successful by most measures than the United States, although not perhaps by as large a margin as is taken for granted in U.S. news media.[37] The combined influence of high stock market prices and a pervasive sense of national success created a climate in which it was natural to attribute to digital technology, as conveniently symbolized by the takeoff of the Internet from 1996 on, a revolutionary step change in productivity and prosperity. The picture of an American people universally and equally enriched by the bounteous harvest of technology had immense appeal. It was, of course, seriously flawed. At the very least it is premature. There is no more reason to extrapolate from four or five years of higher productivity growth than there would have been to draw general conclusions from a similar number of earlier years of depressing statistics.

Even more erroneous is the idea that this benison was evidence of the unique, liberating power of unregulated free-market capitalism. It is common, but it is inaccurate, to say that the new information technology is due to the inspired self-interest of American business and owes nothing to the action of government. The idea of the New Economy is not an economic concept, imposed by the inescapable logic of the numbers. It is a political interpretation, deeply influenced by ideological preconceptions. Those prejudices, in turn, are powerfully influenced by political interests. Microeconomists, including many academics associated with business schools and with conservative research institutes, accept the economic analysis associated with the "rational choice" school. They incline to as little political or regulatory restraint on the operation of the free market as possible. A small group, often associated with the labor movement, argues that the free market has failed us as a society.

In the late 1990s, the latter group seemed to have lost the argument. Some were discouraged, while others hedged their bets. Yet since the turn of the century the balance has shifted. As long as the economy seemed to have performed the miracle of combining rapid growth, full unemployment, and low inflation with a rapid increase in asset values for investments and real estate, the theory of a New Economy was plausible.

A number of myths established themselves. All of them have been demolished or at least thrown into doubt by the events of 2000 and 2001.[38] One was that the business cycle was a thing of the past. Another was that the cycle is still there, but information technology smoothes the cycle. A third myth was that spending on information technology was recession-proof. Profits, fourthly, would rise swiftly for years to come. Some, on the other hand, even went so far as to say that corporate profits themselves were irrelevant to the valuation of stocks. Each of these myths, earnestly put forward by stock analysts and the more uncritical economists, has been blown away. Even though the markets have recovered substantially since September 11, 2001, the principle is unassailed.

No, the business cycle has not disappeared. With the mightiest leaders of the new technology (Intel, Compaq, Cisco, Amazon) shaken like saplings by the harsh winds of recession, it is plain that information technology is at least as exposed to the business cycle as any other sector of the economy. Investment in information technology, for the time being, at least, has slumped. Corporate profits over the whole economy fell by at least 10 percent in 2001. The bleached bones of countless dot.com startups reproach anyone who was foolish enough to invest in them under the illusion that profits did not matter. It would be easy to forgive the apostles of such mythology if it were honest error we were dealing with. But too often it is greed or ambition. Too many of these wilting propositions were inspired by the self-interested ideology of the free market. Too many were expressed in terms of the bogus populism that interpreted any criticism of the perfection of the market—absurdly when the market's profits accrued overwhelmingly to the very best-off—as elitist.

It seems sensible to avoid both the triumphalism of 1999 and 2000 and the alternative view that the economy is headed into prolonged recession. No doubt the cluster of information technologies around the Internet will eventually have very large and very beneficial effects on the economy, and on society. Yet it is plain that, whatever its long-term consequences, the Internet is not the almost unique technosocial event it was portrayed as.

It is probably wise to examine its impact in detail. For example, nineteenth-century technologies (railways, the electric motor, the internal combustion engine) tended to create mass employment in great plants, which in turn brought great cities into existence—Manchester, Pittsburgh, Chicago, Detroit, the Ruhr, and Shanghai—and swelled the population of older ones, including London, New York, Paris, and Tokyo. Great manufacturing plants and seaports demanded great armies of disciplined labor. At first the consequence was overrapid urbanization, social deprivation, and even squalor. By the 1950s these conditions were improving rapidly.

One wave of industrial innovation had been tamed. The new wave of innovation, however, created no immediate need for battalions of unskilled and semiskilled labor. The requirement is for highly trained researchers, programmers, engineers, and the like, capable of working largely on their own initiative. This shift in the nature of the demand for workers is the most obvious single cause of increasing income inequality. Many of the less appealing jobs in the manufacturing sector have already been exported. Semiconductors, to take one obvious example, tend to be made in Asian or Latin American countries. The same is true of mass-produced textiles and assemblies and semifinished goods of many kinds, and this trend will certainly continue, even as some developing countries—India, for example, and Brazil—gradually begin to compete with their own manufactures and processing activities. Ultimately, of course, rising living standards in the United States will also demand secondary workers to do the jobs the most skilled no longer want to do. These will be mostly service jobs, in financial, public, or personal services. Some of this demand for labor has been taken up by women, pouring into the workplace for reasons of their own.

This trend will continue, while some women move more or less rapidly up the ladder into professional and managerial work. Some service jobs, again for complex reasons, are being disproportionately undertaken by members of minorities, though minorities, and especially African Americans, have also been steadily overrepresented among those without work. The service sector has also provided work for many millions of immigrants, most of them from regions that have not sent migrants to the

United States until recently. In the next four chapters we will look at the experience and prospects of immigrants, women, and minorities and of the majority as it has been affected by the changes of the past quarter of a century.

The lens through which we will be able to examine those changes must be the realization that there has not been, and there will not be, a magic transformation scene in which the good fairy of the magic market waves her high-technology wand and turns to gold the base clay of economic reality. Reciting mantras about the free market, in fact (to paraphrase the conservative catchphrase, beloved of Ronald Reagan about government), is not part of the solution. It has been part of the problem.

5

New Immigrants

Immigration is the oldest and most persistent theme in American history, and though the character of immigration has changed drastically within recent years, the nature of the process has remained essentially the same.

> —*Samuel Eliot Morison and Henry Steele Commager,*
> *The Growth of the American Republic*

NOTHING THAT HAPPENED in the United States over the last third of the twentieth century—not terrorism, the explosion of new technology, or the transformation of politics or the end of the Cold War, not even the profound changes in the status and expectations and role of American women—will have more long-term consequences for the future of the United States than the new immigration.

By the end of the twentieth century demographic changes were irrevocably in place that would, by the middle of the twenty-first, utterly transform the genetic and, almost certainly as a consequence, the cultural character of the country. As a result of the New Immigration the United States would cease to be, what in spite of all ideological and environmental influences it had remained since the first European settlements at the beginning of the seventeenth century, a predominantly European country, its people—with identifiable exceptions—Europeans, however hard they strove to be "the American, this new man."[1] No one, at the beginning of the twenty-first century, could predict with certainty precisely how this demographic event would transform American attitudes to, for example, politics, religion, or the rest of the world. But it is pretty safe to say that in the long run the consequences would be comparable with those of, say, the Louisiana Purchase or even the Civil War.

Early in 2001, for example, the Census Bureau reported that over the past decade the Hispanic population, having exceeded expectations by growing by 58 percent in ten years, had drawn almost equal with the black population.[2] There were 35.4 million blacks, the census calculated, and 35.3 million Hispanics. The Asian population had surged ahead at an even faster rate, by 74 percent, to 11.6 million. The highest growth rate in any census category, the 92 percent increase in the number of people identifying themselves as Native Americans, suggested a new and—to most— welcome trend: more and more Americans did not mind identifying themselves as members of groups that were once discriminated against. But the census's main lesson was a simple one: the process whereby white Americans of European descent were headed toward becoming a minority in the United States was rolling forward even faster than the demographers had predicted.

In 1965, the same year in which he signed the Voting Rights Act, Lyndon Johnson put his name to another piece of legislation that would in the long run change American demographics as much as the former act would transform its politics. This was the Hart-Celler Immigration and Nationality Act. (Strictly speaking it consisted of amendments to the McCarran-Walter Act of 1952.)[3] Again, this was an act of public policy whose consequences, if not wholly unintended, were certainly not clearly foreseen. For the 1965 immigration legislation, motivated by a wish merely to correct an injustice between two groups of emigrants from Europe, ended up by setting off what has come to be called the Second Great Migration. That will in time end the predominantly European character of the population.

Americans, it has been well said, are a self-chosen people. With the exception of the one-eighth of the population who are descended in whole or in part from African slaves, all but a handful[4] of Americans are descended from forebears who chose to emigrate from other countries either to the British North American colonies (before 1783) or to the United States. About 1 million people left Europe to settle in America during the rough century and a half before independence,[5] and a substantial proportion of the modern population, especially in the South, is descended from those original immigrants of colonial days.[6] For roughly one hundred years after independence, an average of 170,000 men, women, and children came to the United States every year, with a significant upward bump in the curve in the late 1840s and early 1850s, after the Irish famine and the repression that followed the revolutions of 1848 across Europe.

Then, in the 1880s, the pace of immigration sharply increased. As before, the causes of this First Great Migration were complex. They included frustration with the closing down of economic opportunities in Europe after the recession of 1873; the desire to escape long and harsh periods of military conscription, especially in the czarist empire; reports of the availability and productivity of new lands after the opening up of the Midwest by the transcontinental railroads; and active recruiting by those same railroads and by other American employers. By a strange historical circularity that has not been widely noticed, the development of the United States itself helped to swell the tide of migrants from Europe to the Golden West. It was the agricultural depression across Europe, from Scotland to the Ukraine, caused by the importation of cheap American grain after 1870, that headed farmers and their families first into the nearest city and then toward the seaports and on board ships westward bound.

The first Great Migration shifted its course over a period of roughly four decades. At first, most migrants came chiefly, as they had done in colonial times, from northern Europe: from the British Isles, including Ireland, from Germany and from Scandinavia. Later the source of the migration moved east and south, and the emigrants came increasingly from eastern, southeastern and southern Europe: from Poland (then divided among the German, Austro-Hungarian, and Russian empires); from Russia; from Austrian Bohemia and Slovakia, among other provinces, and from Hungary; from southern Italy and Sicily, which had missed out on the growing prosperity of the industrial north of the peninsula; and from Greece.

Overall the shift was dramatic: in 1882, just under 650,000 immigrants arrived in the United States, of whom only 13 percent came from the south and east of Europe, but by 1907 81 percent of the 1.2 million who immigrated in that year came from those countries.[7]

The migrants of the first three-quarters of the nineteenth century, like the 4 million white people who lived in the United States at the time of the first census in 1791, were largely, though not exclusively, Protestants. Many of the largest Roman Catholic group, the Irish Catholics, were English-speaking and all too familiar with Anglo-Saxon politics and other folk-ways.[8] The new immigrants, many of them Roman Catholics from Italy, Poland, and Hungary, some Orthodox Christians, and a significant minor-ity of Jews, were culturally more "different." Their arrival, in the hundreds of thousands every year, provoked a revival of the nativist, anti-immigrant sentiment that had largely subsided since the Civil War.[9] It is an open question, to which we must revert, whether there will be a similar popular objection to the post-1965 migration, and if so how successful it will be.

The first legal barriers went up against Asians, beginning with the Chi-nese Exclusion Act of 1882.[10] The Japanese were excluded by the so-called Gentleman's Agreement of 1907, and the Immigration Act of 1917 banned virtually all Asian immigrants.[11] In the same year legislation was passed ex-cluding idiots, lunatics, those likely to become a public charge, and con-victs from immigrating into the United States. Over the forty years after the Chinese Exclusion Act, a series of other enactments sought to make the immigration of people who were seen as unfamiliar and undesirable in the eyes of the American majority more difficult. Congress, for exam-ple, made immigration a federal responsibility, sought (unsuccessfully) to impose a literacy test on new migrants, proscribed anarchists, epileptics, and beggars, and made a knowledge of English a requirement for natu-ralization. This legislative activity took place against a background of more or less offensive and racist propaganda against immigrants, who were often portrayed in print and in cartoons in the most insulting light.

An act of Congress in 1907 set up the Dillingham Commission, which published its report in no fewer than forty-two volumes in 1912. In the mean-time Congress had extended the list of medical conditions that barred entry to the United States. In the early 1920s the Supreme Court had found that Japanese could not become citizens because they were not "Caucasian." Hindus could not become citizens either. Although they were considered "Caucasians," "in accordance with the understanding of the common man" they were not white.[12] The Dillingham report reflected many of the racialist and indeed racist stereotypes of such anti-immigrant lobbies as the Immi-gration Restriction League. It also drew on the scientific, or pseudoscientific, researches of anthropologists like Franz Boas, of Columbia University. Boas claimed to be an opponent of racism, but his attempt to demonstrate, with skull measurements and the like, the differences between "races" (a term then used for what would now be known as nationalities) had the effect of encouraging the very doctrines he sought to discredit.

More generally, hostility to the new immigration in the late nineteenth and early twentieth centuries was influenced by the vogue for eugenics. Popular opinion, in the educated elites as well as in the wider public, was more influenced by openly racist works like Madison Grant's *The Passing of the Great Race*,[13] which predicted the "decadence" of the "white race" as a result of "interbreeding." There was widespread fear that immigrants of "inferior stocks" would bring with them disease, madness, and "degeneracy."

Serious attempts were made to repatriate groups who were not seen as desirable by the white, Protestant majority. In the period immediately after the Bolshevik Revolution these included some Jews, because they were suspected, in some cases correctly, of sympathy with communism.[14] Later hundreds of thousands of Mexicans were deported, when Depression conditions meant that their labor was no longer needed.[15] In both of these cases, racial or ethnic prejudice is clearly visible in the reasons given for the expulsions. All these different strands of opposition to immigrants in general, and emigrants from Russia, Mexico, and Italy in particular, finally triumphed in the Johnson-Reed Act of 1924.[16] Twice postponed, and only in full effect from 1929, this act established quotas on the basis of the national origins of the population of the United States as of the census of 1920. Total immigration was to be limited to 150,000 people a year, of which more than half would be allotted to applicants from Great Britain, Ireland, and Germany. The annual quota for most individual non-European countries was set at a miserly 100.

Partly as a result of the 1924 act, and partly as a result of the Great Depression, which began in 1929, immigration into the United States dwindled to a trickle and almost dried up altogether in the 1930s. Over the whole period of the First Great Migration, however, a total of some 26 million immigrants arrived in the United States. While a surprisingly large proportion of these returned to their native countries,[17] this was a large enough movement of people to transform the character of the American population in many very significant ways.

The First Great Migration, however, has already been exceeded in numbers by a Second Great Migration, which began as a result of the reform of immigration law in 1965. In thirty-five years this new flood has already brought more than 30 million new immigrants to America.[18] By 2000 28.4 million foreign-born persons were resident in the United States. Just over half of them were born in Latin America, almost exactly a quarter in Asia, and only fewer than one in six in Europe.[19] By the end of the twentieth century, the New Immigration was running at the rate of almost 1 million legal and perhaps one-third of a million illegal immigrants each year.

In rough terms, one-third of Americans are descended from ancestors who immigrated in the eighteenth century and before, one-third from ancestors who migrated in the nineteenth century, and one-third from migrants during the twentieth century.[20] Estimates of the probable ethnic blend of the population in the middle of the twenty-first century must be unreliable, because they depend on so many unknown variables, such as comparative rates of natural increase and future migration. But the estimate of the scholars James P. Smith and Barry Edmonston has received wide acceptance: it is that by the year 2050 the total U.S. population will be 26 percent Hispanic, 8 percent Asian, and 14 percent black.[21] Other estimates are that the proportion of Hispanics in the American population is growing four times as fast as the rest of the population,[22] and that "Hispanics" (many of whom dislike the name) will replace African Americans as the largest minority group as soon as 2005.

These terms are of course confusing, since many "Hispanics" are at least partially of African descent and many are in varying degrees of American Indian, as opposed to European, background. In any case, such projections must always be treated with caution. For one thing, they assume that the children of, for example, Hispanics will continue to be, genetically— so to speak—Hispanic, when in practice many of them may well marry Americans of European or Asian descent. Culturally, too, it is—as we shall see—a very open question to what extent Hispanics will remain distinctively Hispanic, and the same doubts arise, perhaps even more strongly, in relation to Asian Americans. Still, both the contrast, and the speed of the change, are striking. Only thirty years ago, a mere 5 percent of the population were Hispanic and 1 percent Asian, so a careful estimate suggests that the proportion of Hispanics in the population may multiply by five times in eighty years, and the proportion of Asians also by five times in the same period.

The New Immigration is at once extraordinarily diverse in its origins and quite concentrated inside the United States. Where once new Americans came mostly from the British Isles and then from northern Europe, now they come from almost everywhere except Britain and northern Europe.[23] From the 1950s on conditions in Western Europe had improved to the point where the attraction of emigration declined sharply. Long before the 1965 legislation, the British and German immigration quotas were largely undersubscribed.[24] In parts of Latin America, in contrast, economic stagnation and political failures, coupled with glowing portrayals in movies and other media of the attractions of American life, meant that substantial proportions of whole populations would immigrate to the United States if they could. In the Dominican Republic, for example, it is said,[25] with what degree of exaggeration is not clear, that no fewer than two-thirds of the population would like to immigrate to the Unites States, to join the substantial proportion of the population that has already done so. Again, approximately 3 million Puerto Ricans live in the United States, as against under 4 million who remain in the island commonwealth.

Not only has the volume of immigration increased since 1965 to approach and even perhaps exceed the highest levels reached in the late nineteenth and early twentieth century.[26] The source of the new immigration is also completely different. As recently as the 1950s, more than two-thirds of the immigrants admitted came from Europe or Canada, one-quarter from Latin America, and only 6 percent from Asia. By the 1990s, "only 17 per cent of the immigrants originated in Europe or Canada, almost half in Latin America, and 20 per cent in Asia."[27]

The change in both the numbers and the diversity of Asian immigration, in particular, is very striking. Over the 110 years from 1820 to 1930, 377,000 Chinese and 275,000 Japanese, but only 9,000 Indians, were admitted as immigrants to the United States. By 1990 it was estimated that there were 1.26 million Chinese in America, and 1.4 million Filipinos, and perhaps more than 3 million "Arabs," many of them Christians from Lebanon, Syria, Palestine, and Egypt.[28] There were, according to the same authority, over 800,000 each of Vietnamese, Japanese, and Korean immigrants, and 684,000 Indians.[29]

These groups were rather concentrated, both by occupation and geographically. Koreans, for example, have tended to specialize in running family retail businesses: neighborhood markets, greengrocers, liquor stores, and flower shops, and they cluster densely in downtown Los Angeles. There has been a certain amount of return migration to Korea as a result of the success of the South Korean economy and in response to attacks on Korean property during the rioting that followed the Rodney King incident in Los Angeles in 1992.

Many American Arabs work in industrial cities in the Midwest, especially Detroit. Some Vietnamese have stayed close to the four original reception camps opened to receive them after the fall of Saigon in 1975,[30] whereas others have taken to shrimp fishing along the Gulf Coast. Chinese Americans and Japanese Americans have long been highly successful both in business and in science and engineering. Recently they have been joined and even outstripped by emigrants from the Indian subcontinent. By 1980 "Asians"[31] made up 20 percent of the student body at Berkeley and 9 percent at Harvard; of the 1980 freshman class 20 percent were Asian at Columbia, Yale, and Princeton.[32] By 1989 more than half of the doctorates awarded by U.S. universities in engineering and mathematics were going to Asians, and even as early as 1974 more than one-fifth of all physicians and over one-third of hospital interns and residents in the United States were foreign.[33] The most successful group, perhaps, is the highly educated Indians. In 1990 their average income was more than $48,000, or $18,000 higher than the median for the U.S. population as a whole. Some have found work as medical doctors or in Silicon Valley, while other Indians have moved into the Garment District in Manhattan, where they import textiles, often commuting into the city from northern New Jersey. Others again have all but cornered the motel franchising business.[34]

Still, all the Asians put together were dwarfed by the tide of migration from Latin America, and especially from Mexico and the Caribbean. Altogether emigrants from Latin America make up 51 percent of all immigrants to the United States, and of those just under two-thirds come from Mexico. If illegal immigration is included the trend may be even more striking, because the ease of crossing the border between the United States and Mexico means that a very high proportion of illegal immigrants are from

Mexico or Central America. According to one authoritative account, "Mexico is the source of over 95 per cent of unauthorized aliens apprehended."[35] This presumably includes both those caught crossing the border and those found to be living illegally inside the United States.

Historically, emigration from Latin America, and especially from Mexico, has been different in character from emigration from Europe and also from Asian immigration. For one thing, the first large Spanish-speaking American populations became American not by free choice but by conquest.[36] Again, where Europeans were taking the decisive step of crossing an ocean, a decisive and expensive step for poor laborers and their families from Ireland, Sicily, or the Ukraine, Mexicans had only to travel over a land frontier that was not, in the nineteenth and early twentieth centuries, heavily defended. Lastly, Mexican immigrants did not find themselves isolated as one among many blocks of immigrants, all speaking different languages, and therefore with the strongest motive to learn English as soon as possible, but as a large minority and often a majority locally, and therefore able to retain—for better or for worse—their own language and culture. They came from a country that, by the late twentieth century, was proudly independent, acutely sensitive to any hint of *gringo* arrogance, and with a population more than one-third as large as that of the United States.

After the Mexican War an admittedly scattered population of a few tens of thousands of Spanish-speaking ranchers and their families, *vaqueros*, and *peones* became American willy-nilly.[37] In California, Americans outnumbered the Mexican settlers within a few years after the Gold Rush began, and Anglo businessmen relentlessly squeezed Spanish-speaking landowners out of power over the next generation.[38] By the 1890s, according to the historian Clyde Milner, "the Californios and Hispanos of what had once been northern Mexico lost most of their property."[39] Even in New Mexico, where Anglo predation was less effective than anywhere else, 80 percent of the land had come into Anglo hands by the end of the century.

In Texas, for close to a century (until the 1930s) Mexicans were confronted with de facto and sometimes de jure segregation in housing and education, sometimes, especially in southern Texas, enforced by statute. The Kleberg family, owners of the gigantic King ranch, began the practice, later widely followed in Texas, of voting their Spanish-speaking tenants and employees; in California voters were required to speak English. Altogether, Latinos in Texas and California were treated as half-citizens at best and at worst experienced a status not significantly better than that of African Americans at the same time and place.

The first major wave of Mexican immigration, as opposed to Anglo conquest, in the Southwest, came as a direct result of the Mexican civil war of 1910 to 1920 and lasted up to the passage and implementation of the Johnson-Reed Act. But from 1929 to 1933 came the massive deportations. The strongest voice in favor of allowing Mexicans to stay in the United States came from the big landowners of Texas and the California fruit and vegetable growers, who had come to depend on cheap Mexican "stoop labor." Those same employers treated Mexicans in California as colonial rulers treated their subjects. In the 1920s and 1930s, as California's preeminent historian, Kevin Starr, put it, "white people owned the land, and people of color—368,000 Mexicans most noticeably—did the work."[40] The U.S. agricultural census for 1935 showed that a quarter of the state's agricultural acreage and a third of its produce belonged to just 2 percent of its farmers. California's farms were already highly mechanized, and the growers needed three times as many workers in the harvesting season as they had needed in the spring.[41] Increasingly, nonetheless, Mexicans came to settle. In the first decade of the twentieth century only 50,000 emigrants arrived from Mexico, but in the third the number was almost half a million, ten times as many. The work was hard, backbreaking picking in heat that often passed 100 degrees in the shade, and the work was not done in the shade. The wages were poor, even by the standards of the time: $2.50 to $3.00 for a nine-hour day, with an extra $50 automatically if you were white.[42] Race was very much an issue. The Imperial Valley, says Starr, "sustained *de facto* Jim Crow laws through the late 1920s which excluded Mexicans from restaurants, soda fountains, beauty parlors and barber shops, and permitted them to sit only in separate parts of movie theaters." Mexican children, even if they were American born, which they increasingly were, went to separate and unequal schools.[43]

The big landowners, backed by the Associated Farmers organization, working with vigilante groups, sheriffs, highway patrolmen, and all too many judges, enforced their economic interests as if they were the law of the land, which to all intents they were. By 1930, workers—Mexican or others—were being aggressively organized by the communist-influenced Cannery and Agricultural Workers Industrial Union, and over the next few years the farming towns of California, from Santa Clara Valley just south of San Francisco to the Imperial Valley on the Mexican border, were the scene of a series of strikes, beatings, lynchings, and near massacres that brought the state close to civil war. That was the background to the massive repatriations of the 1930s. But once war came again the growers needed labor. They did not want to employ Filipinos, who tended to arrive without women and therefore to cause trouble. They could no longer count on the white migrants, "Okies" and "Arkies," who had replaced many Mexicans in the 1930s. And so the U.S. government initiated the *bracero* program, which deliberately imported Mexicans to work as agricultural labor on California's increasingly mechanized agribusiness farms.

By the 1970s, the Mexican population was important enough from California to Texas that Richard Nixon, that most pragmatic of politicians, made special efforts to woo the Hispanic vote, while at the same time adopting a number of policies that frustrated Hispanic hopes of economic and social advancement. According to some authorities,[44] Nixon was even responsible for the widespread adoption of the term "Hispanic," as opposed to Mexican, Chicano, or Latino, on the grounds that it was the most inclusive of these various words for Americans of Spanish-speaking background.

The term conceals the immense diversity of those to whom it applies. One recent report, in the news magazine *U.S. News*, divided Hispanic immigrants into no fewer than seventeen "major Latino subcultures."[45]

Two-thirds of the Hispanics in America are of Mexican origin.[46] Yet even the Mexicans and their descendants living in the United States are very far from uniform or indeed united. They include citizens and noncitizens; legal and illegal immigrants and their children; some who speak and write English as well as any Anglo and others who can hardly speak English at all; families settled in the United States and indeed a few who have lived nowhere else for centuries and young men and women who have just crossed the border; well-educated professionals and wealthy businessmen, as well as the desperately poor and the pathetically marginal. What the Mexicans have in common, however, is that they all have their roots in a country that is big (almost 100 million people), rapidly progressing after decades of stagnation, and next door.

If you pull back focus and look at all the "Hispanics" in the United States, the diversity is infinitely greater. Another one-seventh of the Hispanic total, or 2 million people, comes from parts of Central and South America, other than Mexico, Puerto Rico, and Cuba. This second category includes professionals from the relatively developed cultures of the Southern Cone and Brazil, as well as predominantly African American settlers from the Dominican Republic and emigrants of largely Native American, though Spanish-speaking, background from Nicaragua, Honduras, El Salvador, and Guatemala. The two next largest groups could hardly be more diverse. The third category comprises the 3 million-plus Puerto Ricans. They are predominantly dark-skinned, relatively poorly educated as a group, disproportionately poor and mostly in the North, indeed mostly in and immediately around New York City and Chicago.

The fourth largest group, the Cubans, are different again. Generalizations ignore individual cases. But the Cubans are far more likely to be rich, white, conservative and Republican, and they are as heavily concentrated in South Florida as the Puerto Ricans are in Greater New York. Cuba was virtually an American colony from 1898 until Fidel Castro overthrew the dictator Batista in 1958. It was also a country where the upper and upper-middle classes, including most landowners, businessmen, and professionals, were white, while agricultural and city workers were largely black or of mixed race. So when Castro took over, and especially after he declared his hand as a communist, the predominantly white business class fled to Florida, taking education, skills, and, if possible, some capital with them. Their economic and political success in southern Florida reflects their energy and a fierce will to succeed; it also reflects the fact that, as a group, they started with significant advantages, like the migrants from southern China who turned Hong Kong into a model of capitalist enterprise after they fled from the Maoist revolution in 1949.

If diversity, indeed, is one of the most salient characteristics of the new immigration, just as it was in the old, another is concentration. The foreign-born are more geographically concentrated than the native population, and more likely than natives to live in central cities or in metropolitan areas.[47] In 1993, for example, 71 percent of 904,000 foreign-born went to just six states.

California received the lion's share, 28.8. Another 16.7 percent went to New York, so that over 45 per cent of all immigrants went to just two states. The next four states were Texas (7.5 percent), Florida (6.8 percent), New Jersey (5.6 percent), and Illinois (5.2 percent).[48]

On the ground, the concentration is even greater than that. No fewer than 42 percent of all immigrants, not just Hispanics, went to just five metropolitan areas: New York, Los Angeles, Miami, Chicago, and Orange County, California. There are reasons for this. Immigrants are naturally attracted by the convenience and the sense of psychological security that comes from living in communities of their "landsmen," as the central European immigrants of the early twentieth century used to call them. A Spanish-speaking newcomer from Central America or the Dominican Republic, just as much as a Cuban, finds it easier to settle in, find a job, and buy or rent a home in Miami's Little Havana, where Spanish is the first language, than in a middle-western city, where (other than in Chicago) Spanish speakers are relatively few and far between; while emigrants from central and eastern Europe tend to congregate in the Midwest for precisely the same reason.[49] So much is obvious. What is less self-evident is that this concentration is specifically encouraged by the requirement for family sponsorship in the Immigration and Naturalization Services rules.

From the 1920s until at least the 1950s, American national politics and particularly presidential politics were significantly shaped by the concentration of emigrants from southern and eastern Europe in a handful of big industrial states in the Northeast and the Midwest and especially in New York, Pennsylvania, Ohio, Michigan, and Illinois. A presidential candidate who could carry all or most of those states had an immense advantage because of their weight in the Electoral College. But there was a double leverage at work. The electoral vote of many of those states depended critically on winning majorities in a handful of cities, and in particular New York, Philadelphia and Pittsburgh, Cleveland, Detroit, and Chicago. Immigrants are no longer penned together in cities, but even though many have moved to the suburbs where work is plentiful and opportunities are growing, they are still heavily concentrated in a handful of metropolitan areas: New York, Los Angeles and suburban Orange County, Chicago, Miami, and Houston, each of which, significantly, dominates the population of one of the five most populous states. Within metropolitan areas, there can be quite heavy concentrations of immigrants in certain suburbs (for example, in northern New Jersey, in Port Chester, New York, or in Arlington County, Virginia).

This concentration in and immediately around the biggest cities in the biggest states means that the double leverage could still be at work, though with Spanish American, not European, tribes in a position to benefit from it. So the first vital political question about the impact of the new immigration is whether the new immigrant groups will be able to use their potential leverage in presidential politics as their predecessors did. And the second is, if they have that power, what—if anything—will they use it for? What, if any, specific political issues are likely to unite immigrants in general, and Hispanic immigrants in particular? And the most interesting question of all is, What will they want?

By the 1930s the descendants of the immigrants of the First Immigration had transformed the Democratic Party and pushed its northern wing, at least, in the direction of wanting to create a European-style social democracy called the New Deal. In the second and third decades of the twenty-first century, will the children and grandchildren of the Second Immigration want the political system to deliver anything different from what their "old American" neighbors want?

To some degree, the response of the New Americans will be a function of the experience they have at the hands of the Old Americans. Immigration has always been a painful as well as a liberating experience, as the ancestors of tens of millions of Americans discovered; both the pain and the liberation were perceptively analyzed by the writer Eva Hoffman in her 1990 book *Lost in Translation*.[50] Tens of millions of Americans are proud and happy that they or their parents made the decision to come to America. Many American Jews can reflect that, as historian Irving Howe put it, if they hadn't "but for an accident of geography, we might also be bars of soap."[51] Even before the rise of Nazism, the Jews of Russia and Poland, caught between bureaucratic repression and popular prejudice, had a more urgent reason to emigrate than others. Howe has pointed out that while only two-thirds of all immigrants into the United States between 1908 and 1924 remained in America, the proportion of Jewish immigrants who stayed was 94.8 percent.[52]

For the great majority of the others, too—the Irish, the Germans, the Italians, the Slavs, and Scandinavians—the decision to emigrate was seen as triumphantly justified by the outcome, as America was spared the wars of the twentieth century, the hyperinflation, the rise of communism, and the fear of fascism. At least until well after 1945, high American wages, the cheapness and variety of American consumer goods, the availability of cheap land, and, except during the Depression years, the abundance of opportunity made America seem like the Promised Land for the frustrated working class and the ambitious businessmen of Europe alike. Not for nothing was a sudden stroke of good luck, in half the languages of Europe, known as "an uncle from America." Yet, even for those who did not regret the decision for one moment, the translation into being an American brought with it the grind of learning a new language, the embarrassment, sometimes the humiliation, of appearing strange, different. And there were subtler stresses, too: the impatience of children with parents who could not escape from the folkways of the Old Country, and the grief of parents who saw their children drifting away from them.

Just like their predecessors in the first Great Migration, immigrants of the past decades have faced hostility, discrimination, and exploitation, sometimes from the native American population, sometimes from other immigrants. African American rioters in Los Angeles in 1992 singled out stores owned by Koreans to torch. Vietnamese shrimp fishermen in Texas were victims of persecution from native competitors. All but a handful of the cab drivers at Washington's Dulles airport who formed a union in 1999 to protest what they saw as oppressive conditions imposed by the owner of a monopoly concession from the airport authority came from India, Pakistan, Russia, and Afghanistan.[53] But the boss they were complaining of, Farouq Massoud, emigrated from Afghanistan himself in the early 1960s. After working as a laborer and then as a mechanic, he started his own cab company in 1984 and tendered successfully for the monopoly at Dulles in 1989. Drivers complain that even if they work round the clock and sleep in their cabs in the small hours, they make as little as $12,000 a year, and they estimate that Massoud makes $5.5 million a year. Asked by a reporter from the *Washington Post* whether his profit was excessive, Massoud said, "I'm here to make money. I'm not the federal government. I'm not here to feed these guys."[54]

As their diversity would suggest, immigrants in general, and Spanish-speaking immigrants in particular, have had very different experiences in the United States. Even so, some overall generalizations are possible. For example, the foreign-born—as we have seen—are more likely to be found in great cities and in their suburban fringe. They live in bigger families than native-born Americans do. Families with a foreign-born householder are twice as likely to have five people in them than native households.

Most of these generalizations, however, add up to the fact that the foreign-born are worse off economically than other Americans. They are, for example, more likely to be unemployed.[55] They earn less than natives.[56] The differences are not huge, but they are significant. For example, in 1999 36.3 percent of foreign-born full-time workers earned less than $20,000 a year, against 21.3 percent of native workers, one in three against one in five. The foreign-born, lastly, were more likely than natives to live in poverty (16.8 percent below the poverty level in 1999, as against 11.2 percent of natives).

Those are crude, undifferentiated comparisons. They take no account of the diversity of immigrants. And they ignore the dimension of time. One of the constants for immigrants into the United States continues to be, as it has always been, that over time their condition steadily approximates to that of the nonimmigrant majority. If the second generation is taken into account, this is even more true.

Nevertheless the degree of political radicalism to be found in, for example, the Hispanic communities is conditioned by those communities' experience. And that experience has not been entirely a bed of roses. Historically, Hispanic immigrants, as I have suggested, have not simply earned less than the American average. They have experienced discrimination in various forms, and they continue to do so. Two major grievances, in particular, offset their general wish to fit in to American society and to be good citizens.

One is the determination with which the U.S. government tries to keep them and their compatriots out, and the bellicose style with which it often does so in practice, however good its intentions. And the other is the disagreeable fact that at least a substantial minority of the white majority appears not to be very pleased by the number of immigrants who have come among them. That displeasure is expressed sometimes with sophisticated argument, sometimes in blunt street language, and even occasionally by violence. There is some anecdotal evidence that a surge in patriotism following the September 11, 2001, atrocities in New York and Washington has intensified anti-immigration feeling in some quarters.[57]

In 1994, wrote two *Los Angeles Times* reporters who specialize in the issue, "immigration dominated the California election season. Huge protests marked the incendiary debate surrounding Proposition 187."[58] That was the initiative that called for "a dramatic effort to drive out undocumented aliens and to deter their entry by cutting them off from medical and other public services,"[59] including education for their children. It was described in the official argument on the ballot as "the first giant stride in ultimately ending the illegal alien invasion." On November 8, 1994, California voters passed Proposition 187, although it was immediately challenged by several lawsuits, on the ground, among other things, that it violated both the equal protection and the due process clauses of the Fourteenth Amendment, and on December 14 U.S. District Court Judge Mariana R. Pfaelzer of the Central District of California issued an injunction against its principal provisions pending trial. Governor Gray Davis declined to appeal Judge Pfaelzer's decision and the provisions of Proposition 187 have therefore expired. Still, whatever its legal fate, the proposition was a resounding political demonstration of the anger and frustration felt by millions of Californians—at least at the time—at the extent of immigration, legal and illegal, into their state. Anti-immigrant resentment carried California's Governor Pete Wilson, the Republican who started the campaign behind his opponent, to a landslide reelection. Proposition 227, on the ballot in 1998, reinforced the feeling among many Spanish speakers that their presence was resented. The proposition carried by 61 to 39 percent.[60]

According to Laurie Olsen, one of the leaders of the campaign against it, opinion poll analysis revealed "a reservoir of anger, distrust, and even hate focused on bilingual education, bilingual educators, and immigrants—particularly Spanish-speaking immigrants." Proposition 227, she pointed out, successfully exploited "a set of fears and beliefs of a voting California [that was] unrepresentative of the state—whiter, older, only 15% with children in public schools." A majority of this section of the electorate expressed a "sense of the Spanish ruining this country, the sense of our nation in threat."

The campaign for Proposition 227 was led by Ron Unz, a multimillionaire software developer who had run unsuccessfully for governor of California as a Republican. Skillfully framing his campaign as "English for the Children," Unz used an apparently reasonable proposition—that people who will be living in America need to speak, read, and write English—to veil a neoconservative ideology that attacked bilingual educators as "politically correct" and seeking "to roll back our well-intentioned but failed welfare state."[61] Republican and Speaker of the House of Representatives Newt Gingrich enthusiastically backed "English for the Children," asserting (accurately but irrelevantly) that "English is at the heart of our civilization." There is evidence that in private he encouraged Republican candidates to run on the issue. In the end, however, Gingrich never introduced HR 123, a bill declaring English the sole official language of the U.S. government. Other supporters of the proposition saw the issue in more nakedly ethnic, even racial terms, and used it as a way to argue for restriction of immigration.

At first the triumph of Proposition 227 in California brought out imitators in many states. Within six months after its passage, thirty-seven states had contemplated similar legislation. But it was soon apparent that the high watermark of "English only" had passed. It might seem reasonable at first glance to insist that English was the national language of the United States. There were arguments in favor of, as well as against, teaching English by "immersion" instead of through the medium of another tongue. But on second thought public opinion asked how the dominance of English would be threatened by a few schools in California teaching bilingually, and why upsetting, for example, Spanish- or Chinese-speakers who refused to learn English would serve to unite the country.

Before long, the campaign for Proposition 187 had also backfired. Wilson's stance became an albatross around his neck. He was widely perceived by Hispanic voters, who saw the proposition as a thinly veiled attack on all of them, legal and illegal, as prejudiced against Latinos as such. By 1998, the *Times* quoted Antonio Gonzalez, president of the William C. Velasquez Institute, as saying, "it is foolish to run a campaign that is perceived as beating up on Latinos." Pete Wilson himself became the chief political victim of the issue, and in the 1998 midterm elections both Republicans and Democrats avoided the issue of immigration like the plague.

One reason for this somewhat abrupt turnaround in public opinion was no doubt the sharp improvement in the economy between the early and middle 1990s. Traditionally, when the economy is in the doldrums, immigrants in general, and Hispanics in California in particular, become scapegoats for the electorate's fears and frustrations. With the economy's rebound, the issue of immigration became less salient. Besides, politicians—and especially Republican politicians—had become aware of the strength of the Hispanic vote. In unprecedented numbers, Latinos became U.S. citizens. Tens of thousands of newly naturalized Mexicans registered to vote, and Republican politicians in particular realized their attacks on some immigrants had solidified a bloc of Hispanic voters who could not be ignored.

If the wave of anti-Hispanic feeling that produced Propositions 187 and 227 was short-lived, it did serve as a reminder for many Hispanics that at least in some segments of the California electorate, and among voters in Arizona and Texas as well, prejudice and hostility toward them was not dead. There is no question that many, especially older white Californians, did resent the growth in the Hispanic population and felt threatened by the ubiquitous reminders of the growing presence of Spanish-speakers.

Their fear was reciprocated in the Hispanic population by the heavy-handed behavior of "la Migra," the Border Patrol, formerly the law enforcement arm of the Immigration and Naturalization Service of the U.S. Department of Justice, since 2003 part of the Department of Homeland Security. At their worst, many of its officers did their best to imitate, in their conduct toward Mexican border crossers, the attitudes of the less evolved Alabama and Mississippi sheriffs in the early 1960s toward blacks attempting to register to vote.

The number of Border Patrol agents more than doubled between 1994 and 2000, to more than 8,000. Even so they were a thin line to patrol the 2,100-mile frontier, and the stream of immigrants, legal and illegal, did not abate. With wages as much as eight times higher on the northern side of the line, there was no shortage of Mexicans willing to risk being caught and deported, often with rough treatment. But the stream did shift geographically, from the suburbs of San Diego to the arid hills of southern Arizona, while the flood crossing the bottomlands of the Rio Grande valley in Texas continued unabated. In what was dubbed Operation Gatekeeper, Border Patrol officers were drafted into places like Imperial Beach, California, the extreme southwestern tip of the United States, where illegal immigrants used to squirm through the alleys and backyards of a working-class neighborhood.[62] Sensors were buried underground, and an imposing wall built to keep the immigrants out. It worked. In six years, arrests of illegal immigrants in Imperial Beach fell from 187,000 in 1994 to 19,000 in 2000. Meanwhile, all over Orange County in southern California, local police brought in a tough regime of their own. When businessmen complained that Latinos clogged up retail areas and annoyed customers by selling flowers on medians, police would arrest the Latinos and drive them straight to the INS checkpoint on the border to be deported. Indignant Latino and civil liberties activists pointed out that this amounted to racial profiling and discrimination; but more than 4,000 suspected illegal immigrants in two years were stopped by police on suspicion, and many of them summarily deported.

In spite of the difficulty of sifting illegal immigrants from the more than 40,000 cars a day driving over the border into southern California, the crackdown in the San Diego suburbs worked. But the stream of Mexicans seeking work in the United States was largely diverted to more dangerous routes far to the east. By October 2000 the Border Patrol and other law enforcement agencies had apprehended 724,000 border crossers, compared with 563,000 in the whole of the past year. The numbers appear to be falling. Between October 1, 2001, and April 30, 2002, the Border Patrol picked up 526,000 people, just half the number two years earlier. Some would-be illegal immigrants died, mostly of thirst or heat exhaustion in the rugged Arizona mountains and desert; but deaths also appear to be declining. In 2001 336 people died trying to cross the border, against 377 in 2000.[63] Thirst and heat were not the only dangers the illegal border crossers faced, however. Ranchers, angry at the immigrants trampling their land, destroying fences, and even slaughtering cattle for food, were taking the law into their own hands. One Arizona rancher alone detained more than 1,000 immigrants in 2000.[64] Thirty-two Arizona residents detained immigrants, sometimes at gunpoint. In at least three cases local residents shot immigrants to death. Sometimes, too, the violence against immigrants came not just from private citizens, but also from police and from the Border Patrol itself. A July 1999 report by the national Hispanic organization, the National Council of La Raza, revealed that hate crimes against Latinos, though less common than those against African Americans, or indeed than those against homosexuals, had increased by 20 percent in three years.[65] La Raza blamed the increase on "blatant appeals to racism by politicians," especially those campaigning for Proposition 187. In 1998 the respected international human rights organization, Amnesty International, issued a disturbing report documenting cases of beatings, brutality, and sexual harassment by Border Patrol agents, and said that in the Segundo Barrio in El Paso, only a few miles from the border, parents were so afraid of the patrol's high-handed behavior toward suspected illegals that they would not let their children go to school in the morning without their passports.

Neither undisciplined behavior on the parts of some Border Patrol agents nor occasional outbreaks of vigilantism and racism add up to a serious, generalized climate of violence toward Hispanics. But, coming on top of the Proposition 187 campaigns, there was enough to make many Hispanics, especially recent immigrants, wonder how much hostility the American majority population really felt toward them. So it is natural to ask to what extent Hispanic consciousness is likely to solidify into a Hispanic political movement with an identifiable political agenda.

One observer, Dr. Williams Spriggs of the National Urban League, commented on the report that Hispanics had become virtually as numerous as blacks that "African-Americans have a better partner" to demand "things like improving poverty, education and urban development."[66] This is an expression of hope on the part of an African American leader who would like nothing better than a massive block of some 35 million voters, joining their voices to African Americans' grievances and claims. It may, however, have been wishful thinking.

The evidence suggests that while Hispanics may share a vague aspiration toward a more open and less harsh society, they do not, as a block, identify with black political goals or moods. They are themselves divided along several axes, including race, religion,[67] grasp of English, length of stay in the United States, economic status, and education. Successive political movements among them have emphasized economic and cultural differences. The oldest Hispanic organization in Texas, for example, the League of United Latin American Citizens (LULAC), admitted only those who were already citizens and conducted its proceedings in English, beginning with the Pledge of Allegiance, though even LULAC filed lawsuits against educational discrimination and lobbied for equal treatment. La Raza is not, as its name might suggest, an explicitly racial organization: the name derives from the semimystical theories of the Mexican minister of education, José Vasconcelos, in the 1920s, about *la raza cosmica*, the "cosmic race." Starting in the 1930s, far more aggressive radical movements organized agricultural workers in California, culminating in Cesar Chavez's radical United Farm Workers of America in the 1960s, but Chavez's influence has ebbed away. In terms of party affiliation, Hispanics in California and Texas have been overwhelmingly Democratic, with no more than a Republican residue of 20 percent or slightly more. But in Florida, the Cubans overwhelmingly vote Republican.

Overall, the evidence suggests that immigrants' goals, and their social values, may be less different from those of the white majority than has been assumed. And what is true of them is even truer of Asians. Immigrants choose to come to America for two reasons: in the hopes of prospering, and to enjoy the freedom and accessibility of American culture, including, but not only, material culture. Non-Hispanic immigrants appear to be even less interested than Hispanics in forming or joining radical political movements.

The longer immigrants have lived in America, the less they differ from other Americans. Within twenty years of arriving in the United States, for example, more than 60 percent of immigrants lived in their own homes, and 76 percent of those who had lived in the United States for forty years were naturalized citizens.[68] So far as Hispanics are concerned, in spite of the recent flood of immigrants, legal and illegal, the fact is that 87 percent of Hispanics under the age of eighteen were born in the United States, and the same applies to 48 percent of all those over eighteen.[69]

Hispanic voters endorse candidates who campaign for activist government, civil rights, higher (or at least not lower) taxes, health care, and improved education. But that is a general progressive agenda, shared by many millions of white Americans, and for that matter by Cubans, Republicans though they may be. Cubans may be touchy about international issues and inclined to evaluate most foreign policy and some domestic issues through the litmus test of anticommunism. But aside from them it is not clear that most Latinos in the United States really care strongly about what happens in Latin America. They have after all moved to the United States in part, at least, to get away from the frustrations and the failed political strategies of their homelands. Hispanics in the United States are bound together by language but divided by many other factors. They may be a cultural block but not a political nation. This at least would seem to be the lesson of the 2000 elections.

"These people are not automatic anything," Gloria Molina, a Democratic Los Angeles county supervisor told the *Washington Post* early in the 2000 campaign. "They are certainly not automatic Republicans and they are not automatic Democrats either." The U.S. government confirmed after the presidential election of 2000 that Hispanics favored the Democratic Party by more than two to one,[70] with 44 percent saying they were Democrats, compared to 16 percent who identified themselves as Republicans. A Republican pollster, Lance Tarrance, reported that 45 percent of a sample of Hispanics was "hard-core Democrats" and 30 percent "hard-core Republicans." In California, where Governor Pete Wilson's support for Proposition 187 has not been forgotten or forgiven by Hispanics, Hispanic support for the Republicans was weaker than in Texas, where Governor George W. Bush's "compassionate conservatism" and Spanish sound bites had done their work. But both the survey and the *Post's* reporting suggested that Hispanics do not vote in a predictable way. "The survey suggests," the *Post* reported, "that Latinos are not a voting bloc the way African Americans traditionally have been for Democrats."[71]

On balance, my observation is that, at least where most Hispanics are concerned, real, but not widespread, hostility to Hispanic immigrants is more than outweighed by an ideology that is proud of the diversity and the multicultural ambitions of American society. George W. Bush, conservative, upper-class Republican, stresses his affection for Hispanics and shows off his not-so-bad Spanish, in part because there are many Spanish-speaking voters in Texas, but surely more because he calculates that those who are hostile to Spanish-speakers and Hispanics are less numerous than those who are glad—for many reasons—that the United States has welcomed so many of them.

Immigrants will experience economic exploitation, from the native population and, perhaps just as often, from their fellow immigrants. People will sometimes be rough on them. Neighborhoods will experience the familiar stresses—overcrowding, competition for housing and jobs, reciprocal suspicion, irritation, even sporadic violence—as they have done for more than 100 years in the United States, and as they do today in Paris, or Berlin, or London, or for that matter in the great, bulging cities of South America or of the Indian subcontinent. But that does not, I believe, mean that the New Immigration dooms the new immigrants, as a group, to discrimination and oppression. On the contrary, the likelihood is that, over time, the great majority of immigrants both Hispanic and Asian will gradually become more like the American majority both in status and attitudes. They will, with one great exception, *assimilate*.

The great exception, of course, is, as it has always been, race. The larger issue of race in American society is discussed in a later chapter. But the experience of the last couple of decades suggests that Puerto Ricans, and even more so Dominicans, Haitians, and other Spanish-speaking Afro-Caribbeans will continue to be assimilated, not to the white majority, but to the African American minority. But most Mexicans are not of exclusively European descent and appearance, nor are most Guatemalans or Salvadorans or Hondurans. Does that mean that the white American majority will treat them as belonging to another race, and as such subjected to whatever residual and hopefully diminishing discrimination native African Americans experience?

I think not. Professor Desmond King has pointed out that, as recently as 1952, in the drafting of the McCarran-Walter Act, it was recognized that "the inhabitants of Canada, Mexico or any other independent country in the Western Hemisphere may enter freely as non-quota immigrants," whereas the McCarran-Walter legislation would cut down emigration from Jamaica and each other Caribbean country to 100.[72] Blacks, in other words, had always been distinguished from immigrants. Hispanics had sometimes been distinguished in this way, but not generally—unless they were black.

So, eventually, it can be expected that the great majority of the New Immigrants will "assimilate," in the sense that they will become, at least superficially, indistinguishable from other Americans. Their economic and social profile will become statistically more and more similar: the same number of homeowners, professionals and manual workers, rich and poor, as in the general population.

Does that mean, then, that the New Immigration will have failed to change American society and instead simply contribute more streams of ethnic diversity to a "melting pot" that will ultimately make an American of Korean or Chinese or Mexican descent no different from one of Irish or German or Scots descent?

To make that assumption is, surely, to misunderstand the nature both of assimilation and of ethnicity. Ethnic culture is tougher and more durable than is commonly assumed. The American Irish remain significantly distinct from Americans of Italian or English descent, and so do American Jews, although the Irish have been a major presence in America for 150 years, and Jews for more than 100.

Moreover, immigrants do not assimilate to the society that existed before they, as a group, began to immigrate. They assimilate over time to the new society that has been brought into existence by their immigration, at least if it has been on a big enough scale.

White Americans, in other words, may assume that immigrants will assimilate to them. But in reality they will assimilate to an America that will soon be different, whose majority will no longer be white, no longer of European descent, no longer defined exclusively by the folkways of Yankee Puritans or southern cavaliers.[73]

What will be different as a result of the New Immigration? In a word, everything.

Attitudes to race will inevitably change. Traditional assumptions about the superior energy or morality of the white "race" are already all but universally challenged and widely rejected. In an America where less than half the population is "white," they will become not just offensive but absurd.

The pattern of class conflict and party alignment will be changed. For over a century ethnic diversity and layering has masked class divisions and class interests. In an apparent paradox, the arrival of large numbers of new Americans with their way to make in society—conscious, indeed quite possibly hyperconscious, of social exclusion and unfairness, and therefore determined to extract from government social policies that will help them attain real equality—will increase, not diminish, the extent to which party alignment reflects the different interests of haves and have-nots.

The impact on religious belief and practice is even harder to measure. Traditionally the most significant religious division in the United States was between Protestants and Roman Catholics, and one of the most important consequences of the old immigration was that it hugely increased the numbers of Catholics, first from Ireland, then Italy, then from Poland and such parts of the Catholic Habsburg Empire as Hungary, Slovakia, and Croatia. Relatively few of the new immigrants since 1965 have been Protestant, and those who have been, are largely non-European: members of Christian minorities in Asia and the Middle East, and Protestant converts from Central America. The overwhelming majority of the Hispanics are Catholic.[74] But their influence may well be counteracted by the addition of significant, and energetic, minorities of Asians—not only the Chinese, Korean, Japanese, and Vietnamese, who follow various religions, but also Hindus and Muslims from the Indian subcontinent. Over the past quarter of a century the most significant religious divide in America, at least in its implications for public life, has been within Protestantism, between the more society-oriented churches of the old eastern and midwestern middle and upper middle class (Episcopalians, Presbyterians, Lutherans, etc.) and the traditions that have stressed individual salvation: Baptists, evangelicals, Pentecostals. A new Catholic Church, as much Mexican as Irish, while rejecting South American "liberation theology," might still align itself more with the "social gospel" instincts of the older Protestant churches.

The family structure of the new immigrants is likely to be different from that of the rest of the population in the sense that it will be stronger, both because immigrants have traditionally clung to the family as a way of protecting themselves against the unknown and unpredictable behavior of the host society, and also because—if the expression "Asian values" has any meaning at all—it is true that societies from the Indus Valley to Japan have traditionally stressed the claim the family has on the loyalty of every one of its members.

The new immigration will powerfully affect the context and the purposes of American foreign policy. For a century one of its main themes has been the conflict that was often, and wrongly, seen as dividing "isolationists" and "internationalists." Wrongly, because the so-called isolationists did not seek isolation. They wanted to turn the attention of American foreign policy away from Europe, toward Latin America and what was known as the Orient. They were perfectly happy with intervention and expansion in the Caribbean, Mexico, the Philippines, China, and Japan. More recently their conservative and Republican descendants have been enthusiastic about projecting American power and American business interests, from Chile to Vietnam and Korea by way of the Horn of Africa, Iraq, and Afghanistan. Facile talk about the "Pacific Rim" may ignore the prodigious distances involved, the economic rivalries, and the stubborn national attitudes and interests of, among many others, the Chinese and the Japanese. But the New Immigration has already enhanced American interests in Asia, as well as augmenting the number of Americans who move comfortably through the business and political worlds of "Asia/Pacific."

The United States is likely to become even less interested in and less sympathetic to Europe than it has been since the end of the Cold War. The Middle East will continue to be seen as a vital interest, because of Israel, because of oil, and now because of terrorism. It seems inevitable, though, that the United States will become progressively more involved in the difficult paths of Mexico and Central America toward democracy and economic growth, as well as in Colombia because of the drug trade.[75] And there must be a strong probability that, just as the United States has already been appealed to by rival factions in the politics of the Philippines and Korea and Indonesia, so it may become involved as mediator or arbiter in the coming conflicts over the future relations of China and Taiwan, and perhaps ultimately play a crucial role in the development of China itself. The New Immigration, in other words, will commit the United States, more than ever, to a global role, though not necessarily to one that falls within the tradition known as "internationalist."

To go further is to speculate. That would mean building bricks with far too little straw. To predict the precise shape of the changes the New Immigration will bring about may be hazardous. But not so hazardous as to ignore the overwhelming fact: that a United States where more than half the population is not of European descent will be, in very many significant ways, a different nation from the country led by Franklin Roosevelt or even by Ronald Reagan.

6

New Women

There seem to be many parallels that can be drawn between treatment of Negroes and treatment of women in our society as a whole.
— *Casey Hayden and Mary King, "A Kind of Memo"*

To THE SURPRISE OF MANY, the most lasting transformation of American
society in the 1960s and 1970s involved not race, or a new politics, but the
attitudes, expectations, and life chances of American women. That, too,
was to be partly dissipated in sectarian quarrels and to stutter into disappointment. But the breadth and depth of the revolution in the way women
thought of themselves, and demanded to be thought of by men, did constitute the most significant and lasting of the changes wrought by the troubled
years from the early 1960s to the late 1970s.

All women have been affected by this change. Overall, the achievement
has been impressive. Women's opportunities have broadened. In large areas of society they have made good their claim to be treated as equals. Tens
of millions of lives have been enriched and emancipated. But it has not
been a simple progression toward greater opportunity. Progress has been
made. But there has also been disappointment, pervasive and frustrating.
To understand why, it is first necessary to grasp that there has not been one
women's movement in the United States since the 1960s. There have been
two. One has been primarily economic in its motivation, the other psychological and cultural. The two derive from common causes to some

extent, and they have certainly interacted. But they have never been identical, and to some extent they got in each other's way.

The difference was largely one of social class. On the one hand, there were thousands of women who sought to bring about a revolution in their sex's role in the society. Although by no means all of them came from privileged families, they were mostly from comfortable ones, and they almost all received exceptional educations. On the other, there were millions of other women, some "working class," others "middle class," for whom the revolution was essentially a move from working in the home to working both there and outside it.[1] Many working-class and some middle-class women, to be sure, had always worked outside the home. To some extent the move back into the work force from the 1960s was the reversal of a comparatively short trend for women to take advantage of newfound family prosperity to stay home.

It is easy to see that two different movements were at work, changing women's expectations and experience—one overt and vocal, the other silent and largely the sum of private decisions. It is less easy to demonstrate this with statistical proof or even to be analytically clear about what was happening. We are talking, after all, about individual decisions on the part of well over 100 million women. It would have been hard for any one of them to be absolutely precise about their own motivations, for example whether a decision to continue in education or to go out to work was taken for economic or noneconomic reasons, harder still for anyone to categorize such decisions in clear terms. As an official report by the federal government early in the Clinton administration put it:

> American Women have experienced dramatic changes over the last three decades. . . . More of us are in the labor force than ever before and we are more likely to have continuous lifetime work experience. There has been a remarkable increase in the proportion of mothers who work. This is partly a result of noneconomic factors such as changes in the attitudes of society toward working mothers and the desires of women themselves as well as economic factors such as inflation, recession and unemployment of husbands.[2]

Whereas media attention was caught by the feminist movement— highly intellectual, vocal, indeed obsessed with words and feelings rather than with conditions, media-conscious, and often shaped by a dubious parallel between "women" and ethnic "minorities"—the other, and in the long run more decisive, "women's movement" in terms of changing American society, the movement into the work place, was unpretentious, demotic, economic, apolitical, and deeply pragmatic. Yet the mass movement of women into the work force did inevitably challenge preconceptions about what was normal for women, and what was fair, and over time altered perceptions of women themselves.

Between 1960 and 2000 many thousands of women sought to change their minds and their lives by joining "women's groups." During the same period, many millions of women joined another movement, by way of the classified ad pages into the world of work. The numbers are telling. Between 1950 and 1998 the proportion of women working outside the home in America rose from 33.9 to 59.8 percent.[3] Even more striking, and reflecting an even more dramatic change in one of the fundamental cultural assumptions of the society, the number of married women with young children who were at work rose from 12 percent in 1950 to 40 percent in 1990.

This was not absolutely without precedent. In the nineteenth century many women were obliged to work in factories, in sweatshops, and on farms. In 1900, 6 million women workers made up one quarter of the paid work force. "They worked as teachers, in factory jobs, in the retail trades, in agricultural work, and increasingly in offices, but by far the largest percentage worked in various kinds of public and private domestic service."[4] In the Depression, and in both world wars, the proportion of women who went out to work rose significantly. But the shift was on each occasion trivial compared with the change that has taken place over the past forty years, not as a collective response to national emergency, but spontaneously, as a result of millions of women's voluntary decisions and presumably, in most cases, also with the more or less enthusiastic, more or less grudging approval of the men in their lives.

Why has this happened? It can hardly be put down wholly to economic necessity, even though (as we have seen) during a substantial proportion of the period when this change was taking place, namely from about 1973 until the mid-1990s, the growth of incomes for all but the most prosperous individuals in American society was all but static. No doubt one reason for the increase of women in the labor market was the squeeze between rising expectations, lashed on by the seductive cunning of the advertising industry, and stagnant income. Another was the remarkable growth in the number of women going to university and to professional schools, which made it natural for them to go into employment.

To some degree, it was the result, not of national emergency, but of family emergency: of the need to increase family income to meet a tax bill, to pay college fees, or to pay off debt. In many other cases, it was the direct result of that other trend of the same years, the breakup of marriages, the increase in the divorce rate, and the sharp growth in the number of single parents, mostly mothers.

It is wise to assume, however, that the explanation of the increase in the number of women working was, as the social scientists put it, multifactorial. Women had many reasons for wanting to go out to work when their mothers would not have done so, or to return to work sooner than their mothers would have done.

Some did so because they were isolated, bored, and frustrated in the new, sprawling suburbs, deprived of the company of families, neighbors, and friends offered by the old, crowded city neighborhood. They asked, in their newfound relative prosperity, the question Betty Friedan had asked in her famous book,[5] "Is this all?" No doubt some also wanted opportunities to express themselves, now that the range of work available for women was broadening and the number of women whose education fitted them for these job opportunities had increased. No doubt too, a basic sense of fairness played a part. Increasingly women were being brought up, by their mothers but also by the prevailing atmosphere, the *Zeitgeist*, to ask: "Why can't I have anything a man can have?"

Since the 1960s two immense changes have taken place. Between them they have rendered both the American home and the American workplace almost unrecognizable. The number of American women who go out to work, the variety of work they do, and the level at which they do it have all changed dramatically, even if statistical equality is still far away, and many restrictive ceilings and reactionary attitudes survive.

The massive movement of women into the workplace has also affected the American home. Because more and more women are at work for a bigger and bigger proportion of their lives, they have sought to redefine the division of tasks and responsibilities within their relations with men. They have scarcely achieved equality. Many studies show that women who work are also expected to do more than their fair share of household work.[6] Still, there has been massive change both in patterns of behavior and in assumptions.

For better or worse, the world of children has also been transformed. Mom is much less of a presence. School, contemporaries, the commercial youth culture, and television have all taken some of what was once her sovereign place. Even more significant has been the difference in the way women see themselves, and in the expectations they have of society, of families, of men, and of themselves.

Whether you look at the juridical status of women, though, or at public attitudes to key issues like abortion, or to women's experience of the workplace, the pattern has not been one of linear improvement. Instead, a brief period of exciting, breathless change has been followed by more than two decades of confused movement, now forward, now back, and above all of frustration. If the change has been great, it has also been disappointing, both for those women who consciously sought a revolution in their sex's status, and for those who sought no wider revolution but simply wanted to be treated more fairly as individuals, at work and at home. Expectations have risen, and they have not all been fulfilled.

This has not been mainly a matter of politically driven change—far from it. But two stories from the political world illustrate this pattern of progress giving way to confusion and disappointment: the fate of the Equal Rights Amendment, and the bitter fight over a woman's right to an abortion.

———•·•———

THE FATE of the Equal Rights Amendment (ERA) brings this disappointment into sharp focus. The ERA, drafted by the radical feminist Alice Paul, was first introduced into Congress as long ago as 1923, only three years after American women finally won the right to vote.[7] The modern revival of the long tradition of American feminism in America began with a book and an organization. Betty Friedan's *The Feminine Mystique* was published in 1963. The National Organization for Women (NOW), originally a private group, was thrown open to all in 1966. In 1967, in the full tide of the new desire for revolutionary change, the amendment was taken up by NOW, and at first it looked as though it would be quickly swept into effect. It was overwhelmingly approved (by 354 votes to 24) by the House of Representatives in 1971 and by the full Senate even more decisively (84 to 8) on the following March 22. Within a year, 22 of the 38 states whose ratification would be needed had approved it.

Then things slowed down. Eight states ratified in 1973, three in 1974, one in 1975, and none in 1976. Congress imposed a seven-year deadline for ratification that would expire in 1979. In 1977 Indiana became the thirty-fifth state to ratify. So far it is the last, and it is likely to remain so.

How did such a promising beginning end in failure?

For one thing, opposition began to organize. Phyllis Schlafly, an Illinois housewife, lawyer, and Republican Party activist and the leader of an organization called Eagle Forum/STOP ERA, was the most prominent of those who set out to resist the amendment. She and others appealed with growing success to a familiar litany of the same scares that had been brandished in the campaign to block women's suffrage fifty years before. ERA, opponents warned, would deny a woman's right to be supported by her husband. Privacy rights would be abolished. Women would be sent into combat. Abortion would be freely available, and homosexual marriages would be allowed. States' rights advocates portrayed ERA as federal interference with the rights of states; and business interests, especially the powerful insurance industry, signed up to lobby against a measure that not only threatened cherished assumptions but might also cost them money. In particular, Phyllis Schlafly argued that ERA would stop insurance companies charging lower rates for women, although their actuarial record was better than that of men.

The ERA was important not as a practical measure that would change women's lives—for example, by reducing the income gap between female and male workers. It was rather the statement of a principle that might have reached beyond legal entitlements and practical considerations to change the social and economic patterns, and the psychological mind-set, that produced inequality and injustice. It followed that the ERA did not generate the kind of support from interested parties that is most likely to produce legislative change.[8] Rather it was hoped to make an unmistakable statement of national moral commitment to equality and justice.

Nonetheless, faced with the regrouping of ERA's enemies, NOW and a new umbrella group, ERAmerica, stepped up their lobbying in favor of the amendment. By 1977 more than 450 groups, said to represent 50 million Americans, were pressing for ratification. In October 1977 Representative Elizabeth Holtzman of New York introduced a bill calling for an extension of the deadline for ratification, and after massive demonstrations the Congress voted to set a new deadline of June 30, 1982. But the margins of victory were now far lower than in the original votes on ERA. Thirty-six senators and 189 congressmen opposed the extension. After furious and inconclusive litigation on related questions, ERA became an open issue in the 1980 presidential election. The Democratic Party reaffirmed its support for ERA. But while the Republican Party as such took no position on the question, the Republican candidate, Ronald Reagan, openly and actively opposed the amendment.

After further legal battles, ERA was halted, three states short of ratification, on June 30, 1982. By now it had become an overtly political party issue. An overwhelming 85 percent of congressional Democrats voted yes to ERA, and only 30 percent of Republicans did. Within a month the amendment was reintroduced but in November 1983 the House of Representatives failed to pass ERA by the required two-thirds vote. Ever since, the ERA has been reintroduced into each session of Congress. On every occasion it has been stopped in committee. As Eagle Forum spokesmen never tire of crowing, the Equal Rights Amendment is dead. What they and other opponents of the ERA do not so often address is the long-term political consequences, for the Republican Party and for conservatism, of taking positions that are seen as hostile to progress for women in the direction of greater equality and fairness.[9]

THE SAME PATTERN shows up in the field of abortion law. Rapid progress was followed by stagnation and even reaction in public opinion on an issue of vital importance to many women. The contraceptive pill first became available in 1957.[10] Historians argue whether the appearance of the first oral contraceptive, Enovid, in 1960 caused an increase in sexual activity,[11] or whether a change in sexual mores created the demand for an oral contraceptive. In any case, oral contraceptives were first used mostly by married women. But by the late 1960s young unmarried American women were apparently having sex more often, and starting to have sex younger, than before.[12] Specifically, highly educated young women from famous women's colleges and famous universities were beginning to have sex as often, and as young, as working-class women and women in the South, where teenage marriage had long been common. They were also discovering that contraception, whether by means of the pill or using other techniques, was not as reliable as they had been led to believe.

The number of women wanting abortions consequently increased sharply. But whereas in the past to have an abortion was a shameful act, never to be mentioned, now a more outspoken generation of young women talked about it openly, at first to their women friends, later to the adult world whose disapproval had once seemed so terrifying.[13] And what they said was shocking in several ways. For one thing, it emerged that abortion was far commoner than was generally realized. It was not uncommon for a group of women to start truth telling and discover that everyone present had had an abortion. Some young women had undergone the experience two or three times. And the experience was traumatic. Because abortion was everywhere illegal, pregnant women had the choice of going abroad, to Cuba or to London, or risking an illegal operation. Often such procedures were sordid, crude, and dangerous in the extreme, and with honorable exceptions the doctors who carried them out were greedy and unscrupulous.[14]

In 1967 *Life* magazine, scarcely a radical, still less a feminist publication, reported that 5,000 desperate American women died every year of abortions, self-administered or at the hands of backstreet butchers.[15] That same year, overcoming the opposition of older women who thought the issue was too politically dangerous, younger members of NOW pushed through its first pro-abortion resolution. Also in 1967, a National Association for Repeal of Abortion Laws was founded. By 1969 a group of New York radical feminists calling themselves Redstockings had forced the issue to the attention of mainstream media, including the *New York Times*. On March 21 the Redstockings staged a "speak-out" at a Greenwich Village church. One of those who stopped by to listen was the journalist Gloria Steinem, already a political activist but not yet a feminist. "No one wants to reform the abortion laws," she wrote in *New York* magazine as a result. "They want to repeal them. Completely."[16] Before long "speak-out" meetings were being held all over the United States where women told each other of their own abortion experiences and demanded reform or repeal.

Steinem had had an abortion herself, in an expensive clinic in London's Harley Street.[17] But the decisive impetus to repeal came from a woman whose experience of American life was about as far from Steinem's at Smith College and in Manhattan journalism as you could imagine. Norma McCorvey dropped out of high school in Texas in the ninth grade.[18] Physically and emotionally abused as a child, she spent some time in reform school in Gainesville and was raped as a teenager. The husband she married when she was sixteen beat her. According to her own account, she abused both drugs and alcohol and experimented with lovers of both sexes. She drifted through a number of jobs, including working as a bartender and a carnival barker. Three times pregnant, she never had an abortion: her first child was raised by her mother, her second was brought up by her father, and she gave her third child up for adoption. In 1970, under the pseudonym "Jane Roe," she was the lead plaintiff in a class-action suit that challenged the strict Texas law, which prohibited abortion except on medical advice where the mother's life was in danger, and was to provoke a political and ethical storm that has not yet subsided.[19]

This unlikely progress, and even more unlikely developments that lay ahead for McCorvey, came about because the women's movement in general, and "speak-outs" about abortion in particular, had reached the University of Texas at Austin.[20] Women activists there held weekly meetings to discuss "Women and Their Bodies" and opened a "Women's Liberation Birth Control Center" in a building shared by the local underground paper, the *Rag*. It was this group that came up with the idea of challenging the conservative Texas state law on abortion. Two newly qualified UT law graduates, Sarah Weddington and Linda Coffee, understood that they would have no standing. What they needed was a pregnant woman who could not obtain a remedy in Texas. Most pregnant students wanted an abortion, not a lawsuit. That was why Weddington and Coffee found themselves representing, as "Jane Doe," the hapless McCorvey.

The case reached the U.S. Supreme Court on appeal from the U.S. district court in Texas as *Roe v. Wade*. (Henry Wade was the attorney general of Texas.) It was first argued on December 13, 1971. The justices were not happy with the initial argument, and the case was reargued just under a year later. On January 22, 1973, Justice Harry Blackmun delivered the Court's opinion.[21] To considerable surprise in many quarters, not least among his former conservative associates, Blackmun found that the Fourteenth Amendment to the United States Constitution gave women a fundamental right to obtain abortions. He based this right on a "right to privacy," originally asserted in a number of cases brought against state laws banning contraception, starting with *Griswold v. Connecticut* in 1965. (*Griswold* overthrew a state law that prohibited even married couples from using contraception.) Speaking through Blackmun, the Court held that this right to privacy gave women a right to abort unless the state had a "compelling interest" in preventing the abortion. The Court further found that, although states did have a legitimate interest in protecting the life of the fetus, this interest did not become "compelling" until the fetus became "viable" (that is, able to survive birth), in the third trimester of pregnancy. That meant that, where before the legality of abortion was a matter for state law, after *Roe v. Wade* it was an issue of federal constitutional law, so that a woman's right to have an abortion became a fundamental constitutional right.

The Court's decision in *Roe v. Wade* was hailed by the women's movement with euphoria. It fostered the delusion, wrote Susan Brownmiller in her history of the movement, "that the women's revolution was an unstoppable success. A new day had dawned; anything was possible."[22] But, she added, "those at the heart of the fight knew that our enemies were marshalling their forces for a sustained counterattack." It was true.

It was in 1979 that Beverly LaHaye, wife of a minister, Tim LaHaye,[23] in San Diego, was watching Betty Friedan interviewed on television by Barbara Walters. When Friedan said she represented many women in America, Mrs. LaHaye jumped up from her chair in indignation, saying, "She doesn't represent me, and I bet she doesn't speak for the majority of women in America."[24] She went on to found Concerned Women for America, which now claims to be the nation's largest public policy women's organization. The organization has a membership of 600,000 and a budget of $10 million a year. CWA has developed skilled lobbying techniques both with state legislatures and with Congress. It takes up a whole range of issues related to the family, including strong opposition to abortion, homosexuality, and divorce.

(Mrs. LaHaye's husband, Dr. Tim LaHaye, was one of the founders of the Moral Majority.) On any of these issues hundreds of "kitchen table activists," organized into "prayer chains," were capable of subjecting back-sliding congressmen to a withering fire of messages that made them fear for their reelection. LaHaye once summarized her agenda when she told a CWA audience, "Ladies and Gentlemen, there is a concerted effort in our country to steal marriage and the family from our culture."

The success of CWA has led to a large number of imitators, including Focus on the Family and the Family Research Center, headed by Kenneth L. Connor, who campaigns against "safe sex."[25] He likes to cite a 1996 poll conducted by the University of Chicago showing that those who report the highest levels of sexual satisfaction were those who preserved sexual relations until marriage.

Such campaigns succeeded in injecting the so-called social issues into mainstream politics. Legislators like Senator Jesse Helms (R.-N.C.) picked these issues up, and television pundit and former Nixon aide Pat Buchanan made them principal themes of his presidential campaigns in 1996 and 2000. Unlike conservative women campaigners such as Schlafly and LaHaye, Buchanan sometimes seemed openly hostile to women and to be bidding for the votes of conservative males. "Rail as they will about 'discrimination,'" he wrote in a 1983 column, "Women are simply not endowed by nature with the same measures of single-minded ambition and the will to succeed in the fiercely competitive world of Western capitalism." The real liberators of American women, he wrote in his autobiography, were "not the feminist noise-makers, they were the automobile, the supermarket, the shopping center, the dishwasher, the washer-dryer, the freezer."[26]

By the mid-1980s, a substantial, well-organized political movement was actively attempting to turn back the tide of feminism and present an alternative, conservative vision of the role of women in society.

———◆———

THIS IS ONLY ONE of a number of indications that the progress of the movement for women's equality has been halted. A third of a century on from the early victories, this is a battle only half won. American women have made important and historic gains in status, dignity, and opportunity and in the direction of equality. But they have not achieved what their leaders hoped for thirty years ago. A single pair of statistics measures the progress, and the disappointment.

As early as 1963, the Equal Pay Act provided that employers must provide equal pay for women and men who perform "substantially equal work in the same establishment."[27] This was reinforced by a Supreme Court ruling in 1981[28] and by new definitions of what constituted equal pay laid down by the Equal Employment Opportunity Commission.[29] So do women receive equal pay? In 1966, full-time women workers earned on average 60 percent of men's wages, 3.6 percent *down* in a decade.[30] By 1979 women earned 59.7 percent of what men earned.[31] By 1999 women earned 76.5 percent of what men earned.[32] So women had made a solid gain of around 15 percentage points. But for every three dollars earned by women, men still made four.

Like the women's movement as a whole, the economic experience of women in America over the past three decades divides on class lines. Professional women, including women in academia, in officer grades in the armed services, and in the executive strata of business, have made steady progress, even if it has been disappointing and full equality has still not been achieved. But women without a college education and a professional qualification, who have entered traditional working-class occupations, have had an even more difficult time. In addition to finding themselves excluded from promotion ladders, they have faced harassment, some of it disturbingly unpleasant and even violent.

—•—

IN 1998 the psychologist Virginia Valian published a study of the disappointing progress of women in work. She focused particularly on professional and college-educated women, and brought together the results of a large number of surveys.

In business, for example, she reported that "in 1978 there were two women heading *Fortune* 500 companies; in 1994 there were also two; in August of 1996, there were four."

In 1985 2 percent of top executives were women; IBM, where 7 percent of the executives were women, was exceptional. In 1990 women were less than one-half of 1 percent of the most highly paid officers and directors of 799 major companies. In 1992 3 percent of senior executives were women.

On Wall Street in 1996 8 percent of managing directors of major investment banking and brokerage houses were women. Perhaps most telling, a 1996 review of the 1,000 largest firms in the United States shows that only 1 percent of the top five jobs in these corporations (60 out of 5,000) were filled by women.[33]

Professor Valian found that women were less likely to find themselves in top executive jobs. When they did get there, they were likely to be paid less than men. A 1991 study of 502 men and women with master of business administration degrees from one of the top ten business schools in the United States found that the women earned less than the men. A 1992 study showed that this inequality was general. "Even when education, training, experience, hours worked, occupational specialization, supervisory status and job preferences are accounted for, a substantial unexplained discrepancy in the salaries of men and women remains."[34] A broader study, of 1,500 male and female managers in 1992, concluded that "even when education, training, experience, hours worked, occupational specialization, supervisory status and job preferences are accounted for, a substantial unexplained discrepancy in the salaries of men and women remains."[35]

In the 1970s and 1980s, attracted by the financial rewards and protestations of equal opportunity, as well perhaps as by the hope of changing society, women poured into the legal profession. In 1970 3 percent of all lawyers were women. By 1980 they were 8 percent, and in 1995 23 percent.[36] By 1987 women were 36 percent of new admissions to the bar. Yet in 1991 67 percent of all law firms were all male. In 1980 women were 15 percent of associates but only 2 percent of partners.[37] In 1988 women were 30 percent of associates but only 7 percent of partners. In the big Manhattan law firms, women were 12 percent of partners in 1994, as against 35 percent of the lower grade of associates. In the top 250 firms in the country as a whole, women were 3.5 percent of partners in 1981 and 11 percent in 1992.[38]

The experience of women in medicine has been similar to that of women lawyers. Their numbers have increased; in fact they have doubled in roughly twenty years. Their remuneration is catching up with that of men but has not yet done so. In 1970 there were 334,000 physicians in the United States of whom 25,000, or 7.6 percent, were women. By 1980, that had doubled to 54,000 women doctors, or 11.6 percent of the profession.

By 1998 the number of women doctors had increased to 177,000 (out of 777,000 altogether), so that women doctors were 22.8 percent of the total.[39]

Their professional status, however, remains relatively underprivileged. In 1990 women doctors earned 70 percent as much as men. That was partly explained by the fact that women, no doubt especially those with children, worked shorter hours than men. Adjusted for this difference, their earnings were 87 percent of men's. Women were also concentrated in the lower paying specialities such as general practice, pediatrics, and gynecology.

Both in the law and in medicine, as is the case for MBAs, men and women start on a basis of equality or near equality, but whether in terms of salary or of professional advancement (partnership in law firms, specialities in medicine), inequality soon appears and becomes greater as the lawyer or doctor advances through professional life.

Something similar happens in the academic profession. In 1995 the salaries of full-time male and female academics in the humanities were equal in the first five years. But overall, women in the humanities earned 84 percent of men's salaries ($40,500 compared with $48,000). It was the same in science and engineering. Men and women start out equal, but men soon shoot ahead. "Overall women scientists in universities and four-year colleges earned about 90 percent of men's salaries. Women are less likely to be promoted and less likely to be given tenure. Few, if any, medical schools have women deans. In the law, there was a similar lag until the Clinton administration, led by a lawyer president whose wife was also a brilliant and ambitious lawyer, made a conscious and successful effort to increase the number of women judges.

Between 1980 and 1991 the proportion of federal judges who were women went from 4 percent to 9 percent. It improved dramatically under Carter, and remained roughly constant under Reagan. By 1995, after only three years of Clinton, it had doubled to 18 percent. The situation in state and local judiciaries, however, was much less favorable. The judicial bench illustrates an important fact. The federal government can, if it so wishes, act effectively to improve the opportunities for women.

Another example involves not the president but the Congress. Female participation in high school and college sports exploded in the 1970s but has hardly increased since. The reason is that in 1972 the Congress enacted Title IX of the Educational Amendments Act (which modified the Civil Rights Act of 1964). Compliance was not required until 1978. Title IX banned discrimination in any education program receiving federal aid. As a result, the proportion of girls taking part in high school sports went up from 7 percent in 1971 to 32 percent in 1977–78, but by the beginning of the 1990s that had increased only to 36 percent. There was an ironic twist, too. As a result of Title IX, the number of jobs for coaches and sports administrators increased by almost 50 percent, from 4,208 in 1978 to 5,952 in 1992. This was the result of a measure seeking to increase opportunities for women. But 75 percent of the new jobs went to men![40]

Slowly, painfully, highly educated upper-middle-class women in the United States are inching toward at least a statistical equality in the professions. After all, the professions regulate their own entry. They are led by professional associations that are vulnerable to political and public relations pressures. They have an obvious vested interested in at least seeming to be fair. And many of their members *are* fair; they really do want women to have a fair chance of success. Even so, over the generation from the middle 1970s the number of professionals rose from negligible numbers only to levels that still left women in substantial minorities. By the end of the century, after this much vaunted revolution, even though more than half of medical students were female, women were still only roughly one out of every four doctors. They were one out of every six lawyers, and one out of every ten engineers. One informed view is that it will take another generation for the professions to absorb these bigger cohorts of women.[41]

If one focuses on the highest levels within the professions and in business, the disparity is even more glaring. Although 40 percent of all executive, management, and administrative positions (up from 24 percent in 1976) are held by women, they are mainly stuck in the middle and lower ranks. Top management is overwhelmingly male. A 1990 study of the *Fortune* 500 companies by Mary Ann Von Glinow, of the University of Southern California, showed that women were only 2.6 percent of corporate officers in those companies at the vice president level and above.[42] Those numbers are more than ten years old. But they are not changing fast. Indeed, according to research at the University of Michigan, at the present rate women will not reach equality in the executive suite until the year 2466.[43]

———•◆•———

THERE ARE MANY REASONS for the disappointments experienced by the women's movement over the past thirty years or so. Lower pay for women, for example, is partially explained by a number of factors other than deliberate discrimination. Fewer women than men still earn professional qualifications. Many women choose to interrupt their working life for a longer or shorter period of years in order to look after children. And stereotypes linger. Virginia Valian has argued that the prospects of women are negatively influenced by what she calls "gender schemas." This amounts to saying that women still don't "feel" right to many men for some jobs. Many men are still not quite happy with the idea of women admirals, women brain surgeons, and so on. But there is a certain amount of evidence that we are not just looking at delay, at the survival of obsolescent prejudices. In some ways, things are not just getting better too slowly. They may have been getting worse. Specifically, the progress of women may have been set back by a reaction against the style of the new wave of feminists in the 1960s and 1970s.

As we have seen, political sentiment has shifted in a conservative direction in the United States in many ways. One of them has been a turning against the idea that the government should actively promote equality between different groups in society. Specifically, one strand of the conservative revival since the late 1970s has been a nostalgia for "traditional family values." That has been interpreted in some quarters in ways that seek to reimpose a hierarchical relation between the patriarchal male and the subordinate woman.

All these factors, no doubt, have contributed to the disappointments felt by those who hoped that women would progress more rapidly toward equality. But this disappointment cannot be fully understood except in terms of a strategic decision on the part of the leaders of the women's movement themselves. Their mistake—at least from the point of view of collective political success—was to turn away from pragmatic politics of political power in search of an elusive goal of psychological revolution.

Betty Friedan, the women's movement's first guru, later widely rejected as a reactionary, but a woman whose background lay firmly in the gritty economic wrestling of union politics, understood the danger early. "I didn't think a thousand vibrators would make much difference—or that it mattered who was in the missionary position," she wrote bluntly, "—if unequal power positions in real life weren't changed. . . . it was the economic imbalance, the power imbalance in the real world that subverted sex, or made sex into a power game where no one could win."[44]

——•◆•——

THE PROBABILITY is that far more women went out to work for economic reasons than in the search for self-expression or personal development, though the sales of books marketing methods of self-improvement suggest that such motives should not be underestimated. In the period of stagnant incomes and rising expectations that began in the early 1970s, one income was not enough for many families to live as they wanted to live. Two incomes would be needed, so wives found a job and went out to work. This was the majority women's movement, and it changed the lives of everyone in the United States: not only women but also men and children.

The minority women's movement, strongly implanted in the great graduate schools, in the professions, and in the media, drew its leaders largely, though of course not exclusively, from middle-class and even upper-middle-class women, who were less likely to be impelled to work for economic reasons. The point has been well made that many of the first generation of young feminists grew up in working-class homes but were the first women in their families to attend college.[45] Indeed, "a disproportionate number of leaders and activists came from secular, working-class Jewish activist families."[46] Nevertheless, the first generation of feminism was closely identified with a dozen or so of the great graduate schools, especially those of the Northeast, California, and the Middle West. These were the same schools— Harvard and Columbia, UCLA and Berkeley, Michigan and Wisconsin— that had supplied so many of the white sympathizers of the civil rights movement and the shock troops of the rebellion against the Vietnam War. For the most part highly educated, often in the humanities and the social sciences, these young feminist women were understandably more urgently concerned with personal development, with language and equality of esteem, rather than with wages, child care, or equality of opportunity.

Women of many generations and conditions responded to the American women's movement of the 1960s. Yet it cannot be fully understood unless it is first grasped that it began as part of the New Left. Many of its leaders were the children of families with a radical tradition. Most, indeed almost all, of its leaders had been radicalized in their turn, first by opposition to the Vietnam War or, even more often, by commitment to the civil rights movement and, more broadly, to racial justice and equality. Many were impelled in the direction of feminism by the discovery that, even within the supposedly fraternal ranks of the New Left, they were expected to take second place to their male fellow activists and were expected to type for them, make coffee for them, and indeed to sleep with them.[47]

An even smaller group of women who were to be exceptionally influential consisted of those who were similarly radicalized by their experiences within the ostensibly liberal news media. Bright young women emerged from excellent educations to discover that, at *Time* or *Newsweek,* they would find it hard to become writers but would be expected to serve patiently as researchers for middle-aged journalists who, embarrassingly often, expected them to be their sexual, as well as their professional, handmaidens.[48] These were women of impressive ability. At one time or another they included Susan Brownmiller, Gloria Steinem, Nora Ephron, Ellen Goodman, and many others of equal talent. Most of them had solid and even brilliant academic careers behind them. They were frustrated by being obliged to languish as "editorial assistants" while young men soared past them on the fast elevator to the twelfth floor, and they were furious at being referred to collectively as "dollies." On March 16, 1970, forty-six women at *Newsweek* filed a sex discrimination suit against their employer with the Equal Employment Opportunities Commission. Two days later, their colleagues at *Ladies Home Journal* staged a sit-in. And within two months the women at Time Inc. had also filed suit. Rebellion had broken out at the very heart of imperial New York; it was as if the standard of rebellion had been raised in the corridors of the emperor's seraglio.

Nothing illustrates more absurdly the haphazard nature of the situation in which women found themselves in the 1960s than the circumstances, replete with irony, that made it even possible for the women from

Newsweek and *Time* to sue their employers. The federal law that made sex discrimination illegal was not the result of mature legislative deliberation, still less of feminist insurrection. It was rammed through the Congress by, of all people, that legendary dinosaur, Judge Howard Smith of Virginia, chairman of the House Rules Committee and arch-defender of even the least defensible aspects of the Southern Way of Life. When, after the Kennedy assassination, and at the prompting of President Lyndon Johnson, the Congress was debating serious civil rights legislation, Smith foxily moved an amendment adding the word "sex" to Title VII, the clause that banned discrimination by private employers by reason of race, color, religion or national origin. Smith's motive, needless to say, was not a burning commitment to women's equality. He wanted to recruit northern congressmen who did not approve of equality for women to his southern colleagues who wanted to maintain inequality for blacks. The proposal to ban discrimination by reason of sex would give northerners an excuse to vote against the act without facing the accusation of racism.[49] Smith's ploy backfired. Representative Martha Griffiths, probably the strongest feminist in Congress at that time, succeeded in putting together an opposite coalition to the one Smith was trying to create, between southern congressmen unwilling to offend their women supporters and northern liberals. So Title VII came to ban sex discrimination as well as the racial kind.

The connection between the civil rights movement and the new wave of feminism perhaps explains the prevalence in the women's movement of the emotionally pleasing but treacherous comparison of American women with the African American minority. As Casey Hayden and Mary King put it in the sentence quoted from their influential "Kind of Memo," "There seem to be many parallels that can be drawn between treatment of Negroes and treatment of women in our society as a whole."

The position of white women might be disadvantaged, even oppressed. But they were not a minority, and they included every sociological and political characteristic found among white men. Even so, the parallel went deep for many white feminists. "I cannot imagine a gender system," says one eminent historian, "that is not already racialized nor one that is not rooted in class."[50]

The first white women to become involved in the civil rights struggle were southerners, most of whom came to the movement through the churches.[51] As early as 1960, according to their leading historian, they understood that "the achievement of racial equality required fundamental changes in sex roles."[52] The work of educating southern blacks and helping them to register to vote challenged powerful entrenched interests. The danger was real. By the end of the 1964 Freedom Summer, there had been fifteen murders. Thirty-seven churches (centers of education and voter registration as well as of worship) had been bombed or burned, and there had been more than 1,000 arrests of civil rights workers.[53] But it was not only political and legal barriers that were being tested. Interracial sex, especially where it involved a black man and a white woman, was the deepest and most dangerous of all the taboos of southern society. So, in an atmosphere of excitement and fear, idealistic young white women found themselves thrown together with angry, often impressive young black men. Shared emotion often ended up, as it will do, in bed. The number of interracial relationships was no doubt exaggerated. It was, in any case, enough to anger many black women, as well as many conservative white men.

For the white female volunteers the more immediate discovery was that the young men, so idealistic in their commitment to achieving equality for black people, seemed indifferent to equality for women, of either color. The women, one sympathetic male observer wrote, "made peanut butter, waited on tables, cleaned up, got laid."[54] "In the early 1960s," says Sara Evans, "no radical group saw the oppression of women as a more than peripheral issue."[55]

At a volunteers' meeting at Waveland, Mississippi, two white southern women, Mary King and Casey Hayden, put forward a paper on the subject. A later expanded version, which they called "A Kind of Memo,"[56] raised such questions as "Who sweeps the office floor?" and "Who takes the minutes?" before ending pessimistically: "Objectively the chances seem nil that we could start a movement based on anything as distant to general American thought as a sex-caste system." Gradually, more and more women plucked up the courage to challenge male sexism. At a Students for a Democratic Society (SDS) meeting in Champaign-Urbana, Illinois, in December 1965, women made what has been called the historic decision to exclude men from their discussions.[57] But these were mostly women already committed to radical politics. The sexism they first denounced was not that of the establishment but that of what was considered a radical group, SDS. A decisive moment for many of the tiny group of feminist activists was the way they were shouldered aside when they tried to raise feminist issues at the National Conference for New Politics in Chicago in late 1967.[58] The renewed American feminism of the late 1960s and the early 1970s was influenced and enriched from many sources. But it began as a movement that developed inside the tiny world of the American left, and it never wholly escaped from the high-minded but narrow assumptions of that esoteric and in many respects very marginal milieu.

The American left has been notorious for its inability to follow the revolutionary maxim that in unity there is strength. (For decades the New York socialists had been split into half a dozen factions—Johnsonites, Schachtmanites, Lovestonites, and the rest.)[59] The early feminists found it just as hard as their male predecessors to stick together. Almost from the start, there were bitter divisions between those who wanted political power and those who sought personal liberation, between heterosexual and homosexual women, white women and black women, respectables and bohemians.

The two divisions, in particular, between those who, whether "straight" or lesbian, thought men were the primary cause of resistance to the liberation of women and those who saw men as allies, and between white and black women, would not go away, but would haunt the feminist movement until the end of the century and beyond. Still, for a time they were pushed into the background by a series of flashy successes, well publicized by the media.

The first was the protest against the Miss America ceremony at Atlantic City. The idea came from Carol Hanisch, a farmer's daughter from Iowa who had quit journalism to work as a civil rights activist in Mississippi. The radical women had borrowed the old left-wing technique of consciousness-raising. Women, like the workers of the early twentieth century, needed to be recruited by dramatic action. Hanisch suggested targeting the Miss America pageant, which she saw as "a very oppressive thing." One of those who got the idea was the poet Robin Morgan. "Miss America was perfect for us lefty Women's Liberationists," Morgan said later. "Made to order. She touched capitalism, militarism, racism, and sexism, all in one fell swoop. Capitalism, because they used her to sell the sponsors' products, militarism because she went off to entertain the troops, racism because there had never been a black Miss America at that point, and clearly she was objectified as a woman."[60]

The story was picked up by a young woman reporter at the *New York Post*, which thought the protest might be good for a laugh. Its effect was instant. Oddly enough, the action for which the Miss America protest has passed into legend, the burning of bras, never happened. Not a single bra was burned. What the women did do was to pitch bras, falsies, and other symbols of sexual stereotyping into a trash can.[61]

The Miss America protest had instant resonance, both for jeering, uncomprehending men, and for women. Over the winter of 1968–69, as Richard Nixon settled into the White House and the news from Washington to Vietnam was worse and worse, New York radical women went through a brief mayfly summer of unity and success. They were misunderstood and derided, but for the moment they were also powerful, they had the political and cultural wind in their sails, and in New York they were something that city sometimes values even more highly than intellectual power or political muscle. They were, in a funky but unmistakable way, high fashion. The New York media took up the radical women's cause, only—as we shall see—to kick it downhill once the novelty was over.

At the end of the 1960s and the beginning of the 1970s—rather surprisingly for those who saw them as irremediable pillars of capitalism and phallocracy—the big New York newspapers and magazines suddenly discovered feminism. Not only that: rather than allowing the new ideas to be reported by their own, possibly jaundiced female reporters, they allowed the excited young radical women to describe their own feelings of revolutionary enthusiasm.[62] For a few short years the ideas, and the emotions, of the "women's movement" caught on.

August 26, 1970, was the fiftieth anniversary of the Nineteenth Amendment. To celebrate it, Betty Friedan, already rocking from the assaults of younger women who had raced past her into more radical positions, organized a day of demonstrations billed as Women's Strike for Equality. It was successful far beyond Friedan's hopes. Fifty thousand women strode down Fifth Avenue. The papers were sympathetic. That season three powerful feminist texts were published. One was Shulamith Firestone's *The Dialectic of Sex*, which asserted that men were incapable of love, and women needed to be freed from the trauma of childbirth. Then there was

Robin Morgan's anthology, *Sisterhood Is Powerful*. But the first to appear, and the most spectacularly successful, was Kate Millett's *Sexual Politics*. To her amazement this essay in feminist literary criticism turned her into an icon, her import solemnly analyzed in the *New York Times* and her face staring forth from the cover of *Time* magazine.

Poor Kate Millett's story was a cautionary tale. Pressed both by lesbians and by rivals affronted by her media lionizing, she admitted she was bisexual. Challenged at a public meeting to admit that "bisexuality is a copout," she made the admission that she was a lesbian. The storm of intrusive, intense publicity drove her into depression. But her experience was anything but her own personal misery. From that moment on, the intellectual women's movement was to be chopped into smaller and smaller pieces, into an infinite regress of ever smaller groups, each defined by ever more unconventional tastes, concerns, or commitments.

The feminist intellectuals uncovered one serious issue after another, as well as some that were less serious. They turned inside out accepted views about such varied aspects of American life as education, the fashion industry, makeup, abortion, rape—including "date rape"—prostitution, sexual harassment, sexual abuse, and pornography. They had a genius for shock tactics, a sometimes inspired gift for propaganda. With dogged courage they challenged the most potent taboos of American sexual Puritanism. They talked about orgasm, masturbation, sadomasochism in language that was increasingly angry, sometimes almost unbearably shrill, but always hard to ignore. And with every taboo flouted, every boundary crossed, they isolated themselves more totally, marked themselves off as more irredeemably crazy and irrelevant to the great army of their sisters.

These were the women the feminists had seen themselves as leading, the silent majority who wanted not to flout the conventions or shock the square but to attain such unoriginal and, to many inhabitants of Greenwich Village, such boring treasures as a job, better pay, better chances of promotion, affordable child care, opportunity, and fairness within the framework of traditional, or at least only gradually changing, attitudes to men and to families.

Even by the standards of revolutionary movements, the radical women were spectacularly bad at organizing. Individually, and in small groups, they were brilliant at attracting attention, at propagating new and shocking thought. But of marshaling battalions of like-minded women to storm entrenched opposition they had no idea. Solidarity was always in danger of being interpreted as betrayal. Success was too often sacrificed to the pleasure of hearing one's own, endlessly alternative voice.

There were successes. It was not nothing to persuade a society that is conservative about such matters to stop calling married women Mrs. and to call them and their unmarried sisters alike "Ms." It was liberating, if at times confusing, that women, like men, were now referred to in newspapers by their surnames, and that many married women felt free to use their birth names rather their husbands'.

In the media, in the universities, and to a lesser extent in other professions, the numbers of women and their chances of promotion both rose, though significant progress in opening up politics to women was frustratingly slow, slower indeed than in most other developed democracies. By the end of the century, for example, women had held the highest elective offices in half a dozen countries,[63] yet a woman president of the United States seemed further away than ever.

It is easy to criticize—tempting, sometimes, to jeer at—the first, feminist women's movement. Still, the self-conscious, activist women did provide leadership, ideas and goals for the great majority of women who simply wanted an education, a job, parity of esteem and personal freedom. To put it simply, this was a class division. An essentially upper-middle-class movement to raise women's consciousness in terms of the symbols and language of equality had little understanding of the needs or the assumptions of working-class women who were simply struggling for a better life.

While a small number of well-educated women did succeed in business, the professions and especially academia, 99 percent of secretaries are women, as are 93 percent of bookkeepers, 93 percent of nurses, and 82 percent of administrative and clerical support workers. Women are also the majority of textile workers (91 percent).

Two specific examples illustrate the different agendas, constituencies, and styles of these two women's movements: the attempt on the part of some women to become firefighters and the petering out of the long effort to use unions to improve the conditions of the nation's waitresses, and its replacement by a culture of litigation to break barriers for a minority of ambitious women at the carriage trade end of the restaurant business.

The New York City Fire Department earned a glorious reputation by its gallant response to the destruction of the World Trade Center in September 11, 2001. Its response to the demand from women to join its ranks was less glorious. For a hundred years it had been a male monopoly, indeed the very byword for a proud, macho corps. In 1977, for the first time, New York City allowed women to take the firefighter exam.[64] When 400 women passed the physical part of the test, the city hastily tightened up the requirements for physical agility in the hopes of keeping at least some of the women out.

The United Women Firefighters, led by Brenda Berkman, promptly brought a class action suit for sex discrimination, and five years later 42 women passed new, court-supervised tests and became the first female firefighters in New York's history. (This certainly was feminism in action, even if it was more practical and less theoretical than the feminism of graduate women.) Even then white male firefighters went to extraordinary lengths to prevent Berkman and her colleagues from being allowed to do the dangerous work they sought.

The women encountered what their historian calls "an elemental anger that they would even try."[65] Tactics used by firemen included sending the women hate mail, telephoning death threats, sexual harassment, refusing to speak to them for months on end, and scribbling obscene graffiti against women in firehouses. Some male firefighters also slashed women's tires, urinated in their boots, and tried to lock a woman in a kitchen they had filled with tear gas. One woman was raped, and a number of others assaulted. Another female recruit was put in danger of death when her colleagues abandoned her to put out a dangerous fire on her own in a burning building.

Interestingly, the only support the women received from within the firefighting profession was from the Vulcan Society, the labor organization of the black firefighters, who had themselves experienced discrimination and had to go through a comparable ordeal before being allowed to work as firemen. Yet in the end, after their victory, women still numbered only 0.3 percent of the city's 13,000 uniformed firefighters.

Efforts to organize waitresses into a union date back to the very beginning of the twentieth century.[66] The first waitresses' local was formed in Seattle in 1900, but it was not until the general surge of unionism in the Depression years that any appreciable proportion of American waitresses joined a union.

The Hotel Employees and Restaurant Employees union (HERE) was quick to take advantage of New Deal legislation to make union recruiting easier. By 1940 400,000 waiters and waitresses, a quarter of the industry's entire work force, had joined HERE.

Although HERE was closer in spirit to a CIO industrial union than to the AFL craft tradition, and in centers like Detroit cooperated with big industrial unions like the United Auto Workers, industrial progress for food servers was slow. Not until the very peak of union power in the 1960s did waitresses achieve the forty-hour week. The union was more concerned with traditional issues like the share of work between waiters and busboys (often African American) and a continuing preoccupation with whether the union should include cocktail waitresses and others suspected of permitting a little genteel prostitution.

Suddenly, under the influence of a new generation of college-educated waitresses, the agenda shifted. "In the 1970s," writes Dorothy Sue Cobble, "waitress unionism unraveled further as the younger waitress activists challenged the gender separatism of the older generation. Younger waitresses embraced alternative routes to achieving gender equality. Rather than expand the number of jobs defined as 'female.' They sought equal treatment under the law for men and women."[67]

In spite of two generations of union activism, the discriminatory hiring practices of hotel and restaurant employees continued. Only after the EEOC began to take seriously the enforcement of the sex equality provision of the 1964 Civil Rights Act did things change. The younger generation wanted its share of the higher-paid, more interesting kinds of work, such as formal dining and banquets. They felt more at home with legal challenges than with union solidarity, and they identified the union with precisely the old discriminatory practices they wanted to end. Significantly, even when waitresses did organize, they wanted nothing to do with the long-established unions such as HERE. Equally revealing, two of the first of these new organizing efforts were on the campuses of major graduate schools, one in Harvard Square, and the other in Madison, home of the University of Wisconsin.

So waitresses of the new, middle-class feminist stamp, frustrated by the unions' poor response to their concerns, turned to litigation. In 1976 a twenty-nine-year-old waitress called Jeanne King opened formal dinner service to women at the Four Seasons, 21, and other elite New York restaurants, not through union action but by an American Civil Liberties Union–supported suit that not only bypassed HERE's Local Number 1 but also actually included it as a defendant in the suit.[68]

This was just one example of a shift affecting many kinds of workers, male as well as female, who were turning to the law and claiming protection of their rights, as an alternative to the older tradition of collective union action to protect workers from exploitation. On the face of it, it might not seem to matter whether workers' rights are guaranteed by a union official or by a lawyer, and there are many who would prefer the lawyer, if only out of prejudice against unions. But, as the labor historian Nelson Lichtenstein has argued, there are problems with the rights-based approach to remedying unfair or unsatisfactory working conditions, for women or for other workers.[69] It is not easy or even possible to enforce the rights of millions of workers by litigation. Second, the litigation route depends heavily on bureaucratic expertise. The Equal Employment Opportunity Commission lost an important suit against Sears Roebuck because its case was theoretical, whereas the company produced live women who testified that they did not want high-paying jobs in commission sales. Moreover, litigation has not proved able to tackle the structural crisis in many industries. In the 1970s women workers won their case against AT&T, only to lose the jobs they had won in the downsizing of the 1980s.

Obviously a number of social shifts and trends were involved in this new division between the plodding union work of traditional working-class women and the new, rights-based values of younger, college graduates. Rising divorce rates were only one index of women's weaker attachment to traditional family structures. Women were reassessing the whole sense of their relation to society, and not only in its economic dimension. Presumably, too, the general decline of trust in trade unionism and the trend toward a more litigious society entered into this. But in the replacement of solid, motherly working-class waitress leaders like Bee Tumber from Southern California or Kitty Donnelly from Cleveland, who had hoisted many a heavy tray in their day, by young graduate litigants looking to improve their individual position at the expense of collective advance does portray a suggestive picture of the divergent course of the two women's

movements, the intellectual and the proletarian. It also fits the general pattern of what was becoming in many ways a class society.

———•◦•———

BETWEEN 1950 AND 1990, as we have seen, a solid additional quarter of all
American women moved into the labor market, and the proportion of
married women who worked more than tripled from 12 to 40 percent. Add
in the unmarried mothers, and the magnitude of the change becomes
even more startling. At the same time the consciousness-raising activities
of the intellectual feminists did change the image, and the self-image, of
women in America in a drastic and surely irreversible fashion.

Yet a gap remains between the theory and the practice. Women have
moved into the world of work, and the law has sought to protect them and
to assure them, if not of equality of condition, at least of freedom from discrimination. In 1981, for example, the Supreme Court ruled that claims of
sex-based wage discrimination under Title VII were not limited to claims
of equal pay for equal work.[70]

Still, attitudes are changing, and in general in the direction of a greater
recognition, by legislators and judges, of the persistence and subtlety of the
obstacles women face in the world of work. In 1986, as we have seen, the
circuit court rejected the claims of women employed by Sears Roebuck
that they had been discriminated against. In 1988 that judgment was reversed on appeal. In a partial dissent Judge Cudahy commented severely
on the lower court's findings. He said,

> These conclusions, it seems to me, are of a piece with the proposition that
> women are by nature happier cooking, doing the laundry and chauffeuring
> the children to softball games than arguing appeals or selling stocks. The ste-
> reotype of women as less greedy and daring than men is one that the sex
> discrimination laws were intended to address. . . . There are abundant indica-
> tions that women lack neither the desire to compete strenuously for financial
> gain nor the capacity to take risks.[71]

In spite of all efforts to achieve equality in the workplace, the plain
truth is that American women are very far from having achieved it. Almost 80 percent of working women are still in traditional "female" jobs, as
secretaries, administrative workers, and sales clerks. In the executive

boardroom, women are virtually invisible: less than one-half of 1 percent of top corporate managers are women. These are cold statistical demonstrations that the battle remains much less than half-won.

The same point can be made in the sphere of emotions. At a time when many men complain about women's "equality" in the workplace and in the home, what women see is inequality: inequality of opportunity, inequality of income, inequality of esteem.

The reason for this disappointment is that, right at the beginning of the quarter of a century under review, the progress sought by the women's movement was challenged and to some extent rolled back by a backlash. This coincided chronologically with the general political conservatism of the middle 1970s. A whole series of events made it plain that a significant proportion of American men were deeply unhappy about the change in the status of women, and even more worried about what further challenges to masculine pride and convenience might be on the way.

In some respects, indeed, the turning point came even before the beginning of the period under review in this book, as early as 1975. By that year, the momentum behind the Equal Rights Amendment had ebbed away, and by 1977 its opponents had effectively defeated it.[72] This was, in fact, one of the first issues on which the New Right succeeded in bringing together in an effective coalition the radical right, religious conservatives (many of whom, especially in the South, had previously been reliable Democratic voters) and what have been called "non-metropolitan working and middle classes deeply disturbed by cultural changes and especially changes in sexual mores."[73]

The same pattern can be traced in the response to the Supreme Court's decision in *Roe v. Wade*, although the reaction was slower in coming.[74] One major implication of Roe was that the regulation of abortion was taken away from the states and claimed by the federal judiciary. In the *Webster* case in 1989 and *Planned Parenthood v. Casey* in 1992, the Supreme Court in effect handed back to the states a large part of that power to regulate, or to prohibit, abortion. And opponents of abortion have also made considerable progress in Congress. In 1995 a ban on late-term abortions passed the House of Representatives by 295-136, or enough to defeat an expected veto from President Clinton, but the Senate passed the same bill only by 64 to 36, or by just three votes short of the two-thirds needed to override the presidential veto. In a bizarre footnote, Norma McCorvey herself, the original Jane Roe, switched sides. On August 8, 1995, she was baptized in a Dallas swimming pool by the Reverend Phillip Benham, the national director of the pro-life organization Project Rescue. Not surprisingly, McCorvey's conversion gave a boost to opponents of abortion.

Long before that, the media had changed sides on the women's movement, although, at least as far as the mainstream national media were concerned, the majority remained sympathetic to the pro-abortion case. By the 1980s the media had showcased a whole series of scary threats, which were attributed to the emancipation of women and to their going out to work.[75] Among them were an alleged "man shortage"; the prospect of a "devastating" collapse in economic status for women who got divorced under no-fault legislation; an "infertility epidemic" due to career women postponing child bearing; "emotional depression" threatening single women; and "burnout" striking career women. Never mind that each and every one of these bogeys turned out, on checking, to be based on faulty research or in some cases to be purely imaginary. Newspapers, book publishers, and television gave them immense prominence until they became widely held assumptions. To cite a single embarrassing example, the New York media, almost without exception, gave an excited and approving reception to a certain Dr. Srully Blotnick, who claimed his study of more than 3,000 women showed that work "poisons both the professional and personal lives of women."[76] He also called the women's movement "a smokescreen behind which most of those who were afraid of being labeled egomaniacally grasping and ambitious hid." In spite of his limping prose, his book was published by the Viking Press and enthusiastically reviewed. The talk shows loved him. He was given a column in *Forbes* magazine, the bible of many corporate executives. It turned out that almost everything about him was bogus, from his doctorate, bought from a correspondence school, to his "three tons of files, and 26 gigabytes on disk memory." The reception given to this shabby charlatan suggests just how keen men were to hear ill of the women's movement, and just how willing those who purported to be reputable journalists, publishers, and television executives were to pander to their prejudices.

In other instances, male hostility to women at work went beyond words, and indeed beyond sticks and stones. In one appalling case in early 1978,

the American Cyanamid Company decided, in the interests of "fetal protection," that no fertile woman could work in eight out of ten departments
at its Willow Island, West Virginia, pigments plant, which made women's
beauty products.[77] There had been open hostility on the part of male employees to the hiring of women at the previously all-male plant. One day
women arriving at work were greeted by a slogan stenciled on a beam:
SHOOT A WOMAN, SAVE A JOB. One woman found a violent centerfold in
her locker, with a note fastened to it saying, "This is what I want to do to
you."[78] The women, many of them facing desperate financial situations at
home with several people depending on each of them, were offered the
choice of being surgically sterilized or losing their jobs. Five of them actually had their wombs removed.[79] Those who refused were demoted to
janitors. When the five who had had their wombs removed returned to
work their male fellow workers joked that they had been "spayed" and that
"the veterinarian's having a special."[80]

IT MAY SEEM UNFAIR to end a chapter on the change in women's status over
the past twenty-five years with a horror story. Yet the atrocity at the American
Cyanamid plant in West Virginia was not an isolated case. For example, a
company producing electrical batteries in Vermont, Johnson Controls,
excluded all fertile women from work that involved exposure to lead. Attention had been drawn by the Occupational Health and Safety Agency to the
dangers of lead poisoning, especially to pregnant women and their unborn
babies. Johnson Controls ordered that women working with lead could do so
only if they were surgically sterilized.[81] The United Auto Workers, representing women workers at Johnson Controls, sued, arguing that Johnson Controls was using fetal protection both to discriminate against women and to
avoid cleaning up the plant. In a unanimous decision through Justice Harry
Blackmun in 1991 the Supreme Court found for the union, stating that "concern for a woman's existing or potential offspring historically has been the
excuse for denying women equal employment opportunity." Litigation also
arose when employers, fearing legal consequences under the Pregnancy
Discrimination Act, and arguing that the statute nullified older legislation
protecting women, going back to the historical decision in *Muller v. Oregon*
in 1908, fired women workers because they were pregnant.[82]

In general, the high hopes of progress toward greater freedom and equality that many women had held were checked in the 1980s by several largely unexpected negative developments. The women's movement itself largely imploded, with different factions bitterly at odds with one another. Women who had been colleagues and claimed to be working for similar ends accused one another of greed and self-seeking. The larger political climate turned hostile. So did many in the media. Many men resented, often with surprising ferocity, both the feminists' claims for greater freedom and equality and the mass movement of women into the labor market. Many people were deeply shocked by changes in sexual behavior and by threats, perceived and real, to the structure of the family. Although a comfortable majority of women favored the availability of abortion, a very substantial body of opinion, including many traditionalist Catholics and Jews as well as conservative Protestants, believed the liberalization of abortion to be profoundly immoral.

The rising conservative movement fastened on such views, which in any case most of its leaders sincerely shared. Although the evidence suggests that majorities generally supported the major goals of moderate women's leaders, public concern at the tone and substance of claims made by those perceived as more extreme put the brake on progress.

By the 1990s the evidence suggests that this was changing. Women's patterns of voting strongly suggest that a majority of American women were deeply offended by conservative attitudes and by crude attempts to frustrate their progress. There is strong evidence that working women, in particular, rejected the "government is the problem" philosophy of the Republicans and welcomed government's role in protecting them against economic insecurity. Even more decisive was the impact on college-educated women, especially, of Republican opposition to abortion. A poll taken after the 2000 election by Stanley Greenberg, President Clinton's and then candidate Al Gore's pollster, showed that 39 percent of white college-educated females said that the abortion issue was their main reason for supporting Gore, and 33 percent said it was their main reason for doubt about George W. Bush. In 2000, men supported Bush by 53 to 42 percent, but women supported Gore by 54 to 43 percent.[83]

In this, as in other respects, the long period of reaction against the radical movements of the 1970s seemed to be coming to an end at the millennium. But over most of the last quarter of the twentieth century, the experience both of the politicized feminist movement and of working women in general had been disappointing.

But in that respect, the experience of the women's movement was not unique. African Americans, too, found that the temper of the nation was far more conservative than many of them had supposed.

7

New South, Old Race

It's almost as if we'd given up trying to live together.
—*Sophie Gilliam*

Don't you fall now—
For I'se still goin', honey,
I'se still climbin',
And life for me ain't been no crystal stair.
—*Langston Hughes, Mother to Son*

THE HIGH HOPES of the 1960s for racial equality and harmony were first frustrated, then largely disappointed in the succeeding decades. Individual African Americans were brilliantly successful. The group as a whole was less fortunate. By the middle of the 1970s, the noisy claims of radical black leadership had set off a backlash in large sections of the white majority.

This white resentment was more a response to the stridency of some of these demands, given prominence by the media, than to any very real shift in the balance of political power toward blacks. It also represented a rejection of some of the attempts on the part of white liberals—such as busing and more generally affirmative action—that might have brought about substantial change in the complex codes of prevailing racial attitudes and behavior, if they had been allowed to continue. Yet one of the major themes of American public life over the whole period from 1970 to 2000 was reaction to the perceived threats to deeply embedded patterns of belief and conduct posed by the civil rights and women's movements.

That reaction underlay the growth of conservatism, and especially of working-class conservatism, from the late 1960s, when George Wallace stormed out of Alabama to put the fear of God into liberal Democratic politicians from Maryland to Wisconsin, to the emergence of "Reagan Democrats" in the 1980s.[1] Bill Clinton, alone of major national politicians in the entire period,[2] succeeded in forging a new political coalition out of support from black voters (who in large majority either adored him, or at least liked his style and saw no viable alternative) and from some at least of those bewildered and frustrated white working-class voters who had shifted from their parents' loyalty to the union and to the legacy of Franklin Roosevelt. Those voters had looked for salvation successively from Wallace, Nixon, Reagan, and the southern populist tradition as reinterpreted in Congress by such conservative leaders as Newt Gingrich of Georgia, Trent Lott of Mississippi, or Tom de Lay of Texas. Only at the very end of the period covered by this book were there some signs that the majority of working-class opinion, including that of previous "Reagan Democrats," was coming to accept the value of racial tolerance.[3]

One interpretation of the shifting of the political ballast between the 1960s and the 1990s is that it represented the "southernization" of American politics.[4] The majority of white southerners accepted with good grace that blacks must be juridically equal citizens. But neither they nor northerners could accept active government intervention or positive discrimination to help African Americans achieve full economic and social equality.

This massive rejection of the politics of racial and social revolution had profound consequences for the whole structure of American politics, and we analyze those consequences in some detail in a later chapter. For the present, it is enough to say that, just as most American men refused to go more than a few steps along the road proposed by the feminists, so the great majority of white Americans, both men and women, accepted the goals of fully equal civil rights and citizen equality for black people but jibbed at many of the policies that might have brought those goals nearer.

Statistical evidence confirms that, although a minority of African Americans was able to make progress toward personal goals and in some cases achieve spectacular success, overall progress was spotty. Society, in the North and East as well as in the South, remains deeply segregated, and on most measures, from poverty and imprisonment to exposure to AIDS and family breakdown, blacks were overrepresented in the ranks of the unsuccessful, the deprived, and the unhappy.

174 ... Chapter 7

In the 1960s, at the time of the great movement for civil rights in the South, two assumptions were almost universal, in the North as in the South, and both among those who welcomed and those who resisted change in the racial status quo. One was that change was inevitable, and that as a result of it, African Americans would move, more or less slowly, into equality with whites. And the other was that, in the end, the South must become more like the North.

Both those assumptions were soon proved wrong. Instead, in the long generation since the civil rights movements triumphed with the passage of the Civil Rights Act of 1964 and its legislative twin, the Voting Rights Act of 1965, something very different took place. It quickly became plain that achieving de facto equality in the North would be a tougher proposition than achieving de jure equality in the South.

In the South it had been a question of destroying a complex pattern of legal segregation and racial discrimination sanctioned by immemorial custom and reaffirmed by the "Jim Crow" legislation and jurisprudence of the late 1800s. However deeply engrained "the Southern Way of Life" might be, by the mid-1960s the majority of southerners, and certainly the majority of politically sophisticated southerners, found it hard to deny to blacks their citizen rights. In the North, on the contrary, it was a question not of fulfilling rights long conceded in the post–Civil War constitutional amendments and now proclaimed anew by the Supreme Court under Earl Warren, but of how blacks could achieve de facto equality, or — as President Johnson put it in his most ambitious speech — not just "equality as a right and a theory but equality as a fact and as a result."[5]

This was an altogether different matter. For a start, many northerners, not least the unionized working-class workers and voters, many of them of recent immigrant stock, who formed the foot soldiers of the great Democratic political army, did not see themselves as patricians graciously abolishing feudal iniquities, but as hard-pressed families who had been given no favors themselves in their struggle to swim into the mainstream of American life.[6]

There were philosophical difficulties, too. The principle of theoretical equality of opportunity, embracing Jefferson's high-flown pronouncement that all men were created equal, was quite different from the new-fangled political philosophy that would seek to use the power of government, or as its critics increasingly came to call it, of the "state," to intervene to make people more equal in condition.

Finally there was the common play of instinct and interests. It was one thing for the middle-class citizens of New York or Chicago or Los Angeles to rejoice at the assertion of the American political creed by such high-minded and—to northerners—apparently unthreatening prophets and martyrs as Dr. King. It was quite another to be confronted by what seemed a remorselessly swelling tide of black neighbors, all too many of whom appeared to reject the traditional ethos of middle-class America. However unfairly, they impinged on the northern consciousness as criminals or welfare mothers or drug dealers, politically led, or at least represented, by shrill and unreasonable demagogues. No doubt such pictures in white American heads owed more to deep racial stereotypes than to accurate representations of society. But there it was. By the middle of the 1970s, there had been a massive upheaval in northern opinion against most forms of affirmative action, against the whole idea of government intervention intended to compensate blacks for past injustice, against open housing, and above all against busing.

———•◆•———

IN NEW YORK CITY, capital of media and fashion, the backlash appeared even before the movement of reform had reached its peak. The confrontation between Mayor John Lindsay and his strange coalition of upper-class whites and black radicals in the neighborhoods on the one hand and middle-class white New Yorkers on the other over "community control" in the schools was well under way by the winter of 1966–67.

In 1967 came the "riot" in Detroit. Although the black West Side of Detroit did explode after a heavy-handed police raid on a "blind pig" after-hours club, all but ten of the forty-three people killed were black, and very likely thirty-one of the thirty-three blacks killed were shot by the Detroit police, by the Michigan National Guard, or by the army.[7] It would have been hard for anyone in possession of the facts not to endorse the conclusion of the Kerner Commission that the riot had its origin and ran its murderous course because of "white racism."[8] "Despite these complexities," the report said, "certain fundamental matters are clear. Of these the most fundamental is the racial attitude and behavior of white

Americans towards black Americans. . . . White racism is essentially responsible for the explosive mixture which has been accumulating in our
cities since the end of World War II."⁹

"What white Americans have never fully understood," the report went
on, "—but what the Negro can never forget—is that white society is
deeply implicated in the ghetto. White institutions created it, white institutions maintain it, and white society condones it."¹⁰ And, it might have
added, when it boiled over in anger and frustration, white men with bul-
lets fastened the lid back down on it. Not only had white Americans not
understood that. The great majority of them were also quite unwilling to
listen to such talk, and many were willing to punish any politician or any
leader from any background who offered such an analysis. President Lyndon Johnson himself, who had commissioned the report, was shrewd
enough to distance himself from it.

By 1968, when the ghettos boiled over again after the murder of Dr. King,
the white majority had had enough. There was an outpouring of grief
over King's death. But the response to the wild black rioting that followed
was overwhelmingly unsympathetic. By the following summer, reaction
was in full swing. In New York, the conservative John Marchi defeated
John Lindsay, and a Democrat of the George Wallace school, Mario Procaccino, won the Democratic primary. "The forces of reaction and fear,"
said Lindsay, "have captured both major parties in our city,"¹¹ and Lindsay survived only because the conservative vote was split.

New York was not alone. Most major metropolitan cities experienced
the phenomenon of "white flight." This was not wholly attributable to
white people fleeing to the suburbs to avoid increasingly black neighborhoods. The 1950s, after all, was the decade where many working-class
white people moved to newly accessible suburbs on the Levittown pattern.
Still, the Kerner Commission calculated that 5.8 million white people left
central cities in the 1950s, and that between 1960 and 1966 the rate of white
outflow accelerated, with 4.9 million whites leaving in just six years. If you
leave out Los Angeles and Houston, two cities where (in part because of
their great geographical area) the white population actually increased, the
remaining eight of the nation's ten biggest cities lost at least 3.5 million
white inhabitants, and gained about 1.4 million black ones.

Nowhere was this more extreme than in Detroit, which experienced the worst rioting of the 1960s. By 1970 the city's population, which had touched almost 2 million in the 1940s, was down to 1.5 million, half black and half white, while the suburbs totaled almost 3 million, 95 percent of them white.[12] (Flint, home of General Motors's biggest plants, and a scaled-down version of Detroit, went through exactly the same experience. In the 1960s Flint was 80 percent white, 20 percent black. In the 1990s it was half black, half white, but while the population of the city fell from 190,000 to 160,000, that of surrounding Genesee County rose from 375,000 in 1960 to 430,000 in 1998, with almost one-third of the city population living below the poverty level.)[13]

In January 1974 Coleman Young was elected mayor of Detroit. He was an engaging politician in many ways but also an unashamed old-fashioned "race man," who presented all issues robustly in terms of black versus white. His election was widely taken as meaning that henceforth Detroit would be controlled by blacks. In spite of numerous efforts by the city fathers, from Henry Ford and Max Fisher to Walter Reuther of the United Auto Workers, to attract outside capital, the city continued to decline.[14]

It was not only whites who were fleeing the inner cities after the riot years. The journalist Nicholas Lemann reported that in Chicago "all the ghetto schools, the overcrowding of which was supposed to be a major cause of low achievement levels, have lost enrollment."[15] Everywhere middle-class blacks were leaving the inner-city ghettos for the suburbs. The South Bronx lost 37 percent of its population between 1970 and 1980. More than 100,000 black Chicagoans moved to the suburbs in the 1970s; 224,000 blacks moved from Washington, D.C., to its suburbs, 124,000 from Atlanta to its suburbs, and Lemann suspected that the number of black migrants to the suburbs was still increasing when he wrote in 1986. The population of the Woodlawn neighborhood on Chicago's South Side, an increasingly black area after 1960, continued to decline, from 80,000 in 1960 to 54,000 in 1970, 36,000 in 1980, and a mere 24,000 in 1990; at the same time, commercial and industrial establishments in Woodlawn shrank from 800 in 1950 to no more than 100 in the mid-1990s.[16] There was, Lemann rightly suggested, no mystery to why so many people left the ghettos. "They wanted to feel safe on the streets, to send their children to better schools, and to live in more pleasant surroundings; in particular, riots drove many people away. Probably everyone who could leave did."[17]

The same year, 1974, that saw a black man elected mayor of Detroit also saw the bizarre culmination of racial conflict in Boston, once the citadel of abolitionism and more recently the home of Kennedy liberalism. A few days after Coleman Young took over in Detroit, Judge Arthur Garrity, himself a former Kennedy campaign aide, delivered his judgment in *Morgan v. Hennigan,* an action calling for desegregation of the city's public schools. The Boston school board, Garrity courageously stated, has "knowingly conducted a systematic program of segregation."[18] Between 1940 and 1960 Boston's black population grew from 23,000 to 63,000. Although the city numbered both Malcolm X and Louis Farrakhan (born Louis Eugene Walcott) among its children, race relations appeared to be relatively good until they were disastrously embittered by the threat of busing. In late 1965 a citizen committee, disturbed by the degree of de facto racial segregation in Boston's public schools, recommended busing black children to white schools and vice versa. In November 1967 Kevin White, a liberal with presidential ambitions, was elected mayor, but only narrowly. He won by only 12,000 out of almost 200,000 votes and was run hard by Louise Day Hicks, a self-appointed champion of the white and especially of the Irish working-class,[19] who proclaimed that busing was "undemocratic and un-American."

In Charlestown and South Boston, traditional bastions of Irish Democratic Boston, and in other ethnic neighborhoods, anger against busing boiled over. In September 1974 there was a riot at South Boston High School, and a year later Senator Edward Kennedy was booed in front of the Government Center his brother had caused to be built and was actually forced to run for safety from a contingent of the family's oldest supporters from Charlestown. In 1976, in front of the same building, a black lawyer, a graduate of St. Paul's School, Concord, and Yale, as it happened, was attacked with the staff of the Stars and Stripes by another incensed Charlestownee. A photographer caught the painful bicentennial image of Old Glory pointed like a stabbing spear at a black man's chest.[20]

The idea of combating racial segregation in education by busing children out of their home neighborhoods to achieve "racial balance" was a product of liberal social science crossed with judicial activism. The intention was to counteract the prevailing educational segregation that was widespread and stubborn in both South and north alike. The school systems of southern cities like Atlanta, Winston-Salem, and Richmond, which ought to have been desegregated as a result of *Brown*, remained largely segregated. In July 2002 a new study from the civil rights project of the Harvard education school found that educational segregation continued to intensify throughout the 1990s.[21] Researchers found that much of the progress for black students since the 1960s was eliminated during the 1990s, a decade that brought three Supreme Court decisions limiting desegregation remedies. (The data also show that Hispanics, too, have become increasingly isolated for the last thirty years, with the segregation of Hispanics surpassing that of blacks.) They also concluded that the rapid growth in the numbers of minorities in the suburbs has not produced integrated schools.

The reason, of course, given the American tradition of neighborhood schools, lay in the all but universally established patterns of residential segregation, a clear example of the ways in which the north had been getting more like the South or even—so to speak—surpassing it. In 1990, the last date for which detailed figures are available, northern metropolitan cities were either as segregated residentially as southern cities such as Atlanta, Houston, or Memphis, or even more so.[22]

As a result, though improvement was achieved in individual places (such as the once notorious South Bronx, which was being revived by emigrants from the Caribbean and elsewhere), overall the United States remained to the end of the twentieth century racially segregated both residentially and in primary and secondary education. This pattern is not merely the result of the actions of private individuals. It has been, in the opinion of the author of a thorough study of its history and operation, "the *de facto* policy of local governments and standard operating procedure for individual landowners."[23] But federal and state governments have also played a crucial part in creating and maintaining residential racial segregation. "The United States government reinforced discriminatory norms."[24] For example the Federal Housing Administration (FHA) adopted the practice of "redlining," that is, of operating a discriminatory rating system to prevent blacks (described as "an undesirable element") from receiving home loans. As of the 1990 census, 30 percent of all African

Americans live in neighborhoods that are 90 percent or more black, and a further 62 percent live in neighborhoods that are at least 60 percent black. This pattern, the author further bleakly concludes, "exists to a large degree as a result of intentional discrimination against minorities."[25]

———•———

As MILLIONS OF BLACKS moved north in the 1940s and 1950s, insurance companies and other mortgage lenders developed secret but immovable systems, enforced by redlining and other devices, to keep all but a handful of blacks from buying in white neighborhoods. These genteel economic pressures were too often reinforced by intimidation and in the last resort by violence. (There were firebombings of homes acquired by black families in a dozen white Chicago neighborhoods between 1973 and 1985.)[26]

In the 1970s, the private housing market in Chicago was almost wholly segregated by an unwritten rule, except at the very top end, and this is still essentially true today. The public housing projects are in practice wholly segregated too.[27] When Martin Luther King, in 1966, tried to campaign for "open housing" in Chicago, he got nowhere, and sustained the most damaging political defeat of his career.[28] The same applies, with trivial local variations, in Philadelphia, Detroit, Cleveland, Buffalo, Pittsburgh, Baltimore, Milwaukee, Cincinnati, and every other major city east of the Mississippi, not to mention the great majority of smaller cities like Gary, Wilmington, or New Haven, and it is not so very different west of the Mississippi either, for example, in St. Louis, Denver, or Minneapolis. In the circumstances, it was inevitable that education, too, would be largely segregated.

The Supreme Court had clearly struck down segregation in education, and the Johnson legislative program of the mid-1960s had broadened the prohibition. There could be no doubt: segregation in education, intended or not, was unconstitutional. A series of judges left no hiding place. In *Greene*, in 1968, arising in southside Virginia, the Court ended the possibility of a school district having "free choice."[29] *Swann v. Charlotte-Mecklenburg* (1971) mandated busing and created an integrated school system between the city of Charlotte and suburban Mecklenburg County, but bound only southern school districts where educational segregation had once been legally sanctioned.[30] The *Keyes* case, in Denver, outlawed any arrangements that betrayed a "segregative intent."[31] And in June 1972 in Michigan, in *Milliken v. Bradley,* Judge Steven Roth imposed a scheme that, one editorial commented, would make all previous busing proposals look like class excursions.

The situation in Greater Detroit was inflamed. In working-class Pontiac, home of many auto workers, some of whom were black but many of whom were southern whites, feeling was running high against busing. Two Ku Klux Klan members blew up a dozen buses. Roth, himself a former auto worker, went for a solution that was bold to the point of folly. Altogether 780,000 children would be affected, and more than 300,000 would be bused every day, from ghetto neighborhoods to suburbs, but also in the opposite direction. It would take in not just the city but fifty-three (later eighty-five) suburbs, including Pontiac. The scheme had some logic on its side: by that stage, Detroit's school population was already two-thirds black, whereas with three-quarters of the metropolitan area white, it would be possible, using busing, to arrive at a racial balance close to that in the nation as a whole. But politically, Roth's scheme never stood a chance. It was simply too late. Led by Irene McCabe, a grass-roots antibusing insurrection aroused the Motor City and its suburbs as they had not been stirred since the riots of the Depression. In the 1972 primary, George Wallace won no less than 52 percent of the vote in a state that had been the bastion of labor power and a liberal fief since the 1930s.[32]

When *Milliken* reached the Supreme Court, in early 1974, the Court itself had changed. Warren Burger, not Earl Warren, was now chief justice, and the Court ruled, on a straight 5 to 4 conservative over liberal vote, that Judge Roth had no business drawing the suburban school systems, where segregation was not alleged, into a scheme for remedying segregation in Detroit. Less than ten years after Lyndon Johnson's speech at Howard University, the high-water mark of the liberal faith, the tide had turned. Not only busing, but also the whole idea of government intervention to correct racial injustice, was now headed for disrepute. And in Washington, as well as in Pontiac, Michigan, or Chicago, the north had become a little more like the South.

Busing was only one among the many techniques of what became known as "affirmative action." In the spirit of the Howard speech and of the brief period from 1963 to 1966 when the federal government was firmly committed to compensatory action to undo the injustices and handicaps inflicted on African Americans over centuries, all manner of devices had been invented to ensure equal opportunities for blacks.

Atlanta was only one of the cities, for example, where under a black mayor a certain proportion of the city's contracts, in construction, haulage, and many other kinds of business, was reserved for minorities under what came to be called "set-aside." Minority entrepreneurs (many of whom would have found it hard to complete their contracts without help from mainstream white businesses) were allowed a share of the gravy. Huge projects like the Atlanta airport and the Underground Atlanta project for revamping the city's decaying center were included in the set-aside bonanza. By 1978 the share of minority entrepreneurs in Atlanta's municipal contracts had reached 38 percent, and something similar was true in every other city with a black mayor, which included Los Angeles, Washington, D.C., Houston, Cleveland, and Detroit. Affirmative action was to be found in almost every corner of American life. Altogether some 15,000 companies, with 23 million workers, benefited from minority hiring and contracting targets.[33]

For many whites, one of the most offensive forms of affirmative action was the use by universities of various devices to secure preferential admission for minority students. In 1973 a white student named Allan Paul Bakke discovered that when he was refused admission by the medical school of the University of California at Davis, a number of minority students who had done less well than he did in the entrance tests had been admitted as a result of affirmative action. "I realize," he wrote to the school, "that the rationale for these quotas is that they attempt to atone for past discrimination. But instituting a new racial bias in favor of minorities is not a just solution." In June 1974, having received no satisfaction, he filed suit against the university. The Supreme Court heard oral argument in October 1977, and it was not until June 1978 that an embarrassed court, admitting through Justice Lewis Powell that it was not agreed, came up with a somewhat lame compromise. Bakke, the Court found, had a right to be admitted to the university, but affirmative action was not necessarily illegal. The Bakke case aroused conservatives and libertarians alike. The great Yale jurist, Alexander M. Bickel, called the quota system revealed by

Bakke "invidious in principle as well as in practice," and the Harvard sociologist Nathan Glazer foresaw a nation increasingly divided into racial and ethnic categories, so that "new resentments are created, new turfs are to be protected, new angers arise."[34]

By the end of the 1970s, affirmative action was widely discredited, and the wave of hostility to what were perceived as unfair efforts to favor minorities contributed to the election of Ronald Reagan in 1980. African Americans had struggled even when the weight and wealth of the federal government were unreservedly pledged to help them achieve equality. Now what set in was a reaction in both senses of the word: a response to what was perceived as excessive favoring of black Americans and to what was resented as their ingratitude; but also a reaction in the classic political sense, as a shift occurred in the center of gravity of American political opinion from left to right, from those who would use the power of government to right injustice and diminish inequality, to those who cared for none of those things, and saw government as the oppressive "state."

———•◆•———

IN THE NEW ATMOSPHERE of the mid- to late 1970s, a great division appeared among African Americans. The ablest, the strongest, and the more fortunate thrived. The 1970s was a decade of "firsts" for black people: the first black cabinet secretaries, the first black astronauts, the first black Episcopal bishop, and the first black Wimbledon champion.[35] And that progress continued into the 1980s and the 1990s. Prodigiously talented sports stars—Michael Jordan, Tiger Woods, footballers, boxers, and sprinters innumerable—earned ever more astronomical salaries and became role models for young blacks, golden evidence that it was possible for them, or for a few of them, to "make it." Oprah Winfrey and Bill Cosby earned equally gigantic incomes[36] and almost unprecedented respect from a white majority that was relieved to find African Americans in positions of influence and power who might be critical but were ultimately unthreatening. Whites, says another authority, "expect a certain deportment and demeanour, one that will make whites feel comfortable," in the black people they have chosen for preferment.[37]

It was the same in the law, in politics and government, in academia. Where the first black justice of the Supreme Court, Thurgood Marshall, fought his way there as a challenger of the status quo, Clarence Thomas was nominated first and foremost, not as a jurist or an advocate, but as a black conservative. For every Jesse Jackson, whose political career was the natural continuation of early battles for civil rights, there was a Vernon Jordan, who had traversed from the radical years of the struggle for voting rights to the main board of Coca-Cola, from which he would occasionally take time off to play golf with the president of the United States. For every civil rights lawyer, defending paupers for meager fees, there was a Johnnie Cochrane, commanding high fees as a prominent leader of the criminal bar. It was in a Republican administration that Colin Powell, after seriously considering running for president as a Republican, became secretary of state, while Condoleezza Rice, a former provost of Stanford who had risen through the foreign policy establishment, became national security adviser to a Republican president. It was becoming true that almost all pinnacles of American society could be climbed by African Americans, though certainly events were confirming the suspicion of those who said that the first black man or woman to be president would be a conservative.

Perhaps even more significant for the future than these shining individual triumphs were the millions of blacks who were "making it" in the relatively modest sense that they were going to college, getting excellent grades, holding down good jobs, moving to the suburbs, raising families, carving out for themselves a recognizable simulacrum of the American Dream.

The thing has to be put in that slightly grudging way, for two reasons. For one thing, a very substantial number were not making it at all. For another, a surprisingly large literature has appeared where precisely those African Americans who appeared to have made it exposed their resentment that, for all their apparent success, they had not been truly accepted. Some have come to terms with the balance between the opportunities American society does now offer to blacks, and the insults and obstacles that still accompany them. In a subtle book Shelby Steele, a literature professor at San Jose State University in California, drew up a balance sheet.[38] He described the bargain he had himself made in the early 1970s by subscribing in a general way to a collective black identity vaguely rooted in the consciousness, full of "righteous anger and mistrust of America," derived from the black power movement, while at the same time privately pursuing the opportunities he found American society offered him. Both realities, he found, were true. He continued to experience "racial indignities and slights." But he also found opportunities that were real, a white majority that was not racist, a downward slope toward the Promised Land Martin King had offered, a Promised Land that was "an opportunity, not a deliverance."[39]

Not all successful African Americans feel as upbeat as Steele. Even those who were doing best often felt uneasy, unwanted, excluded. An African American journalist, Ellis Cose, listed what he called "the dozen demons," which bar even the most able and talented of his race from confident membership in the upper strata of an American society that was itself increasingly class-conscious and stratified. His list included the inability to fit in; the sense of exclusion from the club; low expectations; shattered hopes; faint praise; and so on. Again and again, Cose reported, superficially successful black people reported stories that might seem trivial but that rankled deeply, about how white people, often in relatively menial positions, had assumed that they were unreliable or undesirable purely on the basis of their race. He gave telling examples, from the white sentry in Biloxi, Mississippi, who would not accept a black general's two-star identification card to an immensely successful senior partner in a major law firm who found his way barred into his own office by a white junior asking coldly, "Can I help you?"

In 2000 the *New York Times* published the results of one of the most original and illuminating journalistic enterprises for many years.[40] Two editors, Gerald Boyd, who is black, and Sandra Behr Golden, who is white, sent forth a dozen reporters to spend as much time as it took to dig themselves into such diverse worlds as a fragilely integrated church in an Atlanta suburb, or the lurking racial resentments in the sergeants' mess of an army company. The series had no particular theme or angle. It sought only to give striking pictures of "how race is lived in America." One piece, for example, showed how two Cuban immigrants, close friends in Havana who had come to America as boat people, one white, one black, drifted apart in Florida. Within a few short years the white friend was saying of African Americans, "They basically have kids and go on welfare. What else is there to know?" His black friend, not long after reaching Florida on a raft, was stopped by four police cars full of officers with drawn weapons, for no reason given except that, as one cop put it, "I saw so many blacks in the car, I figured I would check you out." "Up until that day," said the black Cuban, "I thought all Cubans were the same. It took a while to sink in, but that incident made me start thinking in a different way."

Most telling of all, Gerald Boyd himself thinks, was the report on the two entrepreneurs, one white (and a great-great-grandson of Julius Rosenwald, the founder of Sears Roebuck), the other a black University of Pennsylvania law school graduate from a modest family in North Carolina. When they launched their successful Internet startup, they saw each other as joint CEOs. They even both acknowledged that Tim Cobb, the black man, was more qualified. But the venture capitalists (white) did not like the idea of joint CEOs. In the end, Cobb insisted that his partner, Jeff Levy, must be the CEO. At first they both became rich men. Then they split up and founded separate companies. Cobb's failed, Levy's prospered. Cobb's wife divorced him. She seems to have blamed his single-minded drive for success—"failure is not an option." It is a complex tale. Its obvious motto, whatever the subterranean subtleties of individual personality, seems simple enough. It is not enough to have millions of dollars, trust funds for your children, a new Porsche and new Range Rover, and vintage champagne to drink. "When things were good," Tim Cobb said, "being black made them better; when things were not so good, it made them worse." Less obviously, it was the black friend in a partnership of equals who brought failure on himself, precisely because he accepted that his less qualified white friend must be the CEO. That was what society, in the insistent shape of the venture capitalists, expected. Not to go along with white expectations could be dangerous, as any black man learns young in America: to go along with them can equally lead to disaster. And even when most visible barriers are removed, blacks can sometimes build a cage for themselves.

—◆—

IN THE MORE THAN a third of a century since the great 1964 Civil Rights Act, the black nation in America has been divided like the biblical sheep and goats. Statistics show that on the average African Americans are likely to have lower incomes, higher unemployment, poor health, and more unstable family lives. They are more likely to commit and to be victims of violent crime, far more likely to end up in prison, likely statistically to die younger.

Still, these average statistics conceal a different and, in some ways, even more troubling reality. A majority has moved closer to the mainstream of American life. A small minority within that majority has been undeniably successful, even though, as we have seen, the psychological price has often been heavy. Still, for more than half of the 30 million African Americans, the past thirty-five years have seen real progress.[41] But a significant minority has not only not made progress. Its members have also drifted down into the painful and often dangerous plight of an underclass.

The statistics are well known but nonetheless horrifying. They demonstrate with chilling precision how, while things have been getting better for some blacks, for others, things have been getting very much worse. Life expectancy for black Americans, the most vital statistic of all, is more than six years less than for whites. In 1940 infant mortality for blacks was about 1.6 times higher than for whites. Fifty years later, it was 2.2 times.[42] Sixty percent of all black children grow up in households headed by their mothers, and one-third of black babies, as opposed to fewer than 3 percent of white babies, are born to unmarried mothers. Black people are almost seven times more likely than whites to die by homicide, and nearly five times more likely to be arrested for murder or manslaughter.

In the mid-1990s, before "welfare reform," 37.2 percent of the mothers on welfare were black. In fiscal year 2000, after "welfare reform," 39 percent of the families on temporary assistance were African Americans. So, at the time of writing, are 46 percent of prisoners in federal, state, and local prisons and jails.[43] In fact the astonishing figure of 32 percent, almost *one-third* of all black men between the ages of twenty and twenty-nine, are either in prison, or, by reason of being on probation or parole, can be sent there at any time. Whereas in 1930, three-quarters of the prison population were white and less than one-quarter black, now black prisoners outnumber whites, so that proportionately blacks are about seven times more likely to be in jail.[44] Black males have a 29 percent chance of serving time in prison at some time in their lives; white males have a 4 percent chance.[45] By 2003 more than 2 million African Americans were serving time in prison. In many ways, while life has become easier for a majority, if a slender majority, of black Americans, for a substantial and probably growing black underclass the life of man, in Hobbes's phrase, is poor, nasty, brutish, and all too often short.

Many, especially in welfare rights organizations, are offended by the phrase, "the tangle of pathologies."[46] Yet it is hard to avoid some such concept to describe the interlocking nature of the problems faced by an underclass in American society in the 1990s that was disproportionately black.

It is true that political and ideological propaganda distorted the scope and nature of this problem. Ronald Reagan's imagining of the "welfare queen," driving her Cadillac and claiming benefits under a dozen names, may have been a wild exaggeration, cynically propagated for the purposes of the 1976 presidential campaign, of the frequency of a banal fraud; yet it seized the public imagination and confirmed an established stereotype.[47] Charles Murray's work, although it is closer to political propaganda than to the social science it claims to be, and contradicts itself in fundamental ways, also printed on the public consciousness the idea that there was an underclass in America, that this was a new state of affairs, and that this underclass was predominantly black.[48]

It is not. But it is in fact disproportionately black. And what is certainly true is that in certain urban ghettos, social pathologies reinforce one another. In Brooklyn and the South Bronx, in North Philadelphia and Boston's Roxbury, in the sprawling projects of the South and West Sides of Chicago, in northeast Washington and elsewhere, blacks are disproportionately likely to be poorly housed, to be unemployed, to grow up in homes headed by mothers, to go to poor schools where low expectations are all the more naturally implanted because they seem so inescapably realistic. In these poverty ghetto neighborhoods, defined as places where 40 percent or more live in absolute poverty,[49] work has disappeared, physically retreating to the suburbs, which poor people, in the absence of public transportation, find it hard to reach. Even in the least promising of these places, there are heroic individuals and beleaguered families that struggle to live by the general American values of self-reliance and hard work, and even some who emerge to be successful in one way or another.[50] But for the most part the urban ghettos are places of despair, where many grow up into an adolescence where work has largely disappeared, to be replaced by fighting, stealing, pimping, and buying and selling heroin and crack cocaine. In a typical week in 1990, only 37 percent of the adult population was working in fifteen black Chicago neighborhoods with a total population of 425,000.[51] In the twenty-one years from 1967 to 1987, Philadelphia lost 64 percent of its manufacturing jobs, Chicago 60 percent, New York City 58 percent, and Detroit 51 percent. But where white industrial workers had some chance of finding new work, for black underclass members that was virtually an impossibility.

This was not just a matter of blind economic forces, like the economic downturn that followed the oil price rise and stagflation of the 1970s. It was also caused, at least in part, by conscious public policy. In the 1980s and 1990s both federal and state governments cut back sharply on aid programs targeted at ghetto areas, and in the process cut the very low-paid, locally accessible jobs that ghetto residents might have taken. Both the Reagan and George H. W. Bush administrations cut back severely on aid to cities. In 1980 federal contributions to city budgets were 18 percent; in 1990 they had fallen by no less than two-thirds to 6.4 percent.[52]

Ghetto poverty was related to the disappearance of low-paid work. But it was also the consequence of an impatient unwillingness, on the part of politicians and presumably of their constituencies, and also of corporate decision makers, to go on paying good money after bad to help people who were increasingly seen by many in the white majority as the authors of their own misfortunes.

The welfare state, both in the wider sense of public and political commitment to government intervention to protect individuals in need and in the narrower sense of welfare for needy families, was withering away. In 1995 President Clinton, perhaps against his better instincts,[53] gave way to conservative pressure both from Republicans in Congress and from his own party and supported welfare "reform" in the shape of the so-called Personal Responsibility and Work Opportunity Reconciliation Act of 1996 (PRWORA).[54] It ended the federal entitlement program, Aid to Families with Dependent Children, which dated back (under a slightly changed name) to the Social Security Act of 1935. It removed guarantees of minimum support for poor children, and it allowed states to design welfare systems with increasingly onerous "workfare" provisions.

The reform worked, in the sense that it has more than halved the numbers of welfare recipients, and arguably in other ways too. (By late 2001 the average monthly number of families receiving federal assistance had fallen from a peak of 14.4 million in March 1994 to 5.3 million, though it is not possible to say how much of this reduction was due to reform, how much to other federal programs, and how much to the relatively prosperous state of the economy.) Critics point out that it has not taken all poor people out of poverty, although the official child poverty rate in 2000 was 16.2 percent, down by one-fifth since 1996. It has also been attacked for being discriminatory, both against women and against people of color. Although poverty rates for African American and also for Hispanic children have fallen, they are still three times higher than the rate for white, non-Hispanic children, though this may largely reflect a higher proportion of minority children living in single-parent families. More than a third of all women recipients reported intrusive behavior, especially inquisition into their sex lives, as part of the procedures they had to go through under the "reformed" welfare system. One in six reported sexual harassment in the workplaces to which they were assigned.

The picture is, in reality, mixed. The heart of the welfare reform legislation was the Temporary Assistance for Needy Families (TANF) program.[55] This replaced AFDC. (As it was enacted in 1996 for six years only, it had to be reauthorized by Congress by October 1, 2002.) TANF is indeed a tough system. It repealed the individual entitlement to welfare. It replaced an open-ended federal payment to the states with a block grant, and although the funding level was fixed, states were given greater flexibility in deciding how their money was to be spent. The program contained strong work requirements, backed up by sanctions for those who failed to comply. It limited to five years the period in which a family could qualify for cash payments.

If that had been all that was happening, the situation of welfare recipients would indeed have been bleak. (Millions of children would be "put to the sword," Senator Daniel P. Moynihan predicted.)[56] However, in other parts of the urban jungle, things looked much brighter. Christopher Jencks, the well-known Harvard sociologist, has admitted that the first five years of welfare reform "inflicted far less economic pain than we expected" and that it has "turned out far better than most liberals expected."[57] The new emphasis on helping low-wage workers has created a significantly better system than existed in 1996. Low-income working

families were benefiting from increases in funding through such programs as Earned Income Tax Credit (EITC), Medicaid, and child care
that can fairly be called dramatic. In 1999, for example, working poor and
"moderate income" families were eligible for $52 billion in federal assis-
tance, as compared to only $6 billion they would have been entitled to
under the old (1984) law.[58] Teen pregnancies have declined dramatically,
the share of children born out of wedlock has leveled off, and the share of
children being raised in two-parent families has increased. The Brookings
study found that "although the great majority of mothers leaving welfare
have found jobs, their earnings are quite low, typically around $7–8 an
hour."[59] Few have health insurance coverage through their employers,
and child care is both scarce and expensive.[60] Even so, work does pay
better than welfare, and a woman with no more than three children can
escape from poverty if she works steadily and gets all the benefits to which
she is entitled. Most important of all, there is little evidence that children
have been harmed by the change from welfare to work.

The worst that can be said in summary is that life for a single African
American mother in the ghetto remains painfully hard after welfare reform; the good news is that a situation that was deteriorating to an intol-
erable extent has been stabilized and, in important ways, relieved.

———◆———

As HOPE CAME in sight for young female ghetto residents, prospects remained grim for many of their brothers and lovers. An eminent sociologist suggested that the welfare state was replaced for many by the prison
state.[61] That might be an overstatement, but the prison population has increased more than sixfold in thirty years, from less than 200,000 in 1970 to
1.3 million in 2000, to which must be added more than 600,000 held in
local jails. The United States has now passed Russia and has the highest
rate of incarceration, with 702 inmates for every 100,000 in the population, compared with the Russian rate of 685 per 100,000.[62]

What was even more remarkable was that this sharp increase in the number of people in prison was happening not in response to a crime wave but
at a time when the crime rate was actually falling, as it has done nationally
since 1992. The number of prisoners was growing because of essentially political changes in sentencing policy and practice, such as "zero tolerance,"

"mandatory minimums," "three-strikes-and-you're-out," and "truth in sentencing." Half the states have qualified for federal funding under a 1994 federal crime bill as a result of having changed sentencing laws to require that certain offenders serve at least 85 percent of their sentence. The swollen prison population, in other words, may have kept offenders off the streets and deterred others. But it reflects not a real increase in crime but a public and political response to a perceived increase that, at least for the past decade, has not been there. And the process is racially unfair.

It has borne most heavily on African Americans. Their number in state prisons has grown by 132 percent in ten years, as against an increase of 109 percent in number of white prisoners. They are also disproportionately likely to be executed. Since capital punishment was reintroduced by the Supreme Court's finding that it was not of itself "cruel and unusual punishment" in 1976, 672 persons, the great majority of them men, have been executed in the United States. At the end of 2000, thirty-seven states and the federal prison system held 3,593 prisoners under sentence of death, a sevenfold increase since capital punishment was reintroduced. All had been convicted of murder. Of that total, 1,990 were white, and 1,535 were black.[63]

This was a marginal reversal compared with the 1960s and early 1970s, when far fewer prisoners were held under sentence of death, but the majority of those were black. In 1975, for example, there were 488 prisoners on death row, 218 of them white, and 262 black.

For 2000, a more detailed breakdown is available: 85 persons were executed in twenty states, 83 of them men and 2 of them women; 49 were white, 35 were black, and 1 was Native American. More than three-quarters of the executions (64) took place in states of the former Confederate South (no fewer than 40 in Texas alone). Another 16 executions were carried out in the two classic border states of Oklahoma and Missouri, bringing the number in southern states to 80 out of 85. The remaining executions were 3 in Arizona, 1 in California, and 1 in Delaware. (In 2001, the number of executions fell significantly, from 85 to 66.)

The statistics do not perhaps bear out the idea that the North was getting more like the South. But the return of capital punishment was a return to a traditionally more severe penal code, and disproportionately so where African Americans were concerned.

In spite of the disproportionate growth in the African American prison population, it could perhaps be argued that over the whole period from 1975 to the beginning of the twenty-first century racial hostilities were easing, or at least that the rigidity of racial barriers was softening. Some indicators suggest that black people were experiencing less discriminatory barriers to success at middle and upper social and economic levels. But unfortunately any such progress was offset by a whole series of high-profile episodes that revealed just how much white hostility, and how much black suspicion, remained two generations after the great triumphs of the civil rights movement and the bold legislative program of the Johnson administration.

By the beginning of the 1990s, a witches' brew of stereotypes, some more or less remotely based on true facts, has poisoned the always-tense relations between working-class whites and blacks, and most acutely between blacks and the police in those big cities with large black populations. Twenty years after the Detroit riot and the Kerner Commission report, the 1988 George Bush campaign's effective use of TV ads blaming Democratic presidential candidate Michael Dukakis for allowing an African American criminal named Willie Horton to leave prison on parole, whereupon he raped one person and murdered another, suggested strongly that at least in some circles white racism was as strong as ever.[64]

A whole string of high-profile cases through the 1990s reinforced the same conclusion. On March 3, 1991, an amateur recorded on videotape the ferocious beating handed out by Los Angeles policemen to an unemployed black man, Rodney King.[65] King was speeding and had recently been released from prison, where he had served a two-year sentence for holding up a grocery store with a tire iron. The camcorder showed King being savagely battered with baseball bats and kicked after being stunned by a "taser," police slang for "Tom Swift's Electric Rifle," an instrument police use to control people being arrested by firing electronic darts into them. Four months later a blue ribbon commission chaired by Warren Christopher, later secretary of state in the Clinton administration, found that racism and the use of excessive force against civilian members of minority groups were routine in the Los Angeles Police Department, a state of affairs neatly summed up in a recorded open computer message from one patrol car to another: "Sounds like it's monkey-slapping."[66]

A few weeks later a seven-year-old black boy, Gavin Cato, was killed in a traffic accident involving a Hasidic Jew in Crown Heights, a Brooklyn neighborhood disputed between African Americans and Hasidic Jews.[67] A crowd of black residents chased Yankel Rosenbaum, who turned out to be a yeshiva student of the Holocaust from Australia, shouting, "There's a Jew! Get him!"[68] Some years later Lemrick Nelson Jr., then aged sixteen, was convicted of stabbing Rosenbaum to death. (Nelson's conviction has been overturned by a court of appeals on constitutional grounds.) Cato's death set off four days of wild rioting in the Brooklyn ghetto.

Two years previously to the day, another sixteen-year-old, Yusuf Hawkins, ventured into the Bensonhurst neighborhood with three friends to buy a secondhand car.[69] He was murdered by three white teenagers. The population there is said to be 65 percent Italian in origin and 25 percent Jewish, and African Americans are so rare that the sight of one brings out overt hostility. In 2001 a student reporter from New York University visited the neighborhood and recorded that on seeing a black teenager a twenty-year-old asked his friends rhetorically, "who's this nigger walking up my block?" One of his friends replied, "I don't know but I saw three niggers on bikes on 18th Avenue before. Let me see them pass by again!"[70]

On April 30 the news broke that the four officers charged with beating Rodney King had been acquitted. The Los Angeles Police Department was taken by surprise at the speed with which rage spread in the city's African American neighborhoods. "Quite frankly," said Daryl Gates, the Los Angeles police chief, "we were overwhelmed."[71] At one point more than 2,000 buildings were on fire, and outraged black youths were attacking firefighters with guns or axes or any other weapons they could lay their hands on." After policemen and firefighters, Korean and other Asian storekeepers were preferred targets.[72]

By the middle 1990s, faced with these repeated and unpredictable outbreaks of mob violence, as well as with a public perception of ever growing violent crime and drug dealing in ghetto neighborhoods, the police and law enforcement agencies generally went on the offensive themselves. In 1996, for example, Amnesty International issued a detailed report on police brutality and excessive use of force by the New York Police Department.[73] It concluded that the large majority of those abused by the police are members of racial minorities, particularly African Americans and people of Latin American descent. Three-quarters of official complaints came from those groups. The report pointed out that after years of attempts to increase the proportion of minorities in the New York police, in 1992 only 11.4 percent of the police were black, compared with 28.7 percent of the general population. Shootings by the New York police actually declined from an average of 63 a year in the early 1970s, but then rose again to 41 in 1990. Altogether 125 civilians were shot dead by the NYPD in 1985 to 1990, only 15 of their killers were charged with criminal offenses.[74] The New York police were by no means the most dangerous to the public, however. Police in Atlanta, Houston, and Kansas City all shot twice as many people as their brethren in New York, and police in Los Angeles and Philadelphia also shot more civilians dead than police in New York, according to the Amnesty report.[75] And over the whole decade from 1990 to 2000 the number of shootings per 1,000 officers was five times higher in Prince George's County, a suburban county immediately east of Washington, D.C., with a large African American population, and three times higher in the District of Columbia itself.[76]

In the 1990s New York's Republican mayor, Rudolf Giuliani, made much of his "zero tolerance" policy on crime, and it is widely accepted that under his mayoralty crime ceased to be the severe problem in New York that it had been for at least twenty years. There is an energetic public and academic debate as to the causes of this reduction in the crime figures. Some attribute it to tough "zero tolerance" policing, some to community policing. But both in New York and elsewhere in the United States tougher police attitudes to criminals, and among them disproportionately to black criminals, were accompanied by a certain ferocity.

In late 1995, Florida became the third state, after Alabama and Arizona, to reintroduce chain gangs.[77] Prisoners were fastened together with a chain attached to their belts and, in at least one case, with ankle shackles. Sheriff Tramel of Columbia County said the purpose was like that of putting offenders in the stocks in the early modern period, "to embarrass them."[78] In 1994 New York officers were all issued 9-millimeter semiautomatic handguns, with a fifteen-round magazine. These weapons, alleged to have a hair-trigger effect, especially after the first shot, may have contributed to a sharp increase in the civil actions brought against New York cops for shooting citizens. Between 1992 and 1995 the city paid out more than $82 million in damages.[79] In February 1999 police mistook Amadou Diallo, an unarmed Guinean street vendor, for a rapist they were pursuing, and shot forty-one rounds at him in seconds, nineteen of which hit, killing the innocent man instantly.[80] Even more shocking for the general public was the case of a Haitian immigrant, Abner Louima, who was unfortunate enough to be arrested in a brawl outside a Brooklyn nightclub.[81] Officers dragged Louima into a precinct bathroom, sodomized him with a broken broomstick, damaging internal organs, then rammed it into his mouth, breaking two teeth with it. In 2001, after four years in which the police covered up a sadistic officer's crime, Louima accepted a settlement of $8.7 million from the city and the Patrolmen's Benevolent Association. Again, New York was not alone in the savagery with which cops sometimes treated suspected criminals, especially if they were blacks and even more so if they were known to be gang members. There have been many allegations that detectives in Area Two, on Chicago's South Side, forced confessions from suspects with torture, including electric shocks to the genitals, asphyxiation, and even the medieval *strappado,* in which a victim is suspended by the arms, then dropped, causing excruciating pain.[82] All reports suggest that African Americans were disproportionately subjected to these assaults and that detectives habitually subjected suspects to racial abuse.

Throughout the 1990s a number of African American politicians, notably the Reverend Alfred Sharpton, skillfully exploited tensions between African Americans, especially those in ghetto neighborhoods, and the white population in general and the police in particular. But the incident that most clearly demonstrated the growing rift in perceptions between blacks and whites was the 1995 murder trial of the football star, O. J. Simpson.

O. J., known as "the Juice," had been a star of authentic magnitude as a football player. He won the Heisman Trophy for the best college player of the year as long ago as 1968, and in his later career with the Buffalo Bills many consider him to have been one of the greatest running backs in the history of pro football, if not indeed the greatest. But he retired in 1979, and when his ex-wife, Nicole Brown, and her friend Ronald Goldman were stabbed to death in 1994, Simpson was returning to obscurity, best known for doing ads for the Hertz car rental firm. His trial for murder lasted for almost the whole of 1995; it was the longest trial ever conducted in California. It cost over $20 million, and more than 150 witnesses were called. It attracted one of the most intense media feeding frenzies in history. Witnesses became better known than the vice president. It is said that 91 percent of the national TV viewing audience watched the trial at one time or another and 142 million people listened on radio or watched on television when the verdict was delivered.[83]

That verdict was that Simpson was not guilty. But the most interesting thing is that it was as if two nations watched two different trials, and two nations responded in diametrically opposite ways to two different verdicts.[84] A large majority of white people were convinced that Simpson was guilty; an even larger majority of black people were sure that he was not.[85] The odd thing is that, though African American, O. J. Simpson was not strongly identified as a black man. He was something of a favorite with white football fans. It has been suggested that many white men reacted against Simpson because they were angry that a "model black man" had let them down.[86] Others, no doubt, were influenced by their resentment at the idea of Simpson having been married to and, according to testimony, having violently abused a younger, blonde wife. That is all speculation. What is certain is that black and white Americans reacted differently, at least in part, because they had different experiences of the criminal justice system. Most white Americans might have criticisms to make of cops, lawyers, courts, or judges. But it is likely that they saw those institutions, at least in principle, as necessary and desirable protection for society, that is, for themselves. The response to the Simpson verdict made it painfully clear that most blacks, however respectable their own lives and however little they might have had personal experience of American justice, did not.

ANDREW HACKER CONCLUDED from his detailed study of the O. J. Simpson trial and of relations between black and white Americans generally that "a huge racial chasm exists, and there are few signs that the coming century will see it closed."[87] There is certainly a rather widespread feeling, on both sides of the racial divide, of weariness, of a bitter disillusion toward attempts to achieve greater equality for black people, of a deep, despairing wish to see the whole tragic dilemma just melt away.

Gerald Boyd, the brilliant African American journalist who was one of the editors of the New York Times series, "How Race Is Lived in America,"[88] told me there were times when he felt so discouraged that he gave up on even attempting to explain to white people how African Americans felt about their history and prospects, and why it mattered. Ellis Cose records a deeply revealing opinion from the college-age daughter of two brilliant and successful African American parents, Stephanie Gilliam. Her mother is a *Washington Post* reporter, her father a successful artist. After graduating from Brown, where she lived mainly with a group of African American students, she told Cose she was not so much angry as surprised to discover how much racism she encountered outside that protected world. "It's almost as if we've given up trying to live together," she said. A poll in 1999 gave a certain confirmation to her feeling. The survey, cosponsored by Zogby International and by the National Association for the Advancement of Colored People found that about half of young adults said racial separation in America was all right "as long as everyone has equal opportunity."[89] The whole thrust of the historic *Brown* decision in 1954 was precisely that equality and segregation are incompatible.

In the 1960s and 1970s, the black and white people of the United States confronted the chasm. Overwhelmingly, blacks wanted to be further integrated into white society. Most whites were happy enough to see that happen, so long as they were not too abruptly confronted with the consequences of change. An influential minority of whites, however, chose to focus not on the aspirations of the well-meaning black majority, but on the minority who did not want to be more closely integrated, or at least who said they did not. Where a majority of whites had supported de jure equality for African Americans, a majority also balked at supporting policies (such as affirmative action) that might produce de facto equality.

The parallel with the history of the women's movement is inescapable. Just as many male Americans, influenced by overtly prejudiced reporting in the media, chose to focus on what they perceived as bizarre and extremist elements in the women's movement, so the white majority, influenced by the style of media coverage, concentrated on what were seen as dangerous aspects of black society. The ordinary hard-working African Americans, a substantial proportion of them beginning to achieve modest and, in some cases, not so modest success, were blotted out by stereotypes: the idler, the mugger, the drug dealer, the welfare queen, the Black Panther.

After thirty-five years and more, the problem is not so much hatred, although there is hatred in some places. It is reciprocal dislike, distrust, and boredom, and the fact that it is becoming acceptable again to voice these feelings. These attitudes are far from universal. But they are common enough that a new Reconstruction, rooted for preference in individual behavior rather than in political movements and government action, is surely overdue.

The United States is hardly unique in having to confront racism. European countries such as Britain and France are hardly much better at dealing with racial prejudice and its social consequences. Even countries like Sweden and Holland, which thought themselves free of the disease, have learned that they were immune only so long as there were few black people in their streets.

In Europe, racism is a legacy of imperialism. In America it is a consequence of slavery. Both were in turn consequences of that extraordinary historical movement we call "the expansion of Europe." It is natural that the victims of those two processes should imagine that racism, in its American or its European form, is somehow inherent in the specifically European heredity. Yet this is not so. Racism appears to be universal. Certainly it is found, in more or less virulent forms, in Africa and in Australia, in China and India, in Russia, in the Middle East and in Latin America, as well as in Europe and North America.

A specific variant of race antagonism has pervaded American history since the days of slavery. Race has profoundly influenced the political and economic geography of the United States from the start. There is no shortage of examples. From the War of 1812 until the Mexican War, territories were admitted as states in rough pairs, one slave, one free: Mississippi in 1817, Illinois in 1818; Alabama in 1819, Maine in 1820; Arkansas in 1836, Michigan in 1837; Florida and Texas in 1845, Iowa in 1846 and Wisconsin in 1848. This was no accident, but the result of conscious attempts, North and South, to keep the balance between states where slavery was legal and free soil. Again, the industrial shape of the country was influenced by the fact that, until after the compromise of 1876, all the transcontinental railroads ran through northern states.

Until the middle of the twentieth century, the South remained as distinct, culturally and politically, from the North as it had been on the day of Emancipation. The relationship between New York and the South remained essentially colonial, with economic power enforcing devices such as discriminatory railroad freight rates to keep the South in its place as a supplier of cheap raw materials and energy. The average incomes of the eleven states of the Old Confederacy trailed the rest of the nation, with exceptions that only proved the rule.

A series of historical events and movements were already at work to change that by 1954, when the Supreme Court handed down its judgment in *Brown*. One was the gradual collapse of the cotton kingdom. By the 1930s cotton had largely gone west, to Arizona and California. Driven by the boll weevil and drawn by high wartime wages, blacks began their vast migration north,[90] which the *Chicago Defender* used to call "the flight out of Egypt." With them, there migrated millions of poor whites from the Deep South and the Appalachians alike, taking their hard attitudes to black people with them.

Two world wars hastened that process. The Cold War helped to transform the once strictly agricultural economy of the South: the one-party system meant that it was southern Democratic chairmen in Washington who began the industrialization of the Sunbelt with air force and navy bases, army camps and aerospace facilities from Cape Canaveral via Huntsville to Houston, from Norfolk by way of Fort Benning and Pensacola to Fort Hood. In the 1970s and 1980s, for the first time, the South boasted metropolitan cities—Charlotte, Miami, Houston, Dallas, Anstin, and preeminently Atlanta—with financial clout, manufacturing industries, and suburban sprawl of their own.

As early as 1973 the Nashville writer John Egerton wrote a book that proclaimed *The Americanization of Dixie: The Southernization of America*.[91] He had something. In 1996 a *New York Times* correspondent in Atlanta at the time, Peter Applebome, made this the theme of his book, *Dixie Rising*, subtitled *How the South Is Shaping American Values, Politics and Culture*.[92] He drummed in his point in enthusiastic paragraphs:

> At a time when a Democratic president like Bill Clinton is coming out for school prayer, going along with sweeping Republican legislation shredding welfare and taking his cues from a consultant, Dick Morris, who formerly worked for southern arch-conservatives like Jesse Helms and Trent Lott; when

race is a fractious national obsession; when the nation's population is steadily moving South; when the Supreme Court is acting as if Jefferson Davis were chief justice; when country music has become America's music of choice and even stock car racing has become a $2 billion juggernaut; when evangelical Christians have transformed American politics; when unions are on the run across the nation much as they have always been in the South; when whites nationwide are giving up on public education just as so many southerners did after integration—in times such as these, to understand America, you have to understand the South.[93]

Culturally, the current was alternating. Country music, the music of the southern white working class, spread nationally.[94] Nascar—stock car racing—once the sport exclusively of southern good ol' boys, was the fastest growing sport in America, "a crossover sports-and-entertainment empire set squarely at the confluence of pop culture, commerce and American mythology,"[95] with a third of the population (half of them women) fans and attendance up by 91 percent since 1990. By 2002 three country music albums opened at number 1 in the charts, including one by Oklahoma-born Toby Keith featuring his patriotic lyric:

> Justice will be served, and the battle will rage
> This big dog will fight when you rattle his cage
> And you'll be sorry that you messed with the US of A
> Cause we'll put a boot in your ass, it's the American way.

The southern passion for sport, including the southern addiction to guns, colonized the north and West.[96] Southern attitudes to the nation, to the military, to labor unions,[97] above all to old-time religion,[98] promoted with a thoroughly modern gift for media and marketing, ceased to be the quaint folkways and belief system of a declining section of the country, presumed doomed to ultimate abolition. They moved into—in some cases, captured—the mainstream.

Conservatism pushed back the liberal orthodoxy that had dominated American politics from the Great Depression and the election of Franklin Roosevelt to the civil rights movement of the 1960s. And conservatism was unmistakably the political ideology of the South. "Most of the prescriptions for change are coming from the South, not the north," wrote Peter

Applebome, "and they are coming almost exclusively from the Right." Although most conservatives would hotly deny it, at the heart of the new conservatism were certain attitudes—to the role of government, to the federal government in particular, to states' rights, to affirmative action, to welfare, to crime and punishment—that were ultimately racial, if not racist, in origin.[99] Many of them were the distinctive beliefs of southern conservatism since Calhoun. That was how, that was why, the ultimate consequence of the civil rights movement was counterintuitive: not to make the South like the north, but to reveal that the north, more than anyone had ever imagined, shared many of the assumptions of the South.

8

New Society

To move to the suburbs is to express a preference for the private over the public.
—*William Schneider, The Suburban Century Begins*

THE GREAT HISTORIAN Richard Hofstadter once said that the turmoil and anguish of the Progressive Era in the early twentieth century could be explained by the fact that the United States was born in the country and had moved to the city.[1] Many of the puzzlements and the frustrations of late-twentieth-century America may be put down to the fact that the United States has now moved out to the suburbs, a type of settlement where great material comfort is often purchased at the cost of loneliness, isolation, and a sense of alienation.

We have looked in some detail at the progress and the disappointments experienced in the last quarter of the twentieth century by three groups—women (especially those who by choice or chance found themselves excluded from the traditional family), immigrants, and African Americans. In aggregate, those three groups exceeded half of the American population. What of the rest, the unpoor, the unblack, the native-born, and the white middle class, male and female?[2]

For them, too, if we look at the whole period from the middle of the 1970s to the end of the century, the overall trend was a steady growth of inequality, briefly interrupted by a recovering confidence and better times from the middle of the 1990s. At the end of the century there was a spike of triumphalism, followed as the new century began by a new time of unease.

Four grand themes define the contradictory forces at work on American society generally between the fall of Richard Nixon and the millennium. The first is the emergence of the suburb as the typical American habitat.[3] The second is the triumph of corporate management, both in its political power and in its influence on society.[4] The third, not unconnected, is the pervasive influence of media, in the widest sense, including news and entertainment cultures that have increasingly penetrated one another.[5] And the last, both cause and consequence of corporate domination, is the increasing recognition of that once supposedly un-American phenomenon, social class, and, in particular, of the spread of financial inequality and educational privilege.[6]

———•◆•———

RAILROADS CONCENTRATE, cars disperse. During the first half of the twentieth century, Americans were moving from farms and small towns into the cities. During the New Deal period, they mostly lived either in town or country. The old norm, of family homesteads clustering more or less close to a small town that offered churches and courthouse, high school, barbershop, and drugstore, was challenged from the beginning of the twentieth century on by the downtown city, with its crowded grid of streets, crowned with a business district of tall skyscrapers, surrounded by a maze of often ethnic neighborhoods.[7]

As late as the New Deal, American politics were to a significant extent the art of accommodating the interests of the cities with the interests of the farmers. "Burn down your cities," said William Jennings Bryan at the Democratic convention of 1896, "and leave our farms, and your cities will spring up again as if by magic; but destroy our farms and the grass will grow in the streets of every city in the country."[8] The cities, as a fashionable exaggeration put it at the time, were "burned down" in the riots of the late 1960s. American agriculture continues to be highly productive, but the Jeffersonian society of owner-farmers and the small towns that served their needs has almost withered away.[9] Bryan and his contemporaries could not have imagined one of the most important demographic shifts of the last quarter of the twentieth century. Both cities and farms have given way to the new American normalcy, that of the suburbs.

Robert Putnam, in his magisterial (if scrupulously inconclusive) study of change in American society, *Bowling Alone*, records the numerical dimensions of this shift[10] and then goes on to draw some intriguing conclusions from them. The Census Bureau divides Americans into three categories in terms of the sort of place where they live. One is those who live outside metropolitan areas, that is, in small towns and in the country. They have declined from 43.9 percent of the population in 1950 to a mere 19.9 percent in 1996.[11] Those who live in the central city of a metropolitan conurbation—in the city of Atlanta, for example, or the city of Detroit, or the five boroughs of New York City—have almost held their own; they have declined only from 32.8 to 30.2 percent. In the meantime, the suburbanites, that is, those who live in a metropolitan area, but not in its core city, have inherited the American earth. Their share in America's population has doubled from 23.3 percent in 1950 to 49.9 percent in 1998[12] and is rising clear past the halfway mark.

This shift—the eclipse of rural and small-town America, the relative marginalization of the city, and the rise and rise of the suburb in all its many forms and varieties—is one of the handful of primary demographic changes that define the America of the present and the near future. It has consequences social, economic, cultural, and, not least, political.

As William Schneider has said, politics has become a conflict between the Democratic cities and the Republican suburbs and the suburbs are winning. "Suburbanization means the privatization of American life and culture," he wrote. "To move to the suburbs is to express a preference for the private over the public."[13]

The rise of the new conservatism, one of the most important political developments of the twentieth century, was essentially a suburban phenomenon. It first gathered strength in the rapidly growing suburbs of southern California, especially in Orange County, around midcentury.[14] While individuals were converted to the new conservatism by ideas percolating down from intellectuals with national reputations like William F. Buckley Jr., Russell Kirk, and Ayn Rand and by national publications like *National Review* and *Human Events*, they were also spread from the grass-roots by spontaneous activism, often over highly local issues, at coffee klatches, school board meetings, bridge clubs, and barbecues. Newly affluent suburbanites, many of them rendered comfortable by the defense and aerospace industries, brought with them, often from the small-town Midwest or the South, traditional religious attitudes and morality. At first they were drawn to conservative activism and then to the Republican Party's conservative wing by fear of communism. In a later phase they were more afraid of such immediate threats to traditional family values as abortion, homosexuality, and pornography, not to mention the supposed threat from lower-class African Americans moving into their neighborhoods. Well before the end of the century, the new conservative suburban culture spread to many parts of the country.

An older set of cultural and political traditions—linked with the particular trajectory of Orange County's economic development, its decentralized spatial organization, its in-migrants, and its powerful entrepreneurs—made it a fertile ground for many manifestations of conservatism, from libertarianism to evangelical Christianity. Similar forces have underwritten the growth of more recent boom regions in the South and West, such as the middle-class communities of Cobb County, Georgia; Scottsdale and the suburbs north of Phoenix, Arizona, in Mariposa County; Fort Worth, Texas, and the suburbs north of Dallas; the affluent suburbs of Jefferson Parish, Louisiana; and Colorado Springs, Colorado, to name just a few.[15]

This was the Sunbelt in the making.

There is an apparent congruence between the growth of suburbs and the trend toward privatization of services, on the one hand, and the growing power of corporate business, as compared with civic, municipal, and public authority. However, the political implications of the move to the suburbs are not necessarily irreversible. There are suburbs and suburbs. Republicans in local, state, and federal governments have prospered by responding to the mood of certain suburbs. But if they ignore the discontents of the less affluent suburbanites, they might have an unpleasant surprise.

——————

ALMOST UNNOTICED, the farmlands were suffering like the cities, though for different reasons.

In 1860, half of all Americans lived on farms. In 1900, in grandfather's time for baby boomers, 39 percent still lived on farms. Between 1940 and 1960 the number living on farms fell by one-half, from 30.8 million to 15.6 million.[16] By 2000, only 1.5 percent lived on farms, despite massive federal subsidies to the remaining farmers—or, more precisely, to a comparatively small number of large farmers.[17] Altogether, it is estimated that the federal government pays $23 billion a year in direct subsidies to farmers, more than it pays for primary and secondary education put together, and far more than it pays in foreign aid.[18] At the same time, thousand of family farmers leave the land every year, and thousands more only hang on in a despairing loyalty to the farm that has been the family home for generations.

Dependent on farming were the small towns that were in many ways the archetypal American settlement from the 1850s to the 1950s. The strengths and weaknesses of their tight community life in its diverse variants were the subject of countless classics of American literature, theater, and film, from Sinclair Lewis to William Faulkner, from Thornton Wilder's *Our Town* to the movies of Frank Capra.

The productivity of American farming is legendary and continues to improve, thanks to new machinery, new pesticides and herbicides, and new, often genetically modified, seed. Yet this technological revolution is beyond the reach of many family farmers. The average income in McPherson County, Nebraska, for example, classic corn-and-pigs family farm country, was under $4,000 in 1997, the last year for which numbers are available.[19]

The farm crisis began in the 1970s, in part, counterintuitively, as a result of the Nixon administration's successful sales of grain to the Soviet Union. Many farmers overexpanded and got heavily into debt; the total of farm debt quadrupled between 1970 and 1985. The result was a wave of foreclosures, and by the middle 1980s, by some accounts, a thousand family farms were being sold every week.[20] At the same time, large farms, whether corporations, partnerships, or sole proprietors, were in a position to invest in new technology and expand at the expense of weak family farmers. Corporations own only 2 percent of American farms, but they dominate most kinds of farming, both on the input side (sales of machinery, seed, and agrichemicals) and in output. Four companies, for example, control 80 percent of United States beef production.[21]

In 1996 Congress, supported in this by the Clinton administration, proposed a dramatic reform intended to end the absurdity of billions of subsidy dollars going to the farmers who needed it least. In a supreme example of the law of unintended consequences, the reform legislation, known as the Freedom to Farm Act, simply made things much worse. Although the idea was to eliminate subsidies over seven years, the legislation made poor farmers ever more dependent on subsidies, while benefiting the rich farmers. By 1999, for example, four out of five farmers in North Dakota were receiving federal subsidy.[22] Yet only 12 percent of the regal subsidy handouts were going to the bottom two-thirds of all farms. Instead of reforming the system, once influential farm lobbyists in Washington and powerful farm interests in the states had gotten to the congressmen, the legislation increased subsidies instead of cutting them and made big farmers bigger still.

More than a generation ago a cotton farmer in the Mississippi Delta said to me that where his daddy had farmed the land, he farmed the corridors of Washington.[23] In 1999 the Environmental Working Group published a report on *The Cash Croppers* confirming that he was not alone.[24] It showed that between 1985 and 1994 the federal government paid out $108.9 billion in farm subsidies. Just 2 percent of all recipients, or about 60,000 corporations, partnerships, and individual farmers, received 26.8 percent of those payments. Some made even more than official U.S. Department of Agriculture figures show because "Mississippi Christmas Tree" paper farms were crafted by lawyers to take maximum advantage of loopholes. Many of these recipients will not even be required to farm a single acre of land; to qualify for payments it will be enough that they received them in the past. It is hard to imagine an arrangement more in conflict both with traditional American ideas of fairness and self-reliance or with modern free-market conservative ideology.

So, as a result of legislation intended to cut out boondoggles and save expenditures, the top 2 percent of recipients of federal largesse, corporate farmers and big partnerships or individual agribusinessmen, stood to receive an average of $281,000 each, to a total of almost $8 billion. Some 368 of these big farmers would receive a million or more each, with no obligation to do any farming; 47 of them, it is calculated, would be eligible to receive more than $2 million, and 7, more than $3 million apiece.

Interestingly, in view of the South's strength in Congress, not to mention this writer's thesis about the increased power and influence of the South nationally, while princely payments under Freedom to Farm will be going to big wheat, corn, and stock farmers in the Midwest and elsewhere, some of the very biggest winners are rice farmers from Texas and Louisiana (864 of them) and something under 3,000 upland cotton farmers, who will make almost $60,000 a year each in federal subsidy for the next seven years. Many of the biggest operators in Mississippi will make more than $1 million each over seven years. This is an ironic commentary on the South's often professed hostility to government intervention.

In the summer of 2001, for the fourth year in succession, Congress voted an additional $4.6 billion for Freedom to Farm, known to small farmers as "Freedom to Fail." More than half the money ($2.4 billion) is expected to go to just twenty congressional districts, headed, of course, by those represented by members of the House Agricultural Committee.

All in all, Freedom to Farm is not a bad symbol of what is happening in politics and in the economy. The incremental wealth created by technological innovation and enterprise is being appropriated in the main by a small elite of corporations and by the already wealthy. Small operators are being squeezed out. Safety nets devised since the New Deal to reduce inequality are being abolished in the name of eliminating waste. The money intended to go to the less well-off goes to those who need it least. Overall, in the name of ending "taxing and spending," government spends as much as ever. The bulk of the money, however, goes not to those who need help most but to well-heeled and well-represented constituents. On the farm, as elsewhere in American life, inequality has increased, is increasing, and ought to be diminished.

———◆———

"THE UNITED STATES," wrote the architectural journalist Philip Langdon in 1994,

> has become a predominantly suburban community but not a very happy one. Today more than three-quarters of the American people live in metropolitan areas, and more than two-thirds of those live in suburbs. Each year development pushes out across more than a million acres. . . . The problem is not

simply that a sensible person can no longer believe in the rightness of turning huge expanses of farmland, forest, desert and other rural landscapes into additional suburbs. The problem is that the suburbs we build are fostering an unhealthy way of life.[25]

Langdon quotes a number of the new town planners who share his view that the effects of unregulated suburbanization have been bad, not just aesthetically or for the environment, but even for the people who travel hours a week in search of "a better place to live." Architect and town planner Peter Calthorpe argues that the close-knit towns of the past provided the potential for collective action and for connections among people of different economic and social classes. Now that compact, multiclass communities are being replaced by single-class suburbs, Calthorpe believes that the result is class division and mutual incomprehension. "Culturally and socially we are split into groups that oppose one another," he says. "People feel isolated and alienated." The husband-wife team of suburban planners Andres Duany and Elizabeth Plater-Zyberk (both incidentally refugees from communist countries, he from Cuba, she from Poland) say essentially the same thing. Community and public well-being are in jeopardy.

It should be said that the views of such "new urbanist" and other critics are by no means universally shared. Tens of millions of Americans, in Lenin's phrase, have "voted with their feet" for the suburbs because they appreciate what suburbs have to offer. Some, like the Demographia consultancy, call themselves "pro-choice" and stress the freedom people have to choose a suburb that suits their life-style. A balanced view comes from the Princeton scholar, J. Eric Oliver, who has analyzed the large 1989–90 Civic Participation Study.[26]

Suburbanization has affected many aspects of personal and social interaction. Yet, in Oliver's view, the consequences of those changes are not well understood. He suggests a tentative conclusion: that while in theory suburbanization offers great promise for American democracy, if only because the units of government are smaller, in practice political fragmentation often encourages higher levels of social segregation. He points out that some suburban communities—he mentions New Rochelle, New York, as an example—do combine the cohesion of a small town with the social diversity of a large city.

It is important to understand the diversity of the American communities lumped together as "suburbs." The Census Bureau recognizes 405 "urbanized areas" in the United States, each of which contains up to several dozen suburbs. Some are wealthy, some impoverished, some Arcadian, some devastated by industrial pollution and decay. Some have roots in long-established small towns, others have sprung up like mushrooms as a result of real estate development.

Even before the beginning of the twentieth century, there were suburbs. Well-to-do families had started moving out to suburbs like those on Long Island Sound and in Westchester County, near New York City, or the Main Line in Philadelphia, or other places where suburban trains could carry a man from his downtown office to a spacious family house where his wife and children enjoyed fresh air and outdoor sports.

In the 1950s suburbs ceased to be the preserve of the well-to-do. Part of the democratization of economic life after World War II was the Levittown phenomenon. Developers and builders, helped by cheap loans and government subsidies, built more modest suburbs for office and factory workers, and the federal funding of roughly 90 percent of the Interstate Highway System in the 1950s accelerated the movement to the suburbs.[27] The highways might have been justified as making it possible to move troops from one side of the continent to the other; their main purpose turned out to be the morning commute into downtown.

It happened in every section of the country: around New York and Miami, Chicago and Saint Louis, Atlanta and Houston, Denver and Seattle. But nowhere was the rush to the suburbs more headlong than in California, where Los Angeles used to be called "nineteen suburbs in search of a metropolis."[28] The San Fernando Valley filled up with suburban communities for the new workers brought out to the West Coast by the defense and aerospace industries, and the same movement girdled San Francisco Bay, where the completion of the Golden Gate and the Bay Bridge in the late 1930s had opened a hinterland.[29] Throughout the 1950s, suburban living, made possible by the freeway, the supermarket, and the suburban shopping mall and reinforced by zoning and tax regimes that gave strong incentives to move out to the suburbs, became more and more the norm.

In the 1960s and especially in the 1970s, these long-established demographic trends were reinforced by white flight. The classic instance was

Detroit. In 1950 its booming automobile and related industries employed hundreds of thousands of white workers, many of them of eastern or southern European "ethnic" origins, and the city had grown from modest origins in the 1900s to be the fourth most populous in the nation. Only 16 percent of the city's population was black. By 1990 African Americans made up three-quarters of the population, which had shrunk from a peak of 2.2 million to little over 1 million.

Those missing white people had not volatilized. They had moved across the city limits into the rapidly growing communities of Macomb and other surrounding counties. In Atlanta, Washington, Baltimore, and most other large American cities, the same thing had happened. Baltimore, for example, was less than one-quarter black in 1950, but almost 60 percent black by 1990. Even more striking, perhaps, was the dramatic increase in the African American population of northern cities where there had never been more than a small black community. The black population of Boston, for example, rose from 5 percent in 1950 to more than 25 percent in 1990, and in New York City from under 10 percent to almost 30 percent.

These rapid demographic changes, of course, had dramatic effects on the cities. Crime increased sharply, at least until the mid-1990s. So did the percentage of single-parent families. White families who could afford it, in cities like New York and Washington, almost abandoned the public school system. Urban politics, once in practice barred to blacks, became something like a black monopoly, with black mayors elected at different times in New York, Los Angeles, Chicago, Detroit, Cleveland, Gary, Atlanta, and Washington.

Even more significant was the change wrought by white flight to the suburbs themselves. They became less homogeneous, and more inclusive. They became multipurpose areas, with office and industrial employment opportunities as well as huge shopping malls and residential accommodations of every kind. Once the word "suburban" had connotations of social splendor, so much so that in the 1950s manufacturers called their fancier station wagons "suburban." Now there were cheap single-family homes, studio apartments, and settlements for singles, gay men, senior citizens, and many different ethnic communities.

They were, however, not mixed up together, as they had been in the traditional city, but divided into socially homogeneous clusters. In effect, suburban homes were segregated by income. "Our society is fraught with many different types of segregation—by race, class, by how recently one has immigrated," writes one of the nation's most respected authorities on planning, "but for the first time we are experiencing ruthless segregation by minute gradations of income. . . . One need only attempt to build a $200,000 house on an empty lot in a $350,000 cluster; the homeowners' association will immediately sue."[30]

Once, immigrants had congregated in inner-city neighborhoods like the Lower East Side or Brooklyn in New York, Charlestown and the North End in Boston, South Philadelphia, or Back of the Yards in Chicago. By the later years of the twentieth century, the new immigrants were leapfrogging these traditional reception areas and heading straight for the suburbs, opening restaurants, small markets, and service businesses of many kinds right where people who could afford to pay were living. The reason was simple: two-thirds of new jobs are in the suburbs, while three-quarters of welfare recipients live in the inner city or in rural areas.[31]

A 2002 report by the Lewis Mumford Center for Comparative Urban and Regional Research in Albany, New York, shows how radically the ethnic composition of suburbs is being transformed by population trends in all the 330 metropolitan areas in the United States. In 1990, only 18 percent of the suburban population was African American. By 2000 that figure had risen to 25 percent. The number of black suburban dwellers grew rapidly, up 38 percent, while the proportion of Hispanics in the suburbs grew by 72 percent and that of Asians by 84 percent. Blacks are more than 20 percent of the population in the suburbs of Atlanta, Washington, Richmond, and New Orleans. Hispanics are 55.8 percent of the suburban population in Miami and 44.7 percent in Los Angeles. The Asian population is more than 10 percent of suburban residents in San Francisco and Oakland; Los Angeles and Orange County; and in the Middlesex-Somerset-Hunterdon area of northern New Jersey. While whites continue to be the most suburban of major ethnic groups, with 71 percent living in the suburbs, more than half of Asians (58 percent) live in suburbs, and nearly half of Hispanics (49 percent).

Once, too, suburbs had been largely dormitories. But by the 1980s areas like King of Prussia outside Philadelphia, the suburbs on Route 128 around Boston, and at Tyson's Corner near Washington, not to mention countless other districts of Houston, Denver, Minneapolis, Atlanta, the Bay Area, southern California, Seattle, or San Diego, had become places of work, with high-rise office buildings and low-rise shopping, warehousing, and research facilities. A new term was coined for them: they were not suburbs but "edge cities."[32] Where once congestion arose from the daily heartbeat of commuters in and out of the city center, now suburban traffic was as much across town as in and out. Metropolitan areas captured nearly 90 percent of the nation's employment growth; and much of this growth occurred in these booming edge cities.

By 1990 many of these edge cities had more office space and retail sales than their respective downtowns. The arrival of the Discovery Channel headquarters in the Washington suburb of Silver Spring, for example, has attracted dozens of film industry and service companies to the previously residential and retail neighborhood.[33] Moreover, immigrants, who once huddled together in inner-city areas, increasingly headed straight for edge city suburbs where they thought they would be able to press on with their ambitions with less interference than downtown.

If suburbs of all kinds claimed to offer individuals irresistible advantages, from cleaner air to better schools and lower taxes, from a community or social perspective the move carried a high price. A 1999 report by the Brookings Institution pinpointed the problems caused by the suburban sprawl of Washington, D.C.[34] The report concluded that the region's "explosive growth" had come at a severe social cost. "The Washington region is divided by race, income, jobs and opportunity. The problems of hyper growth on the one hand and social distress on the other are intertwined." Poor schools in one community drove families to move, causing overcrowding elsewhere and erosion of the tax base in the community they left.

At the same time, two cities as far apart as Milwaukee and Salt Lake City were adopting opposite solutions to the same problem of suburban sprawl.[35] While workers poured concrete to double the lanes of traffic on the highway approaching Salt Lake along the front of the Wasatch Mountains, Milwaukee was tearing down a half-built section of highway that would have cut through the center of the city. "The urban superhighway should be relegated to the scrap heap of history," said Milwaukee's mayor, John O. Norquist. "We have all this experience over the last twenty years," from Los Angeles to Atlanta to Phoenix, says Keith Bartholomew of the University of Utah, "that shows that building and widening freeways do not solve our traffic problems." Yet Utah Governor Leavitt says he has no choice: "as many as 97 percent of the population will not use mass transit." "Report: 98 Percent of U.S. Commuters Favor Public Transportation for Others, gibed the online satirical magazine, the *Onion*."[36]

Nowhere is growth more explosive, highway building more intensive, and the problems of suburban sprawl more intractable than in Atlanta, which now claims the national sprawl title over Los Angeles, measured by low population density.[37] (Greater Atlanta has only 1,370 people per square mile, as against 5,400 in Los Angeles.) Only 427,000 of the 3.2 million people who live in metropolitan Atlanta live in the city. The result is measured in traffic congestion, long and tedious commutes, air pollution, and sixty-nine smog-alert days in 1999. Atlanta's air is now so bad that the federal Environmental Protection Agency has threatened to pull all federal money for highway building there.

Atlanta illustrates the problem of sprawl in its starkest form. Local politicians, environmental experts, and activists are increasingly aware that Atlantans will simply have to change their habits; yet there is very little sign that they will do so. The population of Gwinnett County, only twenty years ago a deeply rural area with plantation houses amid unspoilt woodland and pasture, has tripled in twenty years. There is still absolutely no public transportation in the county, which has just allowed developers to build a mall on 100 acres with shopping for 8,600 cars.

By the 1990s, in fact, the suburbs had become the normal and perhaps also the normative American environment. Except in a handful of cities, notably New York, San Francisco, and Boston, and in a few dozen college towns, they had come to dominate the cultural assumptions of the majority. And that brought with it new political power. In 1960, voters in the city of Chicago cast 35 percent of the statewide vote in Illinois, and the suburbs cast 20 percent. By 1996, the city was down to 20 percent of the vote, and the suburbs voted 40 percent. Similar figures apply to New York, Philadelphia, Boston, and Detroit.[38] Only twenty-five years ago, there were roughly equal numbers of urban, suburban, and rural districts in the House of Representatives. Now suburban districts outnumber urban districts by two to one, and rural districts by three to one.

Suburbanization is not only changing where Americans live. It is also transforming how they live, their view of the world, and what they believe in as well. The new political power of the suburbs helps to explain the "new federalism" policies of the Nixon, Reagan, and George H. W. Bush administrations. It translates into lower budgets for education, transportation, welfare and public services generally in inner cities, with the inevitable consequences in social and physical decay.

Increasingly, however, critics are beginning to point out that the suburbs do not by any means always deliver the enviable living conditions their developers are so good at promising to those who can afford to live there. Earlier in the twentieth century, highly successful suburbs—Chicago's Oak Park, Philadelphia's Main Line, Washington's Cleveland Park, and Boston's Brookline among them—grew on the stem, so to speak, of railroads or streetcar lines. But Henry Ford already saw that the automobile would transform suburbs. "We shall solve the city problem," he said, "by leaving the city." And that is what Americans in their tens of millions did.

The suburbs of the last quarter of the twentieth century were built by the automobile and for the automobile. Their inhabitants have become servants of the automobile and all too often find themselves imprisoned in virtually immobile automobiles. The average speed on the Los Angeles freeways is predicted to fall to eleven miles an hour, by coincidence roughly the average speed of horse-drawn traffic in New York City before the invention of the automobile.[39] Hundreds of thousands of Californians get up at five o'clock or even earlier each morning in the hope of beating rush hour traffic. Many average four hours a day and even more of commuting. The phenomenon has given rise to urban legends, like that of "the Owl," a defense contractor's employee in southern California, who sleeps in his automobile in the company car park four nights a week to avoid a four hour, 110-mile commute.[40]

The most obvious victims of the automobile suburbs are the 80 million Americans who are either too old, too young, or too poor to drive.[41] Many of the poor cannot get to the suburbs, either to live or to work. They find themselves trapped in inner-city neighborhoods that increasingly lack facilities and amenities as commercial enterprises head for the suburbs and city tax bases are eroded. But even "normal," middle-class Americans can be victims of the suburbs too. They include commuters like the Owl, women who work "at work," work at home, and drive hours between the two; soccer moms who spend their lives driving kids; and teenagers themselves who are unable to reach recreational facilities until they have a driver's license and find there is nowhere to hang out but the mall. One should not exaggerate. Many millions find a good life in the suburbs. But many millions more do not.

What has been little noticed is that the suburbs are not, as is sometimes suggested, the entirely voluntary product of myriads of individual decisions permitted by free-market capitalism. They have been created with the help of massive government subsidies, especially of highways. They have been shaped for the benefit of developers by governmental fiat and in particular by local zoning regulations. Above all, the whole movement to the suburbs has been willed, controlled, and conditioned by what collectively can be seen as the most powerful lobby in American history and by the decisions of politicians beholden to or frightened of it. This megalobby brings together the automobile and tire manufacturers, highway builders, and oil companies, as well as home building, retail, and real estate interests.

This coalition may be loosely defined, but it wields immense clout, and has been able to procure massive subsidies. The most obvious is the 90 percent of the cost of interstate highways that is paid by the federal government. Home builders and developers have enjoyed numerous other subsidies. It has been calculated that government subsidies for highways and parking amount to 8–10 percent of the GNP, the equivalent of a fuel tax of \$3.50 a gallon.[42] Given this level of government intervention, the choice for individuals and families who move to the suburbs is eminently rational in economic terms. It may not work out for them in terms of individual happiness, but as a matter of public policy the level of (largely concealed) government subsidies is distorting and wasteful.

The interstate highway system was originally conceived, by pioneer planners like Norman Bel Geddes, as "the townless highway linking highwayless towns." Instead, comment Duany, Plater-Zyberk, and Speck, "this country has allowed the exact opposite to occur. . . . Highways were routed directly through the centres of our cities, eviscerating whole neighborhoods—often, African American neighborhoods—and splitting downtowns into pieces. Meanwhile the commercial strip attached itself like a parasite to the highway between cities, impeding the traffic and blighting the countryside in the process."[43]

The consequence of the way highways have been allowed to stray through cities and act as arteries for the daily ebb and flow of suburban commuting, instead of linking discrete cities, is that dominant cultural phenomenon of American life at the end of the second millennium, the suburban strip. Many writers have pointed out the destructive conse-quences of suburban shopping strips.[44] They distort commercial rents so that local enterprises, especially small businesses, are steamrolled by na-tional chains. They suck economic life out of the old city and town centers, substituting for the community life of the old small town automobile shop-ping in impersonal malls. They are directly responsible for the sad state of many once bustling small-town downtowns. They have damaged and in some cases destroyed communities and civil society.

"At the root of what's wrong with the suburbs," Philip Langdon judges, "is an overreliance on business and money-making."[45] Whether that is ac-cepted or not, it is certainly true that the suburbs have been very largely developed by private enterprise with a minimum of public planning and government regulation, albeit with massive, largely hidden government subsidies. As a consequence, the very fabric of people's lives, the homes where couples bring up their families, the pattern of everyday encounters, has been arranged to suit the interests of private developers. This is espe-cially true in some of the fastest-growing regions of the country, for exam-ple, in California, Texas, and Florida and in the Southwest generally. The result is that the architecture of individual homes, the layout of whole neighborhoods, and even some entire cities have been designed with marketing in mind. In individual homes, this has led to an excessive pro-portion of budgets being spent on the first impression the house makes on a prospective purchaser; and whole suburban developments have been turned inside out so that attractive communal features (parks, golf courses, community centers, and so on) are located where they can be seen from the highway, not where they are most convenient for the inhabitants.

Worst of all, although there is substantial hard survey evidence that this is not what people say they want, developers have made market segmen-tation the basic goal of their designs.[46] Homes are segregated by income and also by "life-style" into "clusters" or "pods." Wealthy people live in neighborhoods where everyone is wealthy, retired folks with other retired folks, "singles" with singles, and minorities with minorities. Like the bad

old division of small towns by the railroad tracks, this "market segmenta-
tion" is nothing other than segregation by race, caste, and class. It is not
yet universal. But in many of the newer suburbs and in whole sections of
the country it is becoming dominant. The Lewis Mumford Center concludes that "where most minority groups members live . . . segregation is
higher *and* more unyielding over time, and minority population growth is
more likely to be associated with the creation or intensification of ethnic
enclaves. Minority suburbs tend to be poorer, less safe, and less capable of
supporting quality public services."[47]

———•◆•———

SEVERAL EMINENT HISTORIANS have sought to interpret the history of the
United States in terms of cycles of one kind of another. One of the most
plausible cyclical theories would be one that saw business dominance as
the norm, or default, and noted how, at intervals of a generation or so, the
reign of the business oligarchs was interrupted by prairie fires lit by anger
at their real or supposed failures.

Thus businessmen and their political advocates or nominees were in
the ascendant in the so-called Gilded Age. Their perceived rascality and
arrogance, coupled with the loss of prestige occasioned by the economic
crises of the 1890s and the panic of 1908, set the scene for the Progressive
Era.

Business returned to the throne in the 1920s, and again in the 1950s. But
businessmen were so seriously discredited by the Great Depression of
1929 that they were exiled from government until the 1950s, when a chairman of General Motors, ensconced in a Republican president's cabinet
largely composed of major corporate executives, expressed as self-evident
truth that what was good for America was good for General Motors. Many
people thought he really meant to say it the other way round.[48]

The failures of big business and its political representatives in the 1950s
were not so much failures of competence—the economy prospered on
the whole in the Eisenhower years—as failures of sensitivity. Business hegemony was shaken in the 1960s by the perceived dullness of the man in the
gray flannel suit. It was also discredited by perceived corporate indifference to the frustrations of women, of the young, and of minorities, and by
real corporate carelessness of the environment. "Do not spindle, fold or

mutilate," was one of the slogans of the 1960s Berkeley students, in mockery of the instruction on the IBM Hollerith cards used in the early mainframe computers.

Richard Nixon's paper-thin victory in the 1968 presidential election, and even more his near landslide in 1972, signaled that public irritation with the rebels of the 1960s had grown stronger than public mistrust of the executive class. In political terms, a hard swing of the political pendulum to the right, due in 1972–73, was delayed for a few years by Watergate. But by the mid-1970s, the conservative revolution that was in the offing was to a significant extent the return, and the revenge, of the businessmen.

It may be that the collapse of the Internet boom, if it leads to a significant recession in the early twenty-first century, will provide the opportunity for another revolt against business hegemony. At the time of writing, it looks as if that revolt has been postponed by the conservative response to September 11 and by the war in Iraq. In the meantime, it has to be said that the twenty years from the fall of Jimmy Carter to the election of George W. Bush was an era of popularity, even adulation, for business and businessmen without parallel since the 1920s. It should be added (because there are few statements that can be made about America whose contradictions are not almost equally true) that this era of business hegemony and admiration of enterprise was also an era of considerable cynicism about business and also a golden age for suing businesses for any and every shortcoming.

Corporate profitability fell slowly over the 1950s and 1960s, then abruptly in the 1970s and the early 1980s. One manufacturing sector after another found itself unable to compete consistently with foreign companies, at first in Europe, then in Japan and in some industries in Korea. From the 1970s on, U.S. corporate managers began to respond with tough, even ruthless new policies. Whereas in the 1960s corporations wanted to give the impression that they were offering their workers, and middle managers, a job for life with regular promotions and increasing remuneration, now managements were determined to be masters in their own houses. The Reagan administration gave them deregulation and an example of tough confrontation in the case of the air traffic controllers.

A whole vocabulary of euphemisms for hard-edged management techniques came into fashion: outsourcing, downsizing, restructuring.[49] Outsourcing often meant buying in parts or partly finished materials from countries where wage levels were far lower than in the United States: Mexico, above all, but also the Philippines, Taiwan, even obscure places like Madagascar and the Andaman Islands, once British prison colonies off the Indian coast. Downsizing was often a euphemism for shedding workers, or for selling off less profitable operations.

The 1980s marked a shift in the balance of economic power from the manufacturing sector to the financial sector. When money is short, the man who has some rules the roost. There was also a power shift from employees generally, especially unionized industrial workers, to top managers and to a lesser degree to (big) shareholders. Of course, top managers themselves were major shareholders, all the more so as the habit of rewarding them with stock options enabled them to build up far greater personal wealth than even the highest salaried executives of the 1950s.

Executive salaries and perks, ostensibly intended to provide incentives for hard work, talent, and responsibility, became increasingly the prerogative of what was in effect a caste. Top executives, sitting on each other's remuneration committees, agreed what fine fellows they were and how richly they deserved to be rewarded, even if only for gallant failure. The ratio between the pay of average workers and remuneration packages, as they were delicately called, of top executives grew steadily. "The face of American capitalism has changed," the *Newsweek* economic commentator Robert J. Samuelson has written. "It is less protective and more predatory. It no longer promises ultimate security or endless entitlement. Instead it preaches the inevitability of change, implying that change is often cruel."[50] The corollary is that the mind-set of the corporate executive class has itself become cruel. It takes responsibility now chiefly for shareholders, that is, to a far greater extent than it would have us believe, for its own members. In the process it is recklessly increasing inequality, and dividing American society as it has not been divided since before the Great Depression. A few examples will serve as reminders of the extraordinary empire of money that results from the general application of the free-market capitalist model to all aspects of life.

——•◆•——

FROM THE NIXON YEARS ON, everything was business. In politics, the Supreme Court's decision in *Buckley v. Valeo* (1976) established that political contributions were in effect a form of "speech," and so protected by the First Amendment. The restrictions on political contributions and expenditures in federal legislation "necessarily reduce the quantity of expression by restricting the number of issues discussed, the depth of the exploration, and the size of the audience reached. This is because virtually every means of communicating ideas in today's mass society requires the expenditure of money." Such restrictions on political speech could only be justified by an overriding governmental interest.[51] This judgment, hamstringing attempts to limit campaign expenditure,[52] coincided with a steady upward march in the level of political contributions, and so with an apparently irresistible rise in the political power of money. There is also the enormous amount of money spent by business lobby groups in Washington. Clever, experienced operatives have figured out countless ways of influencing the political process in their clients' favor. Sometimes this takes the form of inducing politicians to take a certain view by the classic inducements: entertaining, schmoozing, campaign contributions. Sometimes, more subtly, it means supplying busy, none-too-well-informed politicians with ready-made arguments, something that the Heritage Foundation has done with great skill from a conservative point of view. Sometimes it means setting the agenda.

There is very little vote buying, says Doug Bailey, who runs the Hotline for *National Journal*, a specialized magazine about government, based in Washington, D.C. It is rare for candidates to trade their soul. What money buys is access, in an ever busier and more crowded political arena.[53] The Enron scandal of 2001 put this issue squarely before media and public. So deeply has public acceptance of the omnipotence of money entered into the culture that many commentators had difficulty in seeing what was wrong with a situation where a businessman who claimed (and had probably substantially invented) profits in the billions could claim special access and special attention from politicians, including the president and vice president of the United States.

Most of all, especially in electoral politics, money buys TV. Television, says Doug Bailey, has been "a major contributor to the screwing up of our politics." The need for money to buy television spots condemns politicians to make themselves available to contributors, and especially to the people who can deliver other people's money. An enormous proportion of a politician's time is mortgaged to fundraisers and major contributors. Such electoral finance law as has been enacted makes the person who can deliver 500 donors of $1,000 each extraordinarily important.[54] John Podesta, President Clinton's White House chief of staff, spoke to me of the unintended consequences of attempts at campaign finance reform.[55] The intention may have been to reduce the influence of interest groups, he said; the effect has been to increase their influence. Business groups have funded conservative politicians in a more substantial and focused way. In general, politicians and political operatives, at least from the moderate Republican center-right to the liberal fringe, agree with an unusual degree of unanimity that money, the need for it and the quantities sloshing around both in Washington and in major campaigns, has had a seriously troubling effect.

Not the least of these consequences has been the professionalization of politics. There have always been political professionals in Washington and in the more important state capitals. But only in the last quarter of a century has a whole political industry come into existence.

———◆———

IN AN AGE of business hegemony, whose motto is "If you're so smart, why ain't you rich?" not just politics but almost every aspect of American life has become a business. Religion is organized as a business more than ever before, and uses many of the techniques of business: advertising, marketing, the ethos and organizational discipline of sales. As many Americans are both sincerely religious and very well-off financially, both legitimate and disreputable religious organizations have been able to attract fabulous sums.

Television evangelists used their broadcasts to rake in the shekels. Jim and Tammy Bakker, of the PTL network and Heritage USA, are estimated to have made off with $70 million before their efforts collapsed in scandal in 1987.[56] That was then, but in late 2001 the *Los Angeles Times* reported that two more television evangelists, Jan and Paul Crouch, of the Costa Mesa–based Trinity Broadcasting Network, have purchased a palatial Newport Beach house for close to $5 million, with ocean views, "nine bathrooms, a billiard room, a climate-controlled wine cellar, a sweeping staircase and a crystal chandelier."[57] Specialist brokers advertise their ability to lend money to churches at favorable rates.

Major church groups count their investments in billions. Of course, money is needed for church operations, for building new churches, and not least for providing incomes and decent pensions for priests and ministers. The ethical investment movement, too, was growing in our period, with many funds avoiding investment in tobacco, liquor, armaments, or other industries objectionable to religious bodies. Still, the sheer size of church investments is impressive. The Church of Latter Days Saints (Mormons), for example, was reported in 1997 to have $30 billion in assets, including a 300,000 acre cattle ranch in Florida and about $6 billion in income, $5.2 billion in "tithings" (member contributions), and the rest mostly from investments. At the end of the millennium, a time for ecclesiastical stocktaking if ever there was one, the United Methodist Church had $12.6 billion in investments. The investment funds of the U.S. Episcopal Church's Church Pension Group in the United States grew by $2.2 billion, or 52 percent in fiscal 2000, truly an "astonishing performance," as the church's official report called it. Among Catholic institutions, the Christian Brothers Investment Services Inc. managed a portfolio of investment funds for Catholic institutional investors, some described as "aggressive," worth $2.4 billion at the end of 1999.

The financial position of the Roman Catholic Church is hard to calculate, both because it is not notable for transparency and because it is decentralized. The annual revenues of the 18,500 Roman Catholic parishes in America total about $7.5 billion, according to Joseph Harris, the financial officer of a Seattle-based charity which has surveyed one parish in six nationwide.[58] In addition, the 194 Catholic dioceses have their own revenues, made up of a tithing of parish revenues, fund-raising, bequests, and earnings on endowments and investments, including substantial real estate holdings.[59] The Archdiocese of Chicago, for example, had a budget of $996 million in 2001, and the Archdioceses of New York and Boston, and perhaps others, have comparable resources. This wealth is seriously threatened, however, by revelations of widespread sexual misconduct and abuse. At least 300 civil lawsuits alleging sexual abuse by clergy have already been filed, and more are possible. More than 200 priests have been removed from their duties. Dioceses have made secret payments, in one case of as much as $450,000. They also face court judgments. In 1995 the Archdiocese of Santa Fe had to meet abuse settlements estimated at more than $30 million, and in 1997 the Diocese of Dallas had to mortgage property to meet a $30 million abuse settlement. Lawyers are aggressively pursuing numerous suits, and insurers have succeeded in avoiding paying out where criminal behavior was hidden by church officials. While parishioners' giving has not yet been dramatically reduced, many larger donors are very unhappy. Some dioceses, like the Archdiocese of Boston, facing at least eighty-six claims by victims, may be seriously damaged financially. A heavy share of the burden will fall upon poor Catholics, for whom charity giving will be reduced. The church, however, will no doubt remain a vastly wealthy institution.

There is nothing new about the affluence of American churches: Theodore Dreiser denounced it with notable passion in 1926.[60] But in the last quarter of the twentieth century the churches, and especially the big, fast-growing evangelical congregation churches of the South and West, were organized like businesses, with multimillion-dollar budgets, business plans, investments, advertising, and marketing programs. First Baptist Church of Dallas, for example, owns a dozen buildings in downtown Dallas, including two colleges, a research library, racquetball courts, a basketball arena, and much besides.[61] Financial solvency is perhaps not incompatible with spirituality, though there is biblical authority that it is easier for a camel to go though the eye of a needle than for a rich man to enter the kingdom of heaven. But some of the most characteristic of late-twentieth-century American churchmen seemed to stress the temporal aspects of their undoubted success at the expense of the spiritual ones.

——•◆•——

MOST PROFESSIONS moved in the direction of becoming businesses in the last quarter of the twentieth century. Lawyers, in particular, found themselves under intense competitive pressures to make revenue, rather than service, their priority. This development is worrying thoughtful lawyers even at the heart of the American Bar Association itself. "Probably the most significant change accompanying the huge growth has been the evolution from law as a profession to law as a business," wrote Terry Carter in the *American Bar Association Journal* in early 2002. "Profits per partner and revenues are the new measures of success. More than ever, firms are subject to business cycles, as we've seen in the unprecedented layoffs in the early 1990s and again this past year. And also more than ever, the lawyers themselves are in the corporate trenches, giving business advice almost as much as the legal kind."[62]

Concern focuses especially on the system of "billable hours," which came in during the 1960s. It gives lawyers an incentive to maximize the hours, in some cases the minutes, worked for which they bill clients. Lawyers love to tell stories like the one about the big New York law firm that billed a client $16 for a Danish—so much for the pastry, and so much for the time it took the lawyer to eat it. No less a figure than Robert E. Hirshon, president of the American Bar Association, has admitted his unease about the effects of the system. "The billable hour is fundamentally about quantity over quality, repetition over creativity. . . . Increased billable hours are squeezing out other aspects of what it means to be a lawyer."

—◆—

SPORTS, ONCE ALMOST a religion for many millions of Americans, was also increasingly indistinguishable from business. A successful baseball or football franchise automatically made its owner or owners seriously rich. Indeed, it can be argued that George W. Bush was the first president of the United States to acquire fame and fortune as owner of a sports franchise; he assembled the group of investors who bought the Texas Rangers baseball club in 1988, and this deal, which brought him some $15 million, was the first to make him seriously wealthy. Of course, sports stars like basketball's Shaquille O'Neal, golf's Tiger Woods, Pete Sampras in tennis, Dallas quarterback Troy Aikman, or Los Angeles pitcher Kevin Brown earned salaries in the millions, plus even vaster amounts from endorsements, advertising, appearance money, and the rest.[63] It is said that Tiger Woods earned $53 million in 2000, only $9 million of which came from playing golf on the PGA tour. He has contracts with Nike, General Motors, Rolex, and American Express, and a new deal with Disney is reported to be close at the time of writing.[64] In 2002 38 golfers earned over $1 million in prize money alone;[65] counting others' earnings from advertising, endorsements, and so on, it has been estimated that about 120 golfers are expected to make $1 million a year from professional golf in the United States alone.[66] Indeed, in golf, the players are actually evaluated, not by their competitive results as such, but by the amount of money they earned.

The case of Tiger Woods is one of the clearest examples of the way sports stars have become brands. For Nike, as a sports shoe and clothing manufacturer with worldwide markets—and under attack for insensitivity, if not greed, in the ways its products are manufactured in developing countries—Woods's image, from a marketing point of view, is a godsend. He is of course a superb golfer. Perhaps he will turn out to be the greatest who ever played. He is young. And he is of mixed race, with African American, Vietnamese, Latin American, and European genes in his makeup. He is, moreover, quiet, with excellent manners, and so unthreatening to the business types who constitute golf's core market. At the same time, as Guy Kinnings, head of golf at the marketing group IMG Europe points out, the demographics of golf viewers has changed since Woods came on the scene. He "introduced a whole new generation of people to golf that hadn't been there before." Indeed, the next thing, according to some branding experts, is that stars will stop recommending other people's products and start marketing themselves as brands.[67]

Many decades ago Casey Stengel announced with uncharacteristic clarity, "Baseball's business." And back in 1951 Congressman Manny Celler of Brooklyn asked the owner of the Chicago Cubs in a congressional hearing, "You mean baseball is a business, an industry?" "It is a very peculiar business," P. K. Wrigley replied, "but it is a business."[68]

And so it has always been. What was peculiar about the baseball business in the 1990s was that it became the classic example of the "winner take all" economy produced by, and producing, growing inequality. The players' strike of 1994, which closed down an entire season, was seen by many as a watershed. Bob Costas, the NBC commentator, in a widely praised polemic, called the impact for fans, "brutal and long-lasting, and not even the McGwire-Sosa summer of '98, with newspapers daily recording the exploits of two sluggers competing to set the all-time single season home run record, could truly change it."[69] Another commentator said "the separation of baseball business from baseball on the field would no longer be possible."[70]

By the late 1990s the disparity in revenues and therefore in payroll between clubs was so great that from 1995 through 1999, out of a total of 158

Major League Baseball "postseason" games, no club whose payroll fell in the lower half of the industry won so much as a single game.[71]

While television revenue spurted ahead in major markets like New York, millions around the world (many of whom had never played or even watched baseball) bought New York Yankees caps, and ticket prices virtually doubled in a decade, only three out of thirty clubs (Cleveland, Colorado, and of course the Yankees) operated profitably, and club debt rose from $600 million to over $2 billion. The imbalance in economic strength between clubs is graphically revealed if one looks at local broadcasting revenue, cutting out the $15 million cut all clubs receive equally from national revenue. On this basis, in 1999 the Yankees received $58 million, the Chicago Cubs $56 million, and the Atlanta Braves $51 million. Middle-of-the-table clubs like San Francisco and Seattle received $17 million. Kansas City got $6 million—barely a tenth of the Yankees' revenue—the Minnesota Twins had $5 million, and the Montreal Expos a mere $3 million. Moreover, as Bob Costas points out, "It is not only the difference in revenues among individual teams but the synergies between a team and the owner's other businesses that drive payroll inequality. Rupert Murdoch hopes that Kevin Brown will promote his international media interests, and the same applies to other owners."[72]

It speaks volumes for the affection in which the game is held that the president of Yale, the former Senate Majority Leader, a former chairman of the Federal Reserve Bank, and one of Washington's most cerebral journalistic pundits would address its problems.[73] But what these distinguished and dignified figures found was, as they put it, "large and growing revenue disparities exist and are causing problems of chronic competitive imbalance." Or, as the fans in the bleachers might put it, the fix was in. Say it isn't so.

———◆———

As ROBERT D. HUTCHINS, the president of the University of Chicago in the 1940s, pointed out in a famous report on the freedom of the press in the aftermath of World War II, journalism is a "profession grafted on an industry." There could be some argument whether journalism is in fact a profession: most definitions of a profession would say that it had to control recruitment, training, remuneration, and discipline, and none of these attributes applies to journalism. But the news media certainly do have a double character. They are not just grafted on an industry; they are an industry. At the same time they have an absolutely vital public function. They are nothing less than the central nervous system of a modern society, the only means by which citizens can be aware of events, trends, changes, issues, challenges. As such, efficient, responsible, fair, and serious news media are vital to the survival of a society. What has happened over recent decades, and especially since the middle 1980s, is that news media have become increasingly penetrated by the values and techniques of entertainment media. While at their best, American media provide an unprecedentedly rich menu of information about what is happening, only a minority of news outlets even attempt to reach the standards of the best. Television, the most important source of news for most Americans, is generally acknowledged to be less responsible than newspapers.

News media have to succeed as businesses. They must support themselves economically and generate the resources for new investment in technology and talent and better news gathering and analysis. Unless they can justify their performance in terms of public service, and raise money accordingly, they must make profits. They cannot afford to be dull. They must entertain as well as inform. To steer the course between commercial success and public service is admittedly hard. But there is reason to believe that they have concentrated on entertaining at the expense of informing and that the effects on society have been damaging. They must take much of the blame for a startling decline in civic involvement or what is called "social capital."

IN THE MIDDLE 1950S Bob Putnam, as a teenager in Port Clinton, Ohio, was a member of a team of five boys who belonged to a bowling league. Thirty years later, as an eminent political scientist and former dean of the Kennedy School at Harvard University, with a classic study of Italian society under his belt, Putnam was struck by the decline not in bowling, which has continued to grow in popularity when many participation sports have declined, but in bowling leagues. He soon discovered that it was not just bowling leagues that had experienced this decline. All kinds of religious, political, and social institutions had followed the same pattern of decline: churches, synagogues, political clubs, bridge clubs, Veterans of

Foreign Wars and American Legion posts, chapters of the National Association for the Advancement of Colored People, marching bands, union locals. When, after one of the most elaborate surveys ever conducted, he came to sum up his finding, Putnam was careful to avoid pessimism or "declensionism." It was not his view that community bonds had weakened steadily over the course of American history, he insisted. There had been ups as well as downs. But in the past three decades something unusual did seem to have occurred. "The dominant theme," he wrote, "is simple: For the first two-thirds of the twentieth century a powerful tide bore Americans into ever deeper engagement in the life of their communities, but a few decades ago—silently, without warning—that tide reversed and we were overtaken by a treacherous rip current. Without at first noticing, we have been pulled apart from one another and from our communities over the last third of the century."[74]

For the next five years, with the resources of the wealthiest of American universities behind him and the almost overenthusiastic help of dozens of volunteer sleuths combing the literature of half a dozen disciplines for him, Putnam sought an explanation of this most worrying development. Besides searching hundreds of secondary works on almost every aspect of American society, he drew heavily on such data collections as the U.S. government's General Social Survey, Roper Social and Political Trends, and the "life style archive" accumulated by the advertising agency, DDB.[75] What could be responsible for the simultaneous decline in "social capital" or "civic engagement" in so many different fields?

He identified a dozen potential suspects. Could the busyness of the age and the ever growing pressures on time be responsible? Or the relative hard times through which the country passed between the middle 1970s and the middle 1990s? What about the movement of women into the paid labor force? Or should the cause be sought in the disruption of marriage, the growth of the welfare state, or in suburbanization and sprawl themselves? Could recent changes in the structure of the U.S. economy be to blame, or technological changes like television and the Internet?

To cut a very long story short, Putnam eventually eliminated every suspect except one.[76] The available evidence suggested, he concluded, that while modern "busyness," economic distress, and the pressures of two-career families were indeed a modest part of the explanation, none was the primary cause of civic disengagement. Suburbanization, too, might account for something like 10 percent of the decline in community involvement but could not explain all of it, for the simple reason that the same phenomenon of civic disengagement could be seen just as clearly in small towns and rural areas.

No: after exhaustive analysis of a dozen possible villains of the piece, Putnam concluded, tentatively but with conviction, that it was television viewing that must be blamed for the decline in community spirit and communal activity. Between 1950 and 1980 television viewing grew from four-and-a-half hours a day per household to seven hours a day. Television took up nearly 40 percent of the average American's free time, and no fewer than 81 percent of Americans, more than four out of five, report that they watch TV "most evenings."

This immense growth in the dominance of television was not a matter of tens of millions of individual choices, Putnam explained; rather it was generational. Although correlation does not prove causation, studies suggested that television watching, and especially dependence on television for entertainment, was closely correlated with civic disengagement, which was most marked in the younger age groups. He quotes a political scientist as observing that by the time the average member of the baby boom generation had reached sixteen years of age he or she had watched at least 12,000 hours of TV. "There can be little doubt that television reduced the baby boom's contacts with its peers and parents," this scholar observed, "and that the generation made its first contact with the real world through the medium."[77]

"Americans at the end of the twentieth century," Robert Putnam concluded, "were watching more TV, watching it more habitually, more pervasively and more often alone, and watching more programs that were associated specifically with civic disengagement (entertainment, as distinct from news). The onset of these trends coincided exactly with the national decline in social connectedness, and the trends were most marked among the younger generations that are . . . distinctively disengaged."[78]

———•◆•———

IT WAS NOT JUST that Americans were watching more television, though they were. What has been crucial in changing the temper of society into what has been called the "Me Generation" was the change in the character of television and of the messages it conveyed. From the middle 1970s, the television industry was going through a whole series of revolutionary changes. Technological change, the arrival of cable in 1980,[79] and satellite and digital channels vastly increased the number of alternative channels. In the 1950s and 1960s the industry was dominated by the three networks, CBS, NBC, and ABC. Between them, they claimed over 90 percent of the national audience in prime time. By the end of the century that dominance was long gone.[80]

The history of American media in the past hundred years can be divided into three phases. In the first, the period of limited and regulated media, the structure was oligopolistic. The limitations of the electromagnetic spectrum were both a reason for regulating scarcity of wavelengths and an excuse for imposing controls thought desirable for political or social reasons. Around 1980 regulation came under attack from three directions. Technological progress ended electromagnetic scarcity. The new conservative ideology objected to regulation as pernicious in itself. And new business strategies demanded economies of scale, which in turn could be achieved only by mergers across the traditional boundaries between media industries.

Until 1980, the year when everything began to change dramatically, a handful of large firms or clusters of firms dominated electronic media. The Bell system, AT&T and its offshoots, controlled 80 percent of local telephone service and virtually 100 percent of long-distance telecommunications. IBM held 77 percent of the computer market. And 92 percent of the television audience belonged to the three networks, NBC, CBS, and ABC.

The interests of the public and of the consumer were safeguarded, more or less effectively, by relatively tight regulation by the federal government.[81] There was little content regulation in practice, although network programming was supposedly controlled by something called the "Fairness Doctrine." But structural regulation was quite rigid, with limits on the number of AM or FM radio or TV stations that could be owned by a single individual or corporation.

The grip of the almighty trinity of networks and their market share began to loosen in the 1970s. But the great change began with the arrival of

Ronald Reagan in the White House in 1981 and with his appointment of Mark Fowler as chairman of the regulatory body, the Federal Communications Commission. Fowler inaugurated a regime of deregulation. Media corporations that had been limited to seven AM, seven FM, and seven TV stations (7-7-7) were allowed to go to 12-12-12. The new distribution technology, broadband cable, was freed from regulation by the Cable Television Act of 1984.

That year marked the transformation from the age of regulation to the new age of multiple channels. Cable spread rapidly, in part because the quality of terrestrial network pictures was poor, partly because of timid programming obsessed with ratings. The cable audience was too small to measure in 1980, but by 1987 it reached nearly 80 percent of American homes, and by 1992 it reached 98 percent, of whom 65 percent actually subscribed.[82] (Market analysts distinguish three groups: those who are "reached" by cable, in the sense that the physical connection is available to them; those who take advantage of it by subscribing; and those, the "audience," who are actually watching at any one time.) Ted Turner's Cable News Network began to take off after 1980, although — except at moments of exceptional drama such as September 11, 2001 — its audience was always a small fraction of its advertised market "reach."

The business impact on the networks was shattering. Their joint market share fell to little more than half of the audience by the end of the decade. The mighty CBS might have been bought by Turner had it not been for the opposition of Senator Jesse Helms, but then a financier, Larry Tisch, did buy effective control and began to slash payroll and budgets.

Business considerations were transforming the news and entertainment media industries alike. Indeed they would soon merge them into a single industry. Beginning with the *Wall Street Journal* in the early 1960s, media companies, many of them traditionally owned by individuals or families, began to bring their shares to the stock market. Often the motive was to secure family ownership beyond the lifetime of the principal owner and lessen tax liability. When the *Washington Post* challenged the Nixon administration over the Pentagon Papers in 1971, the fact that the stock was about to go public weighed on Katharine Graham and her editors.[83] Gradually newspapers, television networks, and Hollywood studios, not to mention book and magazine publishing and the music business, began to experience the influence of professional managers. Equity prices, analysts' opinions, and bottom-line considerations made themselves felt as never before. Gradually proud journalists and the "talent" in Hollywood alike came to realize that the news business and show business were — after all — business.

The peak year for newspaper advertising was as long ago as 1973. By 1997 newspapers' share of total U.S. advertising revenue had fallen from 29.9 to 22.1 percent, and of that an increasing proportion was "preprints" — stand-alone color inserts — despised by journalists.[84] In 1989 newspaper advertising fell like a stone and did not recover for five years. Television and direct-mail advertising were untouched. Metropolitan daily newspapers, the heart of serious American journalism, and the original news gatherers for much television journalism, were in crisis. They had grown with the great cities, and now people and economic juices were leaving the cities for the suburbs. Only the greatest newspapers maintained their quality. Many others remained profitable for owners but at the cost of ruthless pruning of staff, investments, and quality.

Many mergers, too, created multimedia enterprises. In 1985 ABC merged with Capital Cities. At about the same time General Electric bought NBC, already owned by RCA. In 1985 News Corporation bought the first half of Twentieth Century Fox and, within a couple of years, had become in effect a fourth network. Regulatory obstacles to multiple ownership diminished, while the incentive grew. A conglomerate like Rupert Murdoch's News Corporation could theoretically publish a book, turn it into a movie in the Twentieth Century Fox studio, sell it to the Fox television network, review it favorably in newspapers and on radio stations, and take the profit where it made most business sense. News Corporation was hardly alone. By the end of the 1980s, a substantial proportion of American news and entertainment media was controlled by just six conglomerates: Time-Warner; ABC/Disney; Viacom (owning Paramount and Blockbuster Video); News Corporation; CBS/Westinghouse; and NBC, owned by General Electric.

Many and at times shrill were the voices pointing out the dangers of this degree of concentration. It was apparent that the media conglomerates could theoretically use their market power in ways that could be damaging to consumers, creative talent, and smaller entrepreneurs alike. Indeed, if various lawsuits had not been settled out of court, it might have been possible to show that this is exactly what did sometimes actually happen.[85] In a multimedia corporation with multiple outlets, the "gatekeeper" responsible for the quality of news might be many layers down in the corporate hierarchy and unable to prevail against corporate decisions restricting quality.

Yet the situation from 1984 to the middle 1990s was perhaps not as bad as these voices prophesying woe suggested. For one thing, the old monopolistic system had been destroyed. At least in theory, that offered opportunities for innovation, and in different ways many, like CNN, took advantage of it. It was not as if the trinity of networks had been so passionately committed to quality over profits in their day. Second, if giant media conglomerates were emerging, they were not as overwhelmingly dominant as was often suggested. The largest entertainment companies, for example, Disney, Time-Warner, and Cap Cities, with revenues of $6.3 to $8.5 billion in the mid-1990s, controlled market shares in the whole information and entertainment sector of no more than around 1 percent each.[86]

In specific market sectors, however, the degree of concentration could be distinctly troubling. From 1959 the FCC had attempted to prevent the networks having a financial interest in the production or syndication of the shows they aired. These "FinSyn rules" were finally abolished in 1995. Four years later, vertical integration between producers and networks was the rule. Eight of the top ten prime-time program suppliers were corporately linked to one of the major networks. All of the new CBS series that year listed CBS Productions as a coproducer.[87]

The multichannel age ushered in by the technology of broadband cable and the deregulation of the Reagan administration lasted for only a dozen years. With startling abruptness, the coming of the Internet in the mid-1990s announced the arrival, or at least the imminence, of a third age of media. Pundits thought it would be an age of convergence. Corporate spokesmen assured everyone that "content was king," until it turned out that intellectual property, not talent, would be the measure of content. Promoters promised a world in which the consumer would be king. Every man and every woman would be able to edit their own newspaper, the "Daily Me." They would also be able to download digitally recorded movies, TV, or music at will and enjoy them from a new machine, at once computer, television, and access to telecommunications, in the living room. More to the point, from the view of corporate business, the consumer of the future would be able to shop, bank, and manage a stock market portfolio from home.

By the end of the century, it was plain that this nirvana was not available, or at least not yet. Both business and the consumer were confused. It was plain that in several respects enthusiasts for the new technology had exaggerated and/or misunderstood consumers' attitudes. Not everyone, to take an apparently trivial example, would want to watch movies on a computer or use the computer in the living room for working. More generally, it quickly became apparent that, alluring as the possibilities offered by the Internet might be, few had found out a way of getting paid for providing them. Taxed on the point, John Roos, a senior partner in the most influential law firm in Silicon Valley, admitted that one of the few ways you could make money out of most websites was by selling the thing as quickly as possible to someone who had not yet figured out how hard it was to get paid.[88] "The internet as media," says the acerbic New York commentator Michael Wolff, "has failed. It wasn't interesting to any of the parties involved essentially. People didn't want to pay for content, and there is no way to generate money out of content. It didn't work for advertisers, and it's not going to work for websites. The Internet works as an infrastructure that moves lots of different kinds of information. But in terms of being 'the media business' *per se*—forget about it."[89]

Wolff suggests—plausibly—that the Internet will end up not as an industry but as a universal convenience, like the telephone, a facilitator that will make it possible to move product faster and to communicate with an audience, but not an industry. It is clear that it will have enormous importance for both entertainment and news media. But it is not so clear that it will transform the economy, let alone society.

So one media era ended in the middle 1980s, and another appeared above the horizon in the middle 1990s. On balance, consumers have been the gainers. Technology has made possible a great liberation of the individual citizen, as viewer, communicator, researcher, and citizen. Most families, and most individuals, especially in metropolitan areas, have the choice of several dozen—and, in many cases, hundreds—of channels. The Internet will increase the variety of the ways we can learn about the world. It will also enable a significant slice of workers to work from home, and to do so more or less wherever they choose.

Unfortunately, the capacity of the technology to liberate us is limited by the structures and the strategies of corporate business. Promoters of the corporate ideology spoke much of "choice." Even in the age of network dominance, though, competition did not deliver as much choice as theory might suggest, because network executives, intent on maximizing audience and revenue, would often schedule similar programs against each other. In theory, the cable revolution ought to have given viewers a vast increase in choice; but there, too, the real variety on offer was limited by the need of cable outlets to reach the biggest possible audiences. So the pattern of scheduling that emerged was not so much an infinity of choice as a general sameness of highly commercial entertainment and infotainment, enriched by a certain number of specialist channels offering viewers able to pay for them a great variety of more or less high-quality programming. The arrival of the Internet promised an era of personal liberation. But already great corporate interests are intent on capturing the Internet. The pattern inevitably has corresponded closely with the growing economic and educational inequality in society in the 1990s. It was a new world in which the few were magnificently served, and the many expected to be content with a cultural diet that was highly commercial, tailored to corporate agendas, and so depressingly timid.

Between the end of World War II and the middle 1960s, the news media in America enjoyed what came to be seen in retrospect as a golden age. Characteristically for that age, the news industry had a strongly hierarchical shape. Radio and TV stations were almost all grouped into networks, and the three national TV networks, CBS, NBC, and ABC, had a firm financial grip on their hundreds of affiliates. Similarly, in the newspaper industry, all but a dozen or so of some 1,500 dailies and weeklies had monopoly or quasi-monopoly positions in their markets that, given the growth of advertising, guaranteed strong profits, which in turn helped to explain a slow process of concentration into "chains." This prosperous industry developed professionalism, accompanied by a good deal of responsible soul-searching about standards of fairness and impartiality and the status of journalists.

This comfortable era was ended by the events of the 1960s and 1970s. The civil rights movement, the women's movement, and the campaign against the Vietnam War explicitly challenged the news media's claims to be considered impartial. While "Watergate" temporarily heightened the prestige and popularity of journalism, the era symbolized by such national heroes as Benjamin Bradlee of the *Washington Post* and Walter Cronkite of CBS was coming to an end.

In the 1980s and 1990s a number of trends combined to transform the prestige, the profitability, the professional standards, and the influence of the news media. Especially after the end of the Cold War and the "Grand Narrative" that had kept readers and viewers interested in national and international news since the declaration of war in 1917, the audience for both TV and print news fell away. Management invaded the editorial realm in an unprecedented way. While "advertorial" news crept into magazines and local TV, "infotainment" spread like ground ivy.

The manic media coverage first of the O. J. Simpson trial in 1995 and then of the Monica Lewinsky affair in 1998 served a warning about how much traditional news standards had been eroded by the spread of corporate goals and values in news management.[90] This was made all the worse by the imperative need of old media to compete with online news, even if it meant abandoning traditional practices and safeguards.

This trend accelerated after the mid-1980s, when the stock market upgraded its rating of media stocks and huge conglomerates came into existence, seeking to achieve "synergy" between newspapers, TV, movies, magazines, and even book publishing. By the very end of the 1990s, the concept of "convergence" (meaning the belief that telecommunications, computers, and television would become technologically interchangeable, heralded a new phase of concentration, exemplified by the giant merger of America OnLine with Time Warner. That brought together the biggest Internet server with a major magazine publisher, a big Hollywood studio, and CNN, the flagship of twenty-four-hour television news broadcasting. Within a very few years, the merger was being judged a failure. AOL was in difficulty as a result of accusations of dubious accounting, while the "old media" divisions of the merged corporation were reasserting their weight within it.

In the stressed atmosphere after the atrocities of September 11, 2001, most news media played safe by avoiding controversy. And in the Iraq war of 2003, Fox TV openly discarded traditions of journalistic impartiality and, like right-wing radio talk shows, acted as a cheerleader for conservative and chauvinistic attitudes.

Thirty years of media development seemed to have produced a paradox: never had media been more influential, yet never had news media been so little trusted by their audience. Americans were influenced more and more by advertising and entertainment, less and less by traditional journalism. In this, as in other areas of American life, corporate power and influence, though less and less challenged, were increasingly resented.

———•◆•———

FROM EARLY TIMES Americans had always been proud that, however great the differences of wealth among citizens might be, all Americans considered themselves equal. They attributed particular importance to their freedom from the feudal and aristocratic traditions of Europe. "We Americans worship the almighty dollar!" said Mark Twain. "Well, it is a worthier god than hereditary privilege."

To be sure, African Americans, both under slavery and under the Jim Crow system that succeeded it, had always been the great exceptions to this psychological equality. There were other exceptions, too. Native Americans were long treated as less than full citizens, and so in different ways were Asian and Hispanic Americans. Immigrants were often treated, at least for the first generation, as if they were not full members of American society, but the public school systems consciously sought to turn immigrants into Americans. Unionized industrial workers saw themselves as a class apart, and their union and political representatives were not above waging class war. But the powerful drive to become truly and authentically American carried generation after generation of immigrants into a mainstream, egalitarian culture, and that process is still at work with the great majority of today's immigrants.

What was new in the last quarter of the twentieth century was a sharp increase in inequality, accompanied by class divisions in the realms of culture and attitudes, which were all the more damaging to society for being largely unacknowledged, indeed indignantly denied by many, both of those who benefited from them, and of their victims.

There was, as we have seen, unprecedented financial inequality. Money has always been at the root of class divisions. (Money, the "means of exchange and store of value," is reductively a token of entitlement to a share of resources.) "What is gentility," asked the English common lawyer John Selden in the seventeenth century, "but ancient riches?" The hallowed American belief that there was no hereditary privileged class in America, or—if there was one—it was so small as to be insignificant, was being challenged as never before. As we have seen, such benefits as there had been from the moderate economic growth from 1973 until the mid-1990s had been concentrated on the highest income groups, especially on the tiny minority who owned substantial assets. And although millions took part in the stock market boom of the closing years of the century, the profits of the boom went disproportionately to those who could afford to invest large sums, and those same wealthy investors were more likely to extricate themselves from the downturn without lasting damage.

It is now widely acknowledged that the United States is the most unequal society in the developed world in terms of both income and wealth.[91] International income comparisons are fraught with difficulties, but in the widely accepted Luxembourg Income Study, around 1985, again around 1990, and even more in 1995, the United States came eleventh out of eleven countries studied. That is, it was the most unequal of the developed countries. Yet there is still a general assumption that this inequality does not amount to class division and that America is still free from the debilitating class inequalities of Europe. In reality, all Western European societies have made the reduction and, if possible, the elimination of class inequalities a major political goal for the past fifty years, to the point where the United States is arguably a more stratified society than those of European countries, which once took American "classlessness" as a model.[92]

There are several specific reasons why financial inequality eventually translates into deep and lasting social and political divisions. Education is the most obvious. Growing financial inequality, accompanied by sharp cuts in the funding available for states and cities, produced accentuated educational inequality, especially at the top end of the socioeconomic ladder. This was not an accident. It was the inevitable consequence of the tax rebellion of the late 1970s and the Reagan years, as Peter Shrag has documented. "If California seemed to be a national model of high civic investment and engagement in the 1950s and 1960s, so it has become the lodestar of tax reduction and public disinvestment of the 1980s and 1990s."[93] He charts in painful detail how under the blows of tax rebellion and consequent resource shortage, heavy immigration, and arguments about the language in which teaching should take place, standards have plummeted. Some schools, and not only in rich suburbs like Beverly Hills, do remarkably, one could even say heroically, well. Many schools have poor buildings. In some, parents come to take the children home when it rains because the roof leaks and they are afraid the kids will be electrocuted.[94] Many teachers have poor qualifications or no qualifications at all. Worst of all was the growing disparity between spending per pupil on schools in affluent West Los Angeles suburbs like Westwood and less fortunate areas. The gap in expenditure per pupil in both immigrant and African American neighborhoods in East and South Central Los Angeles was as great as that between white and black schools in the Deep South before desegregation.

——•◆•——

ONCE UPON A TIME, all but a handful of white Americans went to public schools, whether the "little red house on the prairie," maintained by stern but lovable spinsters, or in great systems like that operated by the New York City board of education or Chicago public schools.

In the last quarter of the twentieth century, that began to change. This is not a matter of numerical decline. Rather it is a case of a relatively small but disproportionately influential opinion-forming and executive class that has largely withdrawn its children from public schools, especially in large metropolitan centers (New York, Washington, Chicago, Los Angeles, Boston) at the very time when the elites in these metropolitan centers have, as a result of a number of "nationalizing" economic and cultural trends, increased their influence on society as compared with that of provincial elites.

In 1993–94, when the U.S. Department of Education conducted its most recent Schools and Staffing Survey,[95] there were just fewer than 5 million students in private elementary and secondary schools in the United States. They amounted to 10.7 percent of all students from first to twelfth grade in the country. These private schools varied hugely. Average fees for secondary students were $5,500; but for pupils at member schools of the

National Association of Independent Schools average fees were $20,000 a year, and some elite New England boarding schools cost more than that, in spite of their substantial endowments. Almost exactly half of the private school students (2.5 million) attended Roman Catholic parochial or secondary schools. Roughly another 870,000 attended schools run by traditional Protestant denominations (Episcopalians, Lutherans, and so on), 183,000 attended Jewish schools, and a further 1.7 million, in round terms, attended other independent schools.

There is no overall trend toward private schools, although there was a wave of private school founding in the 1970s. Overall, between 1970 and 1988, private schools held their own with low percentage diminution in numbers, while public school enrollments were falling by roughly 12.5 percent. But the impression is clear: the dominance of public schools has been eroded from two directions. In the South and West, there has been a substantial growth in the number of students attending private day schools, many of them run by evangelical Protestant denominations. Although this is denied, this phenomenon must have been related to the replacement of dual school systems in the decades since *Brown*.[96] Often parents were able to rationalize a decision to send children to a predominantly white private school because such schools offered genuinely pleasant learning environments. However, about two-thirds of all the private schools in America have been founded since the mid-1950s. Nine out of ten of the category designated as "conservative Christian schools" by the Schools and Staffing Survey were founded since the mid-1960s. These schools are smaller than the average of private schools, and far smaller than public schools, and their teachers have lower qualifications on the average. They contained 642,000 students in 1993–94.

Over the same period there has been a withdrawal of middle- and upper-middle-class students from public schools in northern cities. This has taken place for two linked reasons: because parents who remained in the city decided to send their children to private schools, and because parents moved out to suburbs where the proportion of minority families was lower than in the city. This too is hard to measure precisely. Some indication is provided by the fact that over the country as a whole the proportion of students in the category "white non-Hispanic" was more than 10 percentage points higher (77.9 percent) than the proportion in public schools (67.3 percent).

This relatively slight differential, however, probably conceals a much greater disparity that would emerge if the data were correlated with socioeconomic class. The problems of American primary and secondary education are not limited to racial inequality. Class barriers, as well as racial ones, divide young Americans and deny to some the opportunities abundantly available to others. Many reputable studies have confirmed that, as Richard D. Kahlenberg has put it, "Our schools remain highly segregated by economic status."[97]

At the primary and secondary level, the upper middle class increasingly either sent its children to private schools or moved to suburbs with well-funded school systems, achieving social advantages for its children indirectly through the housing market. While some upper-middle-class liberals undoubtedly make a point of principle out of sending their children to public schools or to private schools with high minority enrollment, they are likely to be far outnumbered in the higher income groups by parents who have withdrawn their children from city public schools. Sometimes this is because of the changed racial mix. In New York City, for example, the public schools are 84 percent minority; in Washington, D.C., they are almost 100 percent African American, although the total population is only 60 percent black. More than half the children in the Chicago public schools are African American, and another third are Latino, and only 9 percent are white, though 42.4 percent of the city's population is "white non-Hispanic."

Often, however, parents are not simply making up racial excuses when they point to declines in the quality of public schools and to the class mix. Studies since the Coleman report in 1967 all agree that "a pupil's achievement [seems to be] strongly related to the educational backgrounds and aspirations of the other students in the school."[98] Between 1990 and 1998 New York City, often regarded as the wealthiest city on Earth and in spite of a 10 percent growth in student enrolment, cut the budget for its public schools by $2.7 billion. Seventy-three percent of the city's 1.1 million public school students received free school lunches, just twice the proportion in New York State as a whole. It is not surprising, perhaps, that the *New York Daily News* reported in 2000 that most elected public officials in

244 ._ Chapter 8

New York, including Mayor Rudolph Giuliani, sent their own children to private or parochial schools, and that only two of seven members of the Board of Education sent their children to public schools.[99]

The perception that public schools really are failing the kids who go to them is not confined to what the *Daily News* called "bigwigs," though. In a 1997 NBC News/*Wall Street Journal* survey 58 percent of Americans agreed that "we need to make fundamental changes" in public education. There is also abundant evidence that American schools are poor by international comparative standards, as an international study of twenty-one industrialized countries showed in 1998:

> American twelfth graders ranked nineteenth in math and sixteenth in science. In other subjects, even our fourth grade performance is dismal: on National Assessment of Educational Progress tests conducted in 1997, half of American fourth graders could not identify the Atlantic or Pacific oceans on a map. A 1992 study estimated that roughly 42 million American adults are functionally illiterate.[100]

Such differences in the quality of primary and secondary education inevitably translate to differences in equality of opportunity and so into class divisions in later life, as Kahlenberg explains:

> About 70 percent of Americans stay in the same socioeconomic class in which they were born; the children of poorly educated parents make up just 2 percent of the professional and managerial class. Although the United States prides itself on having less class rigidity than that found in Europe, study after study has found that in fact our rates of social mobility are no better.[101]

These inequalities in high school are perpetuated in the tertiary stage of education. Once again, this was by no means always so. The inequalities, amounting to incipient class stratification, are the direct result of changes in government policies, especially tax cuts, consequent on the success of conservative ideology. The "land grant" state universities, once able to compete on more or less equal terms with the richly endowed private universities, fell increasingly behind, even though they were obliged to charge higher and higher fees.[102] The wealthiest private universities, such as Harvard and Yale, claim never to turn a student away for lack of money.

They speak less of the various arrangements made to favor the children of alumni and significant donors. But if students benefit from private largesse, they have no right to it. The packages given, moreover, are means tested, and they are made up of loans and work opportunities as well as grants. It is easier for poor kids to go to the great Ivy League schools than it was; but it is still far harder for them to get there than for the children of affluent business executives and professionals.

Educational opportunity is more equally available than was the case in the 1920s and 1930s, but it is less equally available than in the years of the GI Bill, when anyone who had been in the service could go to college. It is also less available than in the days of Clark Kerr's reign as president of the University of California, when California, and other states such as New York, offered higher education free for all in-state.

The result is that the proportion of Americans completing a college education (once far higher than in any other country) stuck at not much more than one-quarter, at which level, for the first time in history, it was lower than the percentage completing college in some other countries. Virtually all students completing high school say they want to go to college. Roughly two-thirds begin some kind of higher education course. But only about a quarter complete a four-year education. The chief reason, for most of the dropouts, is simply money. And increasingly even a college degree does not guarantee access to professional and managerial careers, for which postgraduate education is now virtually mandatory.

Education is not the only area in which class divisions have developed between the affluent and the rest. A simple example is the mail. Corporations and upper-middle-class citizens have largely abandoned the U.S. mail in favor of private courier services that charge dollars where the Postal Service charges pennies.

Health care is another instance where the wealthy are able to access a higher standard of care than the rest of the population. With the costs both of medical care and of health insurance escalating rapidly (also far higher than in other comparable countries) the affluent were also measurably healthier than the rest. It is well known that 43 million Americans lack any medical insurance. What is less widely understood is the class dimension of this problem. In 1997 little more than 5 percent of working adults in the

United States with incomes over $65,000 lacked health care insurance, whereas in the group earning $16,000 to $20,000 35 percent were uncovered. Moreover, the problem is getting worse, not better, as fewer workers have long-term jobs and more fall into the short-term, part-time "contingent worker" category. Between 1988 and 1998 the share of workers receiving health insurance from their employer fell from 64.6 to 54.1 percent.

Another explanation of class stratification may be the prevalance of advertising and marketing stressing the acquisition of status. Advertisements for everything from clothes, vacations, automobiles and even alcoholic drinks have long relied on suggesting that the man in the Hathaway shirt, the owner of a Cadillac or an imported sports car, or the drinker of premium liquor has bought his way into an exclusive elite. In the last quarter of the twentieth century campaigns relying on snob appeal were commoner and cleverer than ever.

In a word, by the end of the twentieth century social classes in America were increasingly isolated from one another, and not only by income. The all-powerful upper middle class, with its health insurance and its stock options and its pension plans, largely subsidized by "middle-class welfare," is separated from both working-class and underclass Americans by life-style and opportunities, but also intellectually and—perhaps most important of all—geographically.

Suburbanization was separating an increasingly pauperized inner-city population from the various economic strata of the suburbs.[103] This division was graphically presented in Tom Wolfe's 1989 novel, A Bonfire of the Vanities, in which the wealthy banker who leaves the highway finds himself in what he sees as a terrifying, Third World urban jungle. The upper middle class, which increasingly controlled perceptions of society through its grasp of media of all sorts, literally did not know how "the other half" lived. An increasingly isolated upper middle and upper class sought out even more sheltered and agreeable enclaves, in the East in Manhattan and a few suburban counties near New York, Washington, Boston, and Philadelphia, and in such places as western Connecticut and Massachusetts, Vermont, Cape Cod, and the Hamptons, and—especially in the West—often in gated and guarded "communities," where the bumper stickers on their neighbors' cars comfortably reminded them that their children were attending expensive private schools.

This was accompanied by increasingly open class confidence, occasionally tipping over into arrogance. By the 1990s, open discussion of class in American society, common in the 1930s[104] but almost taboo in the 1950s, was again commonplace.

Law firms and even the best newspapers increasingly recruited from a small circle of well-known graduate and professional schools, as did Wall Street banks and (contrary to mythology) Silicon Valley, itself, after all, little more than a journalistic phrase for the Stanford campus. Interestingly, while the media liked to portray the Internet rich as "laid back" in such symbolic matters as the wearing of suits and ties, in reality a remarkably high proportion of them have come from moneyed upper-middle-class backgrounds and an even higher proportion from private universities.[105]

Finally, educational class distinctions led naturally to intellectual ones. For the first time in American history, again, a small, highly educated upper class was reading a handful of *national* newspapers, especially the *New York Times* and the *Wall Street Journal*. Such people also watched television (PBS, C-Span, CNN) of high quality, but insignificant market share, and listened to the excellent National Public Radio. In the meantime the majority relied for information about the world on the increasingly "infotainment" products of the commercial broadcasting empires, including "shock jock" radio talk shows, which almost invariably took a more or less intemperately conservative and a more or less uncritical probusiness stance. The high-quality newspapers, magazines, public radio, and public television reinforced moderately liberal and moderately conservative ideologies without seriously challenging a mass culture increasingly controlled by a small class of entrepreneurs and inheritors and a larger, but still relatively small, class of corporate executives and professionals.

This stratification, by culture and ultimately by money, was increasingly reflected in politics. Not only did only half the population vote. The half that voted was also on the whole the wealthier half. Little surprise, then, that the interests of the poor and even of the middle class were being slowly squeezed out of the agenda of politics. No surprise, if Washington pundits such as Michael Barone or Irving Kristol maintained that economic issues no longer mattered and that elections were decided by "cultural" factors. No wonder, if elections could be won with the votes of little more than the top two tenths of an increasingly skewed income distribution. But a politician who failed to raise money from those who could afford $1,000 donations was doomed.

A society living in suburbs quite sharply segregated by income, influenced and manipulated by corporate managers through media largely under their control, and obliged, in order to survive and to have any hope of seeing its dreams come true, to be obsessed by money, risked turning away from much that had been best in the American tradition.

9

New World

No peace can last, or ought to last, which does not recognize the principle that governments derive all their just powers from the consent of the governed.
—*Woodrow Wilson, "Peace without Victory," January 22, 1917*

THE PAST QUARTER OF A CENTURY has felt like a switchback ride.[1] Americans have seen their country rise from depths of fear and uncertainty in the 1970s to peaks of triumph and self-confidence in the 1990s, only to be shaken by an unfamiliar feeling of vulnerability on September 11, 2001. Since then they have recovered their confidence again. American military might has triumphed easily, first in Afghanistan, then in Iraq, though military victory has hardly brought either tranquillity or security.

For many decades, America has alternately withdrawn from the outside world, and intervened decisively. Subjectively, Americans have felt capable of transforming the world in their own image and then wondered whether they care to do so. Yet objectively, throughout this period, the power and influence of the United States have continued steadily to expand.

To understand the foreign relations of the United States it is necessary to go further back in history than when domestic political issues are in question. Until the end of the nineteenth century, Americans were for the most part content to cultivate their own immense garden, protected by the tariff and the oceans from the turbulence and injustices of the Old World. Especially in the Mexican War, but also every now and again in the Caribbean and in Japan, they were quite prepared to wage gunboat and dollar diplomacy. It was Theodore Roosevelt and his circle who first put forward the idea that because the United States had grown to maturity as a power, it ought now to play a commensurate part in world affairs.[2] By 1898 America's world role was no longer a dream or a theory, it was a fact. In that year American forces defeated a European power, Spain, and annexed Cuba and the Philippines and also incorporated Hawaii as a territory. Even earlier, the United States had challenged a more formidable European power than Spain, namely Britain, over Venezuela,[3] and became deeply embroiled in the affairs of Mexico, the Caribbean, and the Orient. In several parts of the Caribbean, the United States did not hesitate to land troops and to overthrow local governments, ostensibly to protect American or even European investors. In the case of Panama, the United States detached a large portion of Colombia and created a dependent republic there to facilitate the building of the Panama Canal,[4] a project seen as vital to America's future as a world power because it allowed the navy to move from the Atlantic and the Caribbean to the Pacific.

These interventionist, indeed aggressive, policies reflected the new confidence Americans felt as a result of the rapid growth of their population and economy, and a sense of national energy and creativity. Yet when the First World War broke out in 1914, the United States still did not see any need to be involved, and many Americans felt strongly that they should avoid being entangled. It was another three years before Woodrow Wilson, taking the nation into war against Germany and its allies, acknowledged that the United States was not only a world power but also potentially the strongest of all the powers. The United States contributed decisively with men and money to the victory of Britain and France over the Central Powers, and for a moment it seemed that the peace settlement would be shaped by American ideas and American ideals. Yet within a couple of years the United States had once more retreated into what was called isolationism, from which it was dragged, more than two years after another world war had broken out, only by Japan's attack on Pearl Harbor.

Throughout the forty-three years from the sinking of the *Maine* to the sinking of the Pacific Fleet, and indeed throughout the remaining fifty-nine years of the twentieth century, with the possible exception of the

Depression years from 1929 to 1939, the power and international influence of the United States grew steadily, even though that strength was not evenly reflected in military forces.[5] Yet American attitudes to the power of the United States and to its deployment in the outside world have oscillated wildly. Seen from the outside, in other words, objectively, as a reality that other nations have had to confront, the growth of American power has been rather constant. Seen from within, subjectively, as an element in domestic politics and national psychology, Americans' attitude to their growing involvement in the outside world has fluctuated in a process of action and reaction, flow and ebb.

This enduring conflict between the reality of steadily accumulating American power and changing attitudes to that power has its roots not only in reactions to specific situations in the outside world but also in two of the profound constants of American history: the twin experiences of immigration and the frontier. Immigration peopled the United States with men and women whose attitude to the rest of the world (originally toward Europe but later toward other continents) was that they thanked God that they had left it behind and that they hoped they would have as little to do with the Old World as possible. The frontier, on the other hand, built into the American psyche an expectation of steady expansion. These two aspects of the American experience, and the attitudes they engendered, set the templates for the development of American foreign policy as a repeated alternation between the impulse to take advantage of America's growing economic, military, and political strength to export American ideas and values to the rest of the world and a desire on the other hand to avoid "entangling alliances" and other forms of involvement by which a corrupt outside world might soil the purity of the American experiment.

Throughout the American Century, as American power and influence grew both absolutely and relatively, that dualism between the ambition of the frontiersman and the reluctance of the immigrant has continued to set the terms for debate over foreign policy.

———•◆•———

BY THE END OF THE 1970S many well-informed Americans felt that the country's position in the world had been seriously weakened. Many ordinary Americans, in the sense of people who had no special reason to study foreign policy, were sure of it.

The economy faced aggressive competition, from Western Europe and especially from East Asia. The government had been humiliated by a series of defeats, from the fall of Saigon in 1975 to the failure of the Carter administration to rescue the American hostages from Iran in 1980. The Soviet Union was challenging American allies in many parts of the developing world, from Afghanistan to Angola, and also competing aggressively in the central strategic balance.

Only ten years later, the Soviet empire worldwide was collapsing and with it—at least until China reached maturity as a power—all serious geopolitical competition to the United States. In 1989 Moscow allowed, if it did not actively encourage, the emancipation of its satellite regimes in Eastern Europe, and by the end of 1991 the Soviet Union itself had actually disappeared. In that same year President Bush was able to organize a virtually worldwide coalition to free Kuwait and destroy the military power of Iraq. Moreover, the collapse of communism was an ideological victory. Although not everyone, everywhere accepted all components of the dominant American ideology of democracy and free markets, that ideology seemed in the ascendant.

Throughout the 1990s many Americans liked to proclaim the United States as "the last superpower." The proposition was undeniable. What was not always noticed was that it amounted to claiming primacy in a contest in which no one else was engaged. No other democracy even attempted to match the American investment in military assets. Successive administrations sought to use this monopoly of ultimate military power, and America's economic weight, cultural appeal, and technological dynamism, to change the world according to its own ideals and interests. At the end of the millennium, America was triumphant everywhere. Technological prowess seemed, through the alchemy of the stock markets, to have been turned into an unprecedented machine for the creation of unlimited wealth. Other technologies seemed to offer the prospect of military dominance with minimum risk of casualties.

Then, in 2001, once again, as in Vietnam and in the energy crisis of the 1970s, the limits of power reappeared. The technology boom collapsed. The economy fell into recession again. And the long arm of international terrorism, long feared but essentially ignored, demonstrated that no country was invulnerable. Once again, the United States confronted the unpalatable lesson that even the weak, ignored, can be dangerous. It also faced the reality of a world once again, in one way or another, at war.

Over the quarter of a century from the middle 1970s to the end of the millennium, America's real position in the world may not have changed so much as that Manichaean contrast between light and darkness might suggest. American military power was never seriously threatened, not even by terrorists who tried to destroy its central nervous system by crashing an airliner into the Pentagon.[6] Whatever they may have thought they could achieve, not even demented fanatics could have supposed that in that way or any other way they could destroy American military predominance. American military resources, whether measured in missiles, nuclear warheads, ships, aircraft and infantry divisions, or in the industrial and technological capacity to replace them, were essentially undiminished. The United States was spending more on the military than all other countries combined. American economic and political influence, though not unchallenged, remained preeminent.

It was Americans' perception of their position, influenced by sporadic and intermittently frenetic media attention and by political campaigns, alternately alarmist and complacent, acting now upon unrealistic expectations of invulnerability and exceptionalism, now on a perception of deadly threat, that changed. The public was given an exaggerated impression of violent swings from impotence to omnipotence and back again. After Vietnam, it was not the resources that were in question, but the will to use them, and the purposes for which they would be used.

——◆——

IT NEVER RAINS but it pours. Early in 1979 the shah fled from Iran. On February 1 the Ayatollah Khomeini arrived back in Tehran from Paris, where he had been living in exile. Within weeks the Islamic revolution in Iran was complete. Western expatriate managers packed their bags, shot their family pets, and left the oilfields at the head of the Persian Gulf. At the end of March, at the very moment when President Jimmy Carter succeeded in persuading representatives of Israel and Egypt to sign the historic Camp David peace accords, Saudi Arabia cut its oil production, and by a hideous coincidence the nuclear plant at Three Mile Island near Harrisburg, Pennsylvania, was closed by an accident that sent hundreds of thousands of gallons of radioactive water pouring into the reactor building.

Americans, accustomed to a profusion of oil and gas, had first experienced the frustration of waiting in line at gas stations in 1973, after the Organization of Petroleum Exporting Countries raised the price of oil from $2 a barrel to $13.50. It was a hard lesson for the citizens of the world's most powerful country, a first lesson in the strength of the weak. Now, six years later, after the Iranian revolution, there were gas lines again. One of their victims was Clifton Garvin, the chairman of Exxon, the world's biggest oil company.[7] The manager of his local gas station on the Post Road in Greenwich, Connecticut, saw him and offered to let him jump to the front of the line. Helpfully, he offered to explain to the other drivers who he was. Garvin said he would rather wait in safe anonymity. Another who was becalmed for forty-five minutes in a gas line, in this case at an Amoco station on Connecticut Avenue in Washington, was Carter's domestic policy adviser, Stuart Eizenstat.[8] He belted off a furious message telling the president that "nothing else has so frustrated, confused, angered the American people — or so targeted their distress at you personally."

Jimmy Carter had already focused on the energy crisis as his most urgent priority. He gave four speeches, political sermons in which he tried in vain to call for a sense of shared purpose. He borrowed a phrase from William James: energy conservation was "the moral equivalent of war." People mocked his solemnity with the acronym: meow.

In July the leaders of the seven biggest industrial nations met in Tokyo to discuss the crisis that was afflicting all of them. It was, Carter remembered, a nasty meeting.[9] The oil crisis was not only keeping America waiting in line; it was also threatening international peace and economic stability. Cutting out a planned vacation in Hawaii, the exhausted president flew straight back to Washington. Keen to fire two cabinet secretaries for suspected disloyalty, he demanded the resignation of the whole body, then headed for Camp David. He summoned a motley group of advisers, and then emerged to make the most extraordinary television speech of his presidency.[10] It became know as the "malaise speech," though in fact he did not use that word. Instead he spoke, with vatic intensity, about a national crisis of confidence. At times apparently close to hysteria, he mixed together practical considerations of energy policy and a plan for a vast program for manufacturing synthetic fuel with wild sermonizing about the longing for meaning, the American spirit and "faith in the future of this nation."[11] Eighteen months later, Carter had been defeated by Ronald Reagan, his fate sealed by his inability to end the ordeal of fifty American hostages taken prisoner by Islamic fanatics in Iran.[12]

That was the lowest point. But the second half of the 1970s saw one frustrating and humiliating experience after another, until it really did look as though the United States, squandering that commanding position in the world it had won by a century of economic progress, by victory in two world wars, and by the determination with which it had defended the free world in the Cold War, had turned into what Richard Nixon warned it might become, "a pitiful helpless giant."[13]

The position of the United States in the world did appear to be seriously diminished. For the first time in history the country was becoming dependent on oil imports. By 1973 they had reached 36 percent of consumption.[14] Later that proportion went over 50 percent. At the same time, U.S. steel plants began to import iron ore from Brazil and elsewhere for the first time. In many manufacturing sectors, U.S. industry was failing to compete. The knowledgeable worried about the decline of U.S. competitiveness, as measured particularly in comparison with Japan and what were coming to be called the Asian "tigers." Financially, the United States faced foreign account deficits, though not yet the budget deficit of the Reagan years. Herbert Goodman, a Gulf Oil executive, expressed the change concisely.[15] He spoke of the "enormous credibility and respect enjoyed by the United States." Then, he said, it began to fade: "It was the ebbing of American power—the Romans retreating from Hadrian's Wall."

It was not just oil. There was the trauma of the final collapse in Vietnam. Horrified Americans watched U.S. Marines beating off loyal Vietnamese who were trying to cling to the skids of the departing helicopters.[16] There were a number of other defeats, other challenges. In the Middle East, the Arab states came closer than ever before to inflicting defeat on Israel in the 1973 war.[17] Although in retrospect the Camp David agreement of 1978 enhanced U.S. power in the region by drawing Egypt from the Soviet to the American sphere of influence, this was far from clear at the time.

Under Leonid Brezhnev the Soviet Union had tested and challenged U.S. power at a number of "choke points" around the world, especially in Africa. Revolution broke out against the ancient emperor Haile Selassie in Ethiopia early in 1974.[18] By the end of 1977 Major Mengistu Haile Mariam was the undisputed Ethiopian leader. At war with Somalia, he turned to the Soviet Union, which, beginning in 1977–78, poured billions of dollars' worth of arms into the country by air and sea. The Soviet Union pulled off an even more important strategic coup in Angola in the middle 1970s.[19] When the country became independent from Portugal at the end of 1975, it faced chaos, with three separate independence movements fighting one another. Thanks to 10,000 to 12,000 Cuban troops, the MPLA faction in Luanda won the civil war and in October 1976 the MPLA signed a treaty of friendship and cooperation with the Soviet Union, which projected Soviet power close to southern Africa and central Latin America.

There, too, revolutionary Marxist movements seemed to be on the march. The democratically elected Marxist government in Chile was overthrown, with American help, in September 1973. In Central America Soviet allies were more successful. In 1979 a coalition led by the Sandinista rebels overthrew the pro-U.S. regime of Anastasio Somoza Debayle.[20] It began as a broad national movement for democracy, but before long the Sandinistas, too, abandoned their claims to be considered democrats and turned toward the Soviet Union.

In short, with Washington's attention distracted by the Watergate crisis and its aftermath, the Soviet Union made substantial progress in the middle 1970s toward reducing American influence in the developing world. For many patriotic Americans, President Carter's attempt to renegotiate the Panama Canal treaties in the same years was a further blow to pride and national interests.

These were peripheral dangers. The main event was still the strategic contest with the Soviet Union, and there too the conventional wisdom at the time was that the United States was in severe danger. The idea that the United States was losing the Cold War entered the mainstream of political debate with the establishment by President Ford of the Team B inquiry into the strategic balance and with the gradual conversion of the Republican Party to the alarmist assessment of the Committee on the Present Danger.[21]

In retrospect, this conservative assessment in the 1970s seems almost fantastically wide of the mark. So far from threatening the United States with defeat, the Soviet Union was on the brink of vaporizing. It was, however, a symptom of the rather volatile mood swings through which Americans viewed themselves and their position in the world, abetted by the odd combination of touchiness and indifference with which U.S. media reported the outside world.

By the end of the century, the majority view of the U.S. position in the world, even in the expert foreign policy community, had swung from excessive gloom to almost fatuous complacency. Paul Krugman, Princeton professor and *New York Times* columnist, expressed this view with customary trenchancy in a piece called "America the Boastful":

> After a mere two years of good news America's mood has become startlingly triumphalist. In the view of many business and political leaders . . . we have entered the era of the New Economy. . . . And because we have a New Economy and the rest of the world does not, we have also entered an era in which America is once more indisputably Number One—and the rest of the world must adopt our values, emulate our institutions, if it wants to compete. . . . To anyone with a sense of history, this is all deeply worrying. If pride goeth before a fall, the United States has one heck of a comeuppance in store.[22]

We have seen President Clinton's assessment of the situation of the United States in his January 2000 State of the Union Message. "Never before has our nation enjoyed, at once, so much prosperity and social progress with so little internal crisis and so few external threats."[23]

He was not by any means alone. In a book published in 2001, Dr. Henry Kissinger painted a similar picture of America perched upon a peak of imperial grandeur that resembled nothing so much as a contemporary account of the Diamond Jubilee of Queen Victoria in 1896: "At the dawn of the new millennium, the United States is enjoying a preeminence unrivaled by even the greatest empires of the past. From weaponry to entrepreneurship, from science to technology, from higher education to popular culture, America exercises an unparalleled ascendancy around the globe."[24]

And much more in the same hubristic rhythms. To be fair, Dr. Kissinger did not waste much time before discovering a number of worms in this golden apple, not least the fact that "America's preeminence is often treated with indifference by its own people" and that the United States had failed to develop concepts relevant to the emerging realities. He even went so far as to talk of "smugness."

In an excellent popular history of the Clinton years, *The Best of Times,* the highly respected former *Washington Post* reporter Haynes Johnson wrote,

> America's prospects appeared unlimited. Despite an unattractive tendency to boast loudly of their multiple advantages—"We're number one!"—Americans could make a powerful case that not since the peak of the Roman Empire had another society occupied so dominant a world position as they did at century's end. They enjoyed unprecedented peace and prosperity. Their creation of wealth was unsurpassed, and it was new wealth shared by more members of society than ever before. Driven by the force of their longest continuous peacetime boom, the expanding American economy lifted what was already the highest standard of living in the world to even greater heights. . . . Now, the movement was only up—and up, and up. There was no downside. No threat of another global war existed. . . . No new enemies challenged America.[25]

As we have seen, several of those statements were considerable exaggerations.[26] The gross national product, for example, is normally greater each year than in the previous one, and that is true of all industrial countries, not just of the United States. Nor is it conspicuously true that wealth was shared by more members of society than before; on the contrary, one of the most striking aspects of the Clinton boom was the accelerating inequality between the richest and the rest. Again, it was not entirely true that America had no enemies.

ON DECEMBER 21, 1991, plenipotentiaries of Russia, Ukraine, Belarus, and five Central Asian republics signed the treaty establishing the Commonwealth of Independent States. The Soviet Union was no more. Its fate was sealed the previous August by the dramatic events of the failed coup organized by the KGB chief, Vladimir Kryuchkov. The Soviet Union did not even make it to the date officially foreseen for its dissolution, which was the last day of 1991. Instead, Mikhail Gorbachev, who— for all that he could not in the end make the final separation from the

Communist Party, and so was ousted by Boris Yeltsin—deserves the greatest credit for bringing Russia out of the political and economic chains of communism, resigned on Christmas Day. The next day, attempting to enter his office for a meeting, he found his way barred.

As early as 1989, less than a decade after the culminating American humiliation of the Tehran hostages, the Soviet Union appeared to have conceded defeat when Gorbachev passed the word to Soviet military leaders not to intervene to save communist regimes in eastern Europe.[27] Now, at the end of 1991 it even formally ceased to exist.

The effect of this event on the U.S. foreign policy community, on the military and on American public opinion should not be minimized. For more than forty years, the country had been summoned to a supreme effort. President John Kennedy's inaugural rhetoric did not exaggerate the sense of historic destiny, of peril and fear the Cold War inspired. In the process, the country itself had been mobilized. The national security state had been conjured into existence and had developed considerable inertial momentum. In myriad ways, over more than forty years, the Cold War had motivated or justified profound changes in American life. The wartime draft, for example, had been prolonged. A massive defense and aerospace industrial sector had developed, responsible directly for more than 10 million jobs. The investments in higher education and research made because successive U.S. governments saw themselves as in competition, not to say mortal combat, with the Soviet Union made possible the dramatic new technology of computers and the Internet. (It was, as noted in Chapter 3, the Department of Defense's Advanced Research Projects Agency, not some office in the Department of Commerce or the Office of Education, that oversaw the creation of the Internet. After 1958 even university departments of the humanities were able to attract government funding under the National Defense Education Act.) The largest single infrastructure project in American history, the interstate highway system, was justified as making it easier to shift troops and matériel around the country. Public opinion had been profoundly affected. The country saw itself as committed to what John F. Kennedy called "the long twilight struggle," and its disappearance resembled the ending of a psychological dependency. Indeed it has been plausibly argued that the commitment of the Kennedy and Johnson administrations to the civil rights movement was motivated in large part by the wish to avoid damage to America's reputation in the newly independent states of Asia and Africa.[28] More broadly, the Cold War had evoked a liberal consensus. Liberals and Democrats embraced the anticommunism of conservatives and Republicans; and in return, under the slogan "politics stops at the water's edge," Republicans accepted the interventionist policies of the New Deal, Harry Truman's Fair Deal, and (until 1966) Lyndon Johnson's Great Society. The corollary was that the end of the Cold War removed any justification for consensus liberal policies, which had in any case become intensely irksome to a new generation of conservatives.

———⏺———

INEVITABLY, THE ABRUPT collapse of the Soviet Union, after more than forty years in which competition and conflict with its communist rulers had been one of the basic assumptions of American politics, led to an important debate in the United States about the future of foreign policy. It was not, however, a debate that was candidly presented to the public as a whole or much taken up by politicians. By the early 1990s foreign policy had become to a large degree the concern of a clerisy of experts who moved between international relations departments in the great graduate schools, research institutes and think tanks, and the national security bureaucracy itself. The level of expertise was impressively higher than it had been, for example, in the Inquiry in 1918, when President Wilson's researchers had to send to Stanford's map shop in London for maps of the Balkans, or even at the time of that earlier "great debate" about the Cold War in the 1950s. Yet, whether because the wider public was tired of being asked to consider events and issues in remote countries, or because the society as a whole was more ready to leave policy decisions to experts, there was little widespread discussion of how the United States should react to the abrupt collapse of its adversary.

In the foreign policy community, however, two schools of thought fairly quickly emerged. To put the distinction between them in the simplest terms, one school emphasized the triumph of the West, and especially of the United States; the other, as we shall see, stressed new dangers ahead.

At first there were many who saw the collapse of communism in Eastern Europe and in the former Soviet Union as an opportunity, both ideologically and commercially. Some argued that the United States should supply the leadership for a major effort to rebuild the Soviet economy on capitalist lines, rather as the government of a newly reunited Germany, on a smaller scale, was pouring what eventually amounted to hundreds of billions of dollars into trying, with only partial success, to integrate the eastern part of the country, impoverished by communism, with the wealthy west. (The United States had, after all, attempted something similar in Japan after 1945, with great success, and had contributed critically to the restoration of Western Europe through the Marshall Plan.) Others heaved a sigh of relief that the United States need not be so heavily involved in a naughty world, or wondered from what direction the next threat to domestic tranquillity might come.

These two temperamental schools of thought were summed up by two influential books, published shortly after the fall of communism. Many were impressed by the ideas of the Washington-based conservative historian and student of Hegel, Francis Fukuyama, who argued that the Soviet collapse meant "the end of history" (by which he seems to have meant "the end of historicism," the passing, that is, of the view of history that interprets it as leading to the triumph of one ideology or another). Although Fukuyama's book was more subtle than the interpretation widely put on it, his major theme was a new optimism.[29] "As we reach the 1990s, the world as a whole has gotten better in certain distinct ways. . . . Authoritarian dictatorships of all kinds, both on the Right and on the Left, have been collapsing. . . . The pessimistic lessons about history that our century supposedly taught us need to be rethought from the beginning."[30] Fukuyama was putting into words one widespread response to the collapse of communism: that it meant the triumph of democracy and capitalism and the victory of American values.

The Bush administration committed itself totally to Mikhail Gorbachev, without perhaps fully realizing that, if Gorbachev's adoption of *glasnost* and *perestroika*, openness and restructuring, marked the end of communism, it did not necessarily signify the triumph or even the comprehension of American ideas in Russia. The president and his advisers realized too late that

Gorbachev, having made the crucial break toward democracy and a market economy, had become yesterday's man, replaced by the cruder Yeltsin. While numerous entrepreneurs and eminent economists, led by Harvard's Jeffrey Sachs, went to Moscow, ostensibly as advisers, in reality as missionaries for American free-market capitalism, their influence faded as Russia's economy spiraled downward.[31] It became painfully clear that the United States was not in fact prepared to lead a major program of international investment by both private and public sectors in Russia. Both American and European investors failed to understand that adopting the shibboleths of capitalism, such as stock exchanges,[32] was less important than equipping the Russian economy with the basic capitalist infrastructure: a legal system friendly to investment; a strong and convertible currency; the control of crime; reliable communications—in short, a working civil society.

At the very point where an opportunity existed to bring Russia unambiguously into the Western political and economic system, Washington's attention was distracted by events in the Middle East. The second iconic interpretation of the world after the end, if not of history, then at least of communism, was put forward by a Harvard professor, Samuel P. Huntington. He set himself alongside the ambitious "world historical" or metahistorical theorizers of the 1920s and 1930s such as Oswald Spengler and Arnold Toynbee.[33] Where Fukuyama saw the end of communism as heralding a new world open to American ideas, an alternative, and very influential, interpretation asked in effect where a new threat would come from.

To summarize a complex and honorably tentative analysis, Huntington answered: perhaps from an alliance between Islam and China. In 1993 Huntington published an article in the influential New York journal, *Foreign Affairs*, in which he argued that in the future, "conflict between civilizations"—as opposed to nations—"will supplant ideological and other forms of conflict as the dominant global form of conflict."[34]

Like all works of a particular time, the article reflected contemporary and even topical events, in Huntington's case specifically the Chinese government's repression of students demonstrating for democracy in Tiananmen Square, Beijing (and elsewhere), in June 1989; the conflict among Hindus, Muslims, and the secular state in India over the destruction of the Ayodhya mosque in 1993; and—especially—the Gulf War of 1991. World politics, Huntington posited, were entering a new phase, in which the sources of conflict would not be primarily ideological or economic but "cultural."[35] Nation-states would remain the most powerful actors, but global politics would be dominated by "the clash of civilizations." He argued that there were "seven or eight" major civilizations, depending on whether Africa was allowed to count as one: the Western, Confucian, Japanese, Islamic, Hindu, Slavic-Orthodox, and Latin American. A West "at the peak of its power," he warned, "confronts non-Wests that increasingly have the desire, the will and the resources to shape the world in a non-Western way."

Picking up an idea from Singapore's ambassador to the United Nations, Kishore Mahbubani, Huntington predicted it would be "the West versus the Rest." He asserted that a "Confucian-Islamic" connection was challenging "Western interests, values and power." China's conflicts with the West would incline it to seek partnerships with other anti-Western states. And China's growing need for oil would create an "arms-for-oil" axis between Beijing and Islamic capitals.

Western ideas such as "individualism, liberalism, constitutionalism, human rights, equality, liberty, the rule of law, democracy, free markets, the separation of church and state," Huntington argued, often had little resonance for Muslims, Chinese, Japanese, Hindus, and others. And he acknowledged that many non-Westerners saw the West as "using international institutions, military power and economic power to run the world in ways that would maintain Western predominance." He even conceded that there was "a significant element of truth" in their suspicions.

Many criticisms can be made of Huntington's thesis, and in fact he himself softened some of its apocalyptic, pessimistic tone when he expanded it into a book. Although the tone was ostensibly scholarly, the text betrayed a number of biases, against the developing world, for example, and against Islam in particular. Islam, said Huntington, "has bloody borders." (So did the West during the centuries when it was expanding in North America, the Caribbean, Africa, the Indian subcontinent, and Australia, not to mention the earlier centuries when it was contending with Islam in the Crusades, Spain, the Aegean, and the Balkans.) The Gulf War was arguably not so much a conflict between civilizations as a geopolitically motivated war to prevent Iraq (an aggressive, but far from characteristically Muslim state) from getting too close to the world's largest pool of oil. And the key term, "the West," is itself a Cold War concept, linking Europe to the United States. That begged the important questions whether Europe would see the world as it was seen in the United States, and whether the United States would care whether Europeans did or did not. The Huntington thesis, in short, was interesting not so much in itself as because its vogue chimed with a growing sense in certain circles in the United States that America and its allies might soon find themselves again surrounded by enemies.

—•—

TENSIONS BETWEEN the United States and the Islamic world got worse sooner and more visibly than conflict between America and China. Washington was preoccupied with the collapse of communism in eastern Europe when, on August 1, 1990, President Bush's national security adviser, Admiral Brent Scowcroft, found the president sitting on the treatment bench in the basement medical office in the White House. (The president was suffering from nothing more serious than sore shoulders, characteristically from hitting too many golf balls in practice).[36] Scowcroft's news was utterly disconcerting. Iraq was about to invade Kuwait.

Bush might perhaps have dismissed this as a minor act of bullying by one aggressive Middle Eastern state against a puny and unpopular neighbor. Immediately he saw that two vital principles were involved. First, as Margaret Thatcher put it a few hours later, "if Iraq wins no small state is safe."[37] And, second, Iraq—itself a major oil supplier to the West—was threatening the region at the head of the Persian Gulf, shared unevenly among Kuwait, Saudi Arabia, and Iran, which contained well over half the world's proven oil reserves and a substantial proportion of the oil available for export to the world market.

Bush senior handled the ensuing Gulf War with a sure touch, though the way the war ended left grave problems, for his son as for many others. The president eventually secured a strong resolution from the United Nations, giving him and his allies authority to eject Iraq from Kuwait by force. With considerable skill he threaded his way through different congressional objections to his policy. He also put together a coalition of allies that had few precedents since World War II and the founding of NATO. As well as traditional allies like Britain and France, it included Turkey and Egypt, two countries with a strong Islamist opposition, and both Saudi Arabia, which as the chief sponsor and funder of Islamic resistance to American power was certainly one of the strangest of allies, and Syria, one of the chief supporters of Islamic terrorism. Germany, banned by its constitution from sending troops out of the NATO area, nevertheless sent military aircraft. What was more, President Bush was able to secure backing and substantial financial support even from Japan, whose American-imposed constitution had previously banned such involvement.

The overwhelming character of the alliance's victory over Iraq heightened the sense of American hegemony. Here was the "last superpower," really taking the lead in military action to uphold international law and the international system. The military campaign was short, almost bloodless for the allies, and decisive. Following the strict letter of his mandate from the United Nations, Bush halted the coalition's forces before Saddam Hussein had been overthrown, indeed before the Marsh Arabs in the southern third of Iraq (who, like three-fifths of Iraq's population, belong to the Shi'a branch of Islam) or the Kurds in the northern third had been liberated. (The Kurds were able to achieve a kind of de facto independence; the southern Shia were ruthlessly suppressed by Saddam Hussein.) Instead, U.S. and British aircraft continued to bomb Iraq.

Saddam Hussein remained in power and was able to exploit the divisions that gradually emerged in the coalition against him to maintain himself in power. The dangerous question of what to do about Saddam's determination to acquire weapons of mass destruction was left unresolved, except by a fragile United Nations inspection system, soon brushed aside by the ruthless dictator in Baghdad. At the same time the United States and its allies maintained sanctions against Iraq. They had little effect on Saddam's hold on power, though they weakened his military power and inflicted grave hardship on the Iraqi people.

President Bush had acted successfully as a superpower, implacably determined to eject Iraq from Kuwait, but at the same time willing to work within the limits imposed by diplomacy and the United Nations. He had, however, made two serious mistakes. The first involved Russia and the former Soviet Empire. The Bush administration misread what had happened there. Because of Gorbachev's abrupt change of tack, Americans exaggerated their own role in the collapse of communism, and underestimated the extent to which the peoples and even part of the governments of Eastern Europe and the former Soviet Union had simply had enough of a system that was collapsing of its own rigidity. The truth was that the pressure the Reagan administration put on the Soviet leadership by upping the ante in the arms race (through increased military spending and especially through the Strategic Defense Initiative, an experimental missile defense system) had persuaded Gorbachev and other younger leaders that established communist policies would lead to disaster and there would have to be a drastic change in the whole regime.

So Americans came to believe that they had helped the Russians and other Eastern European peoples to carry out a revolution. The situation was more complicated and less desirable than that. It was true that state property was privatized. It was also true that much of it was simply taken to enrich the very same individuals, former members of the communist *nomenklatura*, who had controlled the economy before. (The idea, for example, that the people of Eastern Europe were motivated to throw off communism by seeing ads on television portraying the profusion of consumer goods in the United States, widely held in the early 1990s, was illusory. If East Germans saw any televised profusion, it was West German, not American.) Many Russians admired and envied the West. Many saw the United States as a potential savior. But as the oppression of communism was replaced by economic collapse, real hardship, and widespread gangsterism, others looked back with nostalgia to the ways when, though you might not be able to speak freely, at least you had a job, a regular income, and personal security, and you could have pride in your country's achievements. So the West, led by the United States, bungled the great opportunity presented by the collapse of the Communist Party in Russia.

The second mistake was to underestimate the resentment and anger U.S. conduct had caused in the world of Islam. The Bush administration showed restraint, in retrospect too great restraint, in ending the war before Saddam had been overthrown. There were, however, political as well as legalistic reasons for that. Iraq was an artificial state, put together by Britain after the fall of the Ottoman Empire, in part to protect the Kirkuk oilfields, in part to block the political power of the Saudi dynasty. It was inherently unstable, held together only by Saddam's cunning and brutality. If Saddam were overthrown, the southern third of the country might well secede. Saudi Arabia and the other Gulf States were not anxious to have a Shi'a state, only too likely to merge with or be taken over by Shi'ite Iran, on their northern borders. Similarly the Turks, faced with a Kurdish insurrection in their eastern provinces, had no desire to see the emergence of a Kurdish secession state in northern Iraq.

The whole of Islam, from Morocco to Indonesia, and from Bosnia to West Africa, was in turmoil. In the coinage of American politics, this was too often crudely interpreted as a conflict between "modernization" (often perceived as Westernization or even Americanization) and "fundamentalism." That way of looking at things was both inaccurate and potentially dangerous. Contrary to Huntington's thesis, Islam is not in modern times so much a civilization as a religion shared (in various forms) by something over a billion people in several dozen countries, as well as by minorities elsewhere. Beyond the Koran, the requirements of their religion (faith, prayer, charity, fasting, pilgrimage) are universal.[38] But Islam embraced the two great branches, Sunni and Shi'a, four major schools of religious law, and countless sects, traditions, and alternative rival interpretations, not to mention national and political rivalries. Although Muslims all read the Koran in the Arabic language, there are many variants of spoken Arabic, as different from one another as Portuguese from Italian or Mandarin from Cantonese, and many Muslims speak other languages, such as Urdu, Farsi, or Turkish, not to mention English, French, German, or Russian. As to civilization, there are Arabs who are completely at home in the modern worlds of Washington diplomacy, New York banking, or London media, others—from Afghanistan to Yemen and from the Gobi to the Sahara deserts—whose societies are essentially unchanged since the thirteenth century.

Modern Islam and its tormenting political divisions and agenda are largely the consequence of an experience almost all Muslims share: the dislocating effects of the end of the five empires under which the great majority of them lived until very recent times:[39] the Ottoman, the British, the Russian, the French, and the Dutch. As a consequence, however different their political philosophies, most Muslims share an anticolonial politics. Infuriatingly for Americans, with their anticolonial heritage, many Muslims lump Americans together with other Europeans as "the West" and see them as the leaders of a new kind of imperial power.

While many parts of the Muslim world have made substantial economic and industrial progress, and many millions of Muslims live in great and relatively sophisticated cities (Istanbul, Cairo, Damascus, Baghdad, Tehran, Lahore, Jakarta), many still live in undeveloped societies like those of, for example, Central Asia, North and West Africa, rural parts of the Middle East, the Indian subcontinent, and the Indonesian archipelago. In many Muslim countries, a militant (*not* "fundamentalist")[40] version of Islam has spread in three sectors of the population especially. One is the rural, undeveloped, and conservative poor. A second consists of many (far from all) of the urban lower middle classes of the great and middling cities. The third, and potentially most dangerous of all, are those young, more or less well educated children of the new elites who sense that the world of Islam is on the eve of revolutionary turmoil and want to put themselves on the right side of the barricades.

The first, the country folk, and especially their religious leaders, are simply afraid that traditional purities and pieties will be corrupted by what they see as Western immorality: Hollywood, advertising, the Internet, sexual laxity in all its insidiously tempting forms. (There is a historical inversion here: in the days of Sir Richard Burton and Gustave Flaubert, it was Westerners who found the Muslim world sexually exciting.) Those in the second group share those fears, while they are at the same time fascinated and repelled by Western wealth and freedom (especially sexual freedom). They are frustrated by the inequalities arising from the import of Western capitalism. Finally they are torn between the comforts of traditional religious belief and social structure, and the excitement of Western (which they see as largely American) technology. Similar tensions torment the third group, the potential leaders; but they are, of course, also acutely aware of political considerations and opportunities.

The United States has forged more or less reliable alliances with the political leadership in many Islamic countries, among them Turkey, Egypt, Saudi Arabia, and Pakistan. But in those four countries, and in others such as Jordan, Algeria, and Indonesia, the political opposition has to a greater or lesser extent taken on an "Islamic" coloration. So "Western" or "modernizing" governments are seen as more or less subject to American military or economic domination. In some cases they are more or less openly at war with an "Islamist" movement popular among many of the rural and urban poor.

Ever since the 1940s, the American relationship with Islamic countries, and especially with the Arabic-speaking Middle East, has been complicated by American support for Israel. For many reasons, that support is not negotiable, and it is right that it should not be. Israel is a democracy, it has the closest links with the United States, and the United States (and, with greater or lesser enthusiasm, the other Western countries)[41] is committed to Israel's survival. However, the issue of American support for Israel (as it is generally seen in the Islamic Middle East and elsewhere) has become a serious barrier to good U.S. relations in the region in the past quarter of a century, even though the United States has to a greater or lesser degree cemented good relations with regimes in such important Islamic countries as Egypt, Turkey, and Saudi Arabia.

In 1973 many in the Middle East saw the United States as having rescued Israel from defeat. (In fact, though Israel was badly shaken by the Arab surprise attack, it did not need American help to win that war.) Then came the Iranian revolution. The mullahs denounced the United States as the "great Satan," and their revolutionary disciples took dozens of American hostages. The United States replied with an ill-fated rescue operation on Iranian territory. Other reasons for resentment were the Gulf War, the sanctions against Iraq, and the continuing bombing of Iraq. Over the past quarter of a century, admittedly with substantial provocation, the United States has bombed or otherwise attacked five Islamic countries: Lebanon, Libya, Iraq, Somalia, and Afghanistan.[42] Osama bin Laden was not alone in resenting the American military presence in Saudi Arabia.

Hardest to eradicate, in spite of decades of sincere American attempts to facilitate peace processes between Israel and its neighbors, is the suspicion that the United States is in the last analysis always on Israel's side. Of course, so long as some Islamic countries or movements intend to destroy the state of Israel, all democratic countries will be on Israel's side. But many in the Islamic world do not understand that, or if they do, they do not share that concern, and there is a sense that on the conservative right in America, in particular, Israel is seen as the ally, and Islam itself as the enemy.

In any case, extremist and terrorist groups were forming in many places in the Muslim world. They were not on the whole drawn from the "wretched of the earth," the impoverished peasantry and stressed urban workers. They were formed by young men and women from the third group mentioned earlier, students and a half-educated intelligentsia that resembled, in a sinister way, the children of officials and bourgeois who nurtured the incoherent rage and revolutionary dreams of the Russian intelligentsia of the nineteenth century. In both cases, vast and unpredictable change led to humiliation and rage and created a murderous spiritual distemper.[43]

———•◆•———

IN SPITE OF his impressive conduct of the Gulf War, George H. W. Bush fell from popularity with startling speed in 1992. Almost his last act was to order an incursion by U.S. Marines into Somalia. Almost the first act of his successor, Bill Clinton, was to countermand that incursion, after the Marines found themselves in a fire fight in which hundreds of Somalis and more than a dozen Marines were killed.

When the Clinton administration took office in 1993, it mounted a concerted attempt to tell the world that it would be devoted to what it called "neo-Wilsonian" ideas. The president, his first secretary of state Warren Christopher, his national security adviser Tony Lake, and Madeleine Albright, then ambassador to the United Nations, all made speeches explaining what this meant. They promised that the United States would be aggressively promoting its own ideals, in which free-market capitalism was explicitly given parity with democracy as one of America's defining beliefs.[44] Nothing could better illustrate the triumph of conservative ideology over the previous twenty years. In the 1960s the United States presented itself to the world as a defender of freedom, and as an opponent of colonialism, not primarily as capitalist. Now capitalism, or free markets, had become almost as important in the American value system, as it was promoted by U.S. officials, as democracy and freedom themselves.

This missionary zeal, however, did not survive President Clinton's domestic tribulations or the devastating, largely unexpected, triumph of the Republicans in Congress under Newt Gingrich in 1994. Only in one field, that of world trade, did the Clinton administration press ahead with what its representatives (like Bush administration officials later) habitu-ally, if unfortunately, described as an "aggressive" trade policy.[45]

During the 1990s, however, government policy was by no means the only or even the most important part of the impact of the United States on the world. Everywhere corporations, many of them American, were hav-ing an impact on the lives and governments of foreign countries in the course of the process loosely known as "globalization." This process was supported by the policies of the new World Trade Organization and by the continuing effects of the "reform" policies of the international finan-cial institutions, especially the International Monetary Fund (IMF) and the World Bank, collectively known as the "Washington consensus."[46] The original ten policy prescriptions were listed as: fiscal discipline; tax reform; secure property rights; steering of investment into more produc-tive areas, including welfare spending; liberalization of interest rates; of trade; and of foreign direct investment; a more competitive exchange rate; deregulation; and privatization.[47]

This is a precise formulation of a general ideological climate that began with the collapse of communism in the late 1980s. For years devel-oping countries had clung to the teaching of a social-democratic "devel-opment economics" first formulated in the 1960s.[48] Suddenly, if in some cases only temporarily and superficially, these countries, including Russia and the other former communist states, were converted to neoliberal eco-nomics.[49] Flush with money, the international capital markets and espe-cially the big investment banks on Wall Street were ready to lend to what were now called, not evolving *peoples* or developing *nations*, but "emerg-ing *markets*." To some extent it was a forcible conversion. The IMF and the World Bank enforced a conditionality on their (concessionary) loans: to deserve them borrowers had to agree to what was known as "structural adjustment," and that in turn, in one form or another, meant acceptance of the Washington consensus.

At first, the process worked well. A number of countries—Chile and Uganda and several of the former communist countries in Eastern Eu-rope prominent among them, and even China—were proudly displayed as evidence of what structural adjustment and free-market capitalism could achieve. The first wave of change in the direction of liberalization, too, was comparatively easy to carry out. Currency could be made convertible, foreign direct investment encouraged, by the executive branches of government. Later attempts at deeper change, involving governance and contested social reforms, required assent from parliaments and cooperation from other components of civil society. The results, too, were quickly visible. So for five years it looked as though the prevailing neoliberal public philosophy of the United States, both through the "Washington consensus" in the public institutions and through prevailing fashions in the private capital markets, was really bringing growth and development to the poorer countries of eastern Europe, Latin America, and Africa, while the "Asian tigers" were showing what deregulated markets and privatized industry could achieve in a favorable climate.

Globalization involved many processes, in many parts of the world. It was not simply a euphemism for expansionism on the part of American corporations. For one thing, European and Japanese corporations were also involved. For another, in many respects what was called globalization was beneficial to developing countries, at least certainly to their elites. The growth in international trade offered one glimpse of hope to developing countries, if they could export on fair terms of trade. Globalization also implied some transfer of Western technology.

In practice, the consequences were mixed—to say the least—from the point of view of poor countries. American food exports, for example, and even food, donated as aid under the PL480 legislation, had long seriously damaged local food production.[50] The terms of trade were far from fair in practice. "Washington consensus" policies such as privatization were often inappropriate and even destructive. Corporate interests, such as those of pharmaceutical companies, were often at odds with those of the people of developing countries. (Farmers in the Philippines and forest tribes in the Brazilian Amazon found American law firms were claiming intellectual property rights over traditional strains of rice or medicinal plants in the wild, and so on.) Pressure to adopt the American free-market ideology was often insensitive, to put it no higher. Neither American officials nor public opinion realized the extent to which they were identified not with democratic change but with sundry oppressive and unpopular elites.

Attitudes to the developing world were sometimes unhelpful. The entire continent of Africa, for example, with almost a billion people, was routinely described in public discussion in the United States as a "basket case," a hideous metaphor at best. American politicians increasingly attacked the United Nations, to which many in developing countries turned as their only friend. Successive administrations failed to pay up American dues. At the same time American public opinion was under the impression that the United States was the world's biggest, if not only, source of foreign aid. That might have been true fifty years earlier, but the reality was now that the United States gave a smaller amount of aid as a proportion of its gross national product than any other developed country. U.S. public policy, for example, on the issue of global warming and environmental pollution, was widely seen as self-interested, or shaped by special corporate interests, especially after the George W. Bush administration came to power in 2001. American public opinion was widely seen as arrogantly indifferent to the rest of the world, and much American journalism reinforced that suspicion.

This is not to say that on every issue the United States was in the wrong and other countries in the right: far from it. Selfishness, cowardice, political subservience to corrupt elites and chauvinism were all but universal in the developing world, and European nations pursued their own interests as selfishly as any. But in many particulars Americans did have a picture in their heads of how they were seen in the world that was dangerously at odds with reality.

After the fall of communism, there was a widespread assumption in the United States that the adoption of the American free-market ideology would bring the world peace and prosperity. A number of financial panics in the 1990s shook this assumption. The 1994 Mexican crisis was only the first of a series of shocks that made everyone, from Western governments to the governments of developing and newly developed countries, to the Washington institutions and the New York markets, reassess their optimistic assumptions about the prospects for "emerging," liberalized economies. An ironic consequence was that the U.S. economy benefited, as elites in developing countries transferred their assets, where they could, into the U.S. dollar, thus reinforcing U.S. markets, though not necessarily to the long-term benefit of the U.S. economy.

Most serious was the Asian crisis, which began with the collapse of the Thai *baht* in the summer of 1996. That led to falling dominoes: to

crises, at first financial, then economic and in the end inevitably political, in Indonesia, Malaysia, Hong Kong, Singapore, Taiwan, and South
Korea. Even the mighty Japanese economy, already suffering the effects
of its own financial instability and "bubble economy," was further damaged. The Russian economy was soon in such desperate shape that the
Russian government devalued the ruble. By 1999 even Jeffrey Sachs,
once a missionary to the Russians for neoliberal economics, was pointing out that ten middle-income nations with a total population of close
to 1 billion people had experienced catastrophic economic crises since
1994.[51]

The spectacular rise of the New York markets concealed worrying instability there, too. In 1998 panic was only narrowly averted after the collapse
of the hedge fund Long-Term Capital Management. By the late 1990s
these successive shocks had led some politicians, bankers, and economists
alike to modify their enthusiasm for the pure milk of free-market economics. No less a figure than the former president of Mexico, Carlos Salinas de
Gortari, a former champion of free-market reforms, summed up the new
mood in an article in February 1999:

> In much of the world the search [is] under way for an alternative to what has
> come to be called neo-liberalism, an alternative that would make the market
> shift—the global turn to markets—more people-friendly. . . . The neo-liberal
> version of the market economy may favor the interests of big international
> business.[52]

Salinas's change of tack is itself not immune from criticism. In the
fat years, his was only one of the governments of developing countries that
found it very convenient to adopt "Washington consensus" reforms if that
was the price to be paid for a flood of foreign investment. After all, private
capital flows to "emerging markets" rose from 0.75 percent of their gross
domestic product in 1990 to almost 4 percent only three years later.[53]

The Washington consensus was only part, if an important part, of a
wider set of assumptions that dominated American views of the new world
created by the end of communism. Developing countries would adopt
American ideas of democracy, it was assumed, and also the American
model of capitalism.[54] But in an even larger sense it was assumed that they
would inevitably come to adopt American culture as a whole.[55]

This was the core meaning of globalization. This was the view of many in the Clinton administration and among opinion formers. It was also the opinion of most ordinary Americans, to judge from surveys. For example, in 1999 the Chicago Council on Foreign Relations published one of a long-established quadrennial series of surveys of public opinion about foreign policy.[56] It noted:

> As a new millennium approaches, Americans feel secure, prosperous and confident. They see the United States as the world's most important and powerful country, with the fear of armed threats from a rival superpower diminished. In an era of increasing globalization, Americans view economic rather than military power as the most significant measure of global strength. Apprehension about economic competition from Japan or Europe has dissipated, as have concerns about immigration. Nevertheless, Americans are alarmed by images of violence at home and abroad. They support measures to thwart terrorists, prevent the spread of weapons of mass destruction and keep defense strong, but shy away from using U.S. troops on foreign soil. American public and leadership opinion on foreign policy today reflects a "guarded engagement" by a largely satisfied superpower.
>
> As in all previous surveys, support for an active role for the United States in the world remains strong, with 61 percent of the public and 96 percent of leaders favoring such activism.

As Dr. Henry Kissinger noted, in a book published at the end of the century, there was no doubt about the preeminence of the United States, militarily, economically, and ideologically.[57] The only question, he thought, was how long, and how enthusiastically, Americans would be willing to support it. Dr. Kissinger pointed to two paradoxes. For one, the United States was powerful enough to carry the day in international relations, "often enough to evoke charges of American hegemony." Prescriptions often reflected either domestic pressures or obsolete Cold War maxims. "The result is that the country's preeminence is coupled with the serious potential of becoming irrelevant to many of the currents affecting and ultimately transforming the global order."[58] The second paradox, according to Kissinger, is that American preeminence is often treated with indifference by the American people. (This represents the survival of the "immigrant" tradition, described earlier.) "Judging from media coverage and congressional sentiments, two important barometers," he wrote, "Americans' interest in foreign policy is at an all-time low."[59]

———◆———

THOSE WORDS WERE PUBLISHED in the summer of 2001. By then the new administration of George W. Bush had already experienced one foreign test with sinister implications for the future. When an American reconnaissance aircraft strayed too close to the Chinese coast, Beijing reacted with startling fury. The incident was skillfully handled and did not permanently impede improvement in Sino-American relations. But it was a disconcerting reminder of just how touchy and also how self-confident the Chinese government had become. Certainly the prospect was that relations with China would remain delicate. Although the Chinese government had enthusiastically adopted the superficial aspects of free-market policies, it remained—more than thirty years after the Nixon-Kissinger "opening"—a communist party dictatorship. The long-held assumption that economic liberalization would lead to political liberty remained unproven. China's government was brutally indifferent to human rights in many ways and many places. Dangerous international issues, especially over Taiwan and North Korea, lay ahead. So too did steady pressure intended to limit the freedoms of the "Special Autonomous Region," Hong Kong. It was as if Samuel Huntington's nightmare of an alliance between the Middle Kingdom and Islam had appeared as a ghost at the feast of millennial prosperity. Another more terrifying apparition was on its way.

———◆———

ON SEPTEMBER 11, 2001, with the suicide bombing of the World Trade Center towers and the Pentagon, interest in foreign policy revived, as one might say, with a vengeance. Once again, as after Pearl Harbor, or after the capture of the American embassy in Tehran in 1979, but if anything with even greater fervor, the country was inflamed by a passion of patriotism, or nationalism, united in the resolution that it must act, justly but effectively, against international terrorism.

Once again, the needle had swung between the twin magnetic poles of the immigrant and frontier traditions, between indifference and activism. Or rather the neoconservative group that had acquired dominant influence over foreign policy in the second Bush administration had forged the two traditions, of proud withdrawal and aggressive intervention, into a single policy.

Where in the Gulf War the elder Bush had put himself at the head of a great international coalition in arms to vindicate decency in international affairs, now the younger Bush reacted as though the United States neither needed nor perhaps even wanted the potentially encumbering help of allies who could contribute relatively little in strictly military terms. A number of respected writers on foreign policy promoted the idea that there was no need for the United States to take much notice of foreign nations and that American leaders should pursue their own sense of the national self-interest.[60] By late 2002, to be sure, the second Bush administration had consented to go to the United Nations for justification for its determination to bring about "regime change" in Iraq; but this was a very different matter from the patient coalition building of the first President Bush. And when influential members of the UN Security Council (France, Germany, Russia, China) were reluctant to approve preemptive war against Iraq, the Bush administration went ahead without UN endorsement, or rather with no more specific authority than that conferred by Resolution 1441.

In fact, when George W. Bush was inaugurated in 2001 he installed in charge of foreign and national security policy a group of officials who had long awaited the opportunity to put into effect their own ideas for a tougher American stance. The intellectual antecedents of this new policy go back to the first Bush administration, and to those within that administration who were critical of the way the first President Bush and his White House and State Department thought about the post–Cold War world in general, and the Middle East in particular. The key figure throughout was Dr. Paul Wolfowitz, a veteran of the Bush, Reagan, and even Carter administrations who served as under-secretary of defense under Secretary Dick Cheney in the first Bush administration and then, as dean of the School of Advanced International Studies at Johns Hopkins University, became the focus of conservative opposition to the foreign and defense policies of the Clinton administration. The working relationship between Wolfowitz and Cheney, a veteran Republican politician who during the Clinton years became chief executive of the oil and engineering conglomerate Halliburton, symbolized the alliance between "neoconservative" intellectuals, many of them with close ties to Israel, and classic Republican conservatives with strong corporate interests.

Even before the first President Bush's defeat in the 1992 election, Wolfowitz supervised the production of a forty-six-page "Defense Policy Guidance" document within the Pentagon. The document was withdrawn as being too controversial after it was leaked to the *New York Times* and the *Washington Post*. It began by asserting boldly that "the number one objective of U.S. strategy after the Cold War should be to prevent the emergence of any rival superpower,"[61] and went on to analyze how this could be done in relation to different regions, including western Europe, East Asia, the territory of the former Soviet Union, and the Middle East.

In 1997, after President Clinton's reelection, which no doubt came as a shock as well as a bitter disappointment to them, a group of neoconservative intellectuals, including Wolfowitz, Richard Perle, Norman Podhoretz, Francis Fukuyama, and others joined with powerful Republican politicians, among them Cheney; Donald Rumsfeld, who had emerged as a leading advocate of national missile defense; Governor Jeb Bush of Florida, brother of George W. Bush; and the unsuccessful presidential candidate, Steve Forbes, to sign the statement of principles of a "Project for the New American Century."[62] This was an initiative launched by William Kristol, editor of the Rupert Murdoch–owned conservative magazine, the *Weekly Standard,* and son of one of the key founders of the neoconservative movement, Irving Kristol, and by his associate Robert Kagan, the author of a number of popular nationalist studies of international politics. One began jauntily "Americans are from Mars, Europeans are from Venus."[63]

When the George W. Bush administration took office in 2001, therefore, the link between the Cheney-Rumsfeld corporate school of conservative Republican politicians and the neoconservative policy intellectuals was already firmly forged. The key jobs in the new administration, with the exception of the secretaryship of state, given to the distinguished soldier, Colin Powell, were distributed to members of this powerful alliance. Rumsfeld became secretary of defense with Wolfowitz as his deputy, while Elliott Abrams, son-in-law of Podhoretz, went to the national security staff at the White House under Condoleezza Rice, and another neoconservative, John Bolton, was assigned as Powell's deputy. This redoubtable coterie of (mainly unelected) conservatives was relatively small and derived its influence disproportionately from the support of universities and foundations. But by the same token it was formidably influential within the world of Washington policy makers and strongly supported by ideological well-wishers in the media.

Even before the events of September 11 the main lines of the Cheney-Rumsfeld-Wolfowitz strategy were clearly defined. They included a strong unilateralist streak, amounting in some individuals and on some issues to open contempt for international opinion, especially that of the Europeans, presumably seen as the most serious potential political and economic rivals. Another strand of the Bush II policy was suspicion of the United Nations and other international organizations, and a third was a strong predilection for the right-wing government of Israel under Prime Minister Ariel Sharon. From an early stage (long before the events of September 11, 2001) those neoconservatives who were unconstrained by the responsibilities of office made no secret of their desire to overthrow the Iraqi dictator, Saddam Hussein, while those in office, led by Wolfowitz, pressed behind the scenes for action. September 11, from the point of view of the dominant neoconservative faction, might be a national tragedy. It was also the vindication of what they had been preaching for a dozen years and the opportunity to put a robust assertion of American power and purpose into effect.

In the short term, easy military victories in Afghanistan and Iraq seemed to show the wisdom of a hard, even aggressive policy. In the middle and long term, however, it was less clear that it would succeed. The second Bush administration understandably did not seem to care that it had bruised the sensibilities and ignored the wishes and interests of relatively influential countries, such as France, Germany, Russia, and China. What was less understandable was that, intentionally or otherwise, it had damaged many of the key structures of the alliance system the United States had built up since World War II, including American relationships with the United Nations, the European Union, and indeed—though in this was surely not the intention—with Britain, the most significant loyal ally. Second, the war in Iraq was bound to have problematic and potentially dangerous consequences for America's relations with the whole vast crescent of Muslim countries that stretches from Morocco to Indonesia and with other countries, from Nigeria to Bosnia to the Philippines, with important Muslim minorities. Within weeks of the Iraq crisis it was plain that U.S. relations with Turkey and Saudi Arabia had been seriously affected. There was a clear danger that regimes in major countries on which the United States had counted as allies, such as Egypt and Pakistan, might be overthrown, in part as a consequence of what was seen in the Muslim world as bringing closer the clash of civilizations.

The Bush administration saw things differently. Its model was that of American help to western Europe and Japan after World War II, though this seemed to ignore the very different histories of those regions from the Middle East. Neoconservative champions evoked an alluring picture of an Iraq transformed by war and invasion into a mission station from which American democracy and the American way of life would be spread. Perhaps. But their vision seemed to misunderstand the nature of some of the most important forces in the Middle East, among them nationalism, Islam, and the determination to be free of foreign intervention. The neoconservative enterprise was bold, and no one could doubt that it was inspired by a sincere desire to bring the benefits of American political and business civilization to the world. Two doubts hung over it.

The first was whether the invasion of two Muslim countries and the apparent determination to bring them, and presumably others, into the orbit of Western civilization was really likely to reduce the danger of terrorism, either in the Middle East or elsewhere. If, as seemed likely, the chief psychological motive for terrorism was the passionate sense of frustration and impotence at American omnipotence, especially when it seemed to be unfairly deployed on behalf of Israel, then bombing was hardly likely to have the desired effect.

More serious still was the question whether the United States would in the long run have either the political will or the economic resources to rebuild the Middle East, let alone the whole world, in its own image. For a while, no doubt, however events unfurl, public opinion will remain fascinated by the world abroad. The end of history, so to speak, will be replaced for a while by the clash of civilizations.

Yet the polarity and the paradoxes will remain. The United States offers the strongest and, on the whole, the most attractive culture in the world.

It possesses the strongest military power, in part because it devotes a higher proportion of its resources to military expenditure than other rich countries. (Even before George W. Bush announced massive increases in defense expenditure in 2002, the United States spent more on the military than all other nations put together.)

The United States is not, though, self-sufficient. It depends on the rest of the world for raw materials, including oil; for immigrants and their ability to bring more little Americans into the world; for markets and investment opportunities; and for investment funds to replace its own low propensity to save.[64] It also needs friends, although that is less obvious and less easy to demonstrate. It is easier in America than in any other country, with the possible exception of China, to believe that your country is self-sufficient. And in its early months, before September 2001, the Bush administration did indeed seem indifferent to the concerns of the rest of the world. This certainly was the interpretation widely placed overseas on, for example, the brusqueness with which the Bush administration dismissed foreign concerns about global warming or international organizations, about its missile defense plans, and later about its treatment of prisoners captured in Afghanistan.

Since the collapse of the Soviet Union, and even more during the rather brief period between the beginning of a stock market–led boom in 1995 and the collapse of the markets in 1999, it was easy to be persuaded that the United States had found the political equivalent of the philosopher's stone that turned all to gold, or—to borrow another metaphor—had repealed the laws of economic gravity. The belief was widespread that, to paraphrase the eminent British military historian Sir Michael Howard, "cultural diversity is a historical curiosity being rapidly eroded by the growth of a common, Western-oriented, Anglophone world culture, shaping our basic values."[65] This, Howard added crisply, "is simply not true." Nor is it. But there were just enough suggestions in the late 1990s that it might be true that it became for many Americans an immensely tempting public philosophy. Indeed, this was probably the organizing belief behind the Clinton administration's "neo-Wilsonian" foreign policy, just as much as behind the harsher neoconservative contempt for foreign opinion.

It is important not to underestimate, as many abroad have done, and as perhaps some administrations in Washington have done, the component of idealism and generosity in the complex way in which the American public views the outside world. In February 2001, for example, the Program on International Policy Attitudes (PIPA) at the University of Maryland published a report on American attitudes to foreign aid and world hunger. It found there has been a "marked decrease in the public's desire to cut foreign aid (so that it is now a minority position), while an overwhelming majority continues to support the principles of giving foreign aid . . . even though there has been no decline in the public's extreme overestimation of the amount of the federal budget that goes to foreign aid."[66]

"Overwhelming majorities" support efforts to alleviate hunger and poverty, and support for aid to Africa is very high. No sooner had the war in Iraq ended in April 2003 but the same program reported that only a small minority of Americans (12 percent) wanted to see the United States "the pre-eminent world leader," while an overwhelming 76 percent said "the U.S. should do its share in efforts to solve international problems with other countries." Sixty-two percent of PIPA's sample continued to say, with U.S. troops actually deployed in a police role in the streets of Iraqi cities, "the U.S. plays the role of world policeman more than it should." This is the same paradox that observers as different as Henry Kissinger and Joseph Nye, among others, have noted.[67] By investing so heavily in defense over more than half a century, the United States has acquired almost unlimited power to influence the rest of the world. But it is far from clear that Americans will want to use it.

———•——

FROM THE VERY EARLIEST periods of American history, long before the Revolution, the seeds had been germinating of what has come to be called American exceptionalism. The second governor of Massachusetts, John Winthrop, was already claiming an exceptional status for the United States. It was to be "a city set upon a hill." Winthrop was a Puritan, and there were echoes in his dream of European Protestant religious exceptionalism, of Luther's "mighty fortress" and of John Bunyan's "Celestial City." Eighteenth- and early-nineteenth-century Americans may have thought of themselves as exceptional; and in some respects their political enterprise was indeed benevolently unique. The nineteenth-century United States did pioneer, for example, a nonfeudal society, a wide franchise, prison reform, advanced ideas of equality, and mass public education. Americans sometimes forget that other societies, too, notably in Europe, but also in Australasia, have made substantial contributions to democracy in government and society.[68] But as of the middle of the nineteenth century the United States had certainly pioneered many ideas and institutions that were in advance of anything to be found elsewhere.

Americans in the age of the frontier, however, did not think of themselves as invulnerable. They knew all too well that dangers, in the shape of "Indians" and wild animals, lay no farther than the edge of the woods. But by the mid-twentieth century, with Europe consumed by war and totalitarian dictators, and the United States alone untouched, the idea of invulnerable strength had been linked to the notion of religious purity in the concept of American exceptionalism. Together they gave a special tinge of salvationism to American patriotism. To immigrants, and especially perhaps to Jewish immigrants and to others—Irish, Polish, Sicilian, for example—whose ancestral memory of Europe was that of persecution and cruelty, the idea of American exceptionalism had, and continues to have, powerful appeal.[69]

It also, however, has an impact on American foreign policy, or rather on America's relations with the outside world. There are, of course, millions of people, tens, even hundreds of millions, who admire and love the United States. It used to be said that every civilized man has two fatherlands, his own and France. It can surely be said now that every progressive-minded man or woman has two countries, his or her own and the United States.

Yet the world is not uniform, and never will be. The interests of the Chinese, the Europeans, the Japanese, let alone the Russians, the Indians, and the Muslims, may be compatible with those of the United States; they are not identical. Not by any means will everyone outside the United States accept automatically that American foreign policy is always in their interest, and it would not be wise for the United States to act, as recent administrations have sometimes appeared to do, as if this were so, or even that it ought to be so. Nor is it necessarily true that the United States is still—as it once was—the spiritual homeland of progressive, liberal, and democratic people across the world. An ominous development is surely that, whereas as recently as the Truman, Kennedy, and Johnson administrations, the United States was generally seen as on the progressive side in the world, since the 1980s, justly or unjustly, America is widely seen as on the side of the rich and powerful, its commitment to "free markets" perceived as a cynical cover for eliminating competition.[70]

The claim of American exceptionalism is not just that the United States is the strongest power in the world, though of course it is. It is not just that it is richer, or even, as has been argued,[71] uniquely provided with the cultural means to create wealth. The claim is no less than that American society is *morally* superior. Even that is a claim worth considering seriously, in spite of slavery, of the treatment of Native Americans, of lynching, of the use of nuclear weapons, of persisting inequality. It can be argued that the American contribution to the development of democracy, of the rule of law, and of civilization cancels even those substantial debts in the virtual ledger of national morality. It is unlikely however that the rest of the world's population as a whole (as opposed to some pro-Western elites, especially business elites) will readily accept the claim of *intrinsic* American moral superiority.

In recent years a new claim has been made, again with some initial plausibility. It is that, because of the high levels of immigration over the past thirty-five years, and the much greater diversity of the migrants' origins, the United States is now a "world nation" of a hitherto unseen kind. All that can be said is that the United States is by no means unique in receiving migrants from many parts of the world. The flow of immigrants to the United States, even today, hardly reflects the full diversity of the human family. As we have seen, the United States has not historically been by any means unanimous in wishing to admit all comers, and indeed is not so today.[72]

As to the historical claim to exceptionalism, it is sadly the case that many other nations have previously claimed, and their citizens have believed, that they had "the mandate of heaven" and that it was their God-given destiny to bring their civilization to the world. At different times the British, French, Germans, Russians, Spanish, Portuguese, Dutch, Japanese, and Chinese, not to mention earlier empires from Xerxes to Alexander, have held such beliefs, usually with unhappy results, not only for others but also for themselves.

American exceptionalism, then, is likely to prove an unreliable guide in the long run for American policy toward the rest of the world. The history of the past half century has shown the United States oscillating between engagement and withdrawal, for reasons that lie deep in its own history as well as in the dangerous and unpredictable behavior of others.

In some respects, the United States is now virtually an imperial power, albeit still one that is reluctant to see itself as such. It has hundreds of bases and garrisons in dozens of countries. Its satellites can photograph everywhere and listen in to everything. Its carrier task forces and long-range aircraft can project its military power virtually everywhere.[73] For half a century it has been able to incinerate much of the globe, and now some of its leaders believe they may in the future be technologically in a position to make it physically invulnerable to attack through missile defense. It asserts the right to intervene wherever it can and expects to be the arbiter of any of the world's quarrels that it chooses to enter. Its government interprets international law to allow it a new right of "preemptive self-defense." There is a robustness, verging on arrogance, in all of this. "We need to err on the side of being strong," the influential William Kristol told Fox News television defiantly in April 2003. "And if people want to say we're an imperial power, fine."[74] For more than a century the United States has intervened whenever it chose in the Caribbean and Latin America. More recently it has determined the political fate of Europe, East Asia, and the Middle East. It is dedicated to an ideology that is widely, though not universally, seen abroad as benevolent. Its power is all but irresistible, and its claims little short of universal.

At the same time, most Americans simply do not see themselves as imperialistic. They resent and ridicule any suggestion that they are. Their national political tradition goes back to a rebellion against colonial rule. However much influence American leaders demand, and acquire, in the world, they are usually careful to veil their political power. Increasingly, since the elevation of free-market economics to a place alongside democracy in the American creed, Washington feels free to insist on domestic policies in other nations, which may be sincerely intended to benefit other nations but which certainly benefit American corporate and strategic interests first and foremost. Yet many Americans, perhaps most, are not particularly interested in exerting power around the world, and most sincerely believe that the United States has no imperial ambitions or interests. "America" says the conservative Oxford historian, Niall Ferguson, "is the empire that dare not speak its name."[75]

When the first abolitionists settled at Port Royal in the South Carolina sea islands during the Civil War, they brought with them the gospel and went home owners of handsome plantations.[76] The abolitionist Edward Philbrick made $81,000 there in a single year, a huge income in the money of 1865, combining, said one of his friends, a "noble humanity with honest sagacity and close calculation."[77] Another told his sponsors in Philadelphia that there were fine opportunities for saving souls and also for selling brushes, brooms, knives, forks, soap, combs, candles, and Yankee clocks.[78] Mixed motives continue to inspire American commitment to free trade and the free-market economic system; it is an old American tradition to do well by doing good.

Contradictions remain in American foreign policy between the missionary and the businessman, between the immigrant tradition and that of the frontiersman, between what Bill Clinton and his administration called "neo-Wilsonianism" and the haughty doctrines of Dr. Wolfowitz and William Kristol. This is the American hour, and for the moment the United States can make of it what successive administrations in Washington may want.

After the atrocities of September 11, many commentators thought that their effect would be to focus the American people's attention more closely on the outside world. They did that, all right. Others thought they would force American public opinion to pay more attention to the world abroad. Instead, they seem to have had a hardening effect. Of course the second Bush administration had no alternative but to seek and destroy the perpetrators. Any president would have had to do what George W. Bush did in Afghanistan. But Washington showed little interest in the opinion of other countries. Allies there must be. Military operations in Afghanistan required overflight permissions and bases in Pakistan, Uzbekistan, Tajikistan, and other countries of which most Americans had never heard. Invasion of Iraq is easier if bases in Turkey and Saudi Arabia are available. If other countries, such as Britain, wanted to take part, so much the better. But in Iraq as in Afghanistan war was an American operation, shaped to American feelings and American purposes.

The United States, by asserting the right to attack any country, any-where, that might be found guilty of abetting terrorism, is making an unprecedented claim.[79] Mention, in a presidential speech, of an "axis of evil," with its overtones of the 1940s axis of fascist powers, and other more or less veiled threats suggest that others, too (Iran, Syria, North Korea) might be attacked if Washington thought their government sufficiently "evil" and sufficiently weak. No doubt a Democratic administration might respond in different ways. And, of course, there will be debate in the media and in the academy about how policy should evolve over the months and years.

The effect of the attacks on New York and Washington, though, has been to postpone decision of the essential question. Given that the United States has almost unlimited influence in the world, what will it choose to do with that influence? Will it rely on influence to spread democracy or, in the last analysis, will it use its all but irresistible force? What elements of democracy will it insist on, and what definition of democracy will it adopt? Will it insist that the world must also adopt a neoliberal ideology and a free-market capitalism closely tailored to the American model and to American business interests?

The answers to those questions will affect the entire world. But they will ultimately be domestic decisions, and—for all the inputs of politi-cians, media, think tanks, and unelected public intellectuals of liberal or conservative hue—it will be the American people who will have to make them. There are plenty of evil regimes in the world, many of them as weak as Iraq's. But it seems unlikely that Americans will allow their rulers to embark on a continuing spree of punitive violence in the name of spreading democracy.

10

New Century

This country will not be a permanently good place for any of us to live
in unless we make it a reasonably good place for all of us to live in.
— *Theodore Roosevelt*

EQUALITY AND INEQUALITY make up one of the master themes of American
history. The most salient aspect of the American experience in the last
quarter of the twentieth century, the startling growth of financial and social inequality, was at the same time historically the most uncharacteristic. In 1839 Alexis de Tocqueville began his classic, *Democracy in America,*
with a famous sentence: "Amongst the novel objects that attracted my attention during my stay in the United States, nothing struck me more
forcibly than the general equality of condition among the people."[1]

Ever since then, Americans have been rightly proud of the equality their
society offers. Equality, though, as a political concept, is not as simple as it
looks. For one thing, there is the vexing question: who will be admitted to
equality? As Tocqueville himself understood, African Americans were always the great exception to equality in America, and there have been others. In the 1960s, with great courage, black Americans demanded that this
exception be ended, and with generosity and wisdom the majority of white
Americans and their leaders decided to do what they could to meet that
demand.

Not all white Americans, however, were pleased by the policies they adopted. One defining characteristic of the period covered by this book was the rejection, by a significant proportion of the American people, of the liberal attempt to use government intervention to bring about greater equality for groups who had been excluded from it: not only blacks but also other "minorities"—women, immigrants, homosexuals, and others. Another characteristic of that period was the success of a conservative ideology with roots in that same reaction against the Great Society and its drive for equality.

The idea of equality is not simple. It contains ambiguities. Does American society offer equality of condition or equality of opportunity? The question reveals one of the abiding divisions of politics. If almost everyone accepted that equality was desirable, some—of a liberal mind-set—understood that to mean equality of condition, or at least something as near to that as could be achieved in a fallen world. Others, call them—for want of a better word— conservatives, saw equality as something like that dramatic event on September 16, 1893, when 7 million acres of the Cherokee Strip were opened to settlement in what would become the state of Oklahoma. A hundred thousand would-be settlers lined up in the grassland and, at a signal from a gun, galloped to grab the best land they could get.[2] They started equal, but there was no idea that they should end up that way.

The idea of equality conceals another ambiguity, however. There is financial and economic equality. But there is also social and human equality. Americans have tended to think economic inequality was acceptable, so long as it was accompanied by social equality. That might have been possible in nineteenth-century New England or on the Dakota frontier. It is less plausible in the context of the twenty-first century. A gratifying man-to-man relationship between the rich man and the poor man is unlikely to arise if the two live in segregated suburbs and never achieve human contact beyond a fleeting glimpse from a speeding car.

In the first half of the nineteenth century many Americans were farmers. Indeed, outside the South most were owners of land, a matter for envious wonder among European visitors. Those who were not landowners could look forward to owning land one day. Land in America was abundant and cheap, and for a time the government distributed it on easy terms: loans were available to buy a "quarter section" of 160 acres for $1.25 an acre.

There were wealthy merchants and lawyers from colonial times on. But before the coming of industrialization, American society was relatively equal in material terms, spectacularly so by comparison with Europe.

Well before the end of the nineteenth century that had begun to change. Mines and mills, railroads and streetcar franchises, department stores and oil had created a class of millionaires who were an international byword for wealth, luxury, and ostentation. In the new century the movies, an industry owned by immigrant peddlers and showmen and acted in by brilliant proletarians like Chaplin and Keaton,[3] satirized the pompous rich without mercy. As long as the millionaires delivered the goods of prosperity, though, they might be mocked, but movements to unseat them failed. Even the Great Depression did not wholly change that tolerance of economic inequality. And there was a reason for that.

It lay in the other dimension of American equality. There might be inequality of property. But by and large Americans felt equal as human beings. There were Americans who lived in palaces, ate off gold plates, and generally behaved like European princes. But their superiority was not institutionalized. They might be able to buy privileges, and they did. But the law gave them none. They might control politics, but the fact must be kept hidden. The millionaire might have an income many times greater than his employees. But he would be well advised to speak to them as equals.

Economic inequality, in other words, was made tolerable because of social equality and the dream of opportunity. For white American males, even for immigrants once they had learned to throw off un-American traits, "Jack was as good as his master." And social equality contained the dream that American society offered economic plenty for all. Napoleon claimed that every one of his soldiers carried a marshal's baton in his knapsack. Most Americans clung to the belief that the civilian equivalent of a baton was available to all who would work for it. Some became rich, most did not. So the (in reality largely fictional) promise of equal opportunity for all underlay an American political system that, for all its unreformed oddities, was upheld with the same loyalty and faith by immigrant industrial workers and their unions as by their employers.

The New Deal, the beginning of the American version of the welfare state, was denounced by Republican reactionaries as socialistic. Nothing of the kind. The New Deal was devised to preserve capitalism, not to abolish it. The policies of the Truman as well as the Roosevelt administrations were careful not to tamper with that public philosophy.[4] It was not until the Johnson administration moved from equality of opportunity to equality of condition as its goal that the consensus was threatened.[5] Not coincidentally, it was policies that seemed to break the social compact on behalf of black people that broke the mold.[6]

The politics of the past quarter century have been dominated by the reaction against the idea of a Great Society. There has been a racial dimension to this shift. There have been other dimensions, too: anger at American humiliations abroad; disgust at perceived moral decline, especially in sexual behavior and in the family; resentment of taxation, inflation, and economic change generally. All of this added up, a little perversely, to a rejection of government as the instrument of democracy and the elevation of unregulated free-market capitalism to share democracy's throne at the apex of the American system of belief. (Perversely, because if government failed to win all of its battles against communism in the Third World, free markets were hardly likely to have proved more successful; neither the Coca-Cola Corporation nor Disney was equipped to have won the battle of Ap Bac[7] or rescue the Tehran hostages. Perversely, too, because the "social issues" were scarcely the fault of government: if anything, they should be blamed on market capitalism in the shape of Hollywood, Madison Avenue, and the entertainment industry.)

The dazzling wealth creation of the financial markets in the 1990s made millions of Americans rich, some of them very rich by any historical measure. That wealth may have been more widely distributed than in earlier flush times, such as the Gilded Age of the late nineteenth century or the Jazz Age of the 1920s. But the free-market economy of the 1990s was, by objective measures, less successful in bringing prosperity to the great majority of Americans than the years of the liberal consensus in the 1950s and the early 1960s.[8] Over the twelve years of Republican occupancy of the White House, from 1981 to 1993, the median American wage earner's income fell by 5 percent in real terms. The income of the top 5 percent of taxpayers rose by 30 percent, while the income of the top 1 percent rose by 78 percent.[9] Inequality reigned.

The successes themselves were overstated. There were many—politicians, investment analysts, advertisers, and publicists of many kinds—who had an interest in maintaining that all was for the best in the best of all possible worlds. There were many others—farm workers, industrial workers, waitresses. truckdrivers, hairdressers, nurses, sales clerks, and so on—who knew from their own experience that this rosy version of the nation's experience was a considerable exaggeration.

Yet subjectively most Americans were not dissatisfied with their way of life. The national mood in the late 1990s was on the whole proud, confident, optimistic. No doubt the collapse of communism had much to do with this. After all, for half a century, the challenge of Soviet communism had been the main threat to American security, and the only challenge to American primacy in the world. The mood of the 1990s was already patriotic, overflowing on the right into chauvinism.

The response to the terrorist outrages of September 11 only intensified this mood. Everywhere there were patriotic slogans, sentiments, flags. "Eels over rice $3.95," proclaimed a board outside an Upper East Side fast-food place owned by Japanese immigrants, "God Bless America!"[10] Foreigners remarked on the intensity of American patriotism. Tim Berners-Lee, the Englishman who had invented the World Wide Web and moved from Switzerland to the Massachusetts Institute of Technology because—in spite of his disgust at the corporate takeover of the Internet—he still felt that it was in America that he could best influence its future, remarked shortly after September 11 that all those American flags were an impressive demonstration of unity, but they must also seem pretty frightening when seen from the outside.[11]

Many foreign observers misunderstood the underlying meaning of this demonstration of national feeling. It was not that most Americans were furiously aggressive or vindictive in their feelings toward the rest of the world; but more that they were hurt that others did not seem to share their own love of their country, so strong that it amounted to an ideology, almost to a religion.

From the beginning, however, the components of the American ideology had been slightly more complex and more contradictory than might have been gathered from the more simplistic formulations of high school civics, Fourth of July speeches, and the like. The most obvious exception to these pieties was the racial one. But there have always been others. The American ideal of liberty, originally understood as freedom from a monarch and his government in London, came to mean the freedom of the individual, then the freedom of the slave. But it was also sometimes interpreted as justifying the freedom of the employer to oppress his employees. It was restated in the noble idealism of Franklin Roosevelt's Four Freedoms, but it was also evoked by those who claimed the freedom to defend their homes with assault rifles.

The concept of democracy, too, developed over time, gradually including once excluded groups (manual workers, slaves, Native Americans, persons of oriental descent, women). But if democracy broadened, there were senses in which it also became more shallow. Certainly it was less participatory. Political life and political responsibility, once close to the few in the town meeting or the county caucus, now seemed to the many remote and inaccessible.

If the most striking development in American politics between the fall of Richard Nixon and the end of the twentieth century was the rise of the new conservatism, the most important alteration to the American ideology in that period was certainly the deification of free-market capitalism. It was not only conservatives who wanted to put the free market in the place of government as the chief force shaping American society. Many former liberals, too, accepted the free market's role in place of government almost as uncritically.[12] The conservatives have elevated free-market capitalism into the place once occupied by government. The consequences have been felt in almost every corner of American life.

———•◆•———

THIS BOOK HAS BEEN at some pains to demonstrate that the triumphalist rhetorical picture of American society that was widely held at the end of the twentieth century was overdrawn. Political rhetoric should perhaps not be taken too seriously. But certainly the Candidean picture of society Bill Clinton portrayed in his State of the Union Message, in which all was for the best in the best of all possible worlds, was somewhat at variance with reality.

Inequality, as we have seen, grew. For most ordinary people incomes grew briefly, if at all, after decades of stagnation or even decline. While a small proportion acquired massive capital wealth, most did not. There was a rich stewpot, but people dipped into it with spoons of very different length. Large groups were excluded. Many women. Farmers, or all but rich ones. Most members of minorities, especially blacks. Many immigrants. All but a lucky few of industrial workers. Many service workers. Most of those with less than a four-year college degree or professional qualifications. A large and arguably growing underclass. These were not trivial, marginal groups, to be contrasted with a happy majority singing and marching into sunlit uplands. They added up to a substantial majority of the population.

Worse, by many objective measures, American society was coming to resemble the traditional, horizontally stratified societies of Europe—not the social-democratic Europe of the twenty-first century but the Europe of, say, the 1920s,[13] while European societies, struggling with plenty of problems of their own, were nonetheless getting more equal.[14] The upper fifth, even the upper third of an American society now sharply stratified by income differences, had access, either directly or through health maintenance organizations, to excellent health care. At least 15 percent at the opposite end of the spectrum had access only as a favor. In between, there was concern, worry. (The new interest in personal health—even, to take a striking example, the 1980s craze for running—was at least in part bred by fear of medical bills.)[15]

Again, excellent education was available, but it cost money. Hard as private schools and suburban school systems might try to make good quality education available to some of the less well off, the old American ideal, of good free education available to all, was in retreat. In such centers of opinion-forming as New York, Washington, and Los Angeles, it had all but vanished. Any parents who could afford private education for their children grabbed it gratefully.

Far more than in earlier generations, Americans were segregated into suburbs that reflected narrow gradations of income, which—absent dramatic rates of social mobility—meant gradations of social class. There the affluent were far less likely to be aware of the way the other half lived, let alone of the fact that poverty was not necessarily evidence of personal inadequacy or even sin.

The new inequality, and the new class consciousness inextricably consequent on it, were reflected in politics. An absolute majority of congressional districts were now suburban. The politicians of the suburbs tended to focus on the issues that interested middle-class voters, to the exclusion of the bread-and-butter interests that were important to working-class Americans, "America's best-kept secret."[16] The number of politicians, whether in Congress or in state legislatures, who represented working-class districts shrank steadily. While the political muscle of some minorities, especially Hispanics, grew somewhat, the political system as a whole was far more sensitive to the interests of organized lobbying groups. Some of these were classic economic interest groups, some representing labor, more representing business. More represented the concerns of groups (pro-life, pro-choice, pro-Israel, feminist, green, or gray) that were well funded by (mainly upper-middle-income) membership.

The most puzzling single aspect of American society at the close of the twentieth century was perhaps the disappearance of the politics of protest that might have been expected to flourish, given the objective circumstances documented in this book. In part, this can perhaps be attributed to euphoria caused by the collapse of communism. It also owed something to that fear of radical dissent, which dated back to the Cold War. The availability of affordable consumer goods, made possible by outsourcing to Third World manufacturing, both concealed inequality and made it more bearable. Americans were exposed, via the media, but also often in school, to a culture that encouraged patriotic self-satisfaction and discouraged criticism. Again, the political system was firmly in the hands of the comfortable. (To be fair, American media also encouraged all kinds of critics, whistleblowers, and muckrakers.) In part, again, the quiescence of protest politics may have been caused by a decline in faith in what the political system could be expected to achieve. The influence of immigration, too, cannot be discounted: many immigrants, especially in the second generation, have felt a strong need to assert their Americanism with displays of patriotism.

Whatever the reason, many Americans in the last quarter of the twentieth century did not show much interest in the politics of division or resentment. The divisions and the resentments were there, however, and perhaps all the more bitter for not being adequately expressed in the artificially bland political conflicts of two major parties, each of which represented class interests, while seeking to avoid being openly identified with them.

This was the great paradox of American politics at the end of the twentieth century. Never had the ideological differences between the two major
parties been so sharply defined; never had the politicians, locked into the
hunt for money and the game of electoral technique, been so indifferent to
the real interests of the majority of the people they were elected to represent. The comfortable congratulated themselves on their 401(k) plans; the
hungry sheep looked up and were not fed.[17] Strangest of all: while unim-
peachable numbers demonstrate that the sheep were indeed relatively mal-
nourished while the shepherds and their dogs gorged, most Americans kept
their worries to themselves. Most indignantly rejected calls to challenge the
businessmen and their allies who thought of themselves as the masters of
the universe.[18]

The two major parties were divided, for the first time for close to a
century, by economic and social stratification. The Republicans sought
and won the votes of majorities in the more affluent suburbs. The Democrats sought to represent the cities, the rural hinterland, and the poorer
suburbs. Feelings between their rival constituencies were often angry. But
party leadership, at the national level and increasingly in at least urbanized states, depended on political campaigns that required expensive advertising and paid help. The indispensable money could only come either
from the wealthy or from nationally organized bodies, whose representatives, even in the unions, tended to identify with the political class. The
result was tension between insecure and worried citizens with strong feelings and deep divisions, on the one hand, and, on the other, politicians
torn between personifying that suppressed rage (which in some instances
they appear to share)[19] and the need to be smooth and upbeat with their
paymasters. Not the least odd phenomenon of these new politics was the
way men and women who did not conceal the fact that they were rolling
in money seemed furiously bitter against the poor.

No doubt these strange characteristics of the new politics go far to explain
both the widespread hostility to politicians, and the volatile mood swings of
politics. And volatile they certainly were. From 1992 to 2000, George Bush
senior, Bill Clinton, Newt Gingrich, Al Gore—not to mention many of
their less well known rivals and would-be emulators in national politics—all
lived through the exaggerated peaks and troughs of a media environment

that alternately lifted them to adulation, then cast them down into the vortex of disgrace or ridicule.

Although democracy was seen as the defining characteristic of American society, Americans were distinguished from inhabitants of most other democracies by their unusual indifference to politics (although in other Western democracies, too, voter turnout figures declined in the late twentieth century). To be sure, there were enthusiasts for the political game, rather as there were buffs of other specialist activities, especially those, like baseball, that attract enthusiasts for statistics. But participation in voting, as in civil society generally, was low.

Was this the consequence of contentment, as many on the right maintained? Or of impotence and preoccupation with personal survival, as some said on the left?

There was contentment. Those who had shared in the prosperity of the 1990s felt more secure than their grandparents or their parents. They also found more abundant opportunities for relaxation and self-development. One of the talents of a corporate culture premised on consumer satisfaction was for making at least a simulacrum of luxury available for the many. Record numbers of Americans could afford a passable replica of what had once been the life-style only of the rich: to travel, to collect, to escape, to buy designer labels. There was a passion for sports, but especially for highly commercialized, professional spectator sports. This seemed connected to that ultimate spectator sport, show business, and to the cult of celebrity and the adulation of the successful. Never had the "lives of the rich and famous" been admired so uncritically.

An optimist could certainly find reasons for believing that, in spite of the growing self-absorption, some social problems were less threatening than they had been. Crime, for example, at least in some places, was less alarming. (Because of the unreliable and distorted nature of most of the numbers, it is hard to say with certainty whether it was actually declining.) The younger generation seemed on average more generous and more tolerant, for example, in its attitudes to people of color and to homosexuals, although hate crimes by young people against both groups were not unknown. Massive imports from developing countries meant the malls were full of affordable, attractive consumer goods; equally massive credit card debt ensured that at least until the end of the twentieth century those goods kept moving out of the stores.

There were freedom and diversity. There was prosperity, albeit of an insecure kind. But there was also anxiety and, for many, a sense of impotence. People increasingly felt that their lives were remote from the levers of power. Perhaps they felt, too, that it was not in the political system, but somewhere in the granite and mirror glass sanctuaries of corporate headquarters that those levers were located. But then the collapse of the dot.com bubble and revelations of false accounting and executive greed suggested that the corporate colossus, too, was a giant with feet of clay.

Conservative politicians were successful in propagating the idea that liberalism, in the sense of the belief that government could properly and effectively intervene with public resources to achieve greater equality, was the self-interested belief of an elite. The idea is false, even absurd. Liberal ideas were not invented by any elite; they were largely developed by the labor movement, by the civil rights movement, and by single-issue protest groups. Most liberals are not wealthy, and most wealthy people are certainly not liberals. A moment's reflection demolishes this idea, yet it has strongly influenced public opinion, in the shape of the damaging doctrine called "market populism," the fiction that corporate business, pursuing its own interests through free markets, protects ordinary citizens more effectively than an elected government working under the restraints of the rule of law.

The capitalist system, in other countries as well as in the United States, and in earlier times as well as in the late twentieth century, has shown over and over again its extraordinary vitality and its incomparable ability to generate wealth by allocating resources to the points in the economy where they will be most fruitful. But when free-market capitalism is unrestricted and unregulated it has a built-in tendency to excess, which causes gross and growing economic inequality.[20] Then the exaggerated absence of equality of condition reduces equality of opportunity. That in turn leads in the end to social injustice and to political instability. This is what happens, not under capitalism properly restrained by democratic government and the rule of law, but under unregulated free-market capitalism once it can dominate government, as it largely does in the United States at the beginning of the twenty-first century.

As early as the 1970s, the legitimacy of much of what government does was denied by conservative dogma. By dint of endless repetition, conservative missionaries persuaded many citizens to accept a new public philosophy and with it a new language. In place of democratic government, they spoke of "the state," a word associated in the public mind with bullies in leather overcoats armed with rubber truncheons. They ceaselessly denounced "bureaucracy," as if it were to be found only in the public sector, when anyone who had encountered the inner workings of a bank, an insurance company, or even an airline knew that gobbledygook and delay were characteristic of large organizations, public or private. They appropriated the word "reform," so that instead of suggesting change that benefited the many, it came to be used of change that benefited only the few.

The effectiveness of government was undermined, first by the demand for tax reductions, then by the Reagan administration's deficit strategy.[21] Corporate management reasserted a social hegemony unknown since before the New Deal. It did so not only by attacking the power of the labor unions but also by using other strategies, such as the export of production. As the power of capital grew, the power of labor and the authority of government both declined. John Kenneth Galbraith's famous countervailing power was progressively and, in the end, decisively weakened.[22] The interests of workers and citizens were left to the mercies of the market, and markets, by definition, have no mercy.

We noticed another ominous historical paradox. The dynamism of the late-twentieth-century economy was to be entrusted to the consumer industry and the Internet, even though those immensely creative technological advances had been created by that same social democratic alliance between interventionist government and responsible industry that was being dismantled by the triumph of free-market dogma.

The hopes of dramatic advance for three substantial segments of the population—for African Americans; for immigrants, especially those from Mexico and the Caribbean; and for women, especially, though not only, for "women" in the sense of those females who by chance or choice lived outside the traditional family structure—followed a similar pattern. Dramatic progress, and the widespread acceptance of new and generous goals, was followed by disappointment. The aspirations of blacks and women for equality and progress were not generally denied, nor were they wholly fulfilled. Native white male sympathy was succeeded by irritation, impatience, and finally a sort of mocking indifference. Confronted by demands from women's and African American leaders, many voters appeared to react more with annoyance at being called on to focus on issues that challenged their own fairness, than with sympathy for the calls of justice. The prevailing individualism and "me-ism" of the 1980s and 1990s was clearly associated with the triumph of free-market values. It made social solidarity unpopular. That ensued logically from the decline of a public philosophy—that of New Deal and Great Society liberalism—that had emphasized fairness and equality.

Four rather profound changes reinforced the gains made by selfishness over what had always been a generous and fraternal society.

The suburb has replaced the country and the city as the typical American habitat, with all its tendencies to social separation and stratification and its tendency to replace collective, democratic government with private and corporate control.

The corporate class, and especially its top layer, has strengthened its grip on society and even on politics. (A direct road leads from wealthy James Buckley's successful contention, in *Buckley v. Valeo*, that spending money is a form of free speech, to the successful campaigns for office of even wealthier Michael Bloomberg or Jon Corzine.)[23] Extravagant rewards for top executives placed them further and further above those who did society's real work.

Many in the media have disseminated and sometimes even worshiped a culture of individualism, consumerism, and nationalism. Money, fashion, and success are too often celebrated, while diversity, community, and solidarity are suspect.

Perhaps most ominous, because so much against the grain of traditional American belief and practice, financial inequality and consumption-driven conformity have bred sharp class divisions, accompanied by largely unchallenged class privilege. People are judged by, often judge themselves by, the things they can afford to buy.

Over the last third of the twentieth century the general acceptance of conservative doctrine, with its uncritical faith in unrestrained free-market capitalism, marked not a return to traditional American values, but a break with the way these had developed at least since the Progressive Era at the beginning of the last century.

———•◆•———

THIS IS NOT an altogether happy picture. In the last quarter of the twentieth century strong trends and forces, ideological as well as economic, have been working to reverse the great achievements of the Democratic and liberal era that ended, we can now see, sometime between 1965 and 1975.

The crucial change was the discrediting of government. This was possible because a substantial proportion of the American population, perturbed by the prospect of racial upheaval, rejected the ideals or the methods of the Great Society program.[24] The methods may have been faulty, but the ideals were not, and in rejecting the methods, American society risked forgetting the ideals.

The free-market era that followed released great creative energies. Helped by a certain ruthlessness, it achieved for a few years a dizzy but in several respects flawed prosperity. It was a period symbolized by shining office buildings rising out of blasted communities. It was in many respects a brilliant time, of unparalleled opportunities for those who were included in its scope. It was nevertheless unhealthy, because prosperity was so extremely unequally distributed, but also because its inequality trivialized the public discourse.

A society that learned from every nozzle of the great media machine, from politician and columnist and pundit alike, that the economy had broken every precedent in its triumphant onward progress, when in truth the boom had been historically unremarkable (except for the stock market), unequally shared, fragile, and brief, was not a society well prepared for trials to come. A politics obsessed with the getting and spending of ever bigger pots of money to elect leaders through "a contrived pageant with pragmatic goals"[25] and to decide questions of public policy on the basis of competing pressures from organized interests was not the best method for making difficult and dangerous decisions at home and abroad.

The presidential campaign of 2000 was in several respects a nadir. The candidates were both privileged products of the American upper class, clumsily pretending to be just plain folks. Both owed their nomination to birth membership in the national political elite, in spite of transparent attempts to deny their elite credentials. They campaigned against Washington, as if they were two sockless sharecroppers, one from hardscrabble Texas and the other from a mountain county in East Tennessee. The campaign was lackluster and unedifying. Many observers felt that the defeated challengers, Senator Bradley on the Democratic side and Senator McCain in the Republican camp, tried more seriously than the two nominees to offer straight thinking about national issues.

The result in any event was a dead heat. The subsequent maneuvers displayed the media, the legal profession, and finally the Supreme Court of the United States in the worst light. The winner was consequently perhaps the least legitimate chief magistrate the republic had chosen since Rutherford B. Hayes. His charm, if eccentric, was an asset. As to his other personal qualifications, it could not be said that they included either brilliant intellectual gifts, long experience, unchallenged integrity, or proven sagacity. In office, he surrounded himself with associates of few credentials in electoral politics, bred mainly in the all too often sycophantic atmosphere of private research foundations and appointed office.

Only a fool, said J. P. Morgan, would "go a bear of the United States," and only a fool would presume to predict the future, even in the short term, of a political system as volatile as the American polity has become. President Bush senior fell from triumph to oblivion in a matter of months. So did Speaker Gingrich and his immediate successor.[26] President Clinton came within a coat of paint of being impeached, and within months left office jaunty and with his popularity unscathed. These peripateias could be blamed on the fickle media. But they also reflected dysfunction in the political system and in particular its remoteness from the realities of ordinary life.

Within nine months after his narrow and questionable election, President Bush junior—through no fault of his own, so to speak—found himself one of the most popular presidents in history. After an uncertain start, he convinced the nation that he shared its sense of outrage and resolution. The attacks on September 11 pushed his rating in the opinion polls as high as victory in the Gulf War did for his father, and, thanks to his decision to attack Iraq, he has stayed up there longer. He appeared to believe that the atrocity of suicide attacks constituted a mandate for tax cuts favoring those least in need of them.

At the time of writing it is exceptionally hard to predict the immediate course of politics. It can be argued that the long conservative hegemony has been running out of steam, at least since George Bush senior was defeated by Bill Clinton in 1992. A number of demographic and political trends appear to support this hypothesis. The Republican Party has lost the support of large and strategically situated constituencies. Women, especially better-educated younger women, have been turned off by Republican opposition to abortion. Hispanics, especially in crucial California, have been angered by insensitive policies. It looks as though California is now a safe Democratic fief.[27] Professionals, as opposed to managers, are the fastest-growing group in a postindustrial society. Many of them are disgusted by corporate antics and Republican ideology, and many, even including doctors, once a reliably Republican profession, have swung strongly toward the Democratic Party. The domination of the Republican Party by neoconservative ideologues may cost it dearly.

Yet it has to be admitted that in the midterm elections of 2002 any swing of the pendulum back toward the Democratic Party, or toward liberal ideas, was well hidden by the surge of popular support President George W. Bush and the Republican Party received after September 11, 2001.[28] It might have been predicted that the popularity of Republicans has been significantly diminished by the stock market collapse, the corporate scandals, and the close association of the second Bush administration with some questionable aspects of corporate culture.[29] Nothing of the kind occurred. Any such reaction against the Republicans seems to have been wiped out by a surge of support for the administration's policies in the Middle East, especially since the successful campaigns in Afghanistan and Iraq. It is at least possible that foreign policy considerations could conceal or delay the operation of a political pendulum swinging back toward the Democrats.[30] Equally, untoward developments or sheer frustration in the Middle East or elsewhere in the world abroad could tarnish the Bush administration's shining armor.

Taken together, these and other recent episodes suggest that it is not just the political system, but also the nation's mood, that is febrile and unpredictable. This is hardly surprising, given that the citizens now receive more than 80 percent of their information about the world at home and abroad from a television news culture that is, under corporate pressures for short-term profit growth, alternately flippant and frenzied.

The skills and energies of the American people guarantee that the economy will survive even the damage done by excited vaporings about a "New Economy." The tested strength of Constitution and institutions proved their solidity once again, as they did in earlier trials such as Watergate. The essential good sense of the American people is largely unaffected by the shallow but inflamed picture of themselves and the world served up daily and hourly by the news media. Their vast energies may have been distracted by the follies of the boom, but their heads have not been turned by easy victories abroad.

So, to return to the phrase of Thomas Jefferson with which this book began, the country will indeed go on, "prospering and puzzled beyond example in the history of mankind." The great American experiment will continue, and the world will watch it as carefully as ever. One great question, surely, will rivet the attention of observers at home and abroad.

Will the unquestioning faith in untrammeled free-market capitalism, the defining idea of the last quarter of the twentieth century, survive the shocks of the new era unchallenged? Or will a postconservative majority turn back to older and wiser instincts, in a new determination to share the golden harvest of capitalism in accordance with the old American ideal — damaged but still cherished — of individual opportunity within a free but responsible economic system and a fair and equal society under law?

Notes

Introduction

1. Daniel P. Moynihan, "Guiding Principles for Federal Architecture," *Report of Ad Hoc Committee on Federal Office Space*, June 1, 1962. See Godfrey Hodgson, *The Gentleman from New York* (New York: Houghton Mifflin, 2000), p. 79.

Chapter 1

1. This fear was widely held. Bill Clinton, writing as the chairman of the Democratic Leadership Council, wrote in 1991, "I don't want [my child] to be part of the first generation of Americans to do worse than their parents did." "What We Believe," introduction to *The New American Choice*, DLC convention, Cleveland, 1991.

2. The title of a book by a Stanford University historian. David M. Potter, *People of Plenty* (Chicago: University of Chicago Press, 1954). Economic abundance, Potter argued, "has exercised a pervasive influence in the shaping of the American character" (p. 208).

3. It was not until the 1950s that the United States began to import a substantial proportion of its iron ore needs, for example, from Canada, Africa, and Brazil.

4. It was François Guizot, historian and prime minister, who encapsulated the bourgeois spirit of the July monarchy of Louis Philippe (1831–48) with the phrase "Enrichissez-vous par le travail et l'épargne" (make yourself rich by work and saving).

5. *National Election Studies, Guide to Public Opinion and Electoral Behavior*, Liberal-Conservative Self-Identification, (table 3.1) (Ann Arbor: University of Michigan).

6. Polling by Mark J. Penn with assistance from Jennifer Coleman, published in the *New Democrat* (Fall 1998): pp. 30–35.

7. See, for example, William G. Mayer, *The Changing American Mind: How and Why American Public Opinion Changed between 1960 and 1988* (Ann Arbor: University of Michigan Press, 1992), p. 316: "Beyond the hard facts of elections and policy, there was a general intangible sense that somehow liberalism had run its course."

8. A bold, intellectually coherent statement of this view is Martin Anderson, *Revolution: The Reagan Legacy*, rev. ed. (Stanford, Calif.: Hoover Institution Press, 1990), pp. xx–xxi: "Today, it seems that everywhere we look in the world, we see the threads of a new liberty, based on more capitalism and greater prospects for peace."

9. The absurdity of this widely held idea has been well exposed by Tom Frank, *One Market under God* (New York: Doubleday, 2000). Frank has called it "market populism."

10. William Jefferson Clinton, State of the Union Address, January 27, 2000, Office of the Press Secretary, The White House.

11. The phrase is Daniel Patrick Moynihan's; he coined it as the title of a lecture to the Phi Beta Kappa society at Harvard in 1966. He used it however in a very different sense, referring not to business triumphalism but to the impatience of the counterculture.

12. Though not by as much as was generally believed. See Chapter 9.

13. R. W. Apple Jr., "Grand Ideas, Little Time," *New York Times*, January 28, 2000.

14. *Fortune* magazine, June 9, 1997.

15. See, for example, a Negroponte column in *Wired* magazine, May 1, 1994, "Bit by Bit on Wall Street: Lucky Strikes Again," in which he quoted a successful telecommunications executive, Bob Lucky, as saying he no longer read scholarly articles but read the *Wall Street Journal* instead: "To focus on the future of the 'bit' industry, there is no better place to set one's tripod than on the entrepreneurial, business, and regulatory landscape of the United States, with one leg each in the New York, American, and NASDAQ exchanges."

16. Bruce Steinberg of Merrill Lynch, June 6, 1997.

17. Eliot Spitzer, Attorney-General of New York, Affidavit in support of application for an order pursuant to General Business Law Sec. 354, Article 23-A, April 2002, pp. 8–10.

18. Jeffrey Toobin, *Too Close to Call* (New York: Random House, 2001), p. 281. The Supreme Court's decision was in *Bush v. Gore*, December 12, 2001.

19. Toobin, *Too Close to Call*, p. 281.

20. Data from Robert J. Shiller, *Irrational Exuberance* (Princeton, N.J.: Princeton University Press, 2000), p. 6.

21. Kiplinger website <www.kiplinger.com/basics/investing/indexes/nasdaq>.

22. National Bureau of Economic Research website <www.nber.org>, November 26, 2001.

23. Economic Policy Institute website <www.epinet.org/webfeatures/eocnindicators/jobspict>.

24. Paul Krugman, "The Insider Game," *New York Times*, July 12, 2002.

25. The Harken stock sale, the acquisition of the Rangers' stadium with 270 acres of land in Arlington, Texas, and the relationships between George W. Bush and Tom Hicks are spelled out in a remarkable piece of investigative journalism by Joe Conason, "Notes on a Native Son," *Harper's Magazine*, February 2000.

26. A scandal over the corrupt leasing of naval oil reserves in California and Wyoming, by Interior Secretary Albert B. Fall in the Harding administration, to Doheny and Sinclair oil interests.

27. In 1872 the directors of the Union Pacific railroad handed out to leading Republican politicians blocks of stock in the Credit Mobilier of America construction company, with which they had placed excessively profitable contracts.

28. Oscar Wilde, *A Woman of No Importance*, act 1.

29. Godfrey Hodgson, *In Our Time* (Garden City, N.Y.: Doubleday, 1976).

30. Walt Whitman, *Song of Myself*, l. 50.

31. By 2000 only two pieces of the mosaic remained to be put in place, a section of freeway in Los Angeles and, a continent away, the "Big Dig" in Boston, a complex of highways and tunnels said to have offered opportunities for corporate and municipal boondoggling on a heroic scale.

32. Alexandria, Arlington, and Fairfax counties in Virginia and Montgomery County in Maryland.

33. It has been argued that in strictly military terms the United States was victorious in Vietnam. See, for example, Peter Braestrup, *Big Story: How American Press and Television Reported and Interpreted the Crisis of Tet 1968* (New Haven: Yale University Press, 1983). I prefer the judgment of Don Oberdorfer, *Tet* (Garden City, N.Y.: Doubleday, 1971), p. 344: "The irony of the Tet offensive is that the North Vietnamese and the Viet Cong suffered a battlefield setback in the war zone, but still won the political victory in the United States."

34. Daniel Bell, *The End of Ideology: On the Exhaustion of Political Ideas in the Fifties* (New York: Free Press, 1960). It was not long, however, before Bell's friend Seymour Martin Lipset rehabilitated the concept: Lipset, *American Exceptionalism: A Two-Edged Sword* (New York: Norton, 1997). See discussion by John P. Diggins, <www.ou.edu/special/albertatr/sp98/digjust.htm>.

35. There was also, as Gerald Ford took over the presidency and Dr. Henry Kissinger's influence waned, widespread concern in Washington about the dangers of Kissinger's détente policy in strategic and nuclear affairs. This led to the "Team B" reassessment of CIA's national intelligence estimate of the Soviet Union. See Paul H. Nitze, *From Hiroshima to Glasnost: At the Center of Decision* (New York: George Weidenfeld, 1989), pp. 347–55.

36. See Godfrey Hodgson, *The World Turned Right Side Up* (Boston: Houghton Mifflin, 1996), pp. 124–25.

37. Daniel Yergin, *The Prize: The Epic Quest for Oil, Money and Power* (New York: Simon & Schuster, 1991), p. 648.

38. Jimmy Carter, *Keeping Faith: Memoirs of a President* (New York: Collins, 1982), pp. 114–20; William Greider, *The Secrets of the Temple* (New York: Simon & Schuster, 1987), pp. 12–15.

39. Carter, *Keeping Faith*, p. 120.

40. Carter did not actually use that phrase in this speech.

41. A number of sources, including the conservative leader Paul Weyrich, have told the author that vigorous efforts to persuade dozens of conservative Democrat

House members to become Republicans in 1972–73 were foiled only by the advent of the Watergate crisis in the spring of 1973.

42. See, for example, the activities of the Business Roundtable, founded in 1972, and Charls Walker and the American Council for Capital Formation from 1973, described in Robert Kuttner, *Revolt of the Haves* (New York: Simon & Schuster, 1980), p. 238.

43. Robert Kuttner, *Everything for Sale: The Virtues and Limits of Markets* (Chicago: University of Chicago Press, 1996), p. 5.

44. In the last quarter of the twentieth century, since Milton Friedman won the Nobel Prize for economics in 1976, eleven prizes, or close to half of winners of an award open to the entire world, have gone to economists associated for significant fractions of their careers with the University of Chicago. Most have been more or less closely associated with one or another variant of the neoliberal school.

45. The dominance of Wall Street in this period is an awkward exception to the theory that power is seeping away from the Northeast to the South and Southwest.

46. Lawrence Mishel, Jared Bernstein and John Schmitt, *The State of Working America*, 2000–2001 (Ithaca, N.Y.: Cornell University Press, 2001), p. 266.

47. See Greider, *Secrets of the Temple*, p. 39. Citing a study by the Federal Reserve, Greider said "at the top were the 10 per cent of American families that owned 86 per cent of the net financial worth. Next came the 35 per cent of families that shared among them the remaining 14 per cent of financial assets. Below them were the majority, the 55 per cent of American families that, on balance, had accumulated nothing." Greider, of course, was writing in the late 1980s; the numbers, though not the overall point, have changed since then.

48. Joseph Schumpeter, *Capitalism, Socialism and Democracy* (New York: Harper's, 1942), pp. 82–85.

49. See, for example, in a rich literature, Ken Auletta, *Greed and Glory on Wall Street* (New York: Warner, 1987); Michael Lewis, *Liar's Poker* (New York: Norton, 1989); James B. Stewart, *Den of Thieves* (New York: Simon & Schuster, 1991), on the 1980s depredations of Ivan Boesky and Michael Milken.

50. Frank, *One Market under God*, p. xiv.

51. The classic account is by Michael Lewis, "How the Eggheads Cracked," *New York Times Magazine*, January 24, 1999. A more scholarly account is by Joe Kolman, "LTCM Speaks" on the website <www.derivativesStrategy.com>. See also Ibrahim Warde, "LTCM: A Hedge Fund too Big to Fail," *Le Monde Diplomatique*, November 1998.

52. Nelson Lichtenstein, *State of the Union: A Century of American Labor* (Princeton, N.J.: Princeton University Press, 1992), p. 213.

53. Ibid., pp. 213–14.

54. Ibid., p. 228.

55. Bennett Harrison and Barry Bluestone, *The Great U-turn: Corporate Restructuring and the Polarizing of America* (New York: Basic Books, 1988), pp. 28–29.

56. Ibid., p. 29, citing Joseph Grunwald and Kenneth Flamm, *The Global Factory: Foreign Assembly in International Trade* (Washington, D.C.: Brookings Institution, 1985).

57. Kuttner, *Everything for Sale*, p. 75.

58. For example, Daniel Bell, *The Coming of Post-Industrial Society* (New York: Basic Books, 1973).

59. For example, Douglas Fraser of the United Autoworkers, who charged management with waging "a one-sided class war." Lichtenstein, *State of the Union*, p. 236.

60. Bennett Harrison and Barry Bluestone, *Growing Prosperity* (New York: Houghton Mifflin, 2000), p. 253.

61. Elizabeth Drew, *On the Edge: The Clinton Presidency* (New York: Simon & Schuster, 1993); Martin Walker, *Clinton: The President They Deserve* (London: Fourth Estate, 1996), pp. 60–64; Robert B. Reich, *Locked in the Cabinet* (New York: Knopf, 1997).

62. There is a novelistic but essentially plausible description of the part played in this by the consultant Dick Morris in George Stephanopoulos's memoir, *All Too Human: A Political Education* (New York: Little Brown, 1999).

63. Edward N. Wolff, *Top Heavy: A Study of the Increasing Inequality of Wealth in America* (New York, Twentieth Century Fund Press, 1995), p. 2. For example, in the United Kingdom the share of marketable wealth owned by the top 1 percent of the population fell from 59 percent in 1923 to 20 percent and thereafter, in spite of the free-market policies of the Thatcher government, to 18 percent in 1990. The comparable proportions are 21 percent for Sweden and (in 1986) 26 percent for France. In the United States, wealth inequality was at a sixty-year high in 1989, with 39 percent of marketable wealth owned by the top 1 percent, roughly twice the proportion for the United Kingdom and other western European countries.

64. Gwendolyn W. Nowlan and Robert Anthony Nowlan, *We'll Always Have Paris: The Definitive Guide to Great Lines from the Movies* (New York: HarperCollins, 1995).

65. Frank, *One Market under God*, p. 15.

66. Robert Frank and Philip J. Cook, *The Winner-Take-All Society* (New York: Free Press, 1995).

Chapter 2

1. John B. Judis, *William F. Buckley Jr.: Patron Saint of the Conservatives* (New York: Simon & Schuster, 1988), p. 242.

2. Senator James Buckley was the brother of William F. Buckley, founder of *National Review* and *chef d'orchestre* of intellectual conservatism. James Buckley was a senator for New York from 1970 to 1976, endorsed by the Conservative Party as well as by the Republicans. It is fair to say that those who, like Buckley, challenged the Federal Electoral Commission in court included the maverick liberal, Senator Eugene McCarthy of Minnesota, and the American Civil Liberties Union.

3. The bill, which Lincoln signed 104 years earlier to the day, freed only those slaves who had been pressed into the service of the Confederacy. It was the first "emancipation bill."

4. Harry C. McPherson Jr., who was President Johnson's Special Counsel at the time, confirmed to the author that Johnson was well aware of the consequences for the Democratic Party in the South. "There goes the South" is perhaps apocryphal.

5. Reverend James Reeb, beaten to death by three white men who shouted "niggerlover," and Mrs. Viola Liuzzo, shot through the window of her car by a member of the Ku Klux Klan.

6. See Lyndon B. Johnson, *The Vantage Point* (New York: Popular Library, 1971), pp. 161–66. The text is to be found in *Public Papers of the Presidents, Lyndon B. Johnson*, book I, no. 107, "Special Message to the Congress: The American Promise," pp. 281–91.

7. CQ, *Congress and the Nation* 2 (1965–68): 362.

8. According to a map prepared by the Southern Regional Council in the 1960s, there were 136 counties in the South (out of just over 1,000) where more than 50 percent of the population were African Americans. The two with the highest proportion of blacks were both in Alabama: Lowndes (81 percent) and Greene (81 percent). Eleven Mississippi counties were more than 70 percent black, Macon being the highest with 84 percent. (Map in author's possession.)

9. Different authorities have coined different terms for this distinction. Kevin L. Phillips, in his very detailed analysis, *The Emerging Republican Majority* (New Rochelle, N.Y.: Arlington House, 1969), pp. 187–289, writes of the Deep South and the Outer South. Earl Black and Merle Black, *Politics and Society in the South* (Cambridge Mass.: Harvard University Press, 1987), prefer the Deep South and the Peripheral South. V. O. Key Jr., *Southern Politics in State and Nation* (New York: Alfred A. Knopf, 1949), draws no broad distinction, but speaks of black belts, upcountry, and mountains.

10. In a vast literature, see, for example, William Alexander Percy, *Lanterns on the Levee* (New York: Alfred A. Knopf, 1941); John Dollard, *Caste and Class in a Southern Town* (New Haven, Conn.: Yale University Press, 1937); William R. Taylor, *Cavalier and Yankee: The Old South and the National Character* (New York: Brazilin, 1961). Particularly memorable is Percy's recollection of his father's class contempt for poor whites: "They are the sort of people that lynch Negroes . . . that attend revivals and fight and fornicate in the bushes afterwards." The Percys claimed descent from the dukes of Northumberland.

11. John B. Judis and Ruy A. Teixeira, *The Emerging Democratic Majority* (New York: Scribner, 2002), p. 20.

12. Ibid., p. 21.

13. Black and Black, *Politics and Society in the South*, p. 122.

14. CQ, *Congress and the Nation* 2 (1965–68): 362. On August 19 President Johnson announced that more than 27,000 African Americans had been registered in thirteen counties included in the first action by federal registrars, nearly one-third of potential applicants in those areas.

15. Black and Black, *Politics and Society in the South*, p. 134. Massive exclusion was defined as fewer than 24 percent of potential voters being registered.

16. Ibid., p.138.

17. CQ, *Congress and the Nation* 8 (1969–72): 24–25.

18. According to the Census Bureau's official estimates at July 1, 2001, the population of the United States was 284.8 million, of whom 85.8 million, or close to one-third, were resident in the eleven states of the former Confederacy. Another 15 million were resident in the three border states, Maryland, Missouri, and Kentucky, making a total of over 100 million, or well over one-third in this extended South.

19. Although those moderate Republicans who did survive, estimated at about thirty, enabled their party and its conservative leadership to hang on to a majority of eight seats in 2000–2002, and one of them, Senator James Jeffords of Vermont, actually handed over control of the Senate to the Democrats by switching parties in May 2001. See Judis and Teixeira, *The Emerging Democratic Majority*, p. 34.

20. See Mark Wahlgreen Summers, *Rum, Romanism and Rebellion: The Making of a President, 1884* (Chapel Hill: University of North Carolina Press, 2000).

21. There were, of course, class divisions in nineteenth-century American politics, but generally speaking they did not align along party lines.

22. See Tom Frank, *One Market under God* (New York: Doubleday, 2000), pp. xiv–xvii. See also William G. Mayer, *The Changing American Mind: How and Why American Public Opinion Changed between 1960 and 1988* (Ann Arbor: University of Michigan Press, 1992).

23. A strong exponent of this view is Michael Barone, editor of the invaluable annual *Almanac of American Politics* (Washington, D.C.: National Journal). See, for example, his introduction to the 2000 volume, pp. 25–58.

24. See, for example, E. Digby Baltzell, Nelson Aldrich, and Lewis Lapham.

25. David A. Stockman, *The Triumph of Politics* (New York: Harper & Row, 1986), p. 437.

26. Robert J. Donovan, *Conflict and Crisis: The Presidency of Harry S. Truman, 1945–1948* (New York: Norton, 1977), pp. 299–304; Alonzo L. Hanby, *Man of the People: A Life of Harry S. Truman* (New York: Oxford University Press, 1995), pp. 422–25. For Taft, see James T. Patterson, *Mr. Republican: A Biography of Robert A. Taft* (Boston: Houghton Mifflin, 1972), esp. chap. 23.

27. Frank S. Meyer, "Freedom, Tradition, Conservatism," in Meyer, ed., *What Is Conservatism* (New York: Holt, Rinehart and Winston, 1964); Godfrey Hodgson, *The World Turned Right Side Up* (New York: Houghton Mifflin, 1996), pp. 88–90; William A. Rusher, *The Rise of the Right* (New York: National Review, 1993).

28. See Nelson Lichtenstein, *State of the Union: A Century of American Labor* (Princeton, N.J.: Princeton University Press, 2002), pp. 228ff., for the way major corporations and construction companies adapted the Construction Users Anti-Inflation Roundtable (later the Business Roundtable) as an anti-union umbrella organization. See also Hodgson, *The World Turned Right Side Up*, pp. 208–12.

29. Interview with David Smith, research director, AFL/CIO, July 2000.

30. Ibid.

31. Dan T. Carter, *The Politics of Rage: George Wallace, the Origins of the New Conservatism and the Transformation of American Politics* (Baton Rouge: Louisiana State University Press, 1995), p. 12.

32. Laurence I. Barrett, "Reagan Democrats' Divided Loyalties," *Time*, October 31, 1988.

33. President Ronald W. Reagan, First Inaugural Address, January 1981.

34. Martin Anderson, for example, a Columbia, then Stanford economics professor who had been an adviser to Nixon, proclaimed that "the election of Ronald Reagan in 1980 and many of the events that followed were the political results of an intellectual movement building for many years and to a lesser extent throughout the world." Martin Anderson, *Revolution: The Reagan Legacy*, rev. ed. (Stanford, Calif.: Hoover Institution Press, 1990). In an interview, Anderson told me "there has been an intellectual revolution, moving with the power and speed of a glacier."

35. *Perestroika* means "restructuring." It is apparent that the Soviet elite, including especially members of the KGB, sought to preserve the system by adopting reforms. Instead, the reforms led to the collapse of the system.

36. The best account is in Theodore Draper, *A Very Thin Line: The Iran Contra Affairs* (New York: Hill and Wang, 1991). See also Lawrence E. Walsh, *Firewall: The Iran-Contra Conspiracy and Cover-Up* (New York: W. W. Norton, 1997); and Harold Hongju Koh, *The National Security Constitution: Sharing Power after the Iran Contra Affair* (New Haven: Yale University Press, 1990); Daniel P. Moynihan, *Secrecy* (New Haven: Yale University Press, 1998).

37. See Stockman, *The Triumph of Politics*, p. 403. "By 1984," Stockman wrote, "[the White House] had become a dreamland. It was holding the American economy hostage to a reckless, unstable fiscal policy based on the politics of high spending and the doctrine of low taxes. Yet rather than admit that the resulting massive buildup of public debt would eventually generate serious economic troubles, the White House proclaimed a roaring economic success."

38. See, for example, Daniel P. Moynihan, *Came the Revolution* (New York: Harcourt Brace Jovanovich, 1988), pp. 31–34.

39. Since 1974, when Friedrich von Hayek was awarded a Nobel Prize for economics, eleven economists connected with the University of Chicago have been laureates. Between 1990 and 2000, seven University of Chicago economists won the prize, either alone or with one or more colleagues. The great majority have been known for strong free-market ideas and have been more or less disciples of Milton Friedman (Nobel laureate 1976).

40. George H. W. Bush and Brent Scowcroft, *A World Transformed* (New York: Knopf, 1998); Michael R. Beschloss and Strobe Talbott, *At the Highest Levels* (Boston: Little Brown, 1993).

41. Reagan's "job approval" in the polls reached a high of 68 percent in May 1981 (after the assassination attempt) and again in May 1986, much lower than the highs attained by Carter in March 1977 (75 percent), Kennedy from September 1961 to

March 1962 (79 percent), or George H. W. Bush (89 percent after the Gulf War in 1991). His average rating, at 52 percent, was well below the averages for Kennedy (71 percent), Eisenhower (65 percent), or even Johnson (56 percent). Fred I. Greenstein, *The Presidential Difference: Leadership Style from FDR to Clinton* (New York: Free Press, 2000), p. 235.

42. See Judis and Teixeira, *The Emerging Democratic Majority.*

43. *National Election Studies Guide to Public Opinion and Electoral Behavior,* Liberal-Conservative Self-Identification, 1972–2000 (Ann Arbor: University of Michigan).

44. According to a timeline posted on the web by the prosecuting attorney for Clark County, Indiana, support for the death penalty reached an all time low in 1967; see <www.clarkprosecutor.org/html/death/timeline>. According to the Gallup Poll only 42 percent approved of capital punishment. In that same year an unofficial moratorium on executions began and lasted until 1979 except for the execution of Gary Gilmore in Utah in 1977. In 1972 a Supreme Court decision in *Furman v. Georgia* struck down all capital punishment statutes in all states. In 1987, after the number of executions by the states had begun to increase, the U.S. Supreme Court held in *McCleskey v. Kemp* that statistical evidence of racial disparities in sentencing was not enough to show breach of the constitutional prohibition of cruel and unusual punishment.

45. See Gareth Davies, *From Opportunity to Entitlement: The Transformation and Decline of Great Society Liberalism* (Lawrence: University Press of Kansas, 1996), p. 22; Nathan Glazer, *The Limits of Social Policy* (Cambridge, Mass.: Harvard University Press, 1988).

46. In the section that follows I am greatly indebted to Peter Shrag's excellent *Paradise Lost* (New York: New Press, 1998).

47. Ibid., p. 151.

48. Ibid., p. 152.

49. Ibid., p. 151.

50. Ibid., p. 132.

51. Ibid., p. 90.

52. *Serrano v. Priest,* 5 Cal 3d 600.

53. Shrag, *Paradise Lost,* p. 92, quoting James Richardson, "What Price Glory?" *UCLA Magazine,* February 1997, p. 30.

54. By the middle 1990s crime in California was in fact trending down, but that was not how the media reported and the public perceived the situation.

55. Clarence Lo, sociologist at the University of Missouri, quoted in Schrag, *Paradise Lost,* p. 134.

56. Ibid., p. 159.

57. Nelson Lichtenstein, *The Most Dangerous Man in Detroit: Walter Reuther and the Fate of American Labor* (New York: Basic Books, 1985), p. 439. Century Foundation, *What's Next for Organized Labor?* (New York: Century, 1999), p. v.

58. Century Foundation, *What's Next,* p. v.

59. Michael Zweig, *The Working Class Majority: America's Best Kept Secret* (Ithaca, N.Y.: Cornell University Press, 2000), p. 123.

60. Bennett Harrison and Barry Bluestone, *The Great U-Turn: Corporate Restructuring and the Polarizing of America* (New York: Basic Books, 1988), pp. 39–40.

61. Hobbes, *Leviathan: Of the matter, Forme and Power of a commonwealth Ecclesiastical and Civil,* ed. Michael Oakeshott (Oxford: Blackwell, 1946), p. 83.

62. Lee Iacocca, with William Novak, *Iacocca: An Autobiography* (New York: Bantam Books, 1984), p. 232.

63. Phillips, *The Emerging Republican Majority.*

64. William Greider, "An Insider's View of the Election," *Atlantic Monthly*, July 1988.

65. Martin Walker, *Clinton: The President They Deserve* (London: Fourth Estate, 1996), p. 107. See also Christopher Ogden, *The Life of the Party* (Boston: Little Brown, 1994).

66. Interview with Al From, July 2000.

67. William Galston and Elaine Ciulla Kamarck, *The Politics of Evasion: Democrats and the Presidency* (Washington, D.C.: Progressive Policy Institute, September 1989).

68. To be sure, there were others, mostly on the conservative side of the ideological divide, who argued that there was nothing to worry about. "When reformers say that the system is corrupt," says the controvesial FEC appointee Bradley Smith, "perhaps they reveal more than they intend. They reveal a profound lack of faith in the American people, and in the wisdom of voters to elect good men and women and to oust scoundrels." Bradley Smith, *Unfree Speech* (Princeton, N.J.: Princeton University Press, 2001), p. 213.

69. Interview with David Smith, July 2000.

70. Elizabeth Drew, *The Corruption of American Politics: What Went Wrong and Why* (Secaucus, N.J.: Birch Lane Press, 1999), p. 19.

71. Ibid., p. 61.

72. Jeffrey H. Birnbaum, *The Money Men: The Real Story of Fund-Raising's Influence on Political Power in America* (New York: Crown, 2000), pp. 4–5.

73. Charles Lewis and the Center for Public Integrity, *The Buying of the President, 2000* (New York: Avon Books, 2000), pp. 91–95.

74. In the 105th Congress, for example, in 1997–98, fifty-seven bills were introduced to revise campaign finance reform legislation in one way or another. None were enacted. Campaign finance reform remains one of the most controversial and, for politicians, the most unpopular of legislative proposals. Stephen J. Wayne, *The Road to the White House, 2000: The Politics of Presidential Elections* (Bedford: St. Martin's, 2000), p. 302.

75. Ibid., p. 5.

76. The following numbers, derived from a number of original sources, are taken from Wayne, *The Road to the White House, 2000.*

77. Numbers not corrected for inflation.

78. Wayne, *The Road to the White House, 2000,* p. 304.

79. Drew, *The Corruption of American Politics*, p. 44.

80. Website of the Center for Responsive Politics <www.opensecrets.org/2000elect/storysofar/topindivs.asp>. Mr. and Mrs. Abraham were the biggest individual contributors.

81. HR 2356, the "Bipartisan Campaign Reform Act of 2002," reported on AP, March 27, 2002.

82. David S. Broder, "Toothless Watchdog," *Washington Post*, May 29, 2002.

83. Dan Balz and Thomas B. Edsall, "Financial Records Subpoenaed in Fight over Campaign Laws," *Washington Post*, June 26, 2002.

Chapter 3

1. On March 30, 1998, James K. Glassman and Kevin A. Hassett published an article in the *Wall Street Journal* called "Are Stocks Overvalued? Not a Chance." On March 17, 1999, they followed this up with "Stock Prices Are Still Far Too Low." They subsequently turned their bullish arguments into a book, James K. Glassman and Kevin A. Hassett, *Dow 36,000: The New Strategy for Profiting from the Coming Rise in the Stock Market* (New York: Times Business/Random House, 1999). Not to be outdone, David Elias published *Dow 40,000: Strategies for Profiting from the Greatest Bull Market in History* (New York: McGraw-Hill, 1999).

2. Among the invaluable sources for the history of the Internet is the website called Hobbes' Internet Timeline, by Robert H. Zakon <http://www.zakon.org/robert/internet/timeline>. I would like to express my gratitude to this useful outline of a history it has helped me to understand.

3. This idea comes from Michael A. Cusumano and Richard W. Selby, *Microsoft Secrets: How the World's Most Powerful Software Company Creates Technology, Shapes Markets and Manages People* (New York: Simon & Schuster, 1998), p. 13: "the seventh [Microsoft] strategy is really a concluding impression from our observation of everything Microsoft has done since 1975: Attack the future!" The authors devote a whole chapter (pp. 399–449) to expanding this thought.

4. Interview with John Roos, partner in Wilson, Sonsini, Goodrich & Rosati, August 2000.

5. <http://www.cs.washington.edu/homes/lazowska/cra>.

6. Saint Bernard of Claivaux.

7. Michael L. Dertouzos, director of the MIT Laboratory for Computer Science.

8. Cusumano and Selby, *Microsoft Secrets*.

9. Ibid., pp. 136–37. Steve Lohr, *Go To* (New York: Basic Books, 2001), p. 132. But see also James Wallace and Jim Erickson, *Hard Drive* (New York: HarperCollins, 1992), pp. 183–85; and James Wallace, *Overdrive* (New York: Wiley, 1997), pp. 154–55. The buying of Seattle Computer Products' operating system was the crucial step, in the sucess of Microsoft.

10. Lohr, *Go To*, pp. 164–67.

11. Jim Clark and Jim Barksdale.

12. David A. Kaplan, *The Silicon Boys* (New York: HarperCollins, 2000), pp. 230–54.

13. Ibid., p. 304.

14. Michael A. Bellesiles, *Arming America: The Origins of a National Gun Culture* (New York: Knopf, 2000), pp. 233–34.

15. These included universities and research labs in Australia, Denmark, Norway, France, Switzerland, and the United Kingdom.

16. Richard Rhodes, *The Making of the Atomic Bomb* (New York: Simon & Schuster, 1986), pp. 378, 388, 423.

17. John Naughton, *A Brief History of the Future* (London: Weidenfeld & Nicolson, 1999), pp. 53–55.

18. Ibid., pp. 214–17.

19. Kaplan, *The Silicon Boys*, p. 33.

20. From the law firm's website <www.wsgr.com>.

21. Kaplan, *The Silicon Boys*, p. 330.

22. Cusumano and Selby, *Microsoft Secrets*, p. 3.

23. For Berners-Lee and the World Wide Web, see Tim Berners-Lee with Mark Fischetti, *Weaving the Web* (New York: HarperCollins, 1999), and James Gillies and Robert Cailliau, *How the Web Was Born* (New York: Oxford University Press, 2000).

24. Among other sources, the following historical narrative owes much to that in Manuel Castells, *The Rise of the Network Society*, vol. 1, 2nd ed. (Oxford: Blackwell, 2000), pp. 39–69. I would like to acknowledge my debt to this remarkable book.

25. <www.acm.vt.edu/~andrius/worik/microproc/hoff.html>.

26. Cusumano and Selby, *Microsoft Secrets*, p. 149. Zuse was reported to have *started* to build a computer in 1936.

27. Wallace and Erickson, *Hard Drive*, p. 69.

28. Lohr, *Go To*, p. 84. Kemeny was a Hungarian immigrant. He went to Princeton, became Albert Einstein's research assistant, and ended up as president of Dartmouth.

29. Larry Ellison, founder of Oracle, on PBS documentary, *The Nerds, Nerds,* Part II.

30. Xerox PARC's Learning Research divison, to be fair, did try the new technology and its "Smalltalk" language out on schoolchildren in a Palo Alto grade school. They discovered that the adults found it harder to get than the kids.

31. Readers will have been struck by how many of the pioneers mentioned in this chapter were educated at Harvard, Princeton, Stanford, MIT, or elite engineering schools such as Caltech or Carnegie-Mellon.

32. The account that follows is based on that in Kaplan, *Silicon Boys*, pp. 108–18.

33. Ibid., p. 258.

34. Interview with Paul Baran of RAND, quoted in Naughton, *A Brief History of the Future*, p. 107.

35. After 1972 it was called DARPA, for Defense Advanced Research Projects Agency, an effort on the part of the Nixon administration to make ARPA more harnessed to the military's needs.

36. The French government created a network, called Cyclades, linking sixteen computers in different parts of France, in 1973. Cyclades fell victim to the "free-market" approach of the government of Valéry Giscard d'Estaing, which treated the computer industry (previously run by a public body) as an industry like any other and therefore cut off all government funding. By 1979 it was dead. Cusumano and Selby, *Microsoft Secrets*, p. 38.

37. Robert Reid, *Architects of the Web* (New York: Wiley, 1997), p. 3.

38. Ibid., p. 6.

39. Naughton, *A Brief History of the Future*, p. 246.

40. Tim Berners-Lee, *Weaving the Web*, p. 107.

41. Reid, *Architects of the Web*, p. 15.

42. Ibid., p. 18.

43. Ibid., p. 19.

44. Ibid., p. 26.

45. Ibid., p. 34.

46. Wallace and Erickson, *Overdrive*, p. 265.

47. On November 6, 2001, the United States and nine states entered into a consent decree with Microsoft leaving the corporation intact but prohibiting certain discriminatory and retaliatory conduct.

48. The issue is presented in a nutshell by the editing that took place after Microsoft bought Funk & Wagnall's Dictionary. The entry on Bill Gates that described him as ruthless was changed to say "he is known for his personal and corporate contributions to charity and educational organizations." Andrew L. Shapiro, *The Control Revolution* (New York: Century, 1999).

Chapter 4

1. For example President Clinton's chief of staff, John Podesta, cautiously endorsed the view that there was a new economy in a 1999 interview.

2. Robert J. Shiller, *Irrational Exuberance* (Princeton, N.J.: Princeton University Press, 2000), p. 97. Krugman is now at Princeton University and writes regularly in the *New York Times*.

3. George W. Bush, acceptance speech at Republican convention, Philadelphia.

4. Albert Gore Jr., acceptance speech, Democratic nominating convention, Los Angeles, August 17, 2000.

5. "Structural Change in the New Economy," remarks by Alan Greenspan, chairman of the Federal Reserve Board, National Governors' Association, 92nd annual meeting, State College, Pennsylvania.

6. To simplify complex calculations and transactions, even before he was inaugurated Clinton met with Greenspan in Little Rock. The Fed chairman persuaded him that if he could make an early and serious start on reducing the deficits, the bond markets would reward him by lowering interest rates faster than his advisers had told

him would be possible. At an economic planning meeting on January 7, 1993, soon after taking office, Clinton decided to give priority to deficit reduction and in effect rejected his campaign promises to cut taxes. See Martin Walker, *Clinton: The President They Deserve* (London: Fourth Estate, 1996), pp. 164–76. See also Robert B. Reich, *Locked in the Cabinet* (New York: Knopf, 1997), pp. 29–31.

7. Statistics in the following section are taken from an invaluable work of reference, Lawrence Mishel, Jared Bernstein, and John Schmitt, *The State of Working America, 2000–2001* (Ithaca, N.Y.: Cornell University Press, 2001), I would like to express my debt to this exceptional work of economic scholarship.

8. See *Economist*, special report on U.S. productivity, May 10, 2001.

9. *Economist*, October 18, 2001.

10. Mishel et al., *The State of Working America*, p. 25.

11. Robert H. Frank and Philip J. Cook, *The Winner-Take-All Society* (New York: Free Press, 1995), p. 8.

12. Mishel et al., *The State of Working America*, p. 10.

13. Ibid., pp. 7–8.

14. In 1990 Paul Krugman actually published a book called *The Age of Diminished Expectations* (Washington, D.C.: Washington Post Company).

15. Jack E. Triplett, "Economic Statistics, the New Economy and the Productivity Slowdown," *Business Economics* 34, no. 2 (April 1999).

16. DECD data, cited in Mishel et al., *The State of Working America*, p. 373.

17. Mishel et al., *The State of Working America*, p. 359.

18. Ibid., p. 361.

19. Ibid., pp. 378–79.

20. Remarks at New Economy Forum, Haas School of Business, University of California, Berkeley, May 9, 2000.

21. S. Oliner and D. Sichel, "The Resurgence of Growth in the Late 1990s: Is Information Technology the Story?" *Journal of Economic Perspectives* 4, no. 4 (Fall 2000).

22. Frank and Cook, *The Winner-Take-All Society*.

23. Mishel et al., *The State of Working America*.

24. Frank and Cook, *The Winner-Take-All Society*, p. 6.

25. Frank Levy, *The New Dollars and Dreams: American Incomes and Economic Change* (New York: Russell Sage Foundation, 1998), p. 77.

26. Mishel et al., *The State of Working America*, p. 12.

27. Ibid., p. 11.

28. Paul Krugman, "America the Boastful," *Foreign Affairs*, May 1998.

29. Mishel et al., *The State of Working America*, p. 4. The tax break actually averaged $96,250 for the wealthiest 1 percent.

30. Levy, *The New Dollars and Dreams*, p. 24.

31. James K. Galbraith, *Created Unequal* (New York: Simon & Schuster, 1998, new preface, 2000).

32. Mishel et al., *The State of Working America*, p. 218.

33. See Triplett, "Economic Statistics."

34. Alan S. Blinder, "The Internet and the New Economy," Brookings Institution Policy Brief no. 60, June 2000.

35. The figures in the following paragraph are taken from Shiller, *Irrational Exuberance*, pp. 4–9.

36. Robert C. Merton of Harvard and Myron S. Scholes of Stanford, who were awarded the 1997 Nobel Prize for economics for their "new method of calculating the value of [financial] derivatives," were principals in the hedge fund, Long-Term Capital Management. Founded in 1994, the fund tripled investors' assets in three years before collapsing in August 1998, less than a year after Merton and Scholes had been rewarded for their method of assessing value. The fund had gambled $100 billion, and its collapse so threatened the bond markets that it was bailed out by the Federal Reserve.

37. U.S. commentators have tended to exaggerate the poor performance of European economies, especially that of France. Moreover increasing use of purchasing power parity (PPP) in international comparisons conceals the fact that in what used to be the generally used criterion, by which American workers were seen as having far higher incomes than those of industrial competitors, namely exchange rate comparison, workers in several other countries earned more than American workers. Workers in Norway, Switzerland, Sweden, Denmark, and Finland earned more than Americans, and the Japanese earned almost exactly as much. It is true that PPP (originally adopted by international organizations for comparisons between developing countries) more accurately represents lower prices for food and many manufactured goods in the United States; it also tends to conceal the monetary value of services, such as health care, more generally provided free or cheaply by public bodies in other countries. So when Seymour Martin Lipset, for example, in his book (with Gray Marks), *It Didn't Happen Here: Why Socialism Failed: in the United States* (New York: Norton, 2000), suggests that Americans have higher incomes than those of all other countries except Luxemburg, he does not seem to be aware that this is not true by other, once generally used, measures. Ironically, of course, in other respects conservative American commentators tend to insist on the ability of markets, rather than artificial constructs, to determine reality.

38. *Economist*, May 10, 2001.

Chapter 5

1. J. Hector St. John de Crèvecoeur, *Letters of an American Farmer* (Gloucester, Mass.: Peter Smith, 1968).

2. <http://census.gov>, March 14, 2001.

3. Stephan Thernstrom, "Plenty of Room for All," *Times Literary Supplement* (London), May 26, 2000, p. 5.

4. A comparatively small number are descended from indentured servants and other non-African persons who were more or less unfree.

5. George J. Borjas, *Heaven's Door* (Princeton, N.J.: Princeton University Press, 1999), pp. 6–7.

6. Since, apart from African slaves and a small number of emigrants from Germany, France, Holland, and Sweden, the overwhelming majority of those colonial immigrants were from the British Isles, many recent estimates of the ethnic origin of the American population underestimate the British and Irish component.

7. Austria-Hungary, Greece, Italy, Montenegro, Poland, Portugal, Romania, Russia, Serbia, Spain, and Turkey.

8. In rural Ireland, up to the famine, the majority were probably Irish-speaking. But leadership in America came from English-speaking emigrants from Irish cities and towns.

9. John Higham, *Strangers in the Land* (New Brunswick, N.J.: Rutgers University Press, 1955, reprint, 1988), pp. 14–24. "Prevailing conditions and the dominant national ideals of the postwar era militated against nativism without dislodging a sense of superiority" (p. 24). Higham concedes this mood was succeeded by a crisis in the 1880s.

10. It was renewed in 1892 and 1902 and made permanent in 1904. Desmond King, *Making Americans* (Cambridge Mass.: Harvard University Press, 2000), p. 294.

11. Ibid., p. 79.

12. *Ozawa v. United States* (1922); *United States v. Thind* (1923); Haney Lopez, *White by Law: The Legal Construction of Race* (New York: New York University Press, 1996).

13. Madison Grant, *The Passing of the Great Race on the Racial Basis of European History* (London: Bell, 1921).

14. Richard Gid Powers, *Secrecy and Power: The Life of J. Edgar Hoover* (New York: Free Press, 1987).

15. On December 21, 1919, the USS *Buford* sailed from New York bound for Russia with 249 aliens, deported by order of Attorney General A. Mitchell Palmer and the young J. Edgar Hoover, head of the "radical division" of the Justice Department. Between mid-1919 and early 1921 altogether almost 6,000 other "alien anarchists" were arrested with the intention of deporting them. Many were subjected to "third degree" interrogation, that is, physical force, and long periods of solitary confinement. At least 1,000 deportations were ordered, although, thanks to the efforts of federal judges and radical lawyers, comparatively few were actually deported. See Powers, *Secrecy and Power*, p. 116. One careful study states, "during the years of the Great Depression, hundreds of thousands of Mexicans were expelled by immigration officials." King, *Making Americans*, p. 233.

16. Congressman Albert Johnson of the state of Washington linked in his person the populist and the cerebral opposition to immigrants. He had once led a vigilante mob against the (heavily immigrant) Industrial Workers of the World, and he was

a friend of both Prescott Hall of the Immigration Restriction League and Madison Grant. Senator David Reed was an equally convinced though less articulate restrictionist.

17. Samuel Eliot Morison and Henry Steel Commager, *The Growth of the American Republic*, 4th ed. (New York: Oxford University Press, 1980), 2:174, say total immigration from 1820 to 1930 was 37.8 million, of whom 11.6 million, or slightly under one-third, returned to the "Old World."

18. Just as in the First Great Migration, a surprisingly large number of immigrants subsequently return to their original countries, or move to third countries. George J. Borjas and Bernt Brasberg, "Who Leaves? The Out-Migration of the Foreign-Born," *Review of Economics and Statistics* 78 (January 1996): 165–76, calculated that 22 percent of immigrants return home. According to Borjas, the U.S. Bureau of the Census calculates that 25 percent of the immigrants who entered the country in the 1980s and 1990s eventually would leave the United States.

19. U.S. Census Bureau, *Current Population Reports for March 2000*, issued January 2001 <www.bls.census.gov/cps/cpsmain.htm>.

20. Thernstrom, "Plenty of Room for All," p. 5, quoting "the economist Barry Edmonston."

21. James P. Smith and Barry Edmonston, eds., *The New Americans: Economics, Demographic and Fiscal Effects of Immigration* (Washington, D.C.: National Academy Press, 1997), p. 121.

22. See Linda Robins, "Hispanics Don't Exist," *U.S. News*, May 11, 1998.

23. According to the INS website <www.ins.usdoj.gov>, emigrants from Britain were 203,000 in the decade 1951–60, and 13,657 in 1996. From Ireland the number was 48,362 in the ten years from 1951–60 and 1,731 in 1996. The comparable figure for Germany was 478,000 for the decade 1951–60 and just 6,748 in 1996.

24. By 1965 three countries, the United Kingdom, Ireland, and Germany, were entitled to 70 percent of the quota of places for immigrants to the United States, but by 1964 more than half of the British and more than one-third of the Irish places were unclaimed.

25. Thernstrom, "Plenty of Room for All," p. 5.

26. As a proportion of the resident population, of course, recent immigration is much lower than in 1900, when the population was less than a third of what it is today.

27. Borjas and Brasberg, "Who Leaves? The Out-Migration of the Foreign Born," p. 9.

28. David Reimers, *Still the Golden Door: The Third World Comes to America*, 2d ed. (New York: Columbia University Press, 1992), p. 119.

29. Ibid.

30. Gail Paradise Kelly, *From Vietnam to America: A Chronicle of the Vietnamese Immigration to the US* (Boulder, Colo.: Westview Press, 1977), p. 61. The four camps were at Camp Pendleton, near San Diego; Fort Chaffee, Arkansas; Eglin Air Force Base, Florida, and Fort Indian Town Gap, near Harrisburg, Pennsylvania.

31. The term has been used in the United States, at least until recently, to denote people from East Asia (China, Japan, Korea, and Southeast Asia), as opposed to people from the Indian subcontinent or other parts of the Asian continent.

32. Reimers, *Still the Golden Door*, p. 105.

33. Ibid., p. 100.

34. By 1989 Indians owned 40 percent of all smaller motels (with accommodations for fewer than fifty-six) and 25 percent of Days Inn franchises.

35. Alejandro Portes and Ruben G. Rumbaut, *Immigrant America* (Berkeley: University of California Press, 1996), p. 10.

36. To be precise, by the Treaty of Guadalupe Hidalgo in 1848.

37. Luis Fraga, the political scientist at Stanford University, in an interview in August 2000, estimated that perhaps 60,000 Mexicans became Americans as a result of the Mexican War. Clyde A. Milner II estimates that the Mexican population of California alone, not counting Indians, was 14,000 at the beginning of 1848. Milner, *Oxford History of the American West* (Oxford: Oxford University Press, 1994), p. 170.

38. The process is well described in the novel, *The Squatter and the Don*, by María Amparo Ruiz de Burton, ed. and introd. Rosario Sánchez and Beatriz Pita (Houston: Arte Público Press, 1992).

39. Milner, *Oxford History of the American West*, p. 168.

40. Kevin Starr, *Endangered Dreams: The Great Depression in California* (New York: Oxford University Press, 1996), p. 62.

41. Ibid., p. 63.

42. Ibid., p. 65.

43. Ibid.

44. For example, Luis Fraga.

45. Linda Robins, *U.S. News*, May 5, 1998. The seventeen are: immigrant Mexicans in California; middle-class Mexicans in California; barrio inhabitants in projects like Los Angeles's Boyce Heights; Central Americans, especially Guatemalans and Salvadorans in Pico Union, in East Los Angeles; the long-settled Tejanos of the Rio Grande Valley in Texas; newly arrived Mexicans in Houston; Houston's Guatemalan community, full-blooded Maya Indians, many of them converts to Pentecostal Protestant Christianity; Chicago Mexicans; Chicago Puerto Ricans; Miami Cubans, many of them wealthy and conservative; the impoverished Miami Nicaraguans, many of whom came to the United States to avoid the draft during the conflict between the Sandinistas and the Contras in the 1980s; wealthy emigrants from Colombia, Peru, and other troubled nations of South America, mingling with the Cubans in South Florida; Neoyorquinos: New York's Puerto Ricans, working-class or small business owners, concentrated in "Spanish Harlem" on the Upper East Side of Manhattan; the Dominicans clustered in "Quisqueya," their name for Washington Heights at the northern tip of Manhattan; the relatively prosperous Colombians home-based in Jackson Heights, Queens; the original Hispanics of New Mexico, proud of their conquistador heritage but with high unemployment and welfare

dependency; migrant workers scattered in small enclaves from Dodge City, Kansas, to Siler City, North Carolina, and Turner, Maine.

46. U.S. Bureau of the Census, *Current Population Survey March 1999*. Identification as "Mexican" is determined by the respondent and can include those born in Mexico and those "of that heritage."

47. U.S. Census Bureau, *Current Population Reports*, by Lisa Lubbock, January 2001, p. 2.

48. Portes and Rumbaut, *Immigrant America*, p. 34.

49. For example, 15 percent of all persons of Croatian and 15 percent of Serbian origin in the United States live in Ohio, as do 22 percent of Slovaks and no fewer than 45 percent of Slovenes. Ibid., p. 30.

50. Eva Hoffman, *Lost in Translation: Life in a New Language* (New York: Dutton, 1989).

51. Irving Howe, *Land of Our Fathers* (New York: Simon & Schuster, 1983), p. 59.

52. Ibid., p. 58.

53. Tom Jackman, "Dulles Cabbies Feel Overcharged," *Washington Post*, August 9, 1999.

54. Ibid.

55. U.S. Census Bureau, *Current Population Reports*, January 2001, p. 5.

56. Ibid.

57. See reports collected on the website <www.projectusa.org> of Project USA, an organization that lobbies for immigration restriction but is careful to describe itself as "anti-immigration but not anti-immigrant."

58. Patrick J. McDonnell and Ken Ellingwood, "Immigration – the Big Issue of '94 – Disappears from '98 Debate," *Los Angeles Times*, October 23, 1998.

59. Stanley Mailman, "California's Proposition 187 and Its Lessons," *New York Law Journal*, January 3, 1995.

60. James Crawford, "The Campaign against Proposition 227: A Post Mortem," *Bilingual Research Journal* 21 (1) (Winter 1997).

61. Ibid., p. 12.

62. Ken Ellingwood, "Border Town Wary of Plans for a Second Wall," *Los Angeles Times*, January 3, 2001.

63. Mary Jordan, "Mexicans Caught at Border in Falling Numbers," *Washington Post*, May 24, 2002. These numbers may not be strictly comparable with those quoted from other news sources.

64. Pauline Arrillaga, "Climate of Violence Leads to Death in Texas Desert," *Los Angeles Times*, August 20, 2000.

65. Hector Tobar and Claudia Kolker, "Hate Crimes against Latinos on Rise, Study Finds," *Los Angeles Times*, July 27, 1999.

66. Genaro C. Armas, "Census: Big Increase in Hispanics," AP, March 12, 2001.

67. While most Hispanics were raised as Roman Catholics, of course, many Central Americans, especially Guatemalans, have been converted to Protestantism by the

substantial missionary efforts of North American evangelical, fundamentalist, or Pentecostal churches.

68. 1990 Census Bureau data, published by National Immigrant Forum and cited in "Study Finds Immigrants Doing Well in America," *New York Times*, July 3 1999.

69. Interview with Luis Fraga, Stanford University, summer 2000. See also Earl Shorris, *Latinos* (New York: Morrow, 1994).

70. Carried out jointly by the *Washington Post*, the Henry J. Kaiser Family Foundation, and Harvard University. William Booth, "A Key Constituency Defies Easy Labeling," *Washington Post*, February 14, 2001, p. A1.

71. "Hispanics Vote 2-1 for Gore over Bush in U.S. Presidential Elections," <www.usembassy.it/file2000_11/alia/ao1114-oh.htm>.

72. King, *Making Americans*.

73. It is now more than forty years since William R. Taylor, in a brilliant study, *Cavalier and Yankee: The Old South and the National Character* (New York: Braziller, 1961), examined, and in examining debunked, the cavalier legend. It is also true that comparatively few European immigrants went to the southern states. But it remains true that, until the full tide of the New Immigration, American culture was largely defined by values, and oppositions between values, imported from Europe.

74. Though in recent years American Protestant missionaries have had some success in converting people of nominal Catholic faith in Central America.

75. On the eve of September 11, 2001, it looked as though the United States was on the point of becoming more involved in Colombia, in terms of military assistance and financial aid, under the so-called Plan Colombia.

Chapter 6

1. See Alice Kessler-Harris, *In Pursuit of Equity* (Oxford: Oxford University Press, 2001), p. 5. "As the capacity of gendered differentiation to generate consensus on social policy diminished, and then became the subject of attack, what once seemed fair came to be perceived as rank discrimination."

2. U.S. Department of Commerce, Economics and Statistics Administration, Bureau of the Census, "We the American Women," September 1993.

3. Howard N. Fatherton Jr., "Labor Force Participation: 15 Years of Change," *Monthly Labor Review*, Bureau of Labor Statistics, December 1999.

4. Kessler-Harris, *In Pursuit of Equity*, p. 25.

5. Betty Friedan, *The Feminine Mystique* (New York: Norton, 1963), p. 11.

6. See, for example, James Thornton, *Chair Wars* (York Beach, Maine: Zoneri, 1997).

7. The following account of the conflict over ERA is based on two accounts found on the Internet: "The History behind the Equal Rights Amendment," by Robert Francis, chair of the National Council of Women's Organization's website: <http://www.equalrightsamendment.org/era.html>; and <http://www.now.org/issues/

economic/cea/history.html>. I have also consulted anti-ERA websites like <http://www. eagleforum.org . . . html>.

8. Jane J. Mansbridge, *Why We Lost the ERA* (Chicago: University of Chicago Press, 1986), pp. 42–43.

9. See, for example, the evidence for the "gender gap." "In the 1980s, women not only began voting disproportionately more Democratic than men—the so-called gender gap—but what is more important they began to vote more Democratic than Republican." John B. Judis and Ruy Teixeira, *The Emerging Democratic Majority* (New York: Scribner, 2002), p. 50.

10. Lara V. Marks, *Sexual Chemistry* (New Haven: Yale University Press, 2001), p. 5.

11. Searle marketed norethynodrel under the trade name Enovid in 1957 as a treatment for gynecological and menstrual disorders. It was approved as an oral contraceptive in May 1960.

12. Marks, *Sexual Chemistry*, is cautious about the relationship between the contraceptive pill and increases in sexual activity among unmarried women and at younger ages. "Although the pill is commonly cited as one of the factors that caused the sexual revolution of the 1970s, surprisingly few scholars have examined in detail its impact on sexual behaviour." Nevertheless she states "the drug . . . had a profound influence on attitudes towards sex and contraception" (p. 3). She adds: "By the 1970s lack of marital status no longer posed an obstacle to access, and the consumer was becoming steadily younger. . . . To some extent it might be argued that the pill merely accelerated a trend begun long before its arrival" (p. 8).

13. The historical account of the new consciousness of abortion is drawn from Susan Brownmiller, *In Our Time: Memoir of a Revolution* (New York: Dial Press, 1999), pp. 102–10.

14. Brownmiller, *In Our Time*, pp. 102–4.

15. Ibid., p. 103.

16. Ibid., p. 109.

17. Steinem was one of fifty-three distinguished signatories to an article "We Have Had an Abortion" in *MS* magazine in the spring of 1972. Others included Judy Collins, Billie Jean King, Lillian Hellman, and Barbara Tuchman.

18. "Who Is 'Jane Roe'?" CNN Special <www.cnn.com/SPECIALS/1998/roe. wade/stories/roe.profile/>.

19. 410 U.S. 113 Supreme Court of the United States, an appeal from the United States District Court for the Northern District of Texas. The case was argued December 13, 1971, reargued on October 11, 1972, and decided January 22, 1973.

20. Brownmiller, *In Our Time*, pp. 118–21.

21. 410 U.S. 113 (1973).

22. Brownmiller, *In Our Time*, p. 135.

23. Tim LaHaye was coauthor of best-selling Christian apocalyptic novels such as Jerry B. Jenkins and Tim LaHaye, *The Remnant* (Wheaton IL: Tyndale House, 2002).

24. See website of Concerned Women for America <www.cwfa.org/history>.

25. The Family Research Council, according to its website, exists to affirm and promote nationally, and particularly in Washington, D.C., the traditional family unit and the Judeo-Christian value system upon which it is built.

26. Jeff Cohen <www.buchanan-own-words.html>.

27. Equal Pay Act of 1963 (Pub. L. 88-38) 29 U.S. Code, 206(d). The EPA, which is part of the Fair Labor Standards Act of 1938, as amended, prohibits sex-based wage discrimination between men and women in the same establishment who are performing under similar working conditions.

28. *County of Washington v. Gunther*, 452 U.S. 161.

29. Website: <http://www.dol.gov/dol/wb/html>.

30. Ruth Rosen, *The World Split Open* (New York: Viking Penguin, 2000), pp. 78–79.

31. U.S. Department of Labor website, Bureau of Labor Statistics, "Women's Earnings as a Percentage of Men's, 1979–1999," table prepared by Women's Bureau, February 2000, annual earnings <www.bls.gov/cps/cpswom2001.pdf,Report 960>.

32. These are weekly earnings. Comparable figures not available. Women's weekly earnings lag behind men's less than annual earnings.

33. Virginia Valian, *Why So Slow? The Advancement of Women* (Cambridge, Mass.: MIT Press, 1998), pp. 191–92. Professor Valian cited numerous book-length studies and articles, among them F. D. Blau and M. A. Ferber, *The Economics of Women, Men and Work* (Englewood Cliffs, N.J.: Prentice-Hall, 1992); S. E. Foster, "The Glass Ceiling in the Legal Profession," University of California at Los Angeles, 1995; N. D. Brooks and M. Groves, "The House That Barbie Built," *Los Angeles Times*, August 23, 1996; G. N. Powell, *Women and Men in Management* (Newbury Park, Calif.: Sage, 1988); J. Fierman, "Why Women Still Don't Hit the Top," *Fortune*, July 30, 1990.

34. T. H. Cox and C. V. Harquail, "Career Paths and Career Success in the Early Career Stages of Male and Female MBAs," *Journal of Vocational Behavior* 39 (1991): 54–75.

35. J. J. Jacobs, "Women's Entry into Management: Trends in Earnings, Authority and Values among Salaried Managers," *Administrative Science Quarterly* 37 (1992): 282–301.

36. Valian, *Why So Slow?* p. 199.

37. Ibid., p. 200.

38. Ibid., p. 201.

39. American Medical Association, Women in Medicine Data Source, April 2001.

40. Valian, *Why So Slow?* p. 211.

41. Private communication from Professor Jay Kleinberg, Brunel University.

42. Website of Feminist Majority Foundation <www.feminist.org>, 1995, citing research by Von Glinow.

43. Ibid.

44. Betty Friedan, *It Changed My Life* (New York: Random House, 1976).

45. For example, by Rosen, *The World Split Open*.

46. Ibid., p. 47.

47. The fullest account of the disillusion produced in many of the women who worked with the Student Non-Violent Coordinating Committee in the southern civil rights movement is Sara Evans, *Personal Politics* (New York: Knopf, 1979). See also Rosen, *The World Split Open*, pp. 96–129. See also, in a large literature, Sally Belfrage, *Freedom Summer* (New York: Viking, 1965); Mary Rothschild, *A Case of Black and White: Northern Volunteers and the Southern Freedom Summers* (Westport, Conn.: Greenwood Press, 1982); Casey Hayden, "Women's Consciousness and the Non-Violent Movement against Segregation 1960–1965: A Personal History," 1989, American Psychological Association.

48. Brownmiller, *In Our Time*, pp. 136–46.

49. Rosen, *The World Split Open*, p. 71, Kessler-Harris, *In Pursuit of Equity*, pp. 239–41.

50. Kessler-Harris, *In Pursuit of Equity*, p. 6.

51. Evans, *Personal Politics*, p. 35.

52. Ibid.

53. Ibid., p. 73.

54. James Weinstein, quoted in ibid., p. 160.

55. Ibid., p. 119.

56. It is published verbatim as an appendix in ibid., p. 235.

57. Ibid., p. 162. The circumstances were confused and accounts differ.

58. Rosen, *The World Split Open*, pp. 128-29.

59. See, e.g., John Patrick Diggins, *The Rise and Fall of the American Left*, expanded ed. (New York: Norton, 1992), pp. 166–67.

60. Brownmiller, *In Our Time*, p. 36.

61. Rosen, *The World Split Open*, p. 160.

62. Brownmiller, *In Our Time*, p. 138.

63. For example, India, Pakistan, Sri Lanka, Britain, Ireland, Israel, Norway, New Zealand.

64. I am indebted for this account of the New York women firefighters' experience to Nancy Maclean, "The Hidden History of Affirmative Action: Working Women's Struggles in the 1970s and the Gender of Class," *Feminist Studies* (Spring 1999), printed from <www.findarticles.com>.

65. Ibid., citing "documents too numerous for individual citation" in United Women Firefighters Papers, box 4, Robert F. Wagner Labor Archives, New York University.

66. The following account of the struggle for waitresses to achieve equality in the workplace draws on Dorothy Sue Cobble, *Dishing It Out: Waitresses and Their Unions in the Twentieth Century* (Urbana: University of Illinois Press, 1991).

67. Ibid., p. 198.

68. Ibid., pp. 198–99.

69. Nelson Lichtenstein, *State of the Union: A Century of American Labor* (Princeton, N.J.: Princeton University Press, 2002), pp. 207–11.

70. *County of Washington v. Gunther*, 452 U.S. 161 (1981).

71. Cudahy, J., dissent in *EEOC v. Sears Roebuck*, U.S. Court of Appeals for the Seventh Circuit, January 1988.

72. Mansbridge, *Why We Lost the ERA*, p. 18.

73. Ibid., p. 15.

74. The Supreme Court's decision in *Roe v. Wade* did not come out of a clear blue sky. Many states, including New York, had already liberalized their abortion statutes before the Supreme Court judgment of 1973.

75. The following paragraphs owe much to the impressive study by Susan Faludi, *Backlash* (New York: Crown Publishers, 1991).

76. Ibid., pp. 6–8.

77. This gruesome story is narrated in ibid. and sourced on depositions in *Christman v. American Cyanamid* (civil action no. 80-0024 N.D. West Virginia).

78. Faludi, *Backlash*, p. 443.

79. Ibid., pp. 447–48.

80. Ibid., p. 448.

81. Lichtenstein, *State of the Union*, p. 201.

82. Ibid., p. 202.

83. Judis and Teixeira, *The Emerging Democratic Majority*, p. 50.

Chapter 7

1. Dan T. Carter, *The Politics of Rage: George Wallace, the Origins of the New Conservatism, and the Transformation of American Politics* (Baton Rouge: Louisiana State University Press, 1995).

2. Jesse Jackson might have done so as well.

3. John B. Judis and Ruy Teixeira, *The Emerging Democratic Majority* (New York: Scribner, 2002). Judis and Teixeira express this opinion cautiously, however. They stress that while Gore won a majority of 49 to 46 per cent among working-class white male voters in large metropolitan areas, and did even better with working-class white women, in rural areas he fared much less well.

4. This case has been developed at length in Michael Lind, *Made in Texas: George W. Bush and the Southern Takeover of American Politics* (New York: Basic Books, 2003).

5. President Lyndon B. Johnson, Howard University speech, June 4, 1965.

6. See, for example, Michael Novak, *The Revolt of the Unmeltable Ethnics* (New York: Macmillan, 1972).

7. Report of the National Advisory Commission on Civil Disorders (the "Kerner Report," after its chairman, Governor Otto Kerner of Illinois).

8. Ibid., p. 10.

9. Ibid., p. 203.

10. Ibid., p. 2.

11. *Newsweek*, June 30, 1969.

12. Tamar Jacoby, *Someone Else's House* (New York: Free Press, 1998), p. 260.

13. David Cohen, *Chasing the Red White and Blue: A Journey in Tocqueville's Footsteps through Contemporary America* (New York: Picador USA, 2001), pp. 63–64.

14. Jacoby, *Someone Else's House*, pp. 252–58.

15. Nicholas Lemann, "The Origins of the Underclass," part 1, *Atlantic Monthly*, June 1986.

16. William Julius Wilson, *When Work Disappears: The World of the New Urban Poor* (New York: Knopf, 1996), pp. 5–6.

17. Lemann, "The Origins of the Underclass."

18. J. Anthony Lukas, *Common Ground: A Turbulent Decade in the Lives of Three American Families* (New York: Vintage, 1986), p. 238.

19. The daughter of a popular, and wealthy, Irish judge, Hicks was a big investor in real estate. Ibid., p. 120.

20. Ibid., pp. 261, 323.

21. The study, *Schools More Separate: Consequences of a Decade of Resegregation*, by Gary Orfield with Nora Gordon (Cambridge, Mass.: Harvard Graduate School of Education, 2001), analyzes statistics from the 1998–99 school year, the latest data available from the National Center of Education Statistics' Common Core of Education Statistics.

22. There are several ways of calculating degrees of residential segregation. These are analyzed in Roderick J. Harrison and Daniel Weinberg, "Racial and Ethnic Segregation: 1990," U.S. Bureau of the Census, March 13, 2001. One measure is absolute clustering, which measures the degree of racial enclave, another is the Gini coefficient, whereby a total absence of segregation scores 0.0 and perfect segregation scores 1.0. By both these measures, several northern metropolitan areas are more segregated than southern metropolises. Thus in terms of absolute clustering Chicago (0.694) or Detroit (0.707) scores higher than Atlanta (0.557), Birmingham (0.627), or Memphis (0.576). Measured by Gini coefficient Cleveland (0.944), Chicago (0.955), or Detroit (0.963) approach more closely perfect segregation than Atlanta (0.841), Houston (0.833), or Memphis 0.853, although all six metropolitan areas are sharply segregated by race.

23. Marc Seitles, "The Perpetuation of Residential Racial Discrimination in America: Historical Discrimination, Modern Forms of Exclusion, and Inclusionary Remedies," *Journal of Land Use and Environmental Law* 14, no. 1 (1998): 2.

24. Ibid., p. 2.

25. Ibid., p. 4.

26. Nicholas Lemann lists them in *The Promised Land* (New York: Knopf, 1991), p. 277.

27. Richard Sennett, the sociologist, grew up in the Cabrini Green project in Chicago in the 1940s and 1950s, when it was still racially mixed, but by the 1960s it was overwhelmingly black. Richard Sennett, *Respect in a World of Inequality* (New York: Norton, 2003), pp. 5–12.

28. Ibid., pp. 235–40.

29. New Kent County. *Green v. County School Board of New Kent County,* 391 U.S. 430 (1968).

30. *Swann v. Charlotte-Mecklenburg Board of Education,* decided April 21, 1971, 402 U.S. 1 (1971).

31. *Keyes v. Denver School Dist.,* 413 U.S. 189 (1973).

32. Wallace won 809,239 votes, against 425,094 for George McGovern and a total of 779,034 votes for all other Democratic candidates; see <www.michigan.gov/documents/MichPrisPrimRefGuide>. On the day of the election, in Maryland, Wallace was shot and paralyzed by Arthur Bremer.

33. Jacoby, *Someone Else's House,* pp. 434–35.

34. Nathan Glazer, "On Being Deradicalized," *Commentary,* October 1970, pp. 74–80.

35. Jacoby, *Someone Else's House,* p. 360.

36. Bill Cosby earned $98 million in two years, Oprah Winfrey $88 million, according to Ellis Cose, *The Rage of a Privileged Class* (New York: HarperCollins, 1993).

37. Andrew Hacker, *Two Nations: Black and White, Separate, Hostile, Unequal,* expanded ed. (New York: Ballantine Books, 1995), p. 217.

38. Shelby Steele, *The Content of Our Character* (New York: St. Martin's Press, 1990).

39. Ibid., p. 175.

40. "How Race Is Lived America," *New York Times,* June 4 and July 16, 2000, occasional series.

41. Lemann, "The Origins of the Underclass," calculated between one-sixth and one-third of the 1.2 million black Chicagoans were members of the underclass.

42. According to the National Center for Health Statistics, in a news release dated August 5, 1999, "black infants continue to die at twice the rate of white infants."

43. Website, The Sentencing Project and Bureau of Justice Statistics, April 2001; see <www.ojp.usdoj/fjs> and <www.sentencingproject.org>.

44. In 1993, black prisoners made up 44.9 percent of the prison population, while 43.2 percent were whites. The difference was made up by 11.9 percent "others," mostly Hispanics.

45. The Sentencing Project and Bureau of Justice website.

46. It was used by Daniel Patrick Moynihan in his famous 1965 U.S. Labor Department report, *The Negro Family: The Case for National Action,* and borrowed by him from the black sociologist Kenneth B. Clark.

47. Lou Cannon, *President Reagan: The Role of a Lifetime* (New York: Public Affairs, 1991). The woman, whose real name was Linda Taylor, was convicted of welfare fraud and perjury for fraudulently using two aliases to collect $8,000. In Reagan's campaign speeches this became eighty names, thirty addresses, twelve Social Security cards, and "veterans' benefits on four non-existent husbands" to the tune of "over $150,000."

48. In *Losing Ground: American Social Policy, 1950–1980* (New York: Basic Books, 1984), Murray blamed the existence of the underclass on the noxious consequences of liberal policies. In *The Bell Curve: Intelligence and Class Structure in American Life* (New York: Free Press, 1995), Richard Herrnstein and Charles Murray argued that underclass membership was largely determined by genetic inheritance, and that this was associated with race.

49. Wilson, *When Work Disappears*, p. 12. The 40 percent figure is taken from Paul A. Jargowsky and Mary Jo Bane, "Ghetto Poverty in the United States, 1970–1980," in Christopher Jencks and Paul E. Peterson, eds., *The Urban Underclass* (Washington, D.C.: Brookings Institution, 1991), pp. 235–73.

50. See Sennett, *Respect*.

51. Wilson, *When Work Disappears*, p. 19.

52. Ibid., p. 49.

53. So George Stephanopoulos suggests in *All Too Human: A Political Education* (New York: Little Brown, 1999), p. 421.

54. It is interesting that, in spite of, or possibly because of, passing legislation that was seen as punitive by a disproportionately African American group, "welfare mothers," President Clinton remained steadily popular with black voters. Many African Americans, of course, have strong "family values" and many were appalled by what was happening to their group in terms of the growth in the number of single mothers and related problems.

55. The discussion that follows draws on Isabel V. Sawhill, R. Kent Weaver, Ron Haskins, and Andrea Kane, eds., *Welfare Reform and Beyond: The Future of the Safety Net* (Washington, D.C.: Brookings Institution, 2002).

56. R. W. Apple Jr., "His Battle Now Lost, Moynihan Still Cries Out," *New York Times*, August 2, 1996. See also Daniel P. Moynihan, "Congress Builds a Coffin," *New York Review of Books*, January 1994, reprinted in Moynihan, *Miles to Go: A Personal History of Social Policy* (Cambridge, Mass.: Harvard University Press, 1996), pp. 44–57.

57. Christopher Jencks, "Liberal Lessons from Welfare Reform," *American Prospect* (Summer 2002): A9–A12.

58. Sawhill et al., *Welfare Reform and Beyond*, chap. 1.

59. Ibid., chap. 9.

60. Ibid., chap. 21.

61. Loie Wacquant, *Les prisons de la misère* (Paris: Editions Raisons d'Agir, 1999), pp. 71–94. Dr. Wacquant, a French sociologist, worked with William Julius Wilson at the University of Chicago and on his research into conditions on Chicago's South Side. "The hypertrophy of the prison state," Wacquant wrote, "corresponds to the atrophy of the welfare state" (p. 71).

62. The Sentencing Project and Bureau of Justice website. Numbers from the Justice Department's Bureau of Justice. By way of comparison, there are 120 prisoners per 100,000 in England and Wales, 90 in Germany and France, 59 in Sweden.

63. Bureau of Justice Statistics website <www.ojp.usdoj.gov/bjs/cp>, last revised January 16, 2002. Of the remaining 62 prisoners under sentence of death, 29 were American Indian, 27 were Asian, 12 were of unknown race, and 339 were Hispanics. There were 54 women on death row.

64. Republican apologists, including William Kristol, Lee Atwater, and the *Wall Street Journal*, have tried to suggest that the Horton issue was first injected into the campaign by Al Gore. Gore did criticize Dukakis's Massachusetts furlough program, but he never mentioned Horton or race. See Timothy Noah, "Did Gore Hatch Horton," <slate.msn.com>, November 1, 1999.

65. The following details are taken from a detailed reconstruction of the Rodney King case in *Oregonian*, March 19, 1991.

66. Robert Reinhold, "Violence and Racism Are Routine in Los Angeles Police, Study Says," *New York Times*, July 10, 1991.

67. Report by Jennifer Marino, "Diversity or Division Report: Race, Class and America at the Millennium," on website <www.nyu.edu/gasaas/dept/journal>, July 18, 2001.

68. CNN website, April 1, 1998.

69. Marino, "University of Division Report."

70. Ibid. See also Judie Glave, "Ten Years Later, Racial Killing Leaves Wounds," AP, August 23, 1999.

71. Robert Reinhold, "Riots in Los Angeles: The Blue Line; Surprised, Police React Slowly as Violence Spreads," *New York Times*, May 1, 1992.

72. Ibid.

73. Amnesty International, "Police Brutality and Excessive Force in the New York City Police Department," AI Index: AMR 51/36/96, <http://www.amnesty.org>.

74. Ibid., para 4.5.

75. Ibid., para 4.2.

76. Michael Powell and Christine Haughney, "Immigrant Tortured by Police Settles Suit for $8.7 Million," *Washington Post*, July 13, 2001, p. A3.

77. Amnesty International, "Florida Reintroduces Chain Gangs," AI Index: AMR 51/02/96, <amnesty.org/ai.nsf/index/AMR510021996>.

78. Ibid.

79. Ibid., para 5.10.

80. Amadou Diallo case timeline on About.com, http://crime.about.com/library/bllfiles/bldiallo.htm>.

81. Powell and Haughney, "Immigrant Tortured by Police Settles Suit for $8.7 Million."

82. See reports in the *Chicago Tribune*, e.g., John Gorman, "'Police Tortured Me,' Cop Killer Says at Suit Hearing," February 24, 1989; John Gorman, "'Torture' Charged in Rights Suit," February 16, 1989; Ken Parish Perkins, "The Bane of Brutality," July 4, 1994; and Doug Cassel, Northwestern University School of Law, "The United States: Torture, Chicago Style," *World View Commentary*, no. 21 (February 24, 1999).

83. Thomas L. Jones, "O.J. Simpson," on website <www.crimelibrary.com/classics4/oj>.

84. Andrew Hacker, *Two Nations* (New York: Random House, 1992, 1995), p. 207, discusses the case at great length: "Black and white Americans analyzed the testimony and evidence in radically different ways. So even before the Los Angeles trial was over, the two racial nations had reached two different verdicts."

85. A *Newsweek* poll before the end of the trial found that 74 percent of whites thought Simpson was guilty, while 85 percent of African Americans thought he was not guilty or that his guilt had not been proved beyond a reasonable doubt. Ibid., p. 212.

86. Ibid., p. 218.

87. Ibid., p. 245.

88. Boyd was subsequently appointed editor of the *New York Times*.

89. Paul Shepard, "Race Rift? Many Shrug," *Atlanta Constitution*, August 17, 1999.

90. It truly was vast. Lemann, "The Origins of the Underclass," calculates that "the number of blacks who moved north, about 6.5 million, is greater than the number of Italians or Irish or Jews or Poles who moved to this country during their great migrations."

91. John Egerton, *The Americanization of Dixie, the Southernization of America* (New York: Harper's Magazine Press, 1974).

92. Peter Applebome, *Dixie Rising: How the South Is Shaping American Values, Politics and Culture* (New York: Random House, 1996).

93. Ibid., p. 16.

94. Bill C. Malone, PBS River of Song project, website <http://www.pbs.org/riverofsong/music/e3-southern_music.html>.

95. *Sports Illustrated*, July 1, 2002.

96. Michael A. Bellesiles, *Arming America: The Origins of a National Gun Culture* (New York: Knopf, 2000). Bellesiles speaks of the "growing militarism" of the antebellum South (p. 404). Bellesiles's scholarship has been challenged, but his argument that gun culture originated in the South seems solidly based.

97. *Sports Illustrated*, July 1, 2002.

98. Mark A. Shibley, *Resurgent Evangelicanism in the United States: Mapping Cultural Change since 1970* (Columbia: University of South Carolina Press, 1996).

99. See Carter, *The Politics of Rage*.

Chapter 8

1. Richard Hofstadter, *The Age of Reform: from Bryan to FDR* (New York: Knopf, 1985), p. 23.

2. The average American voter, wrote the authors of a book that was itself part of the reaction against the liberal consensus, is "unblack, unpoor and unyoung." Richard M. Scammon and Ben J. Wattenberg, *The Real Majority* (New York: Coward-McCann, 1970).

3. William Schneider, "The Suburban Century Begins," *Atlantic Monthly*, July 1992.

4. The classic statement is by Bennett Harrison and Barry Bluestone, *The Great U-Turn: Corporate Restructuring and the Polarizing of America* (New York: Basic Books, 1988).

5. There is a detailed study of the growth and impact of mass media, both news and entertainment, in Jean Folkerts and Dwight L. Teeter Jr., *Voices of a Nation: A History of Mass Media of the United States*, 3rd ed. (Boston: Allyn & Bacon, 1998). A comprehensive and clear-eyed survey of news media is Michael Janeway, *Republic of Denial Press, Politics and Public Life* (New Haven: Yale University Press, 1999).

6. As we have seen, the persisting degree of financial inequality is abundantly documented, for example, in Laurence Mishal, Jared Bernstein, and John Schmitt, *State of Working America*, 2000–2001 (Ithaca, N.Y.: Cornell University Press, 2001). There seems to be almost a taboo against concluding that economic inequality translates into divisions of social class.

7. The National Trust for Historic Preservation has given high priority to preserving old town centers threatened by "sprawl." Richard Moe, the Trust president, has said, "Sprawl drains the life out of existing cities and towns, turning downtowns into ghost towns, too often turning cities into doughnuts with a big dead hole in the center" ("Historic Preservation," St. Paul, Minn., May 14, 1997).

8. William Jennings Bryan, "Cross of Gold" speech, in W. J. Bryan, *The First Battle*, pp. 199ff., reprinted in Henry S. Commager, *Documents of American History* (New York: Appleton, 1963), no. 342, pp. 624ff.

9. Since 1981 the National Trust for Historic Preservation <www.mainst.org/AboutMainStreet/Decline> has been working with no fewer than 1,600 communities that want to rescue "Main Street." The trust states that "throughout the nation . . . downtown businesses closed or moved to the mall, shoppers dwindled, property values and sales tax revenues dropped. . . . Neglected buildings, boarded-up storefronts and empty, trash-strewn streets reinforced the public's perception that nothing was happening downtown."

10. Robert D. Putnam, *Bowling Alone: The Collapse and Revival of American Community* (New York: Simon & Schuster, 2000), pp. 206–7.

11. U.S. Dept. of Commerce, Bureau of the Census, Census of Population and Housing, U.S. Summary table 1.4, "U.S. Population in Urban, Suburban and Rural Areas, 1950–1998," last updated April 20, 2000.

12. Ibid.

13. See Schneider, "The Suburban Century Begins."

14. The process is described in detail in Lisa McGirr, *Suburban Warriors: The Origins of the New American Right* (Princeton, N.J.: Princeton University Press, 2001). Among the many interesting characteristics of the suburban right at the grass roots, McGirr notes, are the relative prosperity of most of its early leaders—almost without exception middle class in income and in some cases, like Walter Knott of Knott's Berry Farm, wealthy entrepreneurs—and the role of military officers.

15. McGirr, *Suburban Warriors*, p. 271.

16. Website: <agnr.umd/users/hort/agri105/landgrant/slide0177>.

17. According to the Heritage Foundation, the top 10 percent of recipients—most of whom earn over $250,000 annually—received 73 percent of all farm subsidies in 2001. This figure represents an increase above the 67 percent of all farm subsidies that they received between 1996 and 2000. Brian Riedl, "Still at the Federal Trough: Farm Subsidies for the Rich and Famous Shattered Records in 2001," Heritage Foundation, Backgrounder #1542, April 30, 2002.

18. For example, by Nicholas D. Kristof, "As Life for Family Farmers Worsens, the Toughest Wither," *New York Times*, April 2, 2000, p. 18.

19. Ibid.

20. "The Ongoing American Farm Crisis," Socialist Action website, October 1999, <www.socialistaction.org>.

21. Kristof, "As Life for Family Farmers Worsens."

22. Steve Cates in North Dakota *Bismarck Telegram*, quoted in Prairie Centre Policy Institute website, <www.prairiecentre.com>, January 28, 2002.

23. Interview with Thad Holt, Greenville, Mississippi, summer 1966.

24. See Environmental Working Group website, <www.ewg.org>.

25. Philip Langdon, *A Better Place to Live: Reshaping the American Suburb* (Amherst: University of Massachusetts Press, 1994), p. 1.

26. J. Eric Oliver, *Democracy in Suburbia* (Princeton, N.J.: Princeton University Press, 2001), chap. 1.

27. The classic history of the American suburb is Kenneth T. Jackson, *Crabgrass Frontier: The Suburbanization of the United States* (New York: Oxford University Press, 1985).

28. John Gunther, *Inside USA* (New York: Harper & Brothers, 1947), p. 43.

29. The Bay Bridge was completed in late 1936 and the Golden Gate in 1937; Kevin Starr, *Endangered Dreams* (New York: Oxford University Press, 1996), pp. 337, 338.

30. Andres Duany, Elizabeth Plater-Zyberk, and Jeff Speck, *Suburban Nation* (New York: North Point Press, 2000), p. 132.

31. Ibid., p. 43.

32. The term was invented by Joel Garreau, *Edge City: Life on the New Frontier* (New York: Doubleday, 1991).

33. Steve Twomey, "Networks' Roots May Make Town Bloom," *Washington Post*, February 14, 2000.

34. D'Vera Cohn, "A Region Divided," Brookings Institution, *Washington Post*, July 28, 1999.

35. Timothy Egan, "Concrete Choices," *New York Times*, July 14, 1999.

36. Robert Siegel et al., *Despatches from the Tenth Circle*, The Onion (New York: Box Tree, 2001), p. 114.

37. David Firestone, "Choking on Growth," *New York Times*, November 21, 1999.

38. William A. Galston and Elaine Kamarck, "Five Realities That Will Shape 21st Century Politics," *Blue Print 1*, No. 1, Democratic Leadership Council, Washington, D.C., fall 1998.

39. "In 1906 the horse drawn traffic in New York moved only at an average speed of 11.5 miles per hour," numerous websites, including <www.polihale.com/display/30103>.

40. Langdon, *A Better Place to Live*, pp. 7–8. Langdon claims the Owl's response to the commuting challenge is vouchsafed for by the *Wall Street Journal*.

41. Andres Duany, Elizabeth Plater-Zyberk, and Jeff Speck, *Suburban Nation: The Rise of Sprawl and the Decline of the American Dream* (New York: Farrar, Strauss and Giroux, 2000), p. 115.

42. Ibid., p. 94.

43. Ibid., p. 87.

44. The point is massively documented by the National Trust for Historic Preservation's Main Street Program. The Trust has even suggested that the historic New England town is generically threatened by the spread of shopping centers like those of Wal-Mart.

45. Langdon, *A Better Place to Live*, p. 76.

46. Duany et al., *Suburban Nation*, p. 104. "Developers ignore hard evidence that people want a neighborhood feel, with neighborhood stores and a library, not country clubs or walls."

47. "The New Ethnic Enclaves in America's Suburbs," a report by the Lewis Mumford Center for Comparative Urban and Regional Research, John R. Logan, director, <www.albany.edu/mumford/census>.

48. Of course, Wilson is usually quoted as having said it the other way round, that what was good for General Motors was good for America, and, as Halberstam says, that may well have been what he thought. But Halberstam follows Ed Cray, *Chrome Colossus: General Motors and Its Times* (New York: W. W. Norton, 1990), p. 7.

49. Notably in the air traffic controllers' strike of 1981.

50. Robert J. Samuelson, *The Good Life and Its Discontents: The American Dream in the Age of Entitlement, 1945–1995* (New York: Random House, Vintage, 1995), p. 120.

51. *Buckley v. Valeo*, 424 U.S. 1, (1976).

52. At the time of writing (February 2002) Congress looks like passing a campaign finance reform statute that would abolish "soft money."

53. Interview with Doug Bailey, July 1999.

54. Jeffrey Birnbaum argues that the most vital people in the world of campaign finance aren't the check writers but the check raisers; the most important are what he calls the "solicitors," people who know lots of people who are willing to donate $100 each to a candidate. Birnbaum, *The Money Men: The Real Story of Fund-Raising's Influence on Political Power in America* (New York: Crown, 2000), p. 50.

55. Interview with John Podesta, Washington, D.C., July 1999.

56. Charles E. Shephard, *Forgiven: The Rise and Fall of Jim and Tammy Bakker and the PTL Ministry* (Boston: Atlantic, 1989).

57. *Los Angeles Times*, November 4, 2001.

58. Quoted in "The Economic Strain on the Church," *Business Week*, April 15, 2002.

59. All figures in this paragraph have been taken from Sam Dillon and Lesley Wayne, "Scandals in the Church: The Money: As Lawsuits Spread, Church Faces Questions in Finances," *New York Times*, June 13, 2002.

60. Theodore Dreiser, *Tragic America* (London: Constable, 1932), chap. 14.

61. First Baptist Church of Dallas website <www.firstdallas.org>.

62. Terry Carter, "Law at the Crossroads," *ABA Journal* 88 (January 28, 2002).

63. In the 1999–2000 season, according to <Infoplease.com.> Aikman earned $6.667 million in salary; O'Neal was paid $17.1 million; Kevin Brown's salary was $15.7 million; Gustavo Kuerten of Brazil headed the Association of Tennis Professionals, earning just over $2 million; André Agassi came second with a mere $1.7 million.

64. <FT.com>; August 20, 2001, citing *Forbes* magazine.

65. U.S. PGA official website.

66. Shane Murray on RTE Interactive Sport, RTE (Radio Telefis Eireann) website, quoting Reuters, April 10, 2001.

67. David Owen and Richard Tomkins, "That's Tiger Power," <FT.com>, August 20, 2001.

68. HR Judiciary Committee hearings, 1951.

69. Bob Costas, *Fair Ball* (New York: Broadway Books, 2001), p. 31.

70. Leonard Koppett, *Concise History of Major League Baseball*, quoted in ibid., p. 31.

71. Ibid., p. 185.

72. Ibid., p. xv.

73. The blue ribbon panel, which included Yale president Richard C. Levin, former Federal Reserve chairman Paul A. Volcker, former U.S. senator from Maine George Mitchell, and columnist George Will, reported in July 2000. Report of the Independent Members of the Commissioner's Blue Ribbon Panel on Baseball Economics, July 2000, Major League Baseball.

74. Putnam, *Bowling Alone*, p. 27.

75. Ibid., p. 59.

76. Putnam's work has come under a salvo of criticism. See, for only two examples, the "review essay" by Steven N. Durlauf, an economist at the University of Wisconsin, who accuses *Bowling Alone* of the "ambiguity and sloppiness which have pervaded the social capital litertature." Steven N. Durlauf, "Bowling Alone: A Review Behavior Essay," *Journal of Economic Behavior and Organization* 47 (2002): 259–73. See also the article of Theda Skocpol, of Harvard, which suggested that enthusiasm for *Bowling Alone* among conservatives meant that the comfortable were calling on the poor to

recreate social institutions they themselves had abandoned. Theda Skocpol, "Unravelling from Above," *American Prospect*, no. 25 (March–April 1996).

77. Paul Light, *Baby Boomers*, pp. 123–25, cited in Putnam, *Bowling Alone*, p. 257.

78. Ibid., p. 246.

79. Ted Turner's Cable News Network, what's on air January 1, 1980.

80. Jean Folkerts and Dwight L. Teeter Jr., *Voices of a Nation: A History of Mass Media in the United States* (Needham, Mass.: Allyn and Bacon, 1998), p. 513.

81. The FCC had no teeth. It never deprived a single station or company of a license, and it was criticized for overly close links to the industry it was supposed to be monitoring. From 1945 to 1971 twenty-one out of thirty-three commissioners went to work for media companies.

82. Folkerts and Teeter, *Voices of a Nation*, p. 512.

83. See Katharine Graham, *Personal History* (New York: Knopf, 1997); Benjamin C. Bradlee, *A Good Life: Newspapering and other Adventures* (New York: Simon & Schuster, 1995).

84. Janeway, *Republic of Denial*, p. 122.

85. James N. Talbott, "The Legal Interface," <www.legalinterface.com>, p. 3.

86. Eli M. Noam, "Media Concentration in the United States: Industry Trends and Regulatory Responses," <www.vii.org>, p. 6.

87. Talbott, "The Legal Interface," p. 4.

88. Interview with John Roos, Palo Alto, California, July 2000.

89. Michael Wolff, "The Internet as Media Has Failed," <www.iwantmedia.com> February 1, 2001.

90. Marvin Kalb, *One Scandalous Story: Clinton, Lewinsky and 13 Days that Tarnished American Journalism* (New York: Free Press, 2001).

91. See OECD data; Luxembourg Income Study; see <www.impath.ceps.ln>.

92. One of the few American studies to address class consciousness is Reeve Vanneman and Lynn Weber Cannon, *The American Perception of Class* (Philadelphia: Temple University Press, 1987). Vanneman and Cannon note that foreign observers have long written "glowing accounts of the U.S. inherited ideology of classlessness, but say the weight of evidence suggests there is little difference in the way American and British workers perceive class divisions" (pp. 147–48). "Just as a massive industrial proletariat was being created [in the United States] America worked hardest at convincing itself of its openness and classlessness."

93. Ibid., p. 275.

94. Ibid., p. 71.

95. U.S. Department of Elections, National Center for Electoral Statistics, 1993–94 Schools and Staffing Survey.

96. Ibid. Only 19 percent of all private schools have no minority school students whatsoever.

97. Richard D. Kahlenberg, *All Together Now: Creating Middle-Class Schools through Public Choice* (Washington, D.C.: Brookings/Century Foundation, 2000), p. 3.

98. James S. Coleman et al., *Equality of Educational Opportunity* (Washington D.C.: Government Printing Office, 1966), p. 22.

99. Cited in David Cohen, *Chasing the Red, White and Blue: A Journey in Tocqueville's first steps through contemporary America* (New York: Picador USA, 2001).

100. Kahlenberg, *All Together Now*, p. 15.

101. Ibid., p. 18.

102. The largest endowments as of 1999–2000 were Harvard, $19.1 billion; Yale, $10.0 billion; Stanford, $8.9 billion; Princeton, $8.4 billion. Only a handful of public universities could compete with the ancient private schools, among them the Texas system, $1.6 billion (enriched by oil properties, symbolized by the "nodding donkey," Santa Rita No. 1, who stands guard over the campus in Austin; Michigan ($3.5 billion); University of California at Berkeley ($2.1 billion) and a few others over $1 billion apiece.

103. See, for example, Kahlenberg. *All Together Now*, pp. 21–22.

104. See, for example, the novels of John O'Hara, John P. Marquand, and other contemporaries.

105. "Certainly," writes Putnam, *Bowling Alone*, p. 174, "in the earlier years of the internet heavy users were predominantly younger, highly educated white males." What was true of heavy users was even more true of the masters of the computer and the Web. Bill Gates went to Harvard (but dropped out). His dorm mate there was Steve Ballmer, CEO of Microsoft. Steve Wood, key programmer, studied physics at Yale (Jennifer Edstrom and Martin Eller, *Barbarians Led by Bill Gates* [New York: Henry Holt, 1998]). Nathan and Cameron Myhrvold and David Wiese came from Princeton. N. Myhrvold also studied at Cambridge with Stephen Hawking. Contrary to mythmaking, a high proportion of all the pioneers of computing and the Internet were educated at a small number of elite private universities, especially Stanford, MIT, and Harvard.

Chapter 9

1. The first section of this chapter is based on an article I originally wrote in 1999. Godfrey Hodgson, "Immigrants and Frontiersmen: Two Traditions in American Foreign Policy," *Diplomatic History* 23, no. 3 (Summer 1999).

2. Ibid.

3. Ernest R. May wrote of President Cleveland's message to Congress about the border dispute between the United States and Britain, "The message was not meant to proclaim America's new might. But it was predicated on strength. By implication it warned Britain and the world of the emergence of a new power." Ernest R. May, *Imperial Democracy: The Emergence of America as a Great Power* (New York: Harcourt Brace Jovanovich, 1961).

4. See Howard K. Beale, *Theodore Roosevelt and the Rise of America to World Power* (Baltimore: Johns Hopkins Press, 1956), pp. 46–48; David McCullough, The *Path between the Seas: The Creation of the Panama Canal, 1870–1914* (New York: Simon & Schuster, 1977), pp. 102–8.

5. As late as September 1939, the U.S. Army was the world's *nineteenth* largest, ahead of Bulgaria but behind Portugal. Five years later 15 million people had served in the U.S. armed forces, and the current strength of the army was about 8.5 million. Eric Larrabee, *Commander-in-Chief* (New York: Harper & Row, 1987); S. E. Morison and H. S. Commager, *The Growth of the American Republic*, 2nd ed. (New York: Oxford University Press, 1950), 2: 673.

6. It seems that the Pentagon may have been a last-minute target of opportunity after the hijacked plane failed to carry out a planned attack on the White House.

7. Daniel Yergin, *The Prize: The Epic Quest for Oil, Money and Power* (New York: Simon & Schuster, 1991), pp. 692–93.

8. Ibid., p. 695.

9. Jimmy Carter, *Keeping Faith: Memoirs of a President* (New York: Harper-Collins, 1982), pp. 112–14. Among the adjectives Carter used to describe the meeting were "acrimonious," "harsh," "bitter," and "unpleasant."

10. Ibid., pp. 116–20.

11. Speeches by Jimmy Carter <www.tamu.edu/scom/pres/speeches/jccrisis>.

12. The most comprehensive account is Warren Christopher et al., *American Hostages in Iran: The Conduct of a Crisis* (New York: Council on Foreign Relations, 1985).

13. Richard Nixon, TV address to the nation after Parrot's Beak incursion into Cambodia, April 30, 1970, cited by Stephen Ambrose, *Nixon: The Triumph of a Politician* (New York: Simon & Schuster, 1989), p. 345.

14. Yergin, *The Prize*, p. 567. Imports rose from 19 to 36 percent in only six years, from 1967 to 1973.

15. Ibid., p. 648.

16. A number of writers have attempted to demonstrate that the North Vietnam and Viet Cong Tet offensive in the spring of 1969 was a failure. Among them, Peter Braestrup, *Big Story: How the U.S. Press and Television Reported and Analyzed the Tet Offensive* (New Haven: Yale University Press, 1983); Gunther Lewy, *America in Vietnam* (New York: Oxford University Press, 1978). It seems plain that it was a tactical failure but a strategic defeat, or more exactly a military failure but a political victory.

17. Henry Kissinger, *Years of Upheaval* (Boston: Little Brown, 1982), p. 494: "Israel has suffered a strategic defeat." Avi Shlaim, *The Iron Wall: Israel and the Arab World* (London: Penguin, 2000), p. 320. The Arabs "demonstrated that Israel was not invincible . . . they restored Arab pride, honor and self-confidence."

18. Library of Congress website <www.loc.gov/rr/international/amed/ethiopia/ethiopia>.

19. Library of Congress website <www.loc.gov/rr/international/amed/angola/angola>.

20. Library of Congress website <www.loc.gov/rr/international/hispanic/nicaragua/nicaragua>.

21. The Team B report was sent to President Ford on December 2, 1976. Since at least 1974, the intelligence community had been increasing its estimates of the

proportion of Soviet GNP devoted to military expenditure. The Committee on the Present Danger was set up at the initiative of Paul Nitze early in 1977.

22. Paul Krugman, "America the Boastful," *Foreign Affairs*, May 1998.

23. President William J. Clinton, State of the Union Message, January 27, 2000, *Public Papers of the Presidents*, 2000–2001, 1: 129–40; <www.gpoaccess.gov>.

24. Henry Kissinger, *Does America Need a Foreign Policy? Towards a Diplomacy for the 21st Century* (New York: Simon & Schuster, 2001), p. 17.

25. Haynes Johnson, *The Best of Times* (New York: Harcourt, 2001), pp. 2–3. It is fair to point out that these "best of times" passages are more than balanced by large sections of the book that deal with the societal downsides of the Clinton years.

26. See Chapter 1.

27. Jack F. Matlock Jr., *Autopsy on an Empire* (New York: Random House, 1995), p. 190, argues that having just extracted himself from Afghanistan, Gorbachev never had the option of maintaining the communist government in the German Democratic Republic or anywhere else in eastern Europe. See also, Cornelia Heins, *The Wall Falls: An Oral History of the Reunification of the Two Germanies* (London: Grey Seal, 1994), p. 190, interview with Dr. Wulf Rothenbächer. Even so, the decision not to intervene was the decisive moment.

28. Dan T. Carter, *The Politics of Rage: George Wallace, the Origins of the New Conservatism and the Transformation of American Politics* (Baton Rouge: Louisiana State University Press, 1996), p. 152; H. W. Brands, *The Strange Death of American Liberalism* (New Haven: Yale University Press), pp. 80–93.

29. Francis Fukuyama, *The End of History and the Last Man* (New York: Free Press, 1992).

30. Ibid., p. 12.

31. To be fair to Sachs, he was an early critic of the Bush and Clinton administration's policies and resigned as he saw "reform" become the cover for Mafia-like financial corruption. He wrote in a book review that "my actual influence on events was essentially zero." Sachs, review of Yegor Gaidar's *Days of Victory and Defeat*, *Washington Monthly*, March 2000.

32. At one time, indeed, there were said to have been more than 200 stock exchanges scattered around the Russian provincial cities. Unfortunately, because they traded only securities denominated in U.S. dollars, they were unable to fullfil the classic function of securities markets, which is to invest the savings of the population, and became markets for pure, or impure, speculation. See Tom Zaitsev, Reuters Foundation Programme, Oxford University, unpublished research paper, 1995.

33. Oswald Spengler, *Der Untergang des Abendlandes: Umrisse einer Morphologie der Weltgeschichte* (Munich: Beck, 1932), translated as *The Decline of the West* (London: Allen & Unwin, 1932): Arnold J. Toynbee, *A Study of History* (London: Oxford University Press, 1934–61).

34. Samuel P. Huntington, "The Clash of Civilisations?" *Foreign Affairs*, summer 1993, pp. 22–49. Later Huntington expanded and modified his thesis in a book, *The*

Clash of Civilizations and the Remaking of World Order (New York: Simon & Schuster, 1996).

35. Huntington, "The Clash of Civilizations," p. 28. "The rivalry of the superpowers is replaced by the clash of civilizations."

36. George H. W. Bush and Brent Scowcroft, *A World Transformed* (New York: Knopf, 1998), p. 302.

37. Ibid., p. 319.

38. See, for example, John L. Esposito, *Islam: The Straight Path* (New York: Oxford, 1991), pp. 89–93.

39. Only Iran was not under colonial rule, though as recently as 1943 it was divided between a British and a Soviet "sphere of influence." The Ottoman Empire collapsed in 1918, and many of the Middle East's political troubles are legacies of the inadequate or self-interested arrangement imposed on the region by the Versailles peace conference, which created the states of Iraq, Syria, Jordan, and Saudi Arabia. Pakistan did not become independent from Britain until 1947, and then with the trauma of partition and massacres, and Bangladesh was not separated from Pakistan until 1971. The North African and West African states did not become independent from France until the 1960s. Indonesia was a Dutch colony until the end of World War II. And the republics of Soviet Central Asia and the Caucasus have been independent for only a decade.

40. "Fundamentalist" is a concept imported from Christianity, where fundamentalists interpret the Bible literally. All Muslims accept the Koran as literally the word of Allah, as it was dictated to his Prophet Mohammed. What are perceived in the United States as fundamentalist Muslims, therefore, are Muslims who are adherents of radical, often anti-Western political movements.

41. Although from time to time public opinion and even governments in Europe reveal impatience with the degree of American solidarity with Israel, political support for Israel is far stronger in Western Europe than many Americans suppose. French governments, for example, are very conscious of the feelings of the world's fourth largest Jewish community, and one of the legacies of Nazi atrocities is that no government of democratic Germany can afford to be seen as other than totally committed to Israel's support.

42. U.S. special forces have also been active in other Muslim countries, including Pakistan and the Philippines.

43. I owe this parallel to a column by the BBC's political editor, Andrew Marr, *Guardian*, October 5, 2001.

44. No one could have been more enthusiastic about the virtues of capitalism than the Reagan administration. But it did not announce to the world that it proposed to advocate capitalism. It hardly needed to do so.

45. Interviews with Jeffrey Garten, Washington, D.C., 1995, and Robert Zoellick, Washington, D.C., 2000.

46. Moises Naim has pointed out that the so-called Washington Consensus covered a multitude of sometimes bitter disagreements, with, for example, eminent

economists using such words as "stupidity" and "cliché-ridden and banal" about each other's ideas. Yet it does seem possible to isolate a number of ideas, call them "free market," "neoliberal," or "ultraliberal" to taste, that dominated the policies of the two big international financial institutions throughout most of the 1990s, although after the financial crises in Mexico, Asia, Russia and Brazil these ideas were being sharply questioned from about 1998 on. See Moises Naim, "Fads and Fashions in Economic Reform: Washington Consensus or Washington Confusion?" Working Draft of a paper prepared for the IMF conference on Second Generation Reforms, published in *Foreign Policy*, October 26, 1999, as "Washington Consensus or Washington Confusion," *Foreign Policy*, Carnegie Endowment, no. 115 (Summer 1999).

47. John Williamson, paper prepared as background for World Bank's *World Development Report 2000*, July 1999, website of Institute for International Economics, p. 2, <www.iie.org>.

48. Development economics originated at Harvard, as much as anywhere else, before the triumph of neoliberal economics in the 1970s.

49. Naim, "Washington Consensus or Washington Confusion?"

50. For example, Nigerian rice producers were unable to compete with subsidized U.S. exports.

51. Jeffrey Sachs, "Creditor Panics: Causes and Remedies," *Cato Journal* 18, no. 3 (1999), <www.cato.org/pubs/journal/cato_journal>. The ten countries were Turkey, Venezuela, Argentina, Mexico, Indonesia, South Korea, Malaysia, Philippines, Thailand, Russia, and Brazil.

52. Carlos Salinas de Gortari and Roberto Mangabeira Unger, "The Market Turn without Neo-Liberalism," *Challenge*, January–February 1999, p. 15.

53. Naim, "Fads and Fashions in Economic Reform," p. 9.

54. European writers tended to point out that the American model was not the only successful one, but this idea is not widely accepted in the United States. See, for example Will Hutton, *The State We're In* (London: Jonathan Cape, 1995).

55. This was the message, for example, of the best-seller by the *New York Times* journalist Thomas Friedman, *The Lexus and the Olive Tree* (New York: Farrar, Straus and Giroux, 2000).

56. John Rielly, ed., *American Public Opinion and U.S. Foreign Policy* (Chicago: Chicago Council on Foreign Relations, 1999).

57. Henry Kissinger, *Does America Need a Foreign Policy? Towards a Diplomacy for the 21st Century* (New York: Simon & Schuster, 2001).

58. Ibid., p. 18

59. Ibid.

60. For example, Walter Russell Mead, *Special Providence: American Foreign Policy and How It Changed the World* (New York: Knopf, 2001); Robert Kagan, "Power and Weakness," *Policy Review*, no. 113 (June–July 2002); Robert Kagan, *Of Paradise and Power: America and Europe in the New World Order* (New York: Knopf, 2003).

61. The classified document, originally drafted by Wolfowitz and originally apparently called *Defense Planning Guidance*, was leaked to the *New York Times*, March 8, 1992, and to the *Washington Post*, March 11, 1992.

62. <www.newamericancentury.org>.

63. Kagan, *Of Paradise and Power*, p. 1.

64. "The American economic 'miracle' of the past decade has been fueled by the $1.2 billion per day in foreign capital inflow that is needed to cover the country's foreign trade deficit, currently running at $450 billion per year. It is these huge inward investment flows that have kept share prices high, inflation and interest rates relatively low, and domestic consumption booming." Tony Judt, "Its Own Worst Enemy," *New York Review of Books*, August 15, 2002, p. 16.

65. Sir Michael Howard, "America and the World," annual Lewin lecture, Washington University, St. Louis, April 5, 1984, cited in Huntington, *The Clash of Civilizations*, p. 310.

66. The Program on International Public Attitudes (PIPA) is jointly sponsored by the Center on Policy Attitudes and by the University of Maryland. Quotations are taken from the executive summary of the report. Respondents regularly say they think foreign aid amounts to 20 percent or more of the federal budget, when the correct figure, including military aid, is under 1 percent. They also habitually exaggerate the proportion of all aid to poor countries that comes from the United States; the true figure is only 16 percent and the U.S. gives a lower proportion in aid than any other developed country. PIPA, *Americans on Foreign Aid and World Hunger, A Study of U.S. Public Attitudes*, February 2, 2001.

67. Joseph Nye, *The Paradox of American Power: Why the World's Only Superpower Can't Go It Alone* (New York: Oxford University Press, 2002).

68. The United States was, for example, slow to give the vote to women, who had won the franchise as early as 1895 in New Zealand. Germany introduced public pensions, also in the 1890s. European social democracy pioneered many reforms subsequently borrowed by the New Deal and the Great Society.

69. See, for example, Daniel Bell, "The End of American Exceptionalism," in Nathan Glazer and Irving Kristol, eds., *The American Commonwealth* (New York: Basic Books, 1976); Ernest Tuveson, *Redeemer Nation: The Idea of America's Millennial Role* (Chicago: University of Chicago Press, 1968); and Seymour Martin Lipset, *American Exceptionalism: A Two-Edged Sword* (New York: Norton, 1996); Seymour Martin Lipset and Gary Marks, *It Didn't Happen Here? Why Socialism Failed in the United States* (New York: Norton, 2001).

70. The late Professor Max Beloff, a devoted and conservative admirer of the United States, pointed out at a conference at Ditchley Park, near Oxford, in 1986, that anti-American sentiment in Britain was traditionally a characteristic of the Conservative Party; only in the 1940s did the Tories become the "American party." One turning point was the vote in the House of Commons on the American loan in December 1945. Labour wanted to accept the loan, but Conservatives opposed it as an attempt to

enforce American domination. See Godfrey Hodgson, "Britons, Americans and Europeans," *Political Quarterly* 59, no. 3 (July–September 1988), pp. 334–42.

71. For example, by the historian David M. Potter, *People of Plenty* (Chicago: University of Chicago Press, 1954), p. 89. Such ideas were more credible in the period immediately after World War II, when the U.S. GNP was more than 50 percent of the world's. Now that the collective GNP of Europe is virtually identical to that of the United States (admittedly for a somewhat larger population), and when, for example, the productivity of French workers is over 97 percent of that of American workers, that is less credible.

72. The ProjectUSA website, <www.projectnsa.org>, for example, diligently collects every scrap of evidence that Americans resent immigrants, and it must be said the evidence is considerable. In June 2000, for example, former Colorado governor Richard Lamm and former Republican senator Alan Simpson published an article in the *Washington Post* asking how the United States would be better off if the population, as the government was projecting, doubled to 571 millions by the end of the twenty-first century. Alan K. Simpson and Richard K. Lamm, "571 Million Americans," *Washington Post*, June 20, 2000, p. A23.

73. Rather illogically, American leaders regularly reproach European nations for their inability to do the same. It is safe to say that if Germany, say, or France, doubled its defense budget and announced its intention of "projecting" power in Asia or Latin America, Washington opinion would not be delighted.

74. Quoted by Maureen Dowd, op. ed. page, *New York Times*, April 30, 2003.

75. Ibid.

76. *An address given by James Miller McKim at Sansom Hall Philadelphia, July 9, 1862* (Philadelphia: Willie P. Hazard, 1862). See also Willie Lee Rose, *Rehearsal for Reconstruction: The Port Royal Experiment* (New York: Bobbs-Merrill, 1964).

77. E. L. Pierce, "The Freedmen at Port Royal," *Atlantic Monthly* 12 (September 1863): p. 311.

78. *An address given by James Miller McKim at Sansom Hall*, p. 21.

79. To be sure, Britain, America, and other powers habitually mounted "punitive" expeditions against groups who defied their wishes in the nineteenth century, for example, in North Africa, but these were rarely attacks on recognized foreign states.

Chapter 10

1. Alexis de Tocqueville, *Democracy in America* (New York: New American Library, 1994), p. 26.

2. There were in fact seven "land runs" between 1889 and 1907. The full story is documented in a scholarly way on a website <www.marti.rootsweb.com>.

3. Charlie Chaplin was born in a South London slum and started as a child actor. Buster Keaton, born in Pennsylvania, was the child of two vaudeville artists and also went on the stage as a young child.

4. See Gareth Davies, *From Opportunity to Entitlement: The Transformation and Decline of Great Society Liberalism* (Lawrence: University Press of Kansas, 1996). Davies argues that although the later New Deal departed somewhat in theory from the older, individualist tradition of American liberalism, it was not until after 1968 that liberals became committed to "entitlement liberalism." See also Alan Brinkley, *The End of Reform: New Deal Liberalism in Recession and War* (New York: Knopf, 1995); J. R. Pole, *American Individualism and the Promise of Progress* (New York: Oxford University Press, 1980).

5. "Not just equality as a right and a theory, but equality as a fact and as a result." President Lyndon B. Johnson, Howard University commencement, June 4, 1965.

6. Dan T. Carter, *The Politics of Rage: George Wallace, the Origins of the New Conservatism, and the Transformation of American Politics* (Baton Rouge: Louisiana State University, 1995), p. 468. See also Dan T. Carter, *From George Wallace to Newt Gingrich: Race in the Conservative Counterrevolution, 1963 to 1994* (Baton Rouge: Louisiana State University, 1999). Carter argues that Wallace was a key figure in the rise of the new conservatism and concludes that Wallace recognized the political capital to be made out of race "in a society shaken by social upheaval and economic uncertainty." The social upheaval, of course, was that caused by the civil rights movement. Carter's thesis is that Wallace's appeal, to voters both southern and northern, was openly racist, and that Richard Nixon in 1968 and other conservative politicians since Nixon, learned to tap into deep, often concealed, springs of racism in voters.

7. This defeat for the South Vietnamese army and its American advisers was only one of the defeats that emphasized how difficult it was going to be to defeat the Viet Cong. See Neil Sheehan, *A Bright Shining Lie* (New York: Random House, 1988), pp. 201–65.

8. See Frank Levy, *The New Dollars and Dreams: American Incomes and Economic Change* (New York: Russel Sage Foundation, 1998), pp. 25–26. Between 1949 and 1959 the GDP grew by 43 percent. See also Robert J. Gordon, "Postwar Macroeconomics: The Evolution of Events and Ideas," and Alan S. Blinder, "The Level and Distribution of Economic Well-Being," both papers in Martin Feldstein, ed., *The American Economy in Transition* (Chicago: University of Chicago Press, 1980).

9. John Cassidy, "Who Killed the Middle Class?" *New Yorker*, October 15, 1995.

10. Personal observation, East 50th Street, New York, October 2001.

11. Conversation with author, October 2001.

12. Bill Clinton, for example, spoke in his 1992 Democratic National Convention acceptance speech of his wish for "a government that understands that jobs must come from growth in a vibrant and vital system of free enterprise." It is plain from Adam Clymer's life of Edward Kennedy (*Edward M. Kennedy: A Biography* [New York: Morrow, 1999]) that Senator Kennedy, in many respects the most loyal liberal in the Senate, accepted a role for the private health insurance industry in the 1990s that he would have found unacceptable in the 1970s.

13. See Chapter 4. See also Edward N. Wolff, *Top Heavy: A Study of the Increasing Inequality of Wealth in America* (New York: Twentieth Century Fund, 1995). Wolff points out that the only three countries where longitudinal studies stretching back to the 1920s are available, are the United States, the United Kingdom, and Sweden. When those series are plotted, they show wealth in the United Kingdom, substantially more unequal in the 1920s than in the United States, becoming less unequal from the 1970s, since when inequality has become steeply more pronounced in the United States. The curve for Sweden is flatter, but inequality has been falling below the level in the United States since about 1950. Wolff comments that "in the early part of this century . . . America appeared to be the land of opportunity, whereas Europe was a place where an entrenched upper class controlled the bulk of wealth. By the late 1980s, the situation appears to have completely reversed, with much higher concentration of wealth in the United States than in Europe. Europe now appears the land of equality" (p. 21).

14. Not counting developing countries like Brazil or India, the two countries that most closely approached American levels of inequality were the two that had most followed American models, Australia and Britain.

15. The Texas populist Kent Hance, running against George W. Bush, a keen jogger, as a Democrat in 1978 twitted him that "the only time folks around here go running is when somebody's chasing them." Frank Bruni, *Ambling into History* (New York: HarperCollins, 2002), p. 122.

16. Michael Zweig, *The Working Class Majority: America's Best Kept Secret* (Ithaca, N.Y.: Cornell University Press, 2000).

17. John Milton, *Lycidas*, p. 125.

18. Tom Wolfe's name for the Wall Street bankers and brokers in his novel, *The Bonfire of the Vanities* (New York: Farrar Straus Giroux, 1987).

19. Newt Gingrich, for a time the most successful Republican politician since Ronald Reagan, is said to have distributed to his followers a list of words they should use to describe Democrats. It included "sick," "traitors," "corrupt," "cheat," and "steal." Quoted in Carter, *From George Wallace to Newt Gingrich*.

20. In part the problem seems to arise because, while much of the vitality and health of capitalism comes from competition, the competitors strive for monopoly. As Adam Smith memorably put it, "People of the same trade seldom meet together, even for merriment and diversion, but the conversation ends in a conspiracy against the public, or in some contrivance to raise prices" (Smith, *Wealth of Nations*, vol. 1, book 1, chapter 10).

21. It is ultimately irrelevant whether this strategy was deliberate, as Reagan's budget director, David Stockman, has admitted, and his arch-critic Daniel Patrick Moynihan has maintained, or simply resulted from the lack of courage to take tough decisions.

22. J. K. Galbraith, *American Capitalism: The Concept of Countervailing Power* (Boston: Houghton Mifflin, 1956).

23. In 2001 Bloomberg was elected mayor of New York and Corzine senator from

New Jersey, after campaigns in which each spent tens of millions of dollars of his own money. The ultimately unsuccessful campaigns for president of Malcolm "Steve" Forbes went far enough to underscore the same point.

24. This political shift was also in part a consequence of the Vietnam War, which ironically brought the Great Society up dead in its tracks anyway.

25. Bruni, *Ambling into History*, p. 101.

26. Speaker Bob Livingston resigned on December 19, 1998, as a result of revelations about his private life.

27. In the summer of 2003 the successful recall of California governor Gray Davis threatened Democratic control without changing the Democratic majority.

28. Dotty Lynch, "Is History on the Democrats' Side?" <cbsnews.com>, July 19, 2002.

29. See, for example, Paul Krugman, "The Insider Game," *New York Times*, July 12, 2002; Joe Conason, "Notes on a Native Son," *Harper's Magazine*, February 2000.

30. Robert Sheer, *Los Angeles Times*, August 6, 2002.

Select Bibliography

Documents

Commager, Henry Steele. *Documents of American History*. New York: Appleton, 1963.

CQ, *Congress & the Nation*. Vols. 1–10. 1963–2000.

Levin, Richard C., George J. Mitchell, Paul A. Volcker, and George F. Will. "Report of the Independent Members of the Commissioner's Blue Ribbon Panel on Baseball Economics." July 2000.

PIPA. *Americans on Foreign Aid and World Hunger: A Study of US Public Attitudes*. February 2, 2001.

Public Papers of the Presidents, John F. Kennedy, 1961. Washington, D.C.: United States Government Printing Office.

Public Papers of the Presidents, Lyndon B. Johnson, 1963–64. Vol. 2. Washington, D.C.: United States Government Printing Office, 1966.

Public Papers of the Presidents, Lyndon B. Johnson, 1968. Vol. 1. Washington, D.C.: United States Government Printing Office, 1969.

Public Papers of the Presidents, William Jefferson Clinton, 2000–2001. Vol. 3. Washington, D.C.: United States Government Printing Office, 2002.

Third International Math and Science Study. 1998.

U.S. Census Bureau. *Current Population Reports*, by Lisa Lubbock. January 2001.

U.S. Department of Commerce, Bureau of the Census. *Census of Population and Housing*, U.S. Summary Table 1.4, "U.S. Population in Urban, Suburban and Rural Areas 1950–1998." Last updated April 20, 2000.

U.S. Department of Commerce, U.S. Bureau of the Census. Website <www.census.gov/>.

Articles and Essays

Apple, R. W., Jr. "Grand Ideas, Little Time." *New York Times*, January 28, 2000.

Armas, Genaro C. "Census: Big Increase in Hispanics." AP, March 12, 2001.

Arrillaga, Pauline. "Climate of Violence Leads to Death in Texas Desert." *Los Angeles Times*, August 20, 2000.

Balz, Dan, and Thomas B. Edsall. "Financial Records Subpoenaed in Fight over Campaign Laws." *Washington Post*, June 26, 2002.

Barone, Michael. Introduction to Michael Barone and Grant Ujifusa, eds., *Almanac of American Politics*. Washington, D.C.: National Journal, 2000.

Barrett, Laurence I. "Reagan Democrats' Divided Loyalties." *Time*, October 31, 1988.

Bell, Daniel. "The End of American Exceptionalism." In Nathan Glazer and Irving Kristol, eds., *The American Commonwealth*. New York, Basic Books, 1976.

Blinder, Alan S. "The Internet and the New Economy." *Brookings Institution Policy Brief, no. 60*, June 2000.

Borjas, George J., and Bernt Brasberg. "Who Leaves? The Out-Migration of the Foreign-Born." *Review of Economics and Statistics* 78 (January 1996).

Broder, David S. "Toothless Watchdog." *Washington Post*, May 29, 2002.

Cassidy, John. "Who Killed the Middle Class?" *New Yorker*, October 15, 1995.

Conason, Joe. "Notes on a Native Son." *Harper's Magazine*, February 2000.

Cox, T. H., and C. V. Harquail. "Career Paths and Career Success in the Early Career Stages of Male and Female MBAs." *Journal of Vocational Behavior* 39 (1991): 59–75.

Crawford, James. "The Campaign against Proposition 227: A Post Mortem." *Bilingual Research Journal*, no. 1 (February 1997): 21.

Dillon Sam, and Lesley Wayne. "Scandals in the Church: The Money. As Lawsuits Spread, Church Faces Questions on Finances," *New York Times*, June 13, 2002.

Dowd, Maureen. op. ed. page. *New York Times*, April 30, 2003.

Ellingwood, Ken. "Border Town Wary of Plans for a Second Wall." *Los Angeles Times*, January 3, 2001.

Firestone, David. "Choking on Growth: A Special Report. In Atlanta, Suburban Comforts Thwart Plans to Limit Sprawl." *New York Times*, November 21, 1999.

Greider, William. "An Insider's View of the Election." *Atlantic Monthly*, July 1988.

Heffron, Florence. "The FCC and Broadcast Deregulation." In John J. Havick, ed., *Communications Policy and the Political Process*. Westport, Conn.: Greenwood Press, 1983.

Hodgson, Godfrey. "Britons, Americans and Europeans." *Political Quarterly* 59, no. 3 (July–September 1988).

———. "Immigrants and Frontiersmen: Two Traditions in American Foreign Policy." *Diplomatic History* 23, no. 3 (Summer 1999).

Huntington, Samuel P. "The Clash of Civilisations?" *Foreign Affairs*, Summer 1993.

Jackman, Tom. "Dulles Cabbies Feel Overcharged." *Washington Post*, August 9, 1999.

Jacobs, J. J. "Women's Entry into Management: Trends in Earnings, Authority and Values among Salaried Managers." *Administrative Science Quarterly* 37 (June 1992): 282–301.

Jordan, Mary. "Mexicans Caught at Border in Falling Numbers." *Washington Post*, May 24, 2002.

Kagan, Robert. "Power and Weakness." *Policy Review*, no. 113 (June–July 2002).

Kristof, Nicholas D. "As Life for Family Farmers Worsens, the Toughest Wither." *New York Times*, April 2, 2000.

Krugman, Paul. "America the Boastful." *Foreign Affairs*, May 1998.

———. "The Insider Game." *New York Times*, July 12, 2002.

Kuttner, Robert. "After Triumphalism." *American Prospect*, November 19, 2001.

Lewis, Michael. "How the Eggheads Cracked." *New York Times Magazine*, January 24, 1999.

McDonnell, Patrick J., and Ken Ellingwood. "Immigration—the Big Issue of '94—Disappears from '98 Debate." *Los Angeles Times*, October 23, 1998.

Maclean, Nancy. "The Hidden History of Affirmative Action: Working Women's Struggles in the 1970s and the Gender of Class." *Feminist Studies*, Spring 1999.

Madrick, Jeff. "In the Shadow of Prosperity." *New York Review of Books*, August 14, 1997.

Mailman, Stanley. "California's Proposition 187 and Its Lessons." *New York Law Journal*, January 3, 1995.

Marr, Andrew. *Guardian*, October 5, 2001.

Meyer, Frank S., ed. "Freedom, Tradition, Conservatism." In *What Is Conservatism?* New York; Holt, Rinehart and Winston, 1964.

Naim, Moises. "Fads and Fashions in Economic Reform: Washington Consensus or Washington Confusion?" *Foreign Policy*, October 26, 1999.

Negroponte, Nicholas. "Bit by Bit on Wall Street: Lucky Strikes Again." *Wired*, May 1, 1994.

"Network's Roots May Help Town Bloom." *Washington Post*, February 13, 2000.

Oliner, S., and D. Sichel. "The Resurgence of Growth in the Late 1990s: Is Information Technology the Story?" *Journal of Economic Perspectives* 4, no. 4 (Fall 2000).

Owen, David, and Richard Tomkins. "That's Tiger Power." <FT.com>, April 12, 2001.

Penn, Mark J., with assistance from Jennifer Coleman. *New Democrat* 1 (Fall 1998): 30–35.

Pierce, E. L. "The Freedmen at Port Royal." *Atlantic Monthly* 12 (September 1863).

Robins, Linda. "Hispanics Don't Exist." *U.S. News*, May 11, 1998.

Sachs, Jeffrey. "Creditor Panics: Causes and Remedies." *Cato Journal* 18, no. 3 (1999), <www.cato.org/pubs/journal/cato_journal>.

Salinas de Gortari, Carlos, and Roberto Mangabeira Unger, "The Market Turn without Neo-Liberalism." *Challenge* 42, no. 1 (1999): 19–35.

Schneider, William. "The Suburban Century Begins." *Atlantic Monthly*, July 1992.

Scott, David Clark. "Ready or Not, Here Comes Wal-Mart." *Christian Science Monitor*, September 29, 1994.

Simpson, Alan K., and Richard K. Lamm. "571 Million Americans." *Washington Post*, June 20, 2000.

Skocpol, Theda. "Unravelling from Above." *American Prospect*, no. 25 (March–April 1996).

Smeeding, Timothy M. "Changing Income Inequality in OECD Countries; Updated Results from the Luxembourg Income Study." Center for Policy Research, Maxwell School, Syracuse University, 2001.

"Study Finds Immigrants Doing Well in America." *New York Times*, July 3, 1999.

Thernstrom, Stephan. "Plenty of Room for All." *Times Literary Supplement*, London, May 26, 2000.

Tobar, Hector, and Claudia Kolker. "Hate Crimes against Latinos on Rise, Study Finds." *Los Angeles Times*, July 27, 1999.

Triplett, Jack E. "Economic Statistics, the New Economy and the Productivity Slowdown." *Business Economics* 34, no. 2 (April 1999).

Warde, Ibrahim. "LTCM, a Hedge Fund Too Big to Fail." *Le monde diplomatique*, November 1998.

Wasserman, Joanne. "Public Lives, Private Schools—Bigwigs Pick Private Ed for Their Kids." *New York Daily News*, April 3, 2000.

Wirtz, Ronald A. "Farming the Government." *FedGazette*, website of Federal Reserve Bank of Minneapolis, October 1999.

Wolff, Michael. Interview in <www.iwantmedia.com>, February 1, 2001.

Books

Ackerman, Bruce, and Anne Allstott. *The Stakeholder Society*. New Haven: Yale University Press, 1999.

Ambrose, Stephen. *Nixon: The Triumph of a Politician*. New York: Simon & Schuster, 1989.

Anderson, Martin. *Revolution: The Reagan Legacy*. Rev. ed., Stanford, Calif.: Hoover Institution Press, 1990.

Auletta, Ken. *Greed and Glory on Wall Street*. New York: Warner, 1987.

Beale, Howard K. *Theodore Roosevelt and the Rise of America to World Power*. Baltimore: Johns Hopkins Press, 1956.

Bell, Daniel. *The Coming of Post-Industrial Society*. New York: Basic Books, 1973.

———. *The End of Ideology: On the Exhaustion of Political Ideas in the Fifties*. New York: Free Press, 1960.

Bellesiles, Michael A. *Arming America: The Origins of a National Gun Culture*. New York: Knopf, 2000.

Berners-Lee, Tim, with Mark Fischetti. *Weaving the Web*. New York: HarperCollins, 1999.

Beschloss, Michael R. and Strobe Talbott. *At the Highest Levels*. Boston: Little Brown, 1993.

Birnbaum, Jeffrey H. *The Money Men: The Real Story of Fund-Raising's Influence on Political Power in America*. New York: Crown, 2000.

Black, Earl, and Merle Black. *Politics and Society in the South*. Cambridge Mass.: Harvard University Press, 1987.

Blinder, Alan S., and Janet L. Yellen. *The Fabulous Decade: Macroeconomic Lessons from the 1990s*. New York: Century Foundation, 2001.

Borjas, George J. *Heaven's Door*. Princeton, N.J.: Princeton University Press, 1999.

Braestrup, Peter. *Big Story. How American Press and Television Reported and Interpreted the Crisis of Tet 1968.* New Haven: Yale University Press, 1983.

Brands, H. W. *The Strange Death of American Liberalism.* New Haven: Yale University Press, 2001.

Brinkley, Alan. *The End of Reform: New Deal Liberalism in Recession and War.* New York: Knopf, 1995.

Brownmiller, Susan. *In Our Time: Memoir of a Revolution.* New York: Dial Press, 1999.

Bruni, Frank. *Ambling into History.* New York: HarperCollins, 2002.

Bush, George H. W., and Brent Scowcroft. *A World Transformed.* New York: Knopf, 1998.

Carter, Dan T. *From George Wallace to Newt Gingrich: Race in the Conservative Counterrevolution, 1963 to 1994.* Baton Rouge: Louisiana State University, 1999.

———. *The Politics of Rage: George Wallace, the Origins of the New Conservatism, and the Transformation of American Politics.* Baton Rouge: Louisiana State University Press, 1995.

Carter, Jimmy. *Keeping Faith: Memoirs of a President.* New York: Collins, 1982.

Castells, Manuel. *The Rise of the Network Society.* Vol. 1. 2nd ed. Oxford: Blackwell Publishers, 2000.

Century Foundation. *What's Next for Organized Labor?* New York: Century, 1999.

Christopher, Warren, et al. *American Hostages in Iran: The Conduct of a Crisis.* New York: Council on Foreign Relations, 1985.

Clymer, Adam. *Edward M. Kennedy: A Biography.* New York: Morrow, 1999.

Cohen, David. *Chasing the Red, White and Blue: A Journey in Tocqueville's First Steps through Contemporary America.* New York: Picador USA, 2001.

Costas, Bob. *Fair Ball.* New York: Broadway Books, 2001.

Cusumano, Michael A., and Richard W. Selby. *Microsoft Secrets: How the World's Most Powerful Software Company Creates Technology, Shapes Markets and Manages People.* New York: Simon & Schuster, 1998.

Davies, Gareth. *From Opportunity to Entitlement: The Transformation and Decline of Great Society Liberalism.* Lawrence: The University Press of Kansas, 1996.

Diggins, John Patrick. *The Rise and Fall of the American Left.* New York: Norton, 1992.

Dollard, John. *Caste and Class in a Southern Town.* New Haven: Yale University Press, 1937.

Donovan, Robert J. *Conflict and Crisis: The Presidency of Harry S. Truman, 1945–1948.* New York: Noton, 1977.

Downie, Leonard, Jr., and Robert G. Kaiser. *The News about the News.* New York: Alfred A. Knopf, 2002.

Draper, Theodore. *A Very Thin Line: The Iran Contra Affairs.* New York: Hill and Wang, 1999.

Drew, Elizabeth. *The Corruption of American Politics: What Went Wrong and Why.* Secaucus, N.J.: Birch Lane Press, 1999.

———. *On the Edge: The Clinton Presidency.* New York: Simon & Schuster, 1993.

Duany, Andres, Elizabeth Plater-Zyberk, and Jeff Speck. *Suburban Nation: The Rise of Sprawl and the Decline of the American Dream.* New York: Farrar, Straus and Giroux, 2000.

Esposito, John L. *Islam: The Straight Path.* New York: Oxford University Press, 1991.

Evans, Sara. *Personal Politics.* New York: Knopf, 1979.

Feldstein, Martin. *The American Economy in Transition.* Chicago: University of Chicago Press, 1980.

Folkerts, Jean, and Dwight L. Teeter Jr. *Voices of the Nation: A History of Mass Media in the United States.* Needham, Mass.: Allyn and Bacon, 1998.

Frank, Robert H., and Philip J. Cook. *The Winner-Take-All Society.* New York: Free Press, 1995.

Frank, Tom. *One Market under God.* New York: Doubleday, 2000.

Friedan, Betty. *The Feminine Mystique.* New York: Norton, 1963.

Friedman, Thomas. *The Lexus and the Olive Tree.* New York: Farrar, Straus and Giroux, 2000.

Fukuyama, Francis. *The End of History and the Last Man.* New York: Free Press, 1992.

Galbraith, James K. *Created Unequal.* New York: Simon & Schuster, 1998; new preface, 2000.

Galston, William, and Elaine Ciulla Kamarck. *The Politics of Evasion: Democrats and the Presidency.* Washington, D.C.: Progressive Policy Institute, September 1989.

Gillies, James, and Robert Cailliau. *How the Web Was Born.* New York: Oxford University Press, 2000.

Glassman, James K., and Kevin A. Hassett. *Dow 36,000: The New Strategy for Profiting from the Coming Rise in the Stock Market.* New York: Times Business/Random House, 1999.

Grant, Madison. *The Passing of the Great Race, or the Racial Basis of European History.* London: Bell, 1921.

Greenstein, Fred I. *The Presidential Difference: Leadership Style from FDR to Clinton.* New York: Free Press, 2000.

Greider, William. *The Secrets of the Temple.* New York: Simon & Schuster, 1987.

Hadden, Jeffrey K., and Anson Shupe. *Televangelism: Power and Politics on God's Frontier.* New York: Henry Holt, 1998.

Halberstam, David. *The Fifties.* New York: Random House, 1993.

Hanby, Alonzo L. *Man of the People: A Life of Harry S. Truman.* New York: Oxford University Press, 1995.

Harrison, Bennett, and Barry Bluestone. *The Great U-Turn: Corporate Restructuring and the Polarizing of America.* New York: Basic Books, 1988.

Hart, Stanley, and Alvin Spivak. *The Elephant in the Bedroom: Automobile Dependence and Denial; Impacts on the Environment.* Pasadena, Calif.: New Paradigm, 1993.

Heins, Cornelia. *The Wall Falls: An Oral History of the Reunification of the Two Germanies.* London: Grey Seal, 1994.

Higham, John. *Strangers in the Land*. New Brunswick, N.J.: Rutgers University Press, 1955, 1988.

Hodgson, Godfrey. *The World Turned Right Side Up*. Boston: Houghton Mifflin, 1996.

Hoffman, Eva. *Lost in Translation: Life in a New Language*. New York: Dutton, 1989, 1990.

Howe, Irving. *Land of Our Fathers*. New York: Simon & Schuster, 1983.

Huntington, Samuel P. *The Clash of Civilizations and the Remaking of World Order*. New York: Simon & Schuster, 1996.

Hutton, Will. *The State We're In*. London: Jonathan Cape, 1995.

Jackson, Kenneth T. *Crabgrass Frontier: The Suburbanization of the United States*. New York: Oxford University Press, 1985.

Janeway, Michael. *Republic of Denial: Press, Politics and Public Life*. New Haven, Conn.: Yale University Press, 1999.

Johnson, Haynes. *The Best of Times*. New York: Harcourt Brace, Jovanovich, 2001.

Johnson, Lyndon B. *The Vantage Point*. New York: Popular Library, 1971.

Judis, John B. *William F. Buckley Jr.: Patron Saint of the Conservatives*. New York: Simon & Schuster, 1988.

Judis, John B., and Ruy A. Teixeira. *The Emerging Democratic Majority*. New York: Scribner, 2002.

Kahlenberg, Richard D. *All Together Now: Creating Middle-Class Schools through Public School Choice*. Washington, D.C.: Brookings, 2000.

Kalb, Marvin. *One Scandalous Story: Clinton, Lewinsky and 13 Days that Tarnished American Journalism*. New York: Free Press, 2001.

Kaplan, David A. *The Silicon Boys*. New York: HarperCollins, 2000.

Kelly, Gail Paradise. *From Vietnam to America: A Chronicle of the Vietnamese Immigration to the US*. Boulder, Colo.: Westview Press, 1977.

Kessler-Harris, Alice. *In Pursuit of Equity*. Oxford: Oxford University Press, 2001.

King, Desmond. *Making Americans: Immigration, Race and the Making of the Diverse Democracy*. Cambridge, Mass.: Harvard University Press, 2000.

Kissinger, Henry A. *Does America Need a Foreign Policy?: Toward a Diplomacy for the 21st Century*. New York: Simon & Schuster, 2001.

——. *White House Years*. Boston: Little Brown, 1979.

——. *Years of Upheaval*. Boston: Little Brown, 1982.

Koh, Harold Hongju. *The National Security Constitution: Sharing Power after the Iran Contra Affair*. New Haven: Yale University Press, 1990.

Kovach, Bill, and Tom Rosenstiel. *Warp Speed: America in the Age of Mixed Media*. New York: Century Foundation Press, 1999.

Kunstler, James Howard. *The Geography of Nowhere: The Rise and Decline of America's Man-Made Landscape*. New York: Simon & Schuster, 1993.

Kuttner, Robert. *Everything for Sale*. Chicago: University of Chicago Press, 1996.

——. *Revolt of the Haves*. New York: Simon & Schuster, 1980.

Langdon, Philip. *A Better Place to Live: Reshaping the American Suburb*. Amherst: University of Massachusetts Press, 1994.

Levy, Frank. *The New Dollars and Dreams: American Incomes and Economic Change*. New York: Russell Sage Foundation, 1998.

Lewis, Charles, and the Center for Public Integrity. *The Buying of the President, 2000*. New York: Avon Books, 2000.

Lewis, Michael. *Liar's Poker*. New York: Norton, 1989.

Lewy, Gunther. *America in Vietnam*. New York: Oxford University Press, 1978.

Lichtenstein, Nelson. *The Most Dangerous Man in Detroit: Walter Reuther and the Fate of American Labor*. New York: Basic Books, 1985.

———. *State of the Union: A Century of American Labor*. Princeton, N.J.: Princeton University Press, 2002.

Lipset, Seymour Martin. *American Exceptionalism: A Two-Edged Sword*. New York: Norton, 1997.

Lipset, Seymour Martin, and Gary Marks. *It Didn't Happen Here? Why Socialism Failed in the United States*. New York: Norton, 2001.

Lohr, Steve. *Go To*. New York: Basic Books, 2001.

Lopez, Haney. *White by Law: The Legal Construction of Race*. New York: New York University Press, 1996.

McCullough, David. The *Path between the Seas: The Creation of the Panama Canal, 1870–1914*. New York: Simon & Schuster, 1977.

McGirr, Lisa. *Suburban Warriors: The Origins of the New American Right*. Princeton, N.J.: Princeton University Press, 2001.

Mansbridge, Jane J. *Why We Lost the ERA*. Chicago: University of Chicago Press, 1986.

Marks, Lara V. *Sexual Chemistry*. New Haven: Yale University Press, 2001.

Matlock, Jack F., Jr. *Autopsy on an Empire*. New York: Random House, 1995.

Mayer, William G. *The Changing American Mind: How and Why American Public Opinion Changed between 1960 and 1988*. Ann Arbor: University of Michigan Press, 1992.

Mead, Walter Russell. *Special Providence: American Foreign Policy and How It Changed the World*. New York: Knopf, 2001.

Miller, James E. *The Baseball Business: Pursuing Pennants and Profits in Baltimore*. Chapel Hill: University of North Caroline Press, 1986.

Milner, Clyde A., II, et al. *Oxford History of the American West*. Oxford: Oxford University Press, 1994.

Mishel, Laurence, Jared Bernstein, and John Schmitt. *The State of Working America, 2000–2001*. Ithaca, N.Y.: ILR, Cornell University Press, 2001.

Morison, S. E., and H. S. Commager. *The Growth of the American Republic*. 2nd ed. 2 vols. New York: Oxford University Press, 1950.

Moynihan, Daniel P. *Came the Revolution*. New York: Harcourt Brace Jovanovich, 1988.

———. *Secrecy*. New Haven: Yale University Press, 1998.

National Election Studies Guide to Public Opinion and Electoral Behavior. Liberal-Conservative Self-Identification, 1972–2000. Ann Arbor: University of Michigan.

Naughton, John. *A Brief History of the Future*. London: Weidenfeld & Nicolson, 1999.

Nitze, Paul H. *From Hiroshima to Glasnost: At the Center of Decision*. New York: George Weidenfeld, 1989.

Oberdorfer, Don. *Tet*. Garden City, N.Y.: Doubleday, 1971.

Oliver, J. Eric. *Democracy in Suburbia*. Princeton, N.J.: Princeton University Press, 2002.

Orfield, Gary, and Susan Eaton. *Dismantling Desegregation: The Quiet Reversal of Brown v. Board of Education*. New York: New Press, 1996.

Patterson, James T. *Mr. Republican: A Biography of Robert A. Taft*. Boston: Houghton Mifflin, 1972.

Phillips, Kevin P. *The Emerging Republican Majority*. New Rochelle, N.Y.: Arlington House, 1969.

Pole, J. R. *American Individualism and the Promise of Progress*. New York: Oxford University Press, 1980.

Portes, Alejandro, and Ruben G. Rumbaut. *Immigrant America*. Berkeley: University of California Press, 1996.

Potter, David M. *People of Plenty*. Chicago: University of Chicago Press, 1954.

Powers, Richard Gid. *Secrecy and Power: The Life of J. Edgar Hoover*. New York: Free Press, 1987.

Putnam, Robert. *Bowling Alone: The Collapse and Revival of American Community*. New York: Simon & Schuster, 2000.

Reich, Robert B. *Locked in the Cabinet*. New York: Knopf, 1997.

Reid, Robert. *Architects of the Web*. New York: Wiley, 1997.

Reimers, David. *Still the Golden Door: The Third World Comes to America*. 2nd ed. New York: Columbia University Press, 1992.

Rhodes, Richard. *The Making of the Atomic Bomb*. New York: Simon & Schuster, 1986.

Rielly, John E., ed. *American Public Opinion and U.S. Foreign Policy*. Chicago: Chicago Council on Foreign Relations, 1999.

Rose, Willie Lee. *Rehearsal for Reconstruction: The Port Royal Experiment*. New York: Bobbs-Merrill, 1964.

Rothschild, Mary. *A Case of Black and White: Northern Volunteers and the Southern Freedom Summers*. Westport, Conn.: Greenwood Press, 1982.

Ruiz de Burton, María Amparo, Rosario Sánchez, and Beatriz Pita, eds. *The Squatter and the Don*. Houston: Arte Público Press, 1992.

Rusher, William A. *The Rise of the Right*. New York: National Review, 1993.

Samuelson, Robert J. *The Good Life and Its Discontents: The American Dream in the Age of Entitlement, 1990–1995*. New York: Random House, 1995.

Schumpeter, Joseph. *Capitalism, Socialism and Democracy*. New York: Harper's, 1942.

Shapiro, Andrew L. *The Control Revolution*. New York: Century, 1999.

Sheehan, Neil. *A Bright Shining Lie*. New York: Random House, 1988.

Shiller, Robert J. *Irrational Exuberance*. Princeton, N.J.: Princeton University Press, 2000.

Shlaim, Avi. *The Iron Wall: Israel and the Arab World*. London: Penguin, 2000.

Shrag, Peter. *Paradise Lost: California's Experience, America's Future*. New York: New Press, 1998.

Smith, James P., and Barry Edmonston, eds. *The New Americans: Economics, Demographic and Fiscal Effects of Immigration*. Washington, D.C.: National Academy Press, 1997.

Starr, Kevin. *Endangered Dreams: The Great Depression in California*. New York: Oxford University Press, 1996.

Stephanopoulos, George. *All Too Human: A Political Education*. New York: Little Brown, 1999.

Stewart, James B. *Den of Thieves*. New York: Simon & Schuster, 1991.

Stockman, David A. *The Triumph of Politics*. New York: Harper & Row, 1986.

Summers, Mark Wahlgreen. *Rum, Romanism and Rebellion: The Making of a President, 1884*. Chapel Hill: University of North Carolina Press, 2000.

Taylor, William R. *Cavalier and Yankee: The Old South and the National Character*. New York: Braziller, 1961.

Tocqueville, Alexis de. *Democracy in America*. New York: New American Library, 1954.

Toobin, Jeffrey. *Too Close to Call*. New York: Random House, 2001.

Tuveson, Ernest. *Redeemer Nation: The Idea of America's Millennial Role*. Chicago: University of Chicago Press, 1968.

Valian, Virginia. *Why So Slow? The Advancement of Women*. Cambridge, Mass.: MIT Press, 1998.

Vanneman, Reeve, and Lynn Weber Cannon. *The American Perception of Class*. Philadelphia: Temple University Press, 1987.

Walker, Martin. *Clinton: The President They Deserve*. London: Fourth Estate, 1996.

Walsh, Lawrence E. *Firewall: The Iran-Contra Conspiracy and Cover-Up*. New York: W. W. Norton, 1997.

Wayne, Stephen J. *The Road to the White House, 2000: The Politics of Presidential Elections*. Bedford: St. Martin's, 2000.

Wolff, Edward N. *Top Heavy: A Study of the Increasing Inequality of Wealth in America*. New York: Twentieth Century Fund Press, 1995.

Yergin, Daniel. *The Prize: The Epic Quest for Oil, Money and Power*. New York: Simon & Schuster, 1991.

Zweig, Michael. *The Working Class Majority: America's Best Kept Secret*. Ithaca, N.Y.: Cornell University Press, 2000.

Websites

<www.abanet.org/buslaw/billable/toolkit/bhcomplete/pdf>
<http://census.gov>
<http://www.eagleforum.org>
<http://www.equalrightsamendment.org/era.html>
<http://www.now.org/issues/economic/cea/history.html>
<www.projectusa.org>
<http://www.zakon.org/robert/internet/timeline>

Index

abortion law, 145–49, 167–68, 328n.74

Abraham, Mr. and Mrs. S. Daniel, 55

Abrams, Elliott, 278

academia, women in, 152

accounting firms, scandals involving, 7

advertising: and class divisions, 246; as free speech, Supreme Court on, 31, 53; politicians' dependence on, 30, 51–52. *See also* marketing

affirmative action: backlash against, 181, 183; opposition to, 172, 175; techniques of, 181–82; in universities, 182

Afghanistan, U.S. invasion of, 279, 280, 286

African Americans, 172–202; capital punishment for, 42, 192; children, poverty rates for, 190; in cities, 212; disappointed hopes of, 172, 299–300; educational segregation of, attempts to combat, 178–79; elected officials, 34; and electoral politics, 33, 173; exclusion from American aspirations for equality, 239, 288; Hispanics compared with, 132; individual success stories, 172, 173, 183–84; inequalities among, 27, 183–84, 186–87; middle class, move to suburbs, 177–78; migration north, 200, 333n.90; perceptions of law and order, O. J. Simpson trial and, 196–97; police brutality against, 193, 194–96; population growth, projected, 117; in prison, 187, 192, 330n.44; progress experienced by, 89, 172, 173, 187, 193; public programs for, reductions in, 189; in public schools, 243; radical leadership of, backlash against, 172; stereotypes about, 198; struggle for equality, resistance to, 172, 173, 198, 289; in suburbs, 213; successful, racism experienced by, 184–85; underclass, problems experienced by, 187–89; and urban politics, 212; Voting Rights Act of 1965 and, 33–34; and women, comparison of experiences of, 157, 163

Aid to Families with Dependent Children, end of, 189

Albright, Madeleine, 270

Allen, Paul, 72, 76

Altair, 76

America Online (AOL), 83; losses in early twenty-first century, 7; merger with Netscape, 84; profits in 1990s, 23; takeover of Time-Warner by, 63–64

American Association of Retired Persons, political clout of, 8

American Cyanamid Company, 169

American Revolution, ideals of, xix

Anderson, Martin, 312n.34

Anderson, Robert B., 45

Andreesen, Marc, 64, 68, 69, 72, 82

Angola, Soviet policies in, 256

anti-communist ideology, and conservative ascendancy, 37

anti-immigrant sentiment: in California, 128–29; in late nineteenth–early twentieth centuries, 115–16, 320n.15; in late twentieth century, 345n.72; after September 11, 2001, 128

Apple, R. W., Jr., 4

Apple Computer: competition with IBM, 77; creation of, 76; founders of, 72; law firm advising, 71; success with earliest models, 77; and Xerox PARC, 73, 76, 77

Applebome, Peter, 200–2

Arab Americans, 119

ARPANET, 72, 81

Arthur Andersen, 7

Asia: financial crisis of 1990s, 273–74; government control of Internet in, 86; immigration and U.S. interests in, 138

Asians: anti-immigrant sentiment and, 115; diversity of, 118–19; educational achievements of, 119; population growth, 113, 117, 118; religious beliefs among, 137; in suburbs, 213; use of term, 322n.31

Atlanta (Georgia): affirmative action in, 182; residential segregation in, 329n.22; suburban sprawl in, 215

AT&T, technological inventions at, 74, 79
Australia: inequality in, 347n.14; role in Internet development, 82
automobile, and suburban sprawl, 216

Bailey, Doug, 222
Bakke, Allan Paul, 182
Bakker, Jim and Tammy, 223
Baltimore (Maryland), white flight from, 212
Baran, Paul, 80
Bardeen, John, 74
Barksdale, Jim, 72, 83
Barone, Michael, 247, 311n.23
Bartholomew, Keith, 214
BASIC software: compressed version of, 76; origins of, 75
Belgium, productivity in, 98
Bell Labs, technological inventions at, 74, 79
Beloff, Max, 344n.70
Benham, Phillip, 168
Bentsen, Lloyd, 22–23
Berkman, Brenda, 163
Berners-Lee, Tim: on American patriotism, 292; egalitarian dreams of, 82, 85; invention of World Wide Web by, 68, 73, 81; on Mosaic software, 82
Bickel, Alexander M., 182
bilingual education, attack on, 129
bin Laden, Osama, 269
Bina, Eric, 82
Birmingham (Alabama), residential segregation in, 329n.22
Birnbaum, Jeffrey H., 51
Blackmun, Harry, 148, 169
Blinder, Alan, 106
Bloomberg, Michael, 54, 300, 347n.23
Blotnick, Srully, 168
Blount, Winton, 20
Bluestone, Barry, 21
Boas, Franz, 115–16
Bolt, Beranek & Newman (BBN), 71, 81
Bolton, John, 279
Border Patrol, Hispanic immigrants and, 130–31, 132
Boskin, Michael, 102
Boston (Massachusetts): black population of, 212; racial conflict in, 178
Boston Globe, praise of U.S. economy in, 87
Boyd, Gerald, 185, 186, 197–98
Bradlee, Benjamin, 238

Bradley, Bill, 55, 302
Brattan, Walter, 74
Breaux, John, 49
Bremer, Arthur, 330n.32
Brezhnev, Leonid, 38, 256
Britain: anti-American sentiment in, 344n.70; government control of Internet in, 86; immigration from, decline in, 118, 321n.23; inequality in, 347n.14; racism in, 199
Brown, Kevin, 228
Brown, Nicole, 196
Brown v. Board of Education of Topeca, 200
Brownmiller, Susan, 148, 156
Bryan, William Jennings, 204
Buchanan, Pat, 149
Buckley, James, 300, 309n.2
Buckley, William F., 30, 37, 205, 309n.2
Buckley v. Valeo, 31, 53, 221–22, 300
Bunyan, John, 282
bureaucracy, 299
Burger, Warren, 181
Burton, Sir Richard, 268
Busby, Horace, 47
Bush, George H. W.: 1988 campaign of, racism in, 193; as classic Republican, 41; foreign policy under, 41; and Gulf War, 264–65; loss of popularity, 270, 302
Bush, George W.: on "axis of evil," 287; business profits of, insider knowledge and, 7–8; campaign spending by, 54; defense spending under, 281; election for president, 6, 59, 302; foreign relations under, 273, 276–80, 286–87; and Hispanic vote, 134; insiders in administration of, 7; McCain-Feingold bill and, 56; neoconservatives in administration of, 278–79; popularity after September 11, 302, 303; in presidential campaign of 2000, 88, 301–2; as sports franchise owner, 226; tax cut under, 18; triumphalism and populism associated with, xviii
Bush, Jeb, 278
Bush, Vannevar, 66, 67–68, 70–71
Bushnell, Nolan, 76
business: government as, 11–12; and Internet, role in development of, 68, 69, 72–73; legal profession as, 225–26; media as, 228–29; politics as, 57–58; religion as, 223–25; sports as, 226–28. See also corporations
business cycle, New Economy and myths about, 109

business hegemony: cyclical theories of, 219–20; motto of, 223; opportunity for revolt against, 220

Business Week, praise of U.S. economy in, 4, 87

busing: idea behind, 178–79; law on, 180–81; opposition to, 172, 175, 178, 181

Caddell, Patrick H., 47

California: anti-immigrant sentiment in, 128–29; educational system in, decline of, 43–44; Hispanic population in, 120, 121–22; immigrants in, 124; party politics in, 303, 348n.27; prisons in, increased spending on, 44; rush hour traffic in, 216; suburban communities in, 205, 211; tax revolt in, 16, 38, 42–44

Calthorpe, Peter, 210

Cambridge University, and computer development, 75

Camp David agreement of 1978, 253, 255

campaign finance reform: first attempts at, 52–53; McCain-Feingold bill and, 56; opposition to, 56–57, 314n.74; unintended consequences of, 223

campaign financing: inflation in costs of, 52, 54–55; key players in, 223, 336n.54; Supreme Court on, 31, 53, 221–22. *See also* campaign finance reform

Cannery and Agricultural Workers Industrial Union, 122

capital punishment: for African Americans, 42, 192; exercise of, 192; support for, in last quarter of 20th century, 42, 313n.44

capitalism: competition and monopoly in, 347n.20; definition of, xix. *See also* free-market capitalism

Carter, Dan T., 39

Carter, Jimmy: choice as presidential candidate, 13; and Democratic Party's weakness, warning about, 47; "malaise speech" of, 15, 254–55; oil crisis and, 15, 253–55; and opportunities for women, 152; and Panama Canal treaties, 256

Carter, Terry, 225

Castro, Fidel, 123

Cato, Gavin, 194

Celler, Manny, 227

CEOs. *See* corporate chief executives

Chaplin, Charley, 290, 345n.3

Chavez, Cesar, 133

Cheney, Richard, 7, 277–78; and Lay, Kenneth, 55–56; and "Project for the New American Century," 278

Chicago (Illinois): black middle-class flight from, 177–78; police brutality in, 196; public schools in, 243; residential segregation in, 180, 329n.22

children: minority, poverty rate for, 190; working mothers and, 143

Chile, U.S. relations with, 256

Chiles, Lawton, 48, 49

China: donations to Clinton campaign, 56; and Islamic world, posited alliance between, 262–63; U.S. relations with, 276

Chinese Exclusion Act (1882), 115

Christian Brothers Investment Services Inc., 224

Christopher, Warren, 193, 270

Church of Latter Day Saints, assets of, 224

cities: African American population of, 212; black middle-class flight from, 177–78; downtown, problems of, 204, 334n.16; vs. farms, 204; ghettos in, lack of work opportunities in, 188–89; police brutality in, 194–96; and politics, 205; public schools in, 242, 243–44; vs. suburbs, 205; white flight from, 176–77, 211–12. *See also* specific cities

civic engagement, decline in, 229–31, 297

Civil Rights Act (1964), 174

civil rights movement: assumptions during, 174; Cold War and government response to, 259–60; disappointments of, 172; sexism in, 158; ultimate consequence of, 202; and women's movement, 157–58, 198

civilizations, clash of, predictions regarding, 262–63, 280

Clark, Jim, 82–83

class divisions, 300; in culture, 239, 247; educational inequality and, 244–45; in Europe, reduction in, 240; financial inequality and, 239–41; immigration and changes in, 136; in party politics, 29–30, 35, 58, 295–96; suburbs and, 210, 246; in women's movement, 140, 150, 162–66

class status: of information technology pioneers, 78, 247, 339n.105; of politicians, 60; and voting behavior, 36, 247–48; and women's experience in work force, 150. *See also* class divisions

Clinton, Bill: and African American voters, 173, 331n.54; challenges to optimistic outlook of, 8; and Chinese donors, 56; conservative ideas embraced by, 22–23, 24, 346n.12; and Democratic Leadership Council, 22, 48, 49, 50; economic policies under, 22–23, 88; election campaign of 1992, 22; foreign policy under, 270–71, 281; on future generations, hardships facing, 305n.1; and Greenspan (Alan), 22, 317n.6; and Harriman (Pamela), 49; impeachment trial of, 4, 59; and opportunities for women, 152; popularity of, 302; and Rich (Denise), 55; State of the Union Address (2000), 2–4, 5, 88–89, 257, 293; welfare reform under, 3, 89, 189–91
Clinton, Hillary Rodham, 54
Cobb, Tim, 186
Cobble, Dorothy Sue, 164
COBOL, 75
Cochran, Thad, 34
Cochrane, Johnnie, 184
Coffee, Linda, 147
Cold War: fear of losing in 1970s, 256–57; impact on American life, 259–60; and Internet, origins of, 65; and liberal consensus, 9, 260; and protest politics, disappearance of, 295; and South, transformation of, 200. See also Soviet Union
Colombia, U.S. involvement in, 138, 324n.75
Commager, Henry Steele, 112
communications, in late twentieth century, 11
community involvement, decline of, 229–31
Compaq, 7
CompuServe, 83
computer(s): mainframe, development of, 70–71, 75, 80; personal, development of, 66–68, 73, 75
computer languages, development of, 67, 75
Concerned Women for America (CWA), 148–49
Connor, Kenneth L., 149
conservatism: Bush (George W.) administration and, 279; and foreign policy, 278; growing identification with, 2, 30, 37; on law of unintended consequences, 29; Republican Party captured by, 30, 37, 38; South and, 201–2; of Southern Democrats, 33; suburban culture and, 205–6, 334n.14; and women's movement, backlash against, 148–49, 167–68, 170

conservative ascendancy, 30; affirmative action and, 183; anti-communist ideology and, 37; downward trend in, 303; indicators of, 42; and inequality, growth of, xv, 18, 22, 23–24; liberal consensus replaced by, 12, 24–25; media and, 46; racial fears and antipathies and, 39, 46, 346n.6; roots of, 14–16, 30, 38, 289, 291
conservative Christian schools, 242
consumer goods, availability of, 297
consumer price index (CPI), overestimation of price inflation by, 102–3
contraception, availability of, 145–46; and sexual revolution of 1970s, 146, 325n.12
corporate chief executives (CEOs): as caste, 221; remuneration for, increase in, 90–91, 300; women, 150–51
corporations: decline in profitability of, in 1950s to 1980s, 220; democracy equated with, 2; donations to Republican Party, 53; employees of, decline in living standards of, 20–21; and farming, 207–9; vs. government, mistrust in, 24; and information technology, development of, 65–66, 70, 73–74; and international relations, 271; and Internet, control of, 85, 86, 237; management techniques of, euphemisms for, 220–21; media, 234–35, 238–39; meltdowns in early twenty-first century, 7; and politics, increased influence on, 30, 221–23, 298; power shift from employees to top managers, 221; recruitment by, class inequality in, 247; social hegemony of, 299; tax revolt and, 43; vulnerability of, 298
Corzine, Jon, 54, 300, 347n.23
Cosby, Bill, 183, 330n.36
Cose, Ellis, 185, 198
Costas, Bob, 227, 228
country music, 201
CPI. See consumer price index
Credit Mobilier, 8, 307n.27
Credit Suisse First Boston, 5
crime, decline in, 3, 191–92, 195, 297
Cronkite, Walter, 238
Crouch, Jan and Paul, 223
Cuban immigrants, 123; party affiliation of, 133
Cudahy, J., 166
culture, U.S.: class divisions in, 239, 247; ethnic, strength of, 136; media and, 237; "southernization" of, 201; world-wide acceptance at beginning of new millennium, 4

CWA. *See* Concerned Women for America

Cyclades, 317n.36

DARPA. *See* Defense Advanced Research Projects Agency

Davis, Donald, 80

Davis, Gray, 128, 348n.27

de Lay, Tom, 173

death penalty. *See* capital punishment

debt: farm, 207; government (*See* deficit); personal, growth of, 23, 91–92, 297–98

Defense Advanced Research Projects Agency (DARPA), 79–80, 81, 259, 316n.35

defense spending, xvi, 253, 281

deficit: Clinton's decision to reduce, 88, 317n.6; foreign capital needed to cover, 344n.64; Reagan administration and, 41, 299, 347n.21

Dell, Michael, 72

democracy: concept of, evolution of, 293; free-market capitalism equated with, xix, 2, 19, 24, 62, 305n.8; after Soviet collapse, 252

Democratic Leadership Council (DLC), 48–49; Clinton and, 22, 48, 49, 50; goals of, 49; new strategy of, 50

Democratic Party: conservative ideas adopted by, 30, 50; discredited in 1960s, 13; dominance until 1960s, 36; donors to, 53; and Equal Rights Amendment, 145; erosion of traditional support base, 13–14, 30, 46; future prospects for, 303; historical characteristics of, 34–35; immigrants' descendants and, 125; social class represented by, 35, 58, 296; in South, 32–33; views on immigrants, 35; Voting Rights Act of 1965 and changes in, 31, 34; weakness of, warnings about, 47–48

Department of Defense, and Internet development, 79–80, 81, 259, 316n.35

deregulation: media, 233; Reagan era and, 17; and stock market, 18–19

Detroit (Michigan): busing in, resistance to, 181; decline of, 177; race riot of 1967 in, 175; residential segregation in, 329n.22; white flight from, 177, 212

developing countries: globalization and, 272; manufacturing jobs moved to, 20–21; U.S. attitudes toward, 272–73

The Dialectic of Sex (Firestone), 160

Diallo, Amadou, 196

Dillingham Commission, 115

Dixie Rising (Applebome), 200–2

DLC. *See* Democratic Leadership Council

Doerr, John, 83

Dominican Republic, immigrants from, 118

Donnelly, Kitty, 165

downsizing, 221

Dreiser, Theodore, 225

Drew, Elizabeth, 51

Duany, Andres, 210, 217

Dukakis, Michael, 40, 49

e-commerce, disappointments related to, 65, 105

e-mail, development of, 71

Eagle Forum/STOP ERA, 144

Earned Income Tax Credit (EITC), 191

Eastern Europe, collapse of communism in, 266

Ebbers, Bernie, 7

economy, U.S., 87–111; boom of late 1990s, inequalities left by, 90–92; Clinton administration policies, 22–23, 88; Clinton's evaluation of, 3; declines in early twenty-first century, 6–7; digital revolution and, 88, 94–96; discontent with, and conservative ascendancy, 16; future of, 304; gloomy prognostications since 1970s, 92–93; glorification at end of twentieth century, 3, 4–5, 87–89, 104, 106–7, 301; illusions about, 26, 95–96, 109; factors responsible for, 98–99, 106–7; and immigration issue, 130; information technology and, 88, 94–96, 109–10; international comparisons of performance of, 93–94, 97–98; loss of competitiveness, 13–14; "new": claims regarding, 87, 88, 100, 104–5; concept of, 106, 108; oil crisis of 1970s and, 13; performance measures for, 99; and presidential election of 2000, 87–88, 89; Reagan administration policies, 40–41; realistic assessment of, xv, 89–94, 100

Edmonston, Barry, 117

education, U.S., 11; bilingual, attack on, 129; in California, decline in, 43–44; college, unequal opportunities for, 244–45; inequality in, 240–41, 242–43, 294; international comparisons of, 244; private, cost of, 241; public, demise of, 241, 242, 243–44. *See also* educational segregation

Educational Amendments Act, Title IX of, 153

educational segregation: attempts to combat, 178–79; legal decisions against, 180–81; residential segregation and, 179

Egerton, John, 200

Eisenhower, Dwight D.: and Defense Advanced Research Projects Agency (DARPA), 79; and southern vote, 33

EITC. See Earned Income Tax Credit

Eizenstat, Stuart, 254

electoral college, Democratic worries about, 47–48

electoral politics: African Americans and, 33, 173; class status and, 36, 247–48; Hispanics and, 122, 130, 133–34, 303; immigrants and, 122, 124–25, 133–34; low participation in, 297; television and, 222–23; women and, 170, 303, 325n.9. See also presidential election(s)

Ellison, Larry, 68, 69

emerging markets, 271

energy crises, 13, 253–55

Englebart, Doug, 66

Enron: Bush administration and, 7; scandal involving, 7, 222

Ephron, Nora, 156

Episcopal Church, investments of, 224

Equal Employment Opportunity Commission, suit against Sears Roebuck, 165

Equal Pay Act (1963), 150, 326n.27

Equal Rights Amendment (ERA), 143–45, 167

equality: ambiguities in concept of, 288, 289; American aspirations towards, exceptions to, 239, 288; as historical characteristic of U.S., xx, 288, 289–90; of opportunity, vs. equality of condition, 290–91; trend toward, Republican efforts to reverse, 23–24. See also inequality

ERA. See Equal Rights Amendment

Estaing, Valéry Giscard, 317n.36

ethical investment movement, 218

Ethiopia, Soviet policies in, 256

eugenics, 116

Europe: average income in, compared with U.S. income, 93, 319n.37; class divisions in, reduction in, 240; exports to U.S., 13; GNP of, 345n.71; immigration from, decline in, 118, 321n.23; and Israel, support for, 342n.41; productivity in, compared with U.S. productivity, 93–94; racism in, 199; U.S. interests in, new immigration and decrease in, 138; wealth inequality in, compared with U.S.,

23, 294, 309n.63, 347n.13. See also specific countries

Evans, Sara, 158

exceptionalism, American, 282–85; skepticism about, xvii

executives. See corporate chief executives (CEOs)

Fairchild, 74

Fall, Albert B., 306n.26

family: division of labor in, changes in, 142–43; immigration and changes in, 137

Family Research Council, 149, 326n.25

farms and farming: in American history, 289; corporations and, 207–9; decline of, 205, 206–7; federal subsidies to, 207, 208–9, 335n.17; inequality in, 209

Farrakhan, Louis, 178

Federal Election Campaign Act (1971), 52

Federal Election Commission, 52

Federal Housing Administration (FHA), redlining policies of, 179

The Feminine Mystique (Friedan), 143

feminist movement, 140–41; backlash against, 148–49, 154, 167–68, 170; divisions within, 159; failures of, 161–62; isolation of, 161; radical strategies of, 159–60; successes of, 162

Ferguson, Niall, 286

Ferguson, Roger W., Jr., 94–95, 105

Ferraro, Geraldine, 48

FHA. See Federal Housing Administration

fiber optic cables, 81

Fidonet, 81

Filo, David, 84

financial crises, international, 273–74

firefighters, female, 163

Firestone, Shulamith, 160

Fisher, Max, 177

Flaubert, Gustave, 268

Flint (Michigan), 177

Florida, immigrants in, 124

Focus on the Family, 149

Forbes, Malcolm "Steve," 54, 55, 278, 348n.23

Ford, Gerald, 13

Ford, Henry, 177, 216

foreign aid, U.S., public attitudes toward, 273, 282, 344n.66

foreign relations. See international relations

FORTRAN, 75

Fortune (magazine), praise of U.S. economy in, 4

Fowler, Mark, 233

Fraga, Luis, 322n.37

France: computer network created in, 317n.36; government control of Internet in, 86; and Israel, support for, 342n.41; productivity in, 98, 345n.71; racism in, 199

Frank, Tom, 19, 306n.9

free-market capitalism: ascendancy of theories supporting, 17, 41; assumptions about, 25; cultural shift to, 18–19; deification of, 293; democracy equated with, xix, 2, 19, 24, 62, 305n.8; Democrats' new faith in, 50; fear to criticize, 98; foreign countries' disillusionment with, 274; government functions replaced by, 293, 298; and inequality, increase in, 24; and information technology, claims regarding, 65, 77–78, 83, 85, 86, 108; and international relations, 270; in political decision making, 56; after Soviet collapse, 252; unregulated, built-in tendency to excess in, 298

freedom: American ideal of, different interpretations of, 292–93; Internet's promise of, 85–86; in U.S. society, 10

Freedom Summer, 158

Freedom to Farm Act (1996), 208–9

Friedan, Betty, 142, 148; *The Feminine Mystique*, 143; on strategic mistake of women's movement, 155; and Women's Strike for Equality, 160

Friedman, Milton, 16, 308n.44

From, Al, 22, 48, 49

frontier experience: and American society, xviii–xix; and expansionism in foreign policy, 251

Fukuyama, Francis, 261, 278

fundraising: growing dependence on, and political changes, 30; key players in, 223, 336n.54; professionalization of, 57. *See also* campaign financing

Galbraith, John Kenneth, 299

Galston, William, 49–50

Garrity, Arthur, 178

Garvin, Clifton, 254

Gates, Bill: and BASIC software, 76; Funk & Wagnall's Dictionary on, 317n.48; and IBM, 73; and information technology, develop-

ment of, 64, 68, 72; and Internet, attempts to appropriate, 83–84; and marketing, 77; myths about, 78; original achievement of, 69; word-processing program introduced by, 76–77

Gates, Daryl, 194

Gebhardt, Dick, 48

Geddes, Norman Bel, 217

Gentleman's Agreement (1997), 115

Germany: government control of Internet in, 86; immigration from, decline in, 118, 321n.23; and Israel, support for, 342n.41; productivity in, 98

Gilliam, Stephanie, 172, 198

Gingrich, Newt, 23, 59, 270; and "English for the Children" campaign, 129; loss of popularity, 302; smear tactics used by, 347n.19; and southern populist tradition, 173

Giuliani, Rudolf, 195, 244

Glazer, Nathan, 183

globalization, 271; disillusionment with, 274; and financial crises of 1990s, 273–74; and international relations, 271, 272; and political power, shift in, 21–22; public opinion about, 275; and stock market, 18–19; and wages in U.S., decline in, 21

Golden, Sandra Behr, 185

Goldman, Ronald, 196

Goldman Sachs, 5

Goldwater, Barry, 33, 37, 54

Gonzalez, Antonio, 129

Goodman, Ellen, 156

Goodman, Herbert, 255

Gorbachev, Mikhail, 40, 41, 258–59, 261–62, 266

Gore, Al, Jr.: defeat in 2000 presidential election, 5–6; in Democratic Leadership Council, 48; on economy, 88; in election campaign of 1988, 332n.64; in election campaign of 2000, 55, 58, 88, 301–2, 328n.3

Gosling, James, 67

government, U.S.: as business, 11–12; control of Internet by, 86; vs. corporations, 24; Democrats' new hostility to, 50; disillusion with, in 1970s and 1980s, 38–39; elaborate nature of, 11; free-market capitalism replacing, 293, 298; and information technology, development of, 25, 65–66, 70, 79–81; and law of unintended consequences, 29; need for, xv; skepticism about, xv, xviii, 2, 11, 45; under-

government (*cont.*)
    mined by conservative policies, 17, 299, 301;
    and women, opportunities for, 152
government subsidies: to farmers, 207, 208–9,
    335n.17; and suburb development, 217
Graham, Katharine, 233
Grant, Madison, 116
Gray, Bill, 48
Great Depression: anti-immigrant sentiment
    during, 116, 320n.15; and liberal consensus,
    9; and party politics, 36; Republican Party
    after, 36
Great Society programs, conservative ascen-
    dancy as reaction to, 30, 289, 291, 301
Greenberg, Stanley, 170
Greenspan, Alan: and Clinton's policies, 22,
    317n.6; on new economy, 88, 94
Greider, William, 47
Griffiths, Martha, 157
Griswold v. Connecticut, 148
Guizot, François, 305n.4
Gulf War, 263, 264–65; unresolved issues after,
    265

Hacker, Andrew, 197
Halliburton, 7
Hance, Kent, 347n.15
Hanisch, Carol, 159
Harken Energy, 7
Harriman, Averell, 49
Harriman, Pamela, 49
Harris, Joseph, 224
Harrison, Bennett, 21
Hart, Gary, 48
Hart-Celler Immigration and Nationality Act
    (1965), 113
hate crimes, 131–32, 297
Hawkins, Yusuf, 194
Hayden, Casey, 139, 157, 158
Hayek, Frederick von, 312n.39
Hayes, Rutherford B., 302
health care, inequality in access to, 92, 245–46,
    294
Helms, Jesse, 149, 233
HERE. *See* Hotel Employees and Restaurant
    Employees union
Heritage Foundation, 222
Hewlett, Bill, 71
Hewlett Packard Company, 71
Hicks, Louise Day, 178

Hicks, Tom, 8
highways, 11, 307n.31; Cold War competition
    and construction of, 259; government subsi-
    dies for, 217; negative impact of, 217; and
    suburbs, 211, 214–15
Hinckley, John W., 40
Hirshon, Robert E., 226
Hispanics, 120–23, 127–33; African Americans
    compared with, 132; ambiguity of term, 117,
    122; in California, 120, 121–22; children,
    poverty rates for, 190; deportations of, 121,
    131; discrimination against, 127–28; diverse
    subcultures of, 122–23, 322n.45; divisions
    among, 132, 133–34; educational segregation
    of, 179; and electoral politics, 122, 130, 133–
    34, 303; illegal border crossings by, 130–31;
    party affiliation of, 133; political radicalism
    of, 127; population growth, 113, 117–18; racial
    distinctions among, 135; religious beliefs
    among, 137, 323n.67; in suburbs, 213; in
    Texas, 120–21. *See also* Mexican immigrants
Hobbes, Thomas, 45, 188
Hoff, Marcian E. "Ted," 75
Hoffman, Eva, 125
Hofstadter, Richard, 203
Holland, racism in, 199
Hollywood, support for Democratic Party, 53
Holtzman, Elizabeth, 145
homosexuals, equality for, rejection of, 289
Hoover, J. Edgar, 320n.15
Horton, Willie, 193, 332n.64
Hotel Employees and Restaurant Employees
    (HERE) union, 164
Houston (Texas), residential segregation in,
    329n.22
Howard, Sir Michael, 281
Hower, Irving, 125
Hughes, Langston, xviii, 172
Huntington, Samuel P., 262–64, 276
Hussein, Saddam: Gulf War and, 265; neocon-
    servatives' desire to overthrow, 279; removal
    of, instability threats associated with, 266–67
Hutchins, Robert D., 228

Iacocca, Lee, 45
IBM: competition with Apple Computer, 77;
    and Microsoft, 73, 76, 78–79; personal com-
    puter developed by, 73, 78; women execu-
    tives at, 150
Illinois, immigrants in, 124

IMF. *See* International Monetary Fund

immigration and immigrants, 112–38; American exceptionalism and, 283; assimilation of, 133, 135–36; in colonial era, 113–14, 320n.6; composition in last quarter of twentieth century, 117; composition in late nineteenth-early twentieth centuries, 114; Democratic Party on, 35; diversity of, 118–23; economic status of, 127; and electoral politics, 122, 124–25, 133–34; equality for, rejection of, 289; and essence of America, xviii, 284; exclusions in late nineteenth-early twentieth centuries, 115–16; First Great Migration, 114–16; and future of U.S., 112–13; geographical concentration of, 119, 123–24; hardships experienced by, 125–26; after independence, 114; and international relations, 137–38, 251; political radicalism of, 127; and protest politics, disappearance of, 295; quotas for, 116; race and, 115–16, 135; reasons for, 133; Republican Party on, 35, 36; return to native countries, xviii, 116, 321n.17, 321n.18; Second Great Migration, 113, 117; and social changes, 135–36; in suburbs, 213, 214; violence against, 131–32. *See also* anti-immigrant sentiment; specific immigrant groups

Immigration Act (1917), 115

imperial power, U.S. as, 285–86

income: of African Americans, recent gains in, 89; decline in last quarter of 20th century, 93, 291; inequality of, 90–91, 96–97, 100, 101–2; international comparisons of, 93, 99, 240, 319n.37, 347n.13; of poorest Americans, recent improvement in, 101, 102; segregation by, in suburbs, 213

Indian Americans, social status of, 119

individualism, in U.S. society, 10; media and, 300

inequality: among African Americans, 27, 183–84, 186–87; conservative ascendancy and, xv, 18, 22, 23–24; economic, tolerance for, 289, 290; economic vs. social, 289; in education, 240–41, 242–43, 294; in farming, 209; financial, and class divisions, 239–41; free-market policies and, 24; growth of, xv–xvi, 23, 100, 203, 239, 288, 291, 293; in health care access, 92, 245–46, 294; information technology and, 110; international comparisons of, 94, 240, 294, 309n.63, 347n.13; in mail use, 245; race-based, 174–75; sex-based,

166–67 (*See also* sex-based discrimination); social impact of, 293–95; stock market boom of late 1990s and, 90–92; of tax burden, 100–1; of wages/income, 90–91, 96–97, 100, 101–2, 240; of wealth, 23, 91–92, 294, 309n.63, 347n.13. *See also* segregation

information technology, 61–86; and business cycle, 109; effect on economy, realistic view of, 109–10; and labor demand, shift in, 110; and "new" economy, 88, 94–96; pioneers of, class status of, 78, 247, 339n.105; printing compared with, 104; and productivity, increase in, 95–96, 105–6; as recession-proof, myth about, 103. *See also* information technology, development of; Internet

information technology, development of, 66–85; Cold War competition and, 259; corporations' role in, 65–66, 70, 73–74; entrepreneurs' role in, 68, 69, 72–73, 79; free-market capitalism and, myth about, 65, 77–78, 83, 85, 86, 108; government's role in, 25, 65–66, 70, 79–81; misunderstanding and illusions about, 61–65; universities' role in, 65–66, 70–72, 78, 81–82

innovations: and Internet development, 74–77, 79–81; and productivity gains, 104, 105

integrated broadband networks (IBNs), 81

Intel: founder of, 72; inventions at, 75; losses in early twenty-first century, 7

international financial institutions, "reform" policies of, 271–72

International Monetary Fund (IMF), 271

international relations, 3, 249–87; American exceptionalism and, 282–84; under Bush (George H. W.), 41, 264–65; under Bush (George W.), 273, 276–80, 286–87; under Clinton, 270–71, 281; conflict between expansionism and isolationism, 251; conservatism and, 278; contradictions between missionary and business incentives, 285–86; corporations and, 271; financial crises of 1990s and, 273–74; free-market capitalism and, 270; frontier experience and, 251; globalization and, 271, 272; history of, 249–50; idealism and generosity of American public, 282; immigration and, 137–38, 251; interventionist policies, 250; isolationism, 249, 250; in last quarter of 20th century, xvi, 249, 253; media reporting on, 253, 257; myth of self-sufficiency, 281; oil crises and, 254–55; par-

international relations (*cont.*)

adoxes in, 275, 282; post–Cold War threats, 262–64; professionalization of, 260; public opinion about, 275; under Reagan, 40; after September 11, 2001, 286–87; Soviet collapse and, 259, 260–61, 274, 278; tensions with Islamic world, 264–70; terrorism and, 252–53; triumphalism at end of twentieth century, 108, 252, 257–58; weakened U.S. position in 1970s, 251–52, 255–56

Internet: Cold War competition and creation of, 259; commercial use of, 65, 81–83, 105; corporate control of, 85, 86, 237; disappointments related to, 105; economic impact of, realistic view of, 109–10; egalitarian dreams about, 82, 85; entrepreneurs' role in development of, 68, 69, 72–73, 79; free-market capitalism and, 77–78, 83, 85, 86; freedom and empowerment promised by, 85–86, 236; government control of, 86; government's role in development of, 25, 65–66, 70, 79–81; illusions about history of, 61–65; inventions preparing ground for, 74–77, 79–81; and media, 235–36; Microsoft's attempts to appropriate, 83–84; military ancestor of, 72; origins of, 65, 66–69; pioneers of, class status of, 78, 247, 339n.105; and productivity growth, questions about, 106; social impact of, 62; software for, development of, 82, 83; stages in development of, 68; and stock market boom, 61, 62; and technological revolution, 61; universities' role in development of, 65–66, 70–72, 78, 81–82

investments: church, 224. *See also* stock market

Iran, Islamic revolution in, 253, 269

Iran-Contra affair, 40

Iraq: as artificial state, 266; and instability threat, 266–67; invasion of Kuwait, 264; war in, 279–80, 286, 287

Ireland, immigration from, decline in, 321n.23

Islam, 267; militant versions of, 268, 342n.40

Islamic world: anticolonial politics of, 267, 342n.39; and China, posited alliance between, 262–63; extremist and terrorist groups forming in, 270; U.S. alliances in, 268–69; U.S. support for Israel and, 269; U.S. tensions with, 264–70, 279–80

isolationism, U.S., 249, 250; immigration and, 251

Israel: European support for, 342n.41; U.S. support for, 269, 279

Jackson, Jesse, 48, 184

Jackson, Thomas Penfold, 84

James, William, 254

Japan, exports to U.S., 13

Japanese Americans, anti-immigrant sentiment and, 115

Jarvis, Howard, 44

Jefferson, Thomas, 1, 9, 304

Jeffords, James, 311n.19

Jencks, Christopher, 190

Jews, immigration to U.S., 125

Jobs, Steve, 72, 73, 76

Johnson, Albert, 320n.16

Johnson, Andrew, 4, 37

Johnson, Haynes, 258

Johnson, Lyndon: campaign spending by, 54; and civil rights legislation, 31, 33, 157, 310n.4; and immigration legislation, 113; and Kerner Commission report, 176; on racial justice, 174, 181

Johnson Controls, 169

Johnson-Reed Act (1924), 116

Jordan, Barbara, 34

Jordan, Michael, 183

Jordan, Vernon, 184

journalism. *See* media

Kagan, Robert, 278

Kahlenberg, Richard D., 243, 244

Kamarck, Elaine Giulla, 49–50

Kay, Alan, 66

Keaton, Buster, 290, 345n.3

Keith, Toby, 201

Kemeny, John, 75

Kennedy, Edward, 178, 346n.12

Kennedy, John F., 54, 101, 259

Kerner Commission, 175–76

Kerr, Clark, 245

Key, V. O., Jr., 29

Keynes, John Maynard, 16

Khomeini, Ayatollah, 253

Kilby, Jack, 74

Kildall, Gary, 78, 79

Kiley, Charles, 72

King, Desmond, 135

King, Jeanne, 164

King, Martin Luther, Jr., 31, 175; campaign for "open housing" in Chicago, 180; murder of, riots after, 176

King, Mary, 139, 157, 158

King, Rodney, 193
Kinnings, Guy, 227
Kirk, Russell, 205
Kissinger, Henry, 257–58, 275–76, 282
Kleiner, Perkins, Caulfield & Byers (KPCB), 72
Korea, exports to U.S., 13
Korean Americans, communities of, 119
KPCB. *See* Kleiner, Perkins, Caulfield & Byers
Kristol, Irving, 247, 278
Kristol, William, 278, 285
Krugman, Paul, 87, 100, 257, 317n.2, 318n.14
Kryuchkov, Vladimir, 258
Kurds, 264
Kurtz, Thomas, 75
Kuttner, Robert, 17
Kuwait, Iraqi invasion of, 264

La Raza, 131, 132, 133
labor demand, information technology and, 110
labor force, women in: class status and experience of, 150, 162; disappointing progress for, 150–54; information revolution and, 110; male hostility to, 163, 168–69; marital status and, 166; movement into, 140, 141–42, 166; prevailing occupations of, 162; wage inequality experienced by, 150, 151
labor unions: campaign donations in 2000 election, 53; concessionary agreements negotiated by, 45; decline in membership, 20, 21, 44–45; and wage declines, 100; litigation as alternative to, 164–65; for Mexican immigrants, 133; and women's issues, support for, 163–64, 169
LaHaye, Beverly, 148–49
LaHaye, Tim, 148, 149, 325n.23
Lake, Tony, 270
Lam, Richard, 345n.72
Landon, Alf, 37
Langdon, Philip, 209, 218
Latin America: migration from, 118, 119–23; U.S. interests in, 138
Latinos. *See* Hispanics
lawyers. *See* legal profession
Lay, Kenneth, 7; and Cheney (Richard), 55–56
Lazowska, Edward D., 61, 66
League of United Latin American Citizens (LULAC), 132–33
Leavitt, Mike, 215

legal profession: as business, 225–26; presidential election of 2000 and, 302; role in information technology development, 71–72; role in politics, 57; women in, 151, 152
Lehmann Brothers, 5
Lemann, Nicholas, 177
Levy, Jeff, 186
Lewis, Charles, 52
liberal consensus, 9, 36–37, 290–91; Cold War and, 9, 260; conservative ascendancy replacing, 12, 24–25; economic orthodoxy of, 16
liberalism: conservative claims regarding, 298; conversion to conservative ideas, 22; decline after Reagan years, 42; erosion of support for, 1–2; as outdated ideology, claims regarding, 49–50, 305n.7. *See also* liberal consensus
Lichtenstein, Nelson, 20, 165
Licklider, J.C.R., 66, 80
Lincoln, Abraham, 31, 309n.3
Lindsay, John, 36, 175, 176
Lipset, Seymour Martin, 99, 319n.37
Liuzzo, Viola, 310n.5
Livingston, Bob, 348n.26
lobbying, 54, 57, 295; by business groups, 222
Long, Gillis, 48
Long Term Capital Management: collapse of, 19, 274; Nobel Prize economists and, 319n.36
Los Angeles (California): Rodney King riots in, 193, 194; suburban communities in, 211
Lost in Translation (Hoffman), 125
Lott, Trent, 34, 173
Louima, Abner, 196
Louisiana, rice farmers in, government subsidies to, 209
LULAC. *See* League of United Latin American Citizens
Luther, Martin, 282

Macintosh computer: development of, 76; vs. IBM's personal computer, 77
Mahbubani, Kishore, 263
mail, class divisions in use of, 245
mainframe computer(s): development of, 70–71, 75; network of, 80
Malcolm X, 178
Manchester University, and computer development, 75
manufacturing jobs, move to developing countries, 20–21

Marchi, John, 176

market exchange rates, as measure of economic performance, 99, 319n.37

market populism, 2, 19, 298, 306n.9

marketing: and class divisions, 246; information technology and, 77; sports and, 227. *See also* advertising

Marshall, Thurgood, 183–84

Massachusetts Institute of Technology (MIT), and information technology development, 70, 71

Massoud, Farouq, 126

Mathias, Charles "Mac," 36

McCabe, Irene, 181

McCain, John, 55, 302

McCain-Feingold bill, 56

McCleskey v. Kemp, 313n.44

McConnell, Mitchell, 55

McCorvey, Norma, 147, 168

McGovern, George, 54, 330n.32

McPherson, Harry C., Jr., 310n.4

media: as business, 228–29, 233; and choice, absence of, 237; conglomerates of, 234–35; and conservative ascendancy, 46; consolidation of ownership, 98, 238; corporate power and, 238–39; criticism discouraged by, 295; cultural diet offered by, 237, 300; deregulation of, 233; erosion of traditional news standards, 238, 303; focus on entertaining vs. informing, 229; foreign relations reporting by, 253, 257; government regulation of, 232, 338n.81; Internet and, 235–36; networks of, 232; news: golden age of, 237–38; vital public function of, 229; news and entertainment, merging of, 233–34; political coverage by, 60; presidential election of 2000 and, 302; and stock market, 233, 238; women in, frustrations of, 156; and women's movement, 160, 168

medicine, women in, 151–52, 153

Memphis (Tennessee), residential segregation in, 329n.22

Mengistu Haile Mariam, 256

Merrill Lynch, misleading statements of, 4–5

Merton, Robert, 19, 319n.36

Mexican immigrants, 119–21; *bracero* program for, 122; in California, 121–22; deportations of, 116, 121, 131, 320n.15; diversity of, 122–23; and electoral politics, 122, 130; illegal border crossings by, 130–31; in Texas, 120–21

Mexico: financial crisis in (1994), 273; *maquiladora* plants in, 20

microprocessor, invention of, 75

Microsoft: antitrust suit against, 71–72, 83, 84, 317n.47; formation of, 72, 76; Funk & Wagnall's Dictionary acquired by, 317n.48; growth of, 73; IBM and, 73, 76, 78–79; and Internet, 83–84; losses in early twenty-first century, 7; motto of, 62; MS/DOS of, 78–79; vs. Netscape, 83–84; word-processing program introduced by, 76–77

middle class: debt of, increase in, 91–92; wages for, smallest gains in, 90; wealth of, reduction in, 91

Middle East: Bush administration policies in, 303; Gulf War in, 263, 264–65; Iraq war in, 279–80; U.S. interests in, 138; U.S. support for Israel and, 269, 279

migration: of African Americans, 200, 333n.90. *See also* immigration

military power, U.S., 251, 253; in early twentieth century, 340n.5; in late twentieth century, 3; spending on, xvi, 253, 281

Miller, J. Irwin, 45

Millett, Kate, 161

Milliken v. Bradley, 181

Milner, Clyde, 120

Miss America ceremony, protest against, 159–60

missile defense, 285

MITS, 76

mobility: frontier experience and, xviii–xix; social, 244. *See also* migration

Molina, Gloria, 134

Mondale, Walter, 49

money: and politics, 30–31, 50–57, 60, 296, 301; and religion, 223–25; and suburbs, 218

Moore, Gordon, Jr., 72, 74

Moral Majority, 149

moral superiority, American, claim regarding, 284

Morgan, J. P., 302

Morgan, Robin, 159–60, 161

Morgan v. Hennigan, 178

Morison, Samuel Eliot, 112

Morris, Dick, 200, 309n.62

Mosaic software, 82, 83

Moynihan, Daniel Patrick: on American government, xvii–xviii; on counterculture, 306n.11; on Reagan's deficit strategy, 347n.21; on welfare reform, 190

Muller v. Oregon, 169
Murdoch, Rupert, 228, 234
Murray, Charles, 188, 331n.48

Napoleon Bonaparte, 290
Nascar, 201
National Economic Council, 22
National Journal, 222
National Organization for Women (NOW),
 143; and abortion rights, 146; and Equal
 Rights Amendment, 143
National Physical Laboratory (NPL), and
 packet switching, 80–81
National Science Foundation (NSF), and In-
 ternet, 81
Native Americans, population growth, 113
Negroponte, Nicholas, 4, 71, 306n.15
Nelson, Lemrick, Jr., 194
Netherlands, productivity in, 98
Netscape: vs. Microsoft, 83–84; origins of, 83
New Deal, 290–91; and party politics, 36; Re-
 publican acceptance of, 37; turn away from,
 39
New Jersey, immigrants in, 124
New Left: weaknesses of, 159; and women's
 movement, 156, 159
New York City: black population of, 212; police
 brutality in, 194–96; public schools in,
 243–44; racial conflicts in, 175, 176, 194;
 women firefighters in, 163
New York State, immigrants in, 124
News Corporation, 234
newspapers: class divisions and, 247; decline
 of, 234
Newsweek (magazine), sex discrimination suit
 against, 156
Nixon, Richard: campaign spending by, 54;
 and devaluation of dollar, 14; and Hispanic
 vote, 122; secretary of labor of, 20; and southern vote, 33; victory in 1968 presidential
 election, 13, 37
Norquist, John O., 214
Nortel, 79
North: African Americans in, barriers to de
 facto equality of, 174–75; black migration to,
 200, 333n.90; residential segregation in, 179,
 329n.22; and South: historical relations between, 199–200; shared assumptions of, 202
Noyce, Bob, 74
NPL. *See* National Physical Laboratory

Nunn, Sam, 49
Nye, Joseph, 282

oil crises, 13, 253–55
Oliner, Steve, 95
Oliver, J. Eric, 210
Olsen, Laurie, 128
Organization of Petroleum Exporting Coun-
 tries, 13
Orwell, George, xix
Osterman, Jack, 79
outsourcing, 220–21

Packard, David, 71
packet switching, 80–81
Palmer, A. Mitchell, 320n.15
Panama Canal treaties, renegotiation of, 38,
 256
Panetta, Leon E., 22
patriotism, American, xvii–xviii; and protest
 politics, disappearance of, 295; after Septem-
 ber 11, 2001, 276, 292
Paul, Alice, 143
pension plans, scarcity of, 92
Perle, Richard, 278
personal computer: development of, 66–67,
 68, 73; idea for, 67–68; motivation for devel-
 oping, 75
Personal Responsibility and Work Opportunity
 Reconciliation Act of 1996 (PRWORA), 189
Pfaelzer, Mariana R., 128
Philbrick, Edward, 286
Philippe, Louis, 305n.4
Phillips, Kevin, 46
PIPA. *See* Program on International Public
 Attitudes
Planned Parenthood v. Casey, 167
Plater-Zyberk, Elizabeth, 210, 217
Podesta, John: on campaign finance reform,
 223; on new economy, 317n.1
Podhoretz, Norman, 278
police brutality, 193, 194–96
political system, U.S., foundation of, xix
politicians: class status of, 60; complicity in
 business of politics, 59; declining quality of,
 51; indifference to majority's concerns, 296
politics, U.S., 29–60; as business, 57–58;
 changes in last quarter of twentieth century,
 29–31; cities vs. suburbs and, 205; class divisions and, 29–30, 35, 58, 295–96; conserva-

politics (*cont.*)
  tive shift in, 30, 31, 41–50; corporations and, 30, 221–23, 298; cultural and economic stratification and, 247–48; cultural factors and, 35–36; economic issues and, 35–36; globalization and shift in, 21–22; ideological rift between political parties, 58–59; immigration and changes in, 136; and interpretation of equality, 289; media coverage of, 60; monetization of, 30–31, 50–57, 60, 296, 301; paradox at end of twentieth century, 58–59, 295–96; professionalization of, 223; public indifference toward, 297; "southernization" of, 173, 200–1; suburbs and, 205–6, 215–16, 294–95; Sunbelt and future of, 46–47; two meanings of, 57; urban, black monopoly over, 212; volatility of, 59, 296–97, 302; Voting Rights Act of 1965 and changes in, 29, 31, 33–34; women in, 162. *See also* electoral politics

poor people: conservative anger against, 296; invisibility of, 98. *See also* poverty

population: aging of, 8; ethnic composition of, projected, 117; growth of minority groups, 113

populism: at end of twentieth century, xviii; market, 2, 19, 298, 306n.9

Potter, David M., 305n.2

poverty: among African American and Hispanic children, 190; among immigrants, 127; rate of, international comparison of, 94; reduction in, late twentieth century, 89; rural, 101. *See also* poor people

Powell, Colin, 27, 184, 278

Powell, Lewis, 182

PPP. *See* purchasing power parity

presidential election(s): of 1964, 37; of 1980, 145, 183; of 1988, 40, 49, 193, 332n.64; of 1992, 22; of 2000 (*See* presidential election of 2000); immigrant groups and, 124–25

presidential election of 2000, 59; campaign spending in, 54–55; economic issues in, 87–88, 89; Hispanic vote in, 134; media discourse during, 5; pretense in, 301–2; validity of results, 6; women's vote in, 170; working-class vote in, 328n.3

prison(s): African Americans in, 187, 192, 330n.44; chain gangs, reintroduction of, 195; growth of, 191–92; spending on, increase in, 44

Procaccino, Mario, 176

productivity: comparisons across different time periods, 103–4; decline in first quarter of 2001, 103; growth in late twentieth century, 89–90; information technology and increase in, 95–96, 105–6; international comparisons of, 93–94, 98–99

professions: as businesses, 225–26; and party politics, 303. *See also* specific professions

Program on International Public Attitudes (PIPA), 282, 344n.66

Progressive Policy Institute, strategy paper by, 49–50

"Project for the New American Century," 278

protest politics, disappearance of, 295

PRWORA. *See* Personal Responsibility and Work Opportunity Reconciliation Act of 1996

Puerto Rico, immigrants from, 118, 123

purchasing power parity (PPP), as measure of economic performance, 99, 319n.37

Putnam, Robert, 205, 229–31

race, attitudes to. *See also* racism: expected changes in, 136; and immigration exclusions, 115–16, 135; interracial relationships and, 158

racial chasm: at end of twentieth century, 198–99; O. J. Simpson trial demonstrating, 196–97, 333n.84

racial conflict: in 1960s, 175–76; in 1990s, 193–94

racial segregation, 173; in education, attempts to combat, 178–79, 180–81; in housing, 176–77, 179–80

racism: and conservative ascendancy, 39, 46, 346n.6; examples of, 185–86; Kerner Commission on, 175–76; against Mexicans in California, 121–22; persistence of, 184–85; southern conservatism and, 202; worldwide manifestations of, 199

Radio Shack, computer developed by, 76

Rand, Ayn, 22, 205

Reagan, Ronald: Congress dominated by, 40; deficit strategy of, 41, 299, 347n.21; and deregulation, 17; economic policy under, 40–41; and Equal Rights Amendment, opposition to, 145; foreign policy under, 40; and media deregulation, 233; and opportunities for women, 152; popularity of, 40, 312n.41; presidential campaign of, 15, 188, 330n.47; and turning point in American politics,

41–42; victory in 1966 California gubernatorial election, 37; victory in 1980 presidential election, 40, 183; on welfare policy, 188, 330n.47

Reagan Democrats, creation of, 39–40

recession, in early twenty-first century, 6

Redstockings, 146

Reeb, James, 310n.5

Reed, David, 321n.16

religion: as business, 223–25; immigration and changes in, 136–37; private schools based on, 242

Republican Party: angry focus on moral issues, 38; and business, corrupt associations of, 7–8, 306n.26, 307n.27; and campaign finance reform, opposition to, 56–57; conservative insurrection in, 30, 37, 38; decline until 1960s, 36; donors to, 53; and Equal Rights Amendment, opposition to, 145; future of, 303; historical characteristics of, 34–35; ideological differences within, 36; popular support after September 11, 303; social class represented by, 35, 58, 296; in the South, 33–34; views on immigrants, 35, 36; Voting Rights Act of 1965 and changes in, 29, 31. *See also* conservative ascendancy

residential segregation, 176–77, 179–80, 294–95; and educational segregation, 179; measures of, 329n.22

Reuther, Walter, 177

Rice, Condoleezza, 184, 278

Rich, Denise, 55

Richards, Martin, 67

Robb, Chuck, 48, 49

Roberts, Ed, 76

Rockefeller, Nelson, 36

Rodrik, Dani, 21

Roe v. Wade, 147–48; backlash against, 167

Rogers, William Barton, 70

Roman Catholic Church, financial position of, 224–25

Roos, John, 236

Roosevelt, Franklin D., 70, 293

Roosevelt, Theodore, 250, 288

Rosenbaum, Yankel, 194

Rosenwald, Julius, 186

Roth, Steven, 181

Rubin, Robert, 22–23, 88

Ruina, Jack, 80

Rumsfeld, Donald, 278

Russia, post-Soviet, 262, 266; stock exchanges in, 341n.33

Sachs, Jeffrey, 262, 274, 341n.31

Saddam. *See* Hussein, Saddam

Salinas de Gortari, Carlos, 274

Salomon Smith Barney, 5

Samuelson, Robert J., 221

Sandinistas, 256

Scantlebury, Roger, 80, 81

Schneider, William, 203, 205

Scholes, Myron, 19, 319n.36

Scowcroft, Brent, 264

SDS. *See* Students for a Democratic Society

Sears Roebuck, antidiscrimination suit against, 165, 166

segregation: educational, 178–79, 179, 180–81; residential, 176–77, 179–80, 294–95, 329n.22; in suburbs, 213, 218–19; types of, 213. *See also* inequality

Selassie, Haile, 256

Selden, John, 240

semiconductors: invention of, 74; price of, 75

Sennett, Richard, 329n.27

September 11, 2001: anti-immigrant sentiment after, 128; Bush administration response to, 280; Bush (George W.) popularity after, 302, 303; foreign relations after, 286–87; media after, 238; neoconservative faction after, 279; and party politics, 303; patriotism after, 276, 292; stock market after, 6

service sector, employment in, 110

sex-based discrimination: challenges to, 158–59; in civil rights movement, 158; employment, 156, 163, 168–69; Supreme Court on, 166; in wages, 150, 151

Sexual Politics (Millett), 161

Shafly, Phyllis, 144

Sharon, Ariel, 279

Sharpton, Alfred, 196

Shi'a, Iraqi, 265

Shockley, William, 74

Shrag, Peter, 43, 240–41

Sichel, Dan, 95

Silicon Graphics, 82

Silicon Valley, 71–72

Simo, Roseanne, 83

Simpson, Alan, 345n.72

Simpson, O. J., trial of, 196–97

Sisterhood is Powerful (Morgan), 161
slavery: impact on American society, xix;
    racism as consequence of, 199
Smith, Adam, 347n.20
Smith, Bradley, 314n.68
Smith, David, 38–39, 50
Smith, Hedrick, 40
Smith, Howard, 157
Smith, James P., 117
Snow, C. P., 75
social class. *See* class divisions; class status
society, American, 203–48; changes in 1960s
    and 1970s, alarm at, 14; characteristics at end
    of twentieth century, 10–12, 294–95; decline
    in civic engagement, 229–31; forces defining,
    in last quarter of twentieth century, 204;
    future of, 304; historical experiences shap-
    ing, xviii–xix; immigration and changes in,
    135–36; impact of inequality on, 293–95. *See
    also* specific social issues
"soft money," 56
Solow, Robert, 87
Somoza Debayle, Anastasio, 256
South: African Americans in, de jure equality
    of, 174; capital punishment in, 192; Cold
    War and transformation of, 200; and conser-
    vatism, 201–2; Democratic Party in, 32–33;
    farmers in, government subsidies to, 209;
    growing influence of, xix, 173, 200–1, 209;
    and gun culture, 333n.96; income inequality
    in, 101; and North: historical relations be-
    tween, 199–200; shared assumptions of, 202;
    politics determined by, 46–47, 173; Republi-
    can Party in, 33–34; residential segregation
    in, 179, 329n.22; subregions of, 32, 310n.8;
    Voting Rights Act of 1965 and changes in,
    31, 310n.4
Southern Democrats, conservatism of, 33
Soviet Union, aggressive foreign policy in
    1970s, 12, 38, 256
Soviet Union, collapse of, 252, 258–59; assump-
    tions about foreign relations after, 274; fac-
    tors leading to, 40; media after, 238; missed
    opportunities after, 262, 266; new threats af-
    ter, 262–64; and politics of protest, disap-
    pearance of, 295; triumphalism after, 108,
    252, 261; U.S. role in, 265–66; and U.S. for-
    eign policy, 259, 260–61, 278
Speck, Jeff, 217
Spengler, Oswald, 262

sports, 297; as business, 226–28; female partici-
    pation in, 152–53
Spriggs, Williams, 132
stagflation, in 1970s, 14; reaction to, 16–17
Stanford University, and information technol-
    ogy development, 70, 71–72
Starr, Kevin, 121
Steele, Shelby, 184–85
Steffens, Lincoln, 59
Steinem, Gloria, 146, 147, 156
Stengel, Casey, 227
stock car racing, 201
stock market: bull run on: beneficiaries of,
    106–7; illusions resulting from, 61, 92; Clin-
    ton's policies and, 23; democracy equated
    with, 2; deregulation and globalization and,
    18–19; future levels of, forecasts regarding,
    107; gains in last quarter of twentieth cen-
    tury, 17–18; guesses reflected in prices of,
    107–8; Internet and boom in, 61, 62; "irra-
    tional exuberance" and catastrophic fall of,
    6; media companies and, 233, 238
Stockman, David, 37, 347n.21
stocks, concentration of ownership of, 92
Stone, Oliver, 24
Strachey, Christopher, 67
Students for a Democratic Society (SDS), sex-
    ism in, 158–59
suburbs, 203, 300; before beginning of 20th
    century, 211; black middle-class flight to,
    177–78; and class divisions, 210, 246; class
    segregation in, 218–19; and conservatism,
    205–6, 334n.14; diversity of, 211, 212; and edu-
    cational segregation, 179; emergence of, 205;
    ethnic composition of, 213; government sub-
    sidies and creation of, 217; immigrants in,
    213, 214; income segregation in, 213, 218–19,
    294–95; negative impact of, 209–10, 214–16,
    334n.7; offices and retail in, 214; and politi-
    cal fragmentation, 210; and politics, 205–6,
    215–16, 294–95; race segregation in, 218–19;
    shopping strips in, destructive consequences
    of, 218; sprawl, problem of, 214–15, 334n.7;
    victims of, 216–17; white flight to, 176–77,
    211–12
Sunbelt: characteristics of, 206; and future of
    American politics, 46–47
Supreme Court: on abortion rights, 147–48,
    167, 328n.74; on affirmative action, 182; on
    campaign financing, 31, 53, 221–22; on capi-

tal punishment, 313n.44; on educational segregation, 180, 181; on equal pay, 150; presidential election of 2000 and, 302; on sex-
based discrimination, 166, 169
Swann v. Charlotte-Mecklenburgh, 180
Sweden: average income in, 93; racism in,
199

Taft, Robert, 36
Taft-Harley bill of 1947, 37
TANF. *See* Temporary Assistance for Needy
Families
tariff regime, and export of manufacturing
jobs, 21
Tarrance, Lance, 134
tax(es): and funding of Internet research, 65;
hatred of, 45; regressive character of, 18; tax
cut of 2001, 18; unequal burden of, 100–1
tax revolt: in California, 16, 38, 42–44; and educational inequality, 240–41; spread of, 44
Teal, Gordon, 74
Teapot Dome, 8, 306n.26
technologies: nineteenth century, impact of,
110; twentieth century (*See* information
technology)
technology companies, losses in early twenty-
first century, 7
television: advertising on, politicians' dependence on, 30, 51–52; cable, spread of, 233;
change in character of, 232; class divisions
and, 247; and decline in community involvement, 231; and electoral politics, 222–
23; news reporting on, lower standards of,
229, 303; political coverage by, 60
television evangelists, 223
Temporary Assistance for Needy Families
(TANF), 190
terrorism: Islamic world and, 270; psychological motive for, 280; and U.S. foreign policy,
252–53. *See also* September 11, 2001
Texas: abortion law in, challenge to, 147; capital punishment in, 192; immigrants in, 124;
Mexican population in, 120–21; rice farmers
in, government subsidies to, 209
Texas Instruments, technological inventions
at, 74
Texas Rangers baseball club, 7
Thacker, Charles, 73
Thatcher, Margaret, 264
Thomas, Clarence, 184

Three Mile Island, 254
Thurmond, Strom, 34
Time (magazine), sex discrimination suit
against, 156
time-sharing technology, 80
Time-Warner, AOL takeover of, 63–64
Tisch, Larry, 233
Tocqueville, Alexis de, 288
tolerance, in U.S. society, 10, 297
towns, small, decline of, 205, 207
Toynbee, Arnold, 262
traffic congestion, suburbs and, 216
transistor, development of, 74
trickle-down effect, lack of evidence regarding,
101
triumphalism: Bush (George W.) and, xviii;
Clinton's 2000 State of the Union Address
and, 2–4, 5, 88–89, 257, 293; economic expansion and, 3, 4–5, 104, 301; fall of communism and, 108, 252, 261; in international relations, 257–58; vs. reality, 293
Tumber, Bee, 165
Turner, Ted, 233
Twain, Mark, 239

underclass, determinants of, 331n.48
unemployed people, invisibility of, 98
unemployment: decline in late twentieth century, 89; and inflation, Keynesian doctrine
on, 16; international comparisons of, 99;
low, and wage gains, 96, 102; rise in early
twenty-first century, 6
unions. *See* labor unions
United Auto Workers, 169
United Farm Workers of America, 133
United Kingdom. *See* Britain
United Methodist Church, investments of, 224
United Nations, U.S. relations with, 273, 279
United States v. Microsoft Corporation, 71–72,
83, 84, 317n.47
United Women Firefighters, 163
universities: affirmative action in, 182; inequalities among, 244–45, 339n.102; and information technology, development of, 65–66,
70–72, 78, 81–82; as investors in new technology, 72; and women's movement, 147,
155, 164
University of California at Berkeley, 43
University of Chicago, and free-market economics, 17, 41, 308n.44, 312n.39

University of Illinois, and Mosaic software, 82, 83
University of Pennsylvania, and computer development, 75
University of Texas: abortion rights activism at, 147; privatization of endowment of, 8
Unz, Ron, 129
Usenet, 81

Valian, Virginia, 150, 151
Vasconcelos, José, 133
Vietnam War, and loss of national confidence, 12, 255, 307n.33
Vietnamese Americans, communities of, 119
violence: against immigrants, 131–32; against women firefighters, 163
Von Glinow, Mary Ann, 153
voting: by African Americans, 33, 173; class status and, 36, 247–48; by Hispanics, 122, 130, 133–34, 303; by immigrants, 122, 124–25, 133–34; low participation in, 297; by women, 170, 303, 325n.9
Voting Rights Act (1965), 31, 174; consequences for American politics/and party realignment, 29, 31, 33–34
Vulcan Society, 163

Wade, Henry, 147
wages: decline in last quarter of twentieth century, 21, 93, 291; gains in late 1990s, 89, 101, 102; gap between middle and highest earners, 90–91; inequality of, 90–91, 100; low unemployment and increase in, 96, 102; for women, inequality in, 150, 151
waitresses, union activity vs. litigation by, 163–65
Wall Street: and glorification of U.S. economy, 4–5; lawsuits against, 5; policies benefiting, in last quarter of twentieth century, 17–18
Wall Street (film), 24
Wallace, George, 39, 172, 181, 330n.32, 346n.6
Walters, Barbara, 148
Warren, Earl, 36, 174, 181
Washington (D.C.): contradictory attitudes toward, 12; growth of metropolitan area around, 11–12; lobbyists in, 54; preoccupation with money, 51; public schools in, 243; suburban sprawl in, 214

Watergate scandal, 13
wealth inequality, 91–92; international comparisons of, 23, 294, 309n.63, 347n.13
Webster case, 167
Weddington, Sarah, 147
Welch, Jack, 7
welfare state: prison state replacing, 191; reform in Clinton years, 3, 89, 189–91; withering away of, 17, 189
Weyrich, Paul, 307n.41
White, Kevin, 178
White, Thomas, 7
Whitman, Walt, 9
Whitney, Eli, 69
Wilde, Oscar, 8
Wilkes, Maurice, 75
Wilson, Pete, 128, 129, 134
Wilson, Sonsini, Goodrich & Rosati, 71–72
Wilson, Woodrow, xvi, 249, 250
Winfrey, Oprah, 183, 330n.36
winner-take-all society, 96–97
Winthrop, John, 282
Wirth, Tim, 48
Wolfe, Tom, 19, 246
Wolff, Michael, 236
Wolfowitz, Paul, 277, 278
women: abortion rights for, 145–49; in academia, 152; and African Americans, comparison of experiences of, 157, 163; and electoral politics, 170, 303, 325n.9; employment discrimination of, 168–69; Equal Pay Act of 1963 and, 150; Equal Rights Amendment (ERA) and, 143–45; equality for, resistance to, 289; in executive positions, 150–51; inequalities experienced by, 166–67; in legal profession, 151, 152; in media, 156; in medicine, 151–52, 153; move into labor force, 140, 141–42, 166 (See also labor force, women in); opportunities for, federal government's role in, 152; in politics, 162; in sports, 152–53; wages for, 150, 151
women's movement(s): achievements of, 139, 143, 162; backlash against, 148–49, 154, 167–68, 170; and civil rights movement, 157–58, 198; class status and divisions within, 140, 150, 162–66; disappointments of, 139, 143–55, 166–67, 299–300; factions within, 159, 170; leaders of, strategic mistake of, 154–56, 159; media coverage of, 160, 168, 170; New Left and, 156, 159; radical, demise of, 159–61; two

versions of, 139–41, 155, 162–66 (*See also* feminist movement); universities and, 147, 155, 164
Women's Strike for Equality, 160
Woods, Tiger, 183, 226, 227
Woolongong University (Australia), and Internet development, 82
work: absence in urban ghettos, 188–89. *See also* labor demand; labor force
workers, decline in living standards of, 20–21
World Bank, 271
World Trade Organization, 271
World War I, U.S. in, 250
World War II: computers built during, 75; productivity after, 103–4
World Wide Web: infrastructure development, 82–83; inventor of, 68, 73, 81; military ances-

tor of, 72; purpose of, conflicting views on, 82. *See also* Internet
Wosniak, Steve, 64, 72, 76
Wrigley, P. K., 227

Xerox PARC, 72, 73; and Apple Computer, 73, 76, 77

Yahoo!: losses in early twenty-first century, 7; origins of, 69, 84; profits in 1990s, 23; Stanford University and, 72
Yang, Jerry, 64, 69, 72, 84
Yeltsin, Boris, 259, 262
Young, Andrew, 34
Young, Coleman, 177

Zuse, Konrad, 75

POLITICS AND SOCIETY IN TWENTIETH-CENTURY AMERICA

Civil Defense Begins at Home: Militarization Meets Everyday Life in the Fifties
by Laura McEnaney

Cold War Civil Rights: Race and the Image of American Democracy
by Mary L. Dudziak

Divided We Stand: American Workers and the Struggle for Black Equality
by Bruce Nelson

Poverty Knowledge: Social Science, Social Policy, and the Poor in Twentieth-Century U.S. History by Alice O'Connor

Suburban Warriors: The Origins of the New American Right by Lisa McGirr

The Politics of Whiteness: Race, Workers, and Culture in the Modern South
by Michelle Brattain

State of the Union: A Century of American Labor by Nelson Lichtenstein

Changing the World: American Progressives in War and Revolution
by Alan Dawley

Dead on Arrival: The Politics of Healthcare in Twentieth-Century America
by Colin Gordon

For All These Rights: Business, Labor, and the Shaping of America's Public-Private Welfare State by Jennifer Klein

The Radical Middle Class: Populist Democracy and the Question of Capitalism in Progressive Era Portland, Oregon by Robert D. Johnston

American Babylon: Race and the Struggle for Postwar Oakland
by Robert O. Self

The Other Women's Movement: Workplace Justice and Social Rights in Modern America by Dorothy Sue Cobble

Impossible Subjects: Illegal Aliens and the Making of Modern America
by May M. Ngai

More Equal Than Others: America from Nixon to the New Century
by Godfrey Hodgson